GHOSTS IN THE MIDDLE AGES

JEAN-CLAUDE SCHMITT

TRANSLATED BY TERESA LAVENDER FAGAN

❧ ❧ ❧ ❧ ❧ ❧ ❧ ❧ ❧

THE UNIVERSITY OF CHICAGO PRESS ✦ CHICAGO AND LONDON

GHOSTS

IN THE

MIDDLE AGES

THE LIVING

AND THE DEAD

IN MEDIEVAL

SOCIETY

Jean-Claude Schmitt, a leading *Annaliste*, teaches at the École des hautes études en sciences sociales in Paris. He is the author of *Gestures*, vol. 1, no. 1 (1984) and of *Holy Greyhound: Guinnefort, Healer of Children.*

The University of Chicago Press, Chicago 60637
The University of Chicago Press, Ltd., London
© 1998 by The University of Chicago
All rights reserved. Published 1998
Printed in the United States of America
07 06 05 04 03 02 01 00 99 98   1 2 3 4 5
ISBN: 0-226-73887-6 (cloth)

Originally published as *Les revenants: les vivants et les morts dans la société médiévale,*
© Éditions Gallimard, 1994.

Library of Congress Catalogin-in-Publication Data

Schmitt, Jean-Claude.
    [Revenants. English]
    Ghosts in the Middle Ages : the living and the dead in Medieval society / Jean-Claude Schmitt : translated by Teresa Lavender Fagan.
        p.   cm.
    Translation of: Les revenants.
    Includes bibliographical references (p.   ) and index.
    ISBN 0-226-73887-6 (cloth : acid-free paper)
    1. Ghosts—Europe—History.   2. Ghosts in art.   3. Death—Religious aspects—Christianity—History of Doctrines—Middle Ages, 600–1500.   I. Title.
GR135.S3613   1998
398'.47'094—dc21   97-38308
                                                                          CIP

During one's lifetime, how many people one encounters! You speak to them, you laugh a little, you share a glass of beer, you sing. But once man is laid to rest beneath a cross, the end, he no longer exists. He is laid to rest and he is silent. He is silent. And if we hear someone respond, it is not from the bottom of the grave, we are simply dreaming. Sometimes someone comes to talk to us. Or to stroll around here and there. Or sometimes he stays seated. As if he weren't dead. Or he takes up a cart, even begins some kind of work. Just like a living man. Like a true living man, not like a dead man. Why—one can never know, but in a dream you never see a dead man in his grave, nor even in the casket where he is laid during the funeral service. In our dreams the dead walk, they are seated in front of a pushcart, gesture to you with their hands. Just like the real living. Perhaps this is why the Lord gave dreams to man, so that he might see, as if they were truly living, those who exist no longer, but whom he would truly like to see again.

JUOZAS BALTUSIS
The Saga of Youza (Vilnius, 1979)

CONTENTS

As the reader will discover, Jean-Claude Schmitt makes abundant use of original texts in this work. Wherever possible, I have used the standard English-language translations of those texts and have cited the appropriate references. When a published translation could not be obtained, I have translated directly from the French version.

Bracketed words and phrases in quotations are Schmitt's additions; all other bracketed material is mine.

AUTHOR'S ACKNOWLEDGMENTS

Throughout the years, this book has gradually been enriched by the suggestions of countless colleagues, students, and friends, both in France and abroad. I would like all of them to know how deeply grateful I am to them. I want particularly to thank Pauline Schmitt-Pantel and Jérôme Baschet for their frank and honest readings, Jean-Claude Bonne and Michel Pastoureau for what they have taught me about medieval iconography, Danièle Alexandre-Bidon for the figured documents that she helped me to locate, and Daniel Fabre and the ethnologists in Toulouse for their generous attention and our longtime friendship on the front lines of historical anthropology. Finally, I want to thank Pierre Nora once again for the confidence he has shown in my work.

The dead have no existence other than that which the living imagine for them. In different ways, depending on their culture, their beliefs, and the time in which they lived, people have attributed the dead with a life in the hereafter; they have depicted the places where the dead reside, and in this way they have imagined the fate that they hope or fear for themselves. Accordingly, imagining death and the future of the dead in the hereafter has formed an essential part of the religious beliefs of all societies. Such imaginings have assumed various but widely recognized forms, among which visions and dreams have always been of primary importance.[1] In some regions the ability of certain people, such as the Siberian shamans, to travel to the hereafter in their dreams or in a state of trance has been fully accepted. Elsewhere, exceptional figures—such as Christ or, following in his footsteps, the saints of Christianity—were believed to have had the power to bring the dead back to life. And everywhere we can find what is usually called a "belief in ghosts."[2]

Apparitions of ghosts represented a reverse movement between the dead and the living in the travels to the hereafter. In the rich literature of visions and voyages into the hereafter—from Book VI of Virgil's *Aeneid* to the *Divine Comedy* of Dante, including *Saint Patrick's Purgatory*—visionaries encountered the souls of the dead whom they themselves had once known on earth or whose names and renown had come to their attention. But the goal of such revelations was not, as a general rule, to account for the fate of a specific dead person in the hereafter (with the exception of certain rulers, in highly "political" visions).[3] Rather, the goal was to reveal to the living, to listeners or readers of the *visio*, the geography of the places of the hereafter: the steep paths, the frozen rivers, the furnaces, and the list of tortures beyond the grave—throughout the centuries the great reservoirs of the Western imaginary. Yet the structure and function of ghost tales differ greatly. In such tales it was not the living who traveled to the beyond but the dead who appeared to the living. Nor was the manifestation of a dead person completely comparable to the apparitions of other supernatural beings, such as angels and demons or even Christ, the Virgin, and the saints. These latter beings usually resided in the hereafter, where they remained invisible except when they occasionally appeared before living men and women. Ghosts, on the other hand, still had one foot on the ground, so to speak: they had just departed from the living, to whom they later appeared and from whom they seemed not to be able to separate themselves. With tales of apparitions of Christ, the Virgin, or the devil, the historian is immediately plunged into all the wealth of the imaginary of Christian society. But with tales of ghosts, the historian is also immediately confronted with all the complexities of the social relationships that existed between the living and the dead, who returned again to visit those still living. Thus, unlike the great visions of the hereafter, ghost tales concentrated on the status of the deceased, who was an ordinary person. Granted, saints also appeared, and they too were dead; their apparitions in the dreams and visions of the living were a favorite theme in hagiography. But saints, according to the very accurate expression of Peter Brown,[4] were "very special dead people," who posed specific problems. I will speak of them only parenthetically, emphasizing instead the apparitions of the ordinary dead, of everyday ghosts.

Ever since the Romantic period, as conveyed in literature and horror films as well as in contemporary comic strips, ghosts have been a part of the required scenery of the Middle Ages as we have been content to imagine it, a Middle Ages of haunted castles, dragons, phantoms, and even vampires. Not everything was fantasy in this nevertheless too facile image: in a highly religious culture (in the sense that everyone accepted the existence and the power of supernatural beings who were generally invisible but always nearby), a culture that was comfortable with death and the dead, a "belief in ghosts" was accepted by all. Let us not, however, conclude that the dead were omnipresent in the concerns and the dreams of the living or that the living expected to see their ancestors rise up before them whenever they turned around! Not every dead person returned, and the dead did not appear to just anyone, anytime, anywhere.

In medieval society, as in many other traditional societies, the specific type of existence attributed to the deceased depended on how the "rite of passage" of death had occurred: the dead generally returned when the funeral and mourning rituals could not be performed in the prescribed way, for example, if the body of a drowning victim disappeared and could not be buried according to custom or if a murder victim, a suicide, a woman who died during childbirth, or a stillborn baby presented the members of the community of the living with the danger of a blemish on their group. Such deaths were generally deemed unlucky. This anthropological and widespread dimension of the return of the dead can be found, among other places, in Western traditions from antiquity to the Middle Ages and even in contemporary folklore.[5] Nevertheless, I believe that the historian of the Middle Ages must broaden the more general anthropological definition of ghosts, using more specific historical considerations. Some of these specific factors are the result of the complex makeup of medieval culture, of the weight of the heritage that gave birth to it: the legacies of Greco-Roman paganism (in which the cult of the dead of the polis, or the people, played a very important role); or the "barbarian" legacies that were brought back through the migrations of Germanic peoples and that were integrated into Christendom during the first millennium. In this regard Claude Lecouteux is to be congratulated for having emphasized the debt that the ecclesiastical and Latin literature of the Middle Ages owed to Germanic traditions. He has shown how the Christian duo of the soul (immaterial and eternal) and the body (material and perishable) has sometimes served only to superficially mask the Germanic pagan concept of a quasi-physical double (*hamr*) that survives after death.[6] According to Lecouteux, many Latin tales that describe ghosts as beings endowed with "corporeity" were derived from such concepts, which can be found in the *Edda* and in certain Scandinavian sagas first written in the twelfth and thirteenth centuries. Like the many studies on the folkloric culture of the Middle Ages, this approach might indeed lead to a richer understanding of the various levels of meaning hidden within the medieval document.

I will, however, hazard another interpretation of medieval ghosts. Although legacies and, consequently, an "archeology" of medieval texts must not be ignored, I intend rather to show how beliefs and the imaginary depend above all on the structures and the functioning of the society and the culture at a given period in time. "Mentalities" consist not only of the ancient layers that survive from earlier thoughts and behaviors but also of the beliefs and the images, the words and the gestures, that fully find their meaning in the contemporary social relations and ideology of a given age. It is by considering this reality that we will understand how the Christian culture of the Middle Ages enlarged the notion of ghosts and created other opportunities for the dead to appear.

The period of my focus (from the fifth to the fifteenth centuries,

3

with particular emphasis on the central Middle Ages) experienced the succession and the combination of traditional beliefs and of the slowly Christianized rituals of "tame death" (according to the term used by Philippe Ariès),[7] of the torment of the "death of the self" (the individual fear of the moment of passing and of the specific judgment that leads the soul toward one of the three principal locations in the Christian hereafter: hell, purgatory, or paradise), and even of the pain of the "death of the other," the concern about the fate of relatives and deceased friends in the hereafter (well before mourning was raised to a more secularized form in the weeping statuary in the cemeteries of nineteenth-century bourgeois Europe). In this complex network of attitudes—some quite ancient, others new—medieval society envisioned the possibility that certain of the deceased could return and visit the living or at least those among the living with whom they had formed ties considered unalterable even beyond death. At the same time, important transformations in social structures led to the redefinition of the individual's position within groups and communities that remained in place well after the passing of any individual member. Kinship groups—both natural and spiritual—as well as monastery communities and communities of noble lineage, of the parish, and of confraternities formed the framework for these new relationships not only between the living but also between the living and the dead. These relationships were inscribed within the realities of the social space through the structuring of the dwelling places of the living—the village, the neighborhood—and the dwelling place of the dead: the cemetery. The proximity of graves and houses supported and justified the living person's intense concern with the dead. Similarly, the religious and material hold that the church and the clerics had over lay society grew appreciably after the beginning of the tenth century. It enabled an inculcation of the faithful with a religious morality centered on the notions of sin, penance, and salvation, culminating at the end of the twelfth century in the "birth of Purgatory."[8] Henceforth all Christians could hope to be saved, but only under the condition that after death, they would undergo salutary punishments—the duration and the intensity of which depended both on personal merits (good and bad acts and repentance at the time of death) and on the suffrages (masses, prayers, and almsgiving) undertaken by relatives and friends for the dead's salvation. Otherwise the dead person might appear to a relative or a close friend to demand the suffrages needed and to ask the living to do the pious works necessary for the dead person's salvation. Eager to support and organize the unity of the living and the dead, the church gladly repeated tales of ghosts. Far from simply being the maleficent dead found in all cultures due to up-heavals or to the fortuitous absence of the rite of passage offered by a funeral, far from simply being the products of old pagan beliefs, these ghosts expressed in a more general way—through their return in phantasms, fears, and the tales of the living—the potential multiple dysfunctions of a good Christian death.

More precisely, Christian attitudes toward the dead, as the medieval church intended to define and impose these attitudes, were entirely contained within the notion of the *memoria*, the "remembrance of the dead."[9] This was a liturgical remembrance, reinforced by inscribing the names of those dead who were worthy of being commemorated into *libri memoriales*, necrologies, and the obituaries of monasteries and convents. The liturgical Memento was recited specifically on the occasion of the masses said for the salvation of the dead person, especially on the anniversary of the death. But this word "remembrance" is in fact misleading, for the goal of the *memoria* was to help the living separate from the dead, to shorten the latter's stay in purgatorial punishment (or in purgatory), and finally, to enable the living to forget the deceased. The rhythm of masses and prayers was therefore increasingly relaxed, and they lasted a limited amount of time: three days, seven days, a month, or a year, rarely longer than that. The inscription of a name in the *liber memorialis* did not promise that the deceased would be glorified forever—this was reserved for saints and kings—but that the deceased would be rapidly included in the anonymity of past generations. Funerary foundations, although termed "perpetual" (just as today we talk of "perpetual concessions" in a cemetery), did not escape the effects of human negligence or of dwindling finances. In practice, they lasted for only a time. The idea of a foundation of masses "in perpetuity" was, moreover, contradictory to the function assigned to suffrages for the dead: to free the souls of the deceased as rapidly as possible from the trials of purgatory in order to provide them a final resting place in heaven. In addition, many of the graves in the cemeteries were anonymous, and periodically the ground was dug up and the graves were emptied to make room for new bodies. Beginning in the eleventh century, lineal and genealogical remembrance experienced a true rise in popularity in aristocratic circles, sometimes benefiting from the support of the written word. But the remembrance remained socially limited and fragile. We must therefore emphasize the degree to which the signs were ambiguous; the *memoria*, as a form of collective memory, was a social technique of forgetting. Its function was to "cool off" the memory under the guise of maintaining it, to soothe the painful memory of the deceased until the memory became indistinct. A classifying technique, the *memoria* put the dead in their rightful place so that the living, if they should happen to recall the names of the dead, could do so without fear or emotion.

In this way we can understand who the medieval ghosts were: the rare dead who, obstinately and for a rather brief period following their death, held the regulated functioning of the Christian *memoria* in check, creating an obstacle to the necessary process of the "act of mourning." Although a tainted image of the Middle Ages—indeed, even certain studies in history or folklore—attempts to convince us that medieval people lived in obsessive cohabitation with all their dead, we must be a bit more discerning. Apparitions of the dead were not the norm for relationships between the living and the dead. The living imagined the dead only when the ritual of separation from the deceased could not be carried out fully, when forgetting proved impossible following a perturbation in the normal course of the rite of passage of death and the funeral services—whether because the close survivors (the widow, the son, the brothers), through greed or negligence, had broken the ritual rules and deprived the soul of the deceased of the salutary support of suffrages from the clerics or whether, according to the living, because the dead person, not having carried out a complete penance before death, now called on the support of family to overcome his or her trials in the hereafter. In all cases, the dead person in question was called back to the "memory" of the living undoubtedly not only for the greater benefit of the dead person's soul but also for that of the church, the great arranger of paid suffrages for the dead. Paradoxically, the medieval church, which in the early centuries had shown great reluctance toward a belief in ghosts, claiming that this belief was a characteristic of "paganism" and of "superstitions," was thus now at the origin of a containment and an exploitation of such beliefs, as can be seen widely in tales of miracles and in the sermons of preachers of that time.

Thus the aim of this book becomes clearer. It concerns the social function of the remembrance of the dead in the Middle Ages. More precisely, if we return to that great subject in history, that is, the memories of societies, our purpose is to look primarily at the apparent opposite: the necessity of forgetting and that which prevents this forgetting. We will in fact look at how medieval people sought to remember their dead but also, above all, at how they attempted to forget the dead and at how some of those dead—the "very special" dead, distinguished by imperfections rather than by holiness—apparently rebelled against the will of the living to forget and thus rekindled their memories, invaded their dreams, and haunted their homes.

Historians and ethnologists commonly speak of a "belief in ghosts." But what does this really mean, and how can the historian ascertain past beliefs? One of the recent advances in the "anthropology of beliefs" is to question the ill-considered uses of the notion of "belief."[10] We must be careful not to reify belief, to turn it into something established once and for all, something that individuals and societies need only express and pass on to each other. It is appropriate to substitute a more active notion for the term "belief": the verb "to believe." In this way a belief is a never-completed activity, one that is precarious, always questioned, and insep-arable from recurrences of doubt. There is nothing less fixed and less assured than this activity of believing: the ethnologist who interviews subjects several times in a row, under different circumstances, quickly becomes aware of this. Faced with a single document written down for all time, the historian is in a different situation. At least the historian too can look carefully at the conditions under which an utterance of belief was made, at the forms and genres of the tales being analyzed, for the essence of beliefs is largely dependent on these forms.

Too often the historian is greatly tempted to separate the belief, whose existence and content are postulated a priori, from the nature of the documents—the different types of texts and images—from which the historian derives information. What the document says or shows is a "belief," and to understand it, the historian need only read ancient texts and describe illustrations. But things are not always so very simple. An elementary analysis may enable us to reveal the importance of the condi-tions under which a document was produced; for example, we may learn all that is implied concerning a tale of an apparition from the twelfth or the thirteenth century by its having been transcribed into Latin by a cleric, whereas the tale was originally told (in what form?) in the vernacu-lar. Such mediations—linguistic, social, ideological—are fully part of the enunciation of the belief as the historian is led to discover it.

The issue of the forms of the enunciation concerns not only the doc-umentary genre but also the very manner in which people of the past spoke of their beliefs. For the historian, as for the ethnologist, moreover, the question is essential. How are we to interpret all those tales, passed down by the literate of the Middle Ages (religious figures, of course, though not particularly credulous), that assert as a given what we have great difficulty admitting: that the dead appeared in full daylight to people who were awake and of perfectly sound mind? Are we to blame, as Lucien Lévy-Bruhl once did, the "primitive mentality" of an age foreign to our own logic, a mentality that would supposedly not have known how to distinguish dream from reality? Everything points away from such an interpretation: some of the clerics who passed on these tales of apparitions were "intellectuals" whose theological and philosophical reasoning and relentlessness in distinguishing the "true" from the "false" were not, in their logical approach, all that different from our own.

If we examine the forms of enunciation of the ghost stories more deeply, we will discover that they appear in two types. The great majority were tales of apparitions transmitted orally and transcribed by a cleric, most often in Latin. These tales were the product of a more or less lengthy chain of informants who referred to an earlier visionary experience of a third party. The person who wrote down the tale never claimed to be the direct beneficiary of the apparition. In certain cases, the apparition is described as occurring in a dream, but most often a vision in a wakeful state is mentioned, because the unfavorable prejudices of the official culture—the culture of the clerics—against dreams in the Middle Ages caused people to speak of wakeful visions when they wanted to reinforce the credibility of a tale. In addition, the dead person (or any other supernatural being) whose apparition was reported is described in these tales in a concrete, almost physical manner: the witness not only states that the ghost spoke clearly but also describes the apparition as if it were a living person and sometimes claims to have touched the ghost and felt its touch. If in certain cases we recognize the lasting weight of pagan traditions here, must we not also consider the *effects of the real*, effects unique to tales told by word of mouth and then put down in writing and thus authenticated? The objectivization of the content of the reported tale went hand in hand with its socialization. Furthermore, do we not, even today, hear of and in turn tell "ghost stories"? By the fact of telling and naming, we give a sort of existence—a presence, a form, even a body and a voice—to what is nevertheless only an imaginary being. In a culture in which the here-and-now and the hereafter were supposed to communicate, "believing in ghosts" meant speaking about them and creating images of them (for example, in miniatures of illuminated manuscripts). It also meant attempting to have others "believe" in them, by using those texts and images for quite real, efficacious ends that benefited the living and, above all, the powerful.[11] For the tales of ghosts favored the promotion of the liturgy of the dead, the development of piety, the attraction

8

of charitable donations, and finally, a reinforcement of the church's hold over Christian society.

But we cannot stop there. In the Middle Ages, what did it mean to each individual "to believe in ghosts"? From the outset we will discover another type of enunciation here, in tales whose numbers are more limited: autobiographical tales. In these tales the person who is writing is not content simply to relate what he or she heard or read; this person claims to have had a personal experience with the dead. Needless to say, here too the historian must exercise caution: since antiquity, literary models of the autobiography have weighed heavily on Western traditions. But in certain cases and especially after the twelfth century, there is no reason to doubt the authenticity of the feelings and impressions expressed in these texts. Autobiographical tales mention visions perceived in a wakeful state, a characteristic of tales relating to others, only in quite specific cases. Instead, autobiographical tales sometimes speak of a strange impression of an invisible presence and most often tell of a dream, a more or less inconsistent and phantasmal oneiric image produced through some distress, mourning, or bad conscience after the death of someone dear. Such tales are much less surprising to us than those of conscious visions: do we not also sometimes dream of a dead relative, and do we not also experience, even in sleep, the pain of the "death of the other"? When the intimate core of subjective belief allows itself to be touched in autobiographical tales, we discover that, for the individual as for the group, for the men and women of the Middle Ages as for those of today, when the "work of mourning"[12] occurs in distress, what is most important is the conflict between the desire to forget and the impossibility of doing so, between the fragility of memory and the will to remember.

In this regard the Middle Ages were not as different from our own culture as we might expect. Granted, for the people of that distant age, ghosts "existed," and this is certainly a great difference between that time and our own. When Saint Augustine asserted that the dead could not return to earth, he was not questioning the reality of the existence of souls in the hereafter but only God's willingness to allow them to appear. If clerics questioned the "truth" or the "falsity" of apparitions, it was not to suggest the impossibility of the existence of the apparitions but rather to assure themselves that the apparitions they were to judge were of divine and not diabolical origin. This was an entire system of belief that— since the Enlightenment and the nineteenth century—has become foreign to most Westerners. This is necessarily the historian's point of departure. Historians need not pretend to espouse the modes of thought of the ancient authors whose writings they discover. Confronted with a considerable number of tales and images, historians must, on the contrary, seek—without giving up anything of their own reason—to understand the logic and the functions of these tales and images. The present work thus aims to be a contribution to a social history of the imaginary. By looking at the subject of medieval ghosts—who existed only through the imagination and in the tales of the people of that time—we will attempt to learn how and why the living (and who among them), in their dreams and tales of visions, bestowed on certain of their dead a semblance of existence, a bodily appearance and a face. Perhaps they did so in order better to understand themselves in their relationships with the oneiric and obsessive images of their deceased relatives; or perhaps, in the guise of an imaginary dialogue with the dead, a dialogue obligingly reported by the clerics, they did so in order better to control the society of the living, the transference of inheritances, and the imposition of moral and social norms.

To attempt to understand a social imaginary in historical terms is the goal of this book, in which the historian's passion for the document—delectable tales and no less astonishing images—rivals the historian's will to discover, in the very materiality of texts and illustrations, in the language, and in the writing and the color, the meaning of the past. Out of this comes the particular form the historian very consciously gives to his or her writing. Indeed, while seeking to analyze and explain, I have found it necessary to adopt the narrative style that characterizes most of the documentation and to follow its transformations through time. For what is important in a tale is not only the general story line, a formal structure that sometimes endures unchanged throughout the centuries and even defies the uniqueness of cultures, but also the variants and the mass of concrete details, in constant renewal, that bear the mark of each historical moment like so many dated and localized intentions of those who created, told, and heard those stories and saw the illustrations. Thus, by mixing the tale with the analysis, I have attempted to restore, to make audible and visible, the words and the dreams of the past.

ONE

THE   REJECTION   OF   GHOSTS

A persistent yet somewhat ambiguous and contradictory refusal to admit the possibility that the dead might return in dreams or perhaps in conscious visions characterized the ecclesiastical culture of the early Middle Ages. One of the principal reasons for this refusal was that beliefs and practices relating to the return of the dead were associated with the "survival" of ancient paganism, whose funerary rituals were universally condemned, domesticated, or hidden. Thus the word *larva*, which in Rome designated the ill-fated souls of the dead, took on, in the Latin of the Christians, the sense of demoniacal spirits and diabolical masks. Necromancy (divination through the dead) came to be called "nigromancy": black magic and the invocation of the devil. We must also cite some positive reasons. Christianity's exclusive preoccupation with the salvation of the soul led to a reduction in funerary practices and in concern for the burial place, the gathering place of maleficent "larvae." The only exception made was for the bodies of saints and their graves, which were reserves of thaumaturgic powers. Only at the grave of such an exceptional dead person, a saint of the church, was it acceptable to await revelations. A saint might even appear in dreams, thanks to a practice that came straight from the pagan sanctuaries and that the clerics were forced to tolerate: incubation, the practice of sleeping in contact with the grave of a saint in the expectation of receiving an oneiric apparition. In a religious way of thinking long fragmented by a fundamental dualism—the antagonism between the devil and the saints, between the phantasmagorias of the former and the controlled apparitions of the latter—there was very little room for ghosts or for the oneiric and ambivalent revelations of ordinary dead people.

Legacies and Counter-Models

The lasting repression of ghosts by the official Christian culture of the
early Middle Ages contrasted, at least in part, with the more conciliatory
attitudes of the different cultures from which medieval Christianity in-
herited certain characteristics: Greco-Roman paganism, "barbarian" cultures that were assimilated at a later date, and biblical models that were
the basis of its ideology. In Greece and in Rome, tales of ghosts were
heard everywhere. In Greek literature from the time of Homer, abundant
accounts tell of the "image" (*eídôlon*) of a recent dead person who, having
died abruptly, sometimes infamously but more often in glory—such as
Patroclus, whose loss Achilles mourns and who stands before him in his
sleep[1]—comes back to haunt the dreams of the living who held the
person dear. Jean-Pierre Vernant has superbly analyzed the motives and
functions of these representations of death and the dead in ancient
Greece: "It is the impossibility of thinking about death from the point of
view of the dead that simultaneously constitutes the horror of death, its
extreme strangeness, its complete otherness, and enables the living to go
beyond death by establishing in their societies a constant remembrance
of certain types of dead."[2] The Roman world is of even more interest to
us. For Lucretius, for example, the *simulacrum* was an immaterial double
that a living person had the illusion of "seeing and hearing face to face"
as if the dead person were still alive. The poet describes the relationship
between the dead person and the double by using the model of cicadas
or snakes sloughing their shells or skins.[3] But it was above all the ill-fated
dead who abounded: those who had died violent deaths and who were
seeking vengeance, tarnished souls who were wandering near their
graves, the dead who were lacking final burial places (*insepulti*), suicides
(*biothanati*), women who had died in childbirth. The rituals linked to remembering the dead were of primary importance. Some were forbidden
in principle, and necromancy was even punishable by death. But others
were legally acceptable: the *manes* had their altars and their domestic effigies. In February the *parentalia* were celebrated on the model of funeral
services, with a banquet in honor of the ancestors. However, the *lemuria*
did not include a banquet, and a propitiatory gesture—throwing black
beans, which were believed to be the food of the dead, over one's left
shoulder—was used by the *pater familias* to appease the ill-fated dead.[4]

 We know of ancient Germanic cultures for the most part only
through later texts, but such texts convey traditional and perhaps very

ancient representations of those cultures: notably, the anonymous *Edda*, which was composed between the tenth and the twelfth centuries but the content of which goes back to the seventh century; and Scandinavian and Icelandic sagas, written between the twelfth and the fourteenth centuries at a time when Christianity was already well established in northern Europe. Examples include *Eyrbyggja saga* or *saga of Snorri the Chieftain*, written around 1230, *Laxdoela saga*, probably written around 1250, and *Saga of the Inhabitants of Val of Svörfud*, reworked around 1300. In these tales the dead, or *draugr*, return in great numbers, mutilating and killing anyone they encounter, wiping out entire regions, forcing people and animals to leave their dwellings.[5] Unlike the ghosts of classical antiquity, these dead are not described as "images." They seem to be endowed with real bodies, as if the cadavers themselves, having returned to life, had left their graves. Heroic tales also tell of the battle, to the grave, between a dead person and a living person who attempts to take the dead person's weapons. In *Thordar saga*, Skeggi enters the tomb of King Hrolf of Denmark and steals his sword Skofnung. In *Reykdoela saga*, the hero Thorket takes the sword of Skefil from the bottom of his grave, but the dead man appears to Thorket in a dream and demands that his weapon be returned to him. The story of Asvith and Asmund, told in Latin by Saxo Grammaticus (1149–1216) in his *History of the Danes*, is similar: Asvith dies prematurely, and his friend Asmund, who promised never to leave him, is lowered into Asvith's grave along with ample provisions. Sometime later Asmund is found disfigured and covered with blood but alive. He gives the following account: every night Asvith came back to life. After devouring the horse and then the dog that had been buried with him, Asvith attacked his friend and tore off one of Asmund's ears. Asmund was forced to cut off Asvith's head and stick a pike through his body to keep him from moving.[6] In *Saga of Grettir*, the hero robs the grave of Karr, whom Grettir finds seated on his throne. Grettir carries off Karr's treasure and his sword, but Karr grabs Grettir's wrist, and they fight furiously until Grettir cuts off Karr's head and takes flight. Later, when Grettir becomes the shepherd for Thordall and Gudrun, he decapitates and burns the body of the terrible Glam, who had devastated the countryside and destroyed the herds.[7] What is striking here is the terrifying violence and the "corporeity" of these ghosts, who could be definitively overcome only through the destruction of their cadavers. As we shall see, Christianity had no small amount of difficulty eradicating such beliefs.

Ghosts and the Bible

The almost complete absence of ghosts in the Bible must also have aided the desire of the Christian culture to reject the notion of ghosts. Several passages in the New Testament even show much hesitation regarding a cult of the dead. "Let the dead bury their dead," said Jesus (Matt. 8:22). "God is not the God of the dead, but of the living" (Matt. 22:32). Granted, many dead people are brought back to life by Jesus (and later by some of his disciples), but such a miracle—the most remarkable there was, according to the later classifications of medieval hagiographers— was not comparable to the return of a ghost.[8] It prefigures Christ's own resurrection three days after his Passion. It also anticipates the universal resurrection of the dead at the end of time.

At the time of the transfiguration, Jesus appears in glory flanked by Moses and Elias.[9] Beyond the fact that the latter two were not ordinary figures but were—at the very least—sorts of "saints," tradition held that they were not dead and that they, like Enoch, were raised up, alive, to earthly paradise. Several passages in the New Testament may be interpreted as explicit refusals of a belief in ghosts. When Jesus walks on the water, his disciples become afraid and believe it is the apparition of a "spirit," and Jesus must reassure them (Matt. 14:26; Mark 6:49). Undoubtedly for the same reason, Jesus tells the holy women not to be afraid when he appears to them after his resurrection (Matt. 28:10). It is no less significant that the apostles, informed by the women, do not believe them and suspect they have been dreaming (Luke 24:11). When Jesus finally appears to the disciples, they are "terrified and affrighted, and supposed that they had seen a spirit." Jesus thus encourages them to "handle" him, since "a spirit hath not flesh and bones," and he eats with them to give them additional proof that he is indeed alive (Luke 34:37). This episode is echoed in the scene of the miraculous freeing of Peter in Acts of the Apostles (12:15): the disciples, not wanting to believe the servant woman, Rhoda, who tells them that Peter is standing outside the door, call her "mad" and assert that the figure is his "angel." However, the most successful New Testament text that seemed to deny any possibility of the dead appearing to the living is the parable of Lazarus and the rich man (Luke 16:27–31). Not only does Abraham tell the rich man that in the hereafter there is no possibility of passing between the realm of the blessed (the Bosom of Abraham) and that of the damned, but he refuses to allow Lazarus to return to earth to forewarn the brothers of the rich man against the torments that await them after death. It is indeed in this way that Saint Augustine would interpret the parable: the idea that the dead might return to earth is out of the question.

The only true biblical ghost tale appears in the Old Testament. Yet this story is interpreted quite negatively because it concerns a tale of necromancy. This tale, of the medium woman of Endor, is told at length in 1 Samuel (1 Sam. 28) and is repeated, with a few changes, in 1 Chronicles (10:13–14) and in Ecclesiasticus (46:23) (*The New English Bible with Apocrypha* [Oxford and Cambridge, 1970] numbers the verse in Ecclesiasticus differently, as 43:20). This story has inspired many commentaries, beginning in the first centuries of the church, and even a relatively rich iconography, starting in the twelfth century.

The biblical text describes an act of necromancy that the medium carries out clandestinely on behalf of King Saul, who had prohibited such practices. The king consults this woman because he knows he has been abandoned by God because of his crimes, and he wants to know the outcome of the battle that he will wage the next day with the Philistines. The procedure used to evoke the dead man is not described, but the biblical text specifies that only the medium sees Samuel and that she describes him to Saul as "an old man who comes up covered with a mantle." Then Saul and Samuel have a long conversation, at the end of which Saul is informed that he will die the next day.

From the time of the Greek and Latin church fathers (notably Saint Augustine) to that of the scholastic theologians, the exegesis has attempted to understand the nature of this apparition. There is a wide range of interpretations. Was the dead man resuscitated? Was it Samuel's "spirit" that showed itself? Did the medium take advantage of the king through some deception? Did the devil raise up a "phantasm" that looked like Samuel? Or did Satan himself assume Samuel's appearance? In the twelfth century, the Parisian theologian Peter Comestor (d. 1169) summed up all these hypotheses quite well: "On the subject of this evocation some say that the evil spirit appeared looking like Samuel, or that it was his fantastic image (that is, raised up by the devil) that appeared there, which was called 'Samuel.' Others say that with God's permission it was indeed the soul of Samuel, covered by a body, that appeared; but for others it was a body that was resuscitated and received the life of a spirit, while Samuel's soul remained in its resting place."[10] Consequently, at that time all interpretations seemed possible. Two centuries later, on the contrary, the diabolical interpretation prevailed, though it was less interested in the figure of Samuel and focused increasingly on the medium and Satan.

Viewed within a very long time frame (from the twelfth to the seventeenth centuries), the corresponding iconography conveys this evolution quite well. In a miniature from the *Bible historiale* by Guyart des Moulins, from the first quarter of the fifteenth century, we see the devil enter the picture for the first time, as if to preside over the conversation of the medium and evil King Saul, while Samuel is standing apart (illus. 1).[11] This iconography tended to merge, beginning in the first half of the sixteenth century (in a painting by Jacob Comelisz in Amsterdam, 1526), with that of the witches' Sabbath.[12]

Before this time the ways in which Samuel was portrayed show a much greater diversity. Sometimes the ghost is represented in the manner of a resuscitated body (illus. 2): Samuel's eyes are open, but his dark-brown face contrasts with the white skin of the medium and the king; his body is completely covered in wrappings, which give him the appearance of a mummy; and he is standing up in his grave.[13] Clearly this representation borrows its characteristics from the conventional iconography of Christ's resurrection of Lazarus. Even the king, who is hiding his face in his mantle so that he will not be recognized by the medium, recalls the gesture of Christ's companions, who cover their noses so as not to smell the stench of Lazarus's cadaver.

Sometimes the ghost is portrayed with the characteristics and clothes of a living man (illus. 3). Only reading the accompanying text enables one to know that the figure is a dead person. This illustration is as old as the earlier one, since it is found in a late-twelfth-century manuscript of Peter Lombard's *Commentary on the Psalms*.[14] The iconography continued to the end of the thirteenth century in the illustrations of the *Bible historiale*.[15]

Sometimes Samuel appears as a living-dead in motion, completely naked, barely covered in a shroud that floats on his head and over his shoulders (illus. 5, 6).[16]

Finally, sometimes the transparent shroud reveals the body underneath (illus. 4).[17] In this last case, the medieval illustration announces the modern image of a ghost. But this ghostly appearance derives only from the nature of the clothing, for if the face of the dead man seems extremely pale, the same is true of the other figures in the illustrations.

The iconography of this biblical tale therefore fluctuates between several formulas, but they all give the dead man a full body, fully fleshed, and all show him dressed at least in his shroud if not in the clothing he

was supposed to have been wearing while he was alive. These representations should be compared with those that illustrate contemporaneous
tales of apparitions of ordinary dead people. For the time being, let us
simply emphasize the possibility, in a certain type of illustration at least,
of a negative and even a diabolical connotation in the evocation of Samuel by the medium of Endor. This type of image corresponds to the unfavorable judgments that, in Augustinian tradition, were generally associated with ghosts.

Augustine and Evodius

Augustine (354–430), the bishop of Hippo, was the true founder of the
Christian theory of ghosts. This theory showed three principal characteristics, all of which tended toward a strong restriction against apparitions of the dead. Such apparitions were considered if not impossible,
then at least highly unusual. It was neither the body nor even the soul
of the dead person that appeared but only the "spiritual image"; these
"spiritual images" were quite often introduced by demons into the minds
of people while they were asleep. One therefore had to beware of
dreams.

Tertullian (c. 160–c. 230) had already fought the notion that seeing
a dead person in a vision would enable one to see that person's very soul.[18]
Rather, demons were passing themselves off as relatives of the living who
received the apparitions and who, through an exorcism, could be forced
to confess their true nature. It might have been a "personal demon" who
haunted a man throughout his life and caused him to act badly.[19] As for
Lactandus (c. 250–c. 325), he combined in the same condemnation the
opinion of the people (vulgus) who believed that "the souls of the dead
wander around the graves and the remains of their bodies," and the idea
of idols, which were themselves "semblances of the dead." The true God
had no need of such "images."[20] And yet, ghosts appeared: even Ambrose
of Milan—Augustine's own teacher—emotionally described the dream
in which his dead brother Satyrus appeared to him.

Augustine addressed the issue of ghosts in a much more systematic
and complete way, in a detour from a more comprehensive reflection on
death and the dead, visions and dreams, angels, demons, and saints. We
should note that some of Augustine's writings on this subject are of an
epistolary nature: their interest lies, then, in the confrontation between
Augustine's opinions and those of his correspondents, Evodius (in letter

158) and then Paulinus of Nola (in the treatise *On the Care to Be Given to the Dead*).

In one letter, his correspondent Evodius resumes a dialogue with which Augustine and he had been familiar for a long time. Younger than Augustine, Evodius had also been converted in Milan and then had followed his friend to Rome and to Thagaste, where he became one of the first monks before becoming the bishop of Uzalis near Utica. In response to Evodius's questions, Augustine wrote his treatises on the soul (*De quantitate animae*) and on free will (*De libero arbitrio*). The method of the dialogue is always the same: Evodius feigns doubt (*simulata dubitatio*) in order to give Augustine completely free reign to develop his arguments. For Evodius, there is no doubt about the reality of apparitions of the dead; they occur in great numbers and serve to announce future events, which indeed do come to pass.[21] "More than once" he heard that many dead people returned, both day and night, to the houses they had once known. People who were awake encountered them on their way. According to the stories, many of the dead came at a certain time during the night to the places where their bodies were buried, that is, primarily to the basilicas, where prayers are said over the tombs. Evodius cites the trustworthy testimony of a very holy priest who had seen a multitude of dead with luminous bodies coming out of the baptistery. Evodius claims to have carried out a true investigation, an *inquisitio*, in the course of which all his information proved to be consistent. He cannot therefore convince himself that everything he has heard is just a web of fables: in Evodius's opinion, the dead visit the living in their dreams and even when they are awake. These *visitationes* are not fantasies (*fantasia*: the word has a very strong diabolical connotation); they are as true as Joseph's dreams in the Holy Scriptures. Evodius himself was the beneficiary of announcements, which proved to be true, from three dead monks (Profuturus, Privatus, and Servilius). He thus calls on the wisdom of Augustine to give him advice, notably concerning the very complex case of his young secretary, who had just died prematurely at the age of twenty-two.

We must untangle the somewhat snarled thread of that story to reconstruct the chronology, rigorously established by Evodius, of the rituals that accompanied the death of the young man and of the signs, in the form of visions and apparitions, that announced and followed the death. These rituals and signs reveal the coherence of a micro-society galvanized by the death and its consequences: it brought together living people, others who were dead, and finally, others who would very shortly die. This milieu was the one in which Evodius lived, and he writes his account from what he was told by those who were living near him. It is noteworthy, however, that at no time does he speak about any apparition of which he personally was the beneficiary but only about the visions or dreams of others. For the sake of clarity, let us establish the sequential stages of the tale.

1. When the young secretary is near death, a fellow student who had died eight months earlier appears in a dream to announce that he "has come to get his friend."

2. The very day of his death, the young man summons his father, who is a priest, and exchanges, three times, a kiss of peace with his father, whom he begs to come soon and join him in death. This wish was very soon to be granted.

3. Scarcely does Evodius's young secretary die when another "man"—supposedly a dead man, but his identity is not specified—appears in the same house to a half-awake old man. The dead man holds a laurel branch and a written document in his hand (we do not know what the document is). Although mysterious, this apparition must signify that the dead man will be saved.

4. Indeed, while prayers are being offered for three days for the salvation of the deceased, on the second day the widow Urbica, who leads a holy life, sees in a dream a deacon, someone who had himself died four years earlier. He is busy preparing a palace as shiny as silver where he can welcome the young secretary who died "the day before." He works alongside the servants of God, virgins and widows, while an old man gleaming in whiteness (*senex candidus*: is this God himself?) orders two figures who are just as white (angels) to draw the young man from his grave and lead him up to heaven. This celestial vision thus confirms the blessed destiny of the dead man.

5. Finally, on the third day the dead man himself appears in a dream to one of his brothers, who asks him a series of questions. Does he know he is dead? (He answers in the affirmative.) Was he received by God? (Yes.) What does he want? ("I have been sent," he answers, "to fetch my father.") The priest/father, in the company of the old bishop Theasius, looks to the monastery to be consoled for the loss of his son. The brother who was dreaming wakes up, and he tells his vision to the bishop, who is reluctant to disturb the priest with such news. But just as was announced, the father dies four days after the *visitatio* of his son, seven days after his son's death.

This series of oneiric visions is composed of at least three apparitions of different ghosts (the deacon who had died four years earlier, the student who had died eight months earlier, and finally the young man himself), all of whom serve the same purpose: either to announce to someone the coming death of someone else (the young man, then his father) or to reveal the destiny of a dead person in the hereafter (the young man, who is saved). These dead inform the living about death and the dead, but they do not ask the living for suffrages, even though the young man expresses his gratitude for the prayers that those close to him said for his salvation. This is notably different from the actions of ghosts in the central Middle Ages.

Evodius's letter also inscribes the dead man's revelations within a particular space, that of grave sites, which were increasingly concentrated in churches, near the tombs of saints (*ad sanctos*). In Evodius's writings, what is the weight given to *simulata dubitatio*? It is difficult to guess Evodius's own convictions, but Augustine could hardly have accepted everything Evodius presented to him. We can see this for ourselves through Augustine's response to another letter, that of Paulinus of Nola.

Augustine and Paulinus of Nola

In 421 Paulinus, the bishop of Nola in Campania, wrote to his friend Augustine, the bishop of Hippo, that he had given in to the wishes of a noblewoman, Flora, to have her dead son buried in the Saint Felix basilica in Nola. Paulinus assumes that the *ad sanctos* burial place is beneficial to the dead, and he seeks Augustine's advice on the matter. The answer Augustine ultimately sends him is a veritable treatise "on the care to be given to the dead" (*De cura pro mortuis gerenda*, c. 421–424).[22]

In this treatise Augustine does not share Paulinus's point of view. In Augustine's opinion Christians, unlike pagans, must not concern themselves with the bodies of the dead. Only the soul is important, and for its salvation they must pray to God. The pomp of funeral services and the state of the burial place are important only to the living, who are thus consoled in their time of grief ("*magis sunt vivorum solacia quam subsidia mortuorum,*" chap. II).[23]

Using all the means at his disposal, Augustine attempts to deny the possibility of any communication between the living and the dead. Just as the living know nothing of the destiny of the dead in the hereafter, so the dead know nothing more of the living. He is forced, however, to admit that, based on the reliability of certain visionary tales he has been told, the dead might appear either in a dream or "in other ways" to give relatives some information and even to indicate what they should do for the burial place of the dead. In chapter X he tells the story he heard in Milan: while some unscrupulous creditors were demanding that a young man pay the debt his father supposedly had not paid before dying, the dead man appeared to the son in a dream and revealed to him where the receipt for the payment could be found.

But such an apparition occurred unbeknownst to the dead person, in the same way that we might dream of a living person without that person knowing anything about it. Thus, at the very moment when Augustine was hearing this tale in Milan, he himself, without his knowledge, was appearing in a dream to the rhetorician Eulogius of Carthage. This man, unable to understand a difficult passage of Cicero, dreamed that Augustine was dictating the solution to him. Naturally, Augustine knew nothing of that dream. "On the other side of the sea, at that very same moment I was doing something else entirely, perhaps I was falling asleep, and in any case I was not thinking at all of his concerns" (chap. XI).

"How does this occur?" Augustine wonders. As often happens when he asks a difficult question that he does not want to evade, Augustine is content to admit: "I do not know."[24] In fact, reducing apparitions of the dead to the realm of dreams that the living have of each other enables him to deny that the dead themselves can move around as spirits and truly enter into the minds of the living. In any event, the apparition is not a man, whether living or dead, or his soul, or of course his body. The apparition is a "semblance of the man" (similitudo hominis), an "image" (imago), completely foreign to the consciousness of the person whom it depicts as living.

The dead, just like the living, are therefore unaware that people, dreaming, see them "imaginarily" (imaginaliter) (chap. XII). The spirits of the dead (spiritus defunctorum) have no reason to involve themselves with the living (chap. XIII). This is, moreover, what is taught by the parable of Lazarus, whom Abraham did not allow to appear to the brothers of the rich man. Granted, the rich man was concerned about his brothers, but he knew nothing of their business on earth. Likewise, we are concerned about our dead, but we cannot know what becomes of them (chap. XIV).

If the dead learn something about the living, it can only be through the intercession of angels who are in contact with each other and who ensure a mediation between the divine kingdom, which is beyond time, and the earthly world, which is in time. And if an exception must be admitted, that is, if some apparitions do occur, these do not involve the ordinary dead but instead involve exceptional figures, such as saints. These apparitions are the counterpart of the *raptus* of Saint Paul, who was carried off from earth to paradise (2 Cor. 12:2). This is, in a certain sense, the reverse direction from that taken, according to the Old Testament, by Samuel, who was conjured by the medium of Endor and who told Saul of his impending death, and similarly by Moses and Elias (at the time of the transfiguration of Christ) (chap. XV). Christian saints also appeared under exceptional circumstances. "We have learned," Augustine cautiously recognizes, "through not uncertain rumors and sure witnesses, that Saint Felix appeared during the siege of Nola by the Barbarians." The caution of the statement is quite revealing: everything must separate the ordinary dead, whose apparitions would be too reminiscent of ancient paganism, from the saints, the elite dead of Christianity and the church. "We must understand that through the work of divine power the martyrs can involve themselves in the affairs of the living, whereas the deceased, by their very nature, cannot" (chap. XVI). In the end, all these phenomena are explained by the mediating powers of the angels: through the grace of God, angels cause people to see, even in their sleep, the images *"in effigie corporis,"* in the guise of the bodies of those, living or dead, with whom they have, or once had, a relationship (chap. XVII).

The Mediating Imagination

If Augustine denied that the living and the dead could have even the slightest direct contact, this was because he wanted to eradicate any form of material worshiping of the dead. The entire conclusion of the treatise discusses the prayers that the living should address to God for the salvation of the souls of the dead. The phenomenon of apparitions is not completely denied, but it is relegated to its rightful place: the realm of the "spiritual vision," which consists of immaterial images produced in various ways in the imagination, especially while a person is dreaming. This is what Augustine demonstrates in a systematic way in his twelve-volume commentary on Genesis, in which he sets forth the Christian theory of the three types of visions: "corporeal," "spiritual," and "intellectual."[25] This distinction was considerably important throughout the Middle Ages. We will therefore devote some time to it.

The Augustinian theory of vision was in part the heir of ancient concepts. It had enormous influence until the twelfth century, when it was then joined to Aristotle's naturalist concepts, transmitted through Arab science. The three types of visions formed a hierarchy, homologous to the hierarchy of the faculties of the soul: corporeal vision depended on the bodily senses; spiritual vision, on the imagination; and intellectual vision, on pure reason.

• At the bottom, the *visio corporalis* was nothing more than the sense of sight. It enabled a person, through his or her corporeal senses, to see material objects. According to our contemporary notion of sight, from the discoveries of Kepler in the seventeenth century, solar light reflected on an object stimulates, on the retina, a nerve impulse that is transmitted to the brain. Ancient and medieval theories were quite different.[26] Some supported "intromission," but without the idea of the reflection of solar light: the object itself emitted into the "medium," separating it from the eye of the *species*, something like particles (according to Democritus and the atomists) or pure appearances (according to the Arab Al Hazen and, in the thirteenth century, Roger Bacon). To talk about the form or the image of the object that is imprinted in the eye, Roger Bacon used the terms *species, lumen, idolum, phantasma, simulacrum, forma, similitudo, umbra,* etc. Although the theory of intromission continued to spread into the thirteenth century, ancient and medieval scholars, from Plato and his commentator Chalcidius to William of Conches in the twelfth century and even beyond, proclaimed much more widely the theory of extramission: the "natural" and then the "spiritual virtue" produced in the body and conducted through the optical nerve from the brain to the eye was a sort of ray emitted by the eye and sent through external light to the object in view; the ray took on the object's shape and color, which was sent back to the eye and from there to the soul.[27] When this interpretation of visual power was finally rendered null and void by the laws of optics and retinal vision, the popular concepts of "fascination" and the "evil eye" remained.[28] All these notions shared the idea of a concrete, physical interaction of the eye and the object through an external medium: *species* circulated and penetrated into the eye, which, far from being passive, exercised its *virtus* over the external world.

• At the highest level, the *visio intellectualis* dominated all other visions, since it came out of man's reason (*mens, ratio*) and aimed for a direct contemplation of God. Regarding vision, it plunged into the unspeakable and the invisible; it was beyond any image. The clerics of the Middle Ages agreed when they said that this experience was reserved for a very small number, such as Saint Paul, who wondered if he had been "caught up to the third heaven, whether in the body or out of the body" (2 Cor. 12:2).

• Finally, Saint Augustine and his continuators reserved a very important place, situated between corporeal sight and intellectual vision, for *visio spiritalis*, through which the "spirit" of man (not the senses of the body or the *mens*, the upper part of the soul) perceived "images" or "semblances" of bodies (and not the bodies themselves). The soul's function that came into play here was the *imaginatio*, the intermediary and mediatory power between *sensus* and *mens*, which received and transformed images. Its role was central: to receive the images perceived by the senses and submit them to the judgment of reason before committing them to memory. It could also receive images of people or things that were not present, but only those that had been previously perceived by the senses, or it could even "imagine at the whim of our fantasy things that are absolutely nonexistent." Afflictions of the body and the mind also had an impact on the imagination, since those who were sick with high fevers and those who were depressed often had such "phantasms," or hallucinations. As we can see, the debate on visions and dreams displays several facets: the tradition of the classification of dreams (from Macrobius to Gregory the Great) intersects the medical discourse that originated in Galen and that was particularly attentive to the body's role in the origins of such phenomena.

If "intellectual vision" was beyond images, corporeal vision and spiritual vision presented more than one analogy. Both of them dealt with *imagines*, either in relation to material objects (corporeal vision) or independent of this perception of objects (spiritual vision). The latter did not perceive bodies, only "semblances of bodies," also named *species, similitudines, figurae, formae, umbrae*; they were "like bodies" (*quasi corpora*) without really being so. During sleep these appearances were oneiric images and all sorts of visions and apparitions, which the *miracula* and *exempla* related in great numbers. Finally, in the insane and the sick, they were hallucinations brought on by fever.

The Ghost: A Body or an Image?

What could be said about the object of the spiritual vision, that is, the dead person who appeared? The question forces us to look back at the foundations of Christian anthropology.

Man was made of a composed and mortal body and of a composed but immortal soul. When a person died, when the vital principle that had "animated" the person was extinguished (for expediency's sake, let us name this *anima*), the body (*corpus, caro*), the carnal and transient envelope of the soul, was interred and destined for a rapid deterioration. According to Saint Augustine, as we have said, the dead body deserved no "concern" (*cura*) beyond reasons of social conventions.[29] On the other hand, the soul, the divine principle that was in man (*animus, spiritus*), did not die: as soon as it "separated" from the body, the soul, unless it was immediately saved or damned, endured "purgatorial" trials (or even, after the twelfth century, went to purgatory after an individual judgment) while awaiting final salvation. It was during this more or less lengthy time, conceived and even measured in the same proportions as terrestrial time, that apparitions of the dead were most likely to occur.

But what exactly appeared? The range of narrative possibilities appears limitless. Some tales relate that a certain deceased person appeared, quite recognizable by the face, the voice, the name, and often even the clothing that the person had worn while alive and, especially, at the time of death. Others tell of the apparition of a soul (*anima*) or a spirit (*spiritus*), this second expression referring back most directly to the nature of "spiritual vision": it was the "spirit-mind" of the living person, the cognitive powers of the soul, that enabled the living person to perceive the "spirit" of the dead person, the immaterial but visible substitute for the invisible soul, presenting the dead person as she or he had appeared while alive. Other tales emphasize the value of appearance, of the incorporeal image of the apparition. Texts sometimes call this *umbra* and make use of the corresponding adjective in the expression *species umbratica:* an "appearance of a shadow," a phantom.[30] What the living saw had only the appearance (*similitudo, forma, species, effigies, imago*) of the living people that those dead had once been. The adverb applied most often to the dead is *quasi:* while they were in fact dead, they appeared "as if" they were alive. This adverb *quasi* is characteristic of all visionary literature, and I consider it very important. It indeed expresses doubt, a hesitation in the face of all those phenomena that were known to be immaterial and that, nevertheless, had all the appearances of the tangible; this is the essence of what was called spiritual (*spiritalis*). The same remark can be made about the phrases so frequently uttered: *visum est sibi* or *videtur sibi videre*, which were used in preference to the active *vidit*. They should be translated as "it seemed to him" or "it seemed to him he had seen," which indicates doubt as to the nature of the object of the "spiritual vision." I also detect evidence here of a passive attitude, one of submission, as if, before seeing a dead person (or an angel or the devil), the living person was first seen by him/it.

Another interesting term is *persona*, generally used to designate a supernatural being (angel, saint, dead person, even Christ) whom the beneficiary of the apparition had not yet identified.[31] This is the case when a dead person broke off from an anonymous group of deceased and was not yet recognized and named. Here we are not far from the theatrical meaning of the words "character" [*personnage* in French] and "mask" (*persona* being, among other meanings, the equivalent of the Greek *prósôpon*). In *De cura pro mortuis gerenda*,[32] Saint Augustine contrasts the *persona* of the dead, that is, the image or the immaterial semblance, to the *praesentia* of the living, who are indeed there "in person." Written at the beginning of the tenth century, *Canon Episcopi* denounces the disguises of the devil, who in dreams takes on the appearance "of *persons* sometimes known, sometimes unknown."[33] We must compare to that word a no less ambiguous noun: *larva* (with its adjective *larvaticus*). This word refers simultaneously to the ill-fated dead of ancient Rome and to masks, following the meaning that prevailed in the Middle Ages.[34]

These names for appearance conform most to the Augustinian theory of an apparition as a "spiritual vision." Let us repeat: for Augustine, what appeared was neither the dead person's body nor the dead person's soul, which was an immaterial essence and had absolutely no reason to come into contact with the living. It was an *imago*, a "spiritual image"—not "corporeal"—that had only the appearance of a body. Let us recall that for Augustine, there was no essential difference between the apparition of the image of a dead person and the apparition of the oneiric image of a friend who lived far away and who was unaware of being the object of a dream. All these images were perceived not by the eyes of the body but by the "eyes of the soul," to which they were brought by angels, both good and evil.[35]

For "spiritual images" were not always formed by themselves in the person's spirit-mind: some were introduced by "foreign spirits," both good and evil.[36] Augustine was the heir of the great pneumatic tradition handed down by antiquity.[37] In the Christianized form that he gives this tradition, angels—subject to divine will—informed people of what they knew through spiritual images. And the same was true of fallen angels, the "evil spirits" who imprinted their false images onto the imagination of men and women, especially during sleep. In both cases the process was the same; it was therefore difficult to distinguish the good angels from the bad (who, according to Saint Paul—2 Cor. 11:14—disguised themselves as "angels of light"). Being able to tell the spirits apart (*discretio spiritum*) assumed that charisma of which the apostle spoke (1 Cor. 12:10).

Thus Augustine was sure that the only "spirits" that ensured a mediation between the hereafter and the here-and-now were angels (among them, the evil angels, demons). It was angels who presented to a person's mind the "spiritual image" of a dead person, in the appearance of the living body of that person. But that apparition had no relation either to the dead person's real body, whose burial place was of no importance, or to the deceased's soul, which was no more interested in appearing. And on these two essential points the Augustinian theory continued to be contradicted throughout the entire Middle Ages. Far from being completely immaterial, "spiritual images" seemed strangely to be endowed with corporeity, both in tales of apparitions and in iconographic representations of ghosts. Moreover, angels and demons were not the only "spirits" likely to move around by themselves; ghosts too did quite well without angelic mediation.

The Descendants of Saint Augustine

De cura pro mortuis gerenda and the commentary on Genesis regarding visions were cited widely and were used by Christian authors throughout the Middle Ages. For example, Julian of Toledo (d. 690) drew inspiration explicitly from them when he wondered "whether the dead can appear visibly to the eyes of the living."[38] Much later, in the twelfth century, Gratian recalled Augustine's opinion that the dead did not know what went on above their graves,[39] and in the same period Honorius Augustodunensis echoed the idea that souls that endured punishment in the afterworld appeared to the living "only with the angels' permission."[40] As for the liturgists, they continued to repeat that during the funeral mass, the body of the deceased had to wait in the vestibule of the church, "for we do not communicate with the dead, since they do not answer us."[41]

However, Augustine's ideas found all their contemporary impact and strength primarily in a twelfth-century treatise that was for a long time erroneously attributed to him: *Liber de spiritu et anima*, which, it is generally agreed today, was most likely written by the Cistercian monk Alcher of Clairvaux (died c. 1165).[42]

In this work, and in completely Augustinian terms, the author examines the multiple meanings and the inclusive relationships of the words that relate to the definition of the soul and to visionary experiences (*animus, anima, spiritus*). He dwells on the three types of visions, and drawing inspiration from Macrobius, he introduces among spiritual visions the classic distinction of the five types of dreams.[43] Having then spoken in turn of angels and demons, he comes to apparitions of the dead (chap. XXIX).

To all appearances, he follows Augustine's teachings to the letter: apparitions are only the "semblances of things" (*similitudines rerum*), not the things themselves; apparitions are produced through "the workings of angels," on God's orders; the dead are unaware of what goes on among the living, just as the living do not know the destiny of the deceased. However, there are some significant alterations in the details. The very fact that apparitions of the dead are the subject of a separate chapter, in the same right as apparitions of angels and demons, immediately grants the former an importance and an autonomy that Augustine never recognized. In addition, the dead are considered to have a concern for the living (*cura de vivis*) equal to the concern that the living have for the dead (*cura de mortuis*). Finally, although the dead themselves cannot see what the living do, they are informed about the living in part by other dead who join them and to whom they listen; they thus learn "what some have permission to reveal and what others need to hear."

A quick reading of *De spiritu et anima* might convince us that it is a completely Augustinian treatise. For the most part, that impression is unavoidable. But subtle differences show that the theory of ghosts, in spite of the authority of the father of the Latin church, has partially given way to the pressure of narrative inflation and of more appealing representations, which gradually gave ghosts a greater importance, more of a presence, and more numerous functions than Augustine could or would ever admit. Examining the evolution of tales of apparitions of the dead from the fifth to the twelfth centuries will enable us to follow these changes step by step, changes that were at first quite slow but that occurred much more rapidly after the year 1000.

Between Saints and Demons

Throughout the early Middle Ages, tales of ghosts were rare. A still profoundly dualistic conception of the world made little room for them between apparitions of God, saints, and angels and those of the devil and demons. For a long time tales of ghosts were largely indistinguishable from hagiography: one of the recognized roles of the Merovingian or Carolingian saint was to exorcise the ill-fated spirits of the dead, which were more or less associated with the "evil spirits" (*maligni spiritus*) that were demons. Heroes of the new faith, the saints put to flight, exorcised, and denounced the evil dead of paganism and "superstition"; after these saints died, their hagiographers strove to set their apparitions apart from those of the other dead. Saint Germanus of Auxerre (according to his hagiographer, Constantius of Lyon, who wrote around 478, some thirty years after the death of his hero) was believed to have rid a house of "evil shadows" that were haunting it because of the presence of cadavers that had not received a worthy burial place.[44] An exceptional model of the Christianity of the Gauls, Saint Martin, according to his hagiographer, Sulpicius Severus (c. 397), addressed the "sordid shadow" of a robber for whom the inhabitants of the town had established a cult as if the robber were a martyr; Saint Martin forced the shadow to reveal his name and to confess his crimes.[45] Here we have a very significant model, one used again by hagiographers for other saints such as the evangelist of Ireland in the fifth century, Saint Patrick, who carried out approximately the same acts.[46]

The church fathers were already tending to associate the ill-fated dead with demons to explain the misfortunes of Christian communities.[47] In the collection *Miracles of the Protomartyr Stephen*, a dying man, Dativus, dreams he is threatened by a mob of dead people, some of whom he knows and who evidently play the role that would be assumed by demons in the medieval visions of the dying.[48] The rituals of exorcism used by the clerics in the early Middle Ages also show how the fear of the evil dead and that of demons were often the same: sprinkling holy water and salt, combined with a formula of conjuration, would cast aside "every shadow, every Satan, all the diabolical workings of the infernal spirits of suicides or of those who wander the earth."[49]

On the opposite side of this society's scale of values, the apparitions of saints were expected and were sought after. We see this in the work of Gregory of Tours (c. 538–594), who in *Liber in gloria confessorum* describes the necropolis or Polyandrion of Autun, the "place of the great majority."[50] Frequent apparitions and mysterious psalmodies indicated the burial places of the blessed minority of Christians who were granted eternal rest. In the basilica dedicated to Saint Stephen right next to the cemetery, two inhabitants who had come to pray were surprised to hear mysterious voices. The spirit of a blessed one chased them away from that holy place, of which they were not worthy. In this way Christianity transformed old beliefs: by seeking to reserve for its saints the privilege of apparition and by using a fear of ghosts to protect its holy places. Gregory of Tours shows this well when he tells about his visit to Lyon in the company of the bishop Nizier. On the gravestone of the bishop martyr Helius, a notice recalls that one night the dead man seized a grave robber and let him go only when he repented of his sins.[51] Therefore the ecclesiastical culture, by slightly transforming the Germanic traditions, "tamed" those traditions relative to the dead who defended their graves against intruders.[52]

The saint thus appeared most often to comfort his flock, to defend his sanctuary, or to put the living on guard against sins and to urge them to prepare for death. These apparitions are legion in all of the hagiographical literature of the early Middle Ages, and this is not the place to study them in great detail.[53] On the other hand, it is important to note that they introduced a narrative model that was then applied in broad terms to all the dead. This is seen clearly in *Life of Saint Amatus*, written perhaps before 700. Well before his death, the saint, the abbot of Remiremont (d. c. 628), had his burial place prepared at the entrance to the Saint Mary basilica. His epitaph was intended to inspire the faithful to pray for him. Three days after he died he appeared to a brother to tell the brother not to mourn his death, for he had earned eternal salvation. But he begged the brother to tell his successor, Romaric, to please conserve his *memoria*. At the end of the year, following the nocturnal service celebrated in his memory, he appeared once again to order that his remains be placed in the crypt of the basilica.[54] In at least two ways this saint, whose memory was piously preserved by the community he had led, presaged the more ordinary ghosts of the later period. To erase the minor sins he had committed, even though he was a saint, he sought and benefited from the liturgical prayers of the monks. Subsequently, his apparitions followed the rhythms of liturgical time, which favored the days that immediately followed the death and, above all, the exact date of the death. That moment, which definitely sealed one's destiny in the hereafter, would be important for all dead. Here it was marked by a liturgical act that was essential to the makeup of hagiographical memory and that, in this regard, resolutely distinguished saints from the ordinary dead: only saints benefited from a solemn transfer of their corporeal remains, the equivalent, in Christian society, of a "second funeral," which in "primitive" societies distinguished those who had access to the rank of the "ancestors."[55]

The Genesis of Medieval Tales

Between apparitions of the ill-fated dead linked to paganism and those of saints, very little room was left for apparitions of the ordinary dead. This period was fixed on the mode of psychomachy, on the antagonism between good and evil; the time had not yet come for an assessment of the destiny of ordinary people, in death as in life. A few tales do, however, exist.

Those written by Pope Gregory the Great (c. 540–604) enjoyed great fame throughout the Middle Ages. Having become pope in 590, around 593–594 Gregory undertook to write down, in the form of *dialogues* with the deacon Peter, a whole collection of Italian hagiographical traditions. Through his friend he aimed at a literate audience of monks and clerics, whom he wanted to convince that saintliness could still flourish in their time and that this saintliness offered moral examples their contemporaries should follow. Book I exalts twelve thaumaturgists. Book II focuses on the single figure of Saint Benedict. In Book III, however, more than thirty saints, often quite recent ones, are presented as examples. Book IV contrasts with the earlier books in that it departs from the hagiographical genre and focuses on the single theme of a person's final hours and of the destiny of the soul after death. In this final book, the death of ordinary Christians is thus taken into account. More than the preceding books, Book IV appears as a treatise in which tales are used to illustrate theoretical assertions on the survival of the soul after death, on the celestial signs that accompany a passing, and on visions of the places in the hereafter. At the end of the book Gregory raises the question of the benefit of an *ad sanctos* burial place, so often sought by his contemporaries; in agreement with Augustine, he considers such a burial of little use and even demonstrates its risks to the deceased who are not worthy of such a site. Rather, he recommends prayer and the offering of masses for the salvation of the soul.

Here the author inserts a tale he claims to have heard from the bishop Felix of Porto: its hero is a priest who was accustomed to going to the baths of Tauriana.[56] This priest was regularly served there by an unknown man to whom, as a symbol of gratitude, he finally offers two "crown-shaped loaves," breads usually intended for the eucharistic sacrifice. The man then reveals that he is the former master of those baths, that he is dead, and that he is atoning for his sins in the earthly place where he committed them. He refuses the rings of bread but asks the priest to offer them up to God on his behalf. He then disappears, thus confirming that he is a "spirit" (*spiritus*).

Book IV of the *Dialogues* contains another analogous tale: that of Germanus, the bishop of Capua, who encounters the spirit of the deacon Paschasius in the public baths of Angulus, where the latter was purging a minor sin. The bishop's prayers delivered the dead man at the end of a few days.[57]

These tales are inscribed within the series of representations of expiatory places that preceded the advent of purgatory, in the formal sense.[58] They also bear witness to the significance, at least in central Italy in the sixth century, of public baths, those shrines—henceforth in ruins—that represent ancient sociability and the *otium* but that are at present offered up, thanks to the water and warm steam, to the investment of the Christian imaginary in death and in the hereafter.

No less famous is the tale of the apparition of the monk-doctor Justus, who died three years before Gregory recounted his story. On his deathbed, Justus confesses to his brother Copiosus that he hid three pieces of gold and thus erred in his vow of poverty. Told of this, Gregory condemns the dying man to isolation (no one would come to see him in his final moments), and then, once he is dead, Gregory forbids anyone from burying the body in the monks' cemetery. But at the end of thirty days, considering the punishment sufficient, Gregory orders that the eucharistic sacrifice be offered every day for the deceased during the following thirty days. Soon Justus appears to his brother Copiosus to announce that on that very day he "has received communion." A quick calculation confirms that mass was celebrated for him for thirty days exactly before showing results.[59] The practice of saying masses for a dead person during the thirty days following death was therefore well established at the end of the fifth century. Using the metaphor of food to be shared with the dead was also encouraged, since it tended to detract Christians from funerary practices—libations, banquets, offerings on the grave—that were too reminiscent of paganism. Thus the *Poem on the Mass of the Dead* by Jacques de Serugh (d. 521) advised the living to invite the dead person to the eucharistic "banquet" but not "to call the dead onto his grave, for he doesn't hear you."[60]

Other references to apparitions of ordinary dead people in the early Middle Ages do exist, but they are most often pulled by the two opposite poles of hagiography and demonology. In Gregory of Tours's *History of the Franks*, a jealous husband who killed his wife and the man he had taken for his rival is assailed in his dreams by his victims, who foretell of his imminent death.[61] And yet, in his voluminous *Ecclesiastical History*, Bede the Venerable (c. 672–735) mentions, alongside a wealth of tales of visions of all sorts, scarcely more than three apparitions of the ordinary dead. These all involve monks and recluses who announce to other religious figures that they will soon die or who give them religious advice: the hagiographic model thus remains very close.[62]

The Development of the Liturgy of the Dead

Beginning in the ninth century, the principal factor in the increase in the number of tales of ghosts was the development of the liturgy of the dead. In the Carolingian period, the system of masses said especially for a dead person on the third, the seventh, and the thirtieth day after death was firmly and coherently established.[63] It was completed by the practice of making offerings to the poor in memory of the deceased using donations bequeathed to the church. This entire liturgy in fact rested on a structure of exchange in which symbolic values were inseparable from the most important material and social effects. We must now illustrate a network of the complex relationships that were established between four distinct groups.

• The legators divided their goods between the church and their heirs; they entreated the latter to look after their souls after death and not to redirect their charitable donations.
• The heirs, in fact, were often tempted to hoard the entire estate and neglect the *memoria* of their deceased relatives.
• The church, primarily the monasteries, received these bequests, with the instructions to pray for the dead and also to redistribute a portion of the gifts to the poor.
• Finally, the poor benefited in part from the alms. Sometimes the recipients represented only a small symbolic number, but often they were a crowd of truly miserable folk. They were considered to be the terres-

trial substitutes for the dead people, since the alms they received made up the "suffrages" that helped in the salvation of the dead. Giving material nourishment to the poor was the same as symbolically "nourishing," through prayers, the dead benefactors' souls in purgatory. The abbey of Fulda was at that time one of the premier places for this type of exchange between the living and the dead. It is therefore not surprising that we find there two ghost tales that directly concern the liturgy of the dead and demonstrate the necessity of suffrages for the deceased.

The *Life* of Rabanus Maurus, abbot of Fulda and archbishop of Mainz, tells of the brutal punishment that the "shadows" of the deceased monks of the monastery inflicted one night in the year 837 on the cellarer Adelhardus. Because he had redirected, for his own profit, the provenders intended for the poor, the deceased legators could no longer benefit from a lessening of their trials in the hereafter. They therefore returned for their revenge.[64] A bit later the continuator of the *Annals of Fulda* recalls how King Louis the Germanic devoted himself devoutly to prayer during Lent in 878. One night his deceased father, Emperor Louis the Pious, appeared to him to entreat him in the name of Christ and the Trinity to pull his father out of the torments of the hereafter. Terrified by this vision, the king had his tale written down and sent it to all the monasteries in the kingdom so that all the monks would pray to God for the salvation of the deceased emperor.[65]

Thus in the ninth century the entire apparatus—institutional, liturgical, narrative—was in place; Saint Augustine's hesitations regarding apparitions of the dead, reservations expressed five centuries earlier, were now definitely discarded. It was henceforth admitted that the dead could indeed appear to the living, much to the benefit of both groups. But it was the living who imagined and told of apparitions. The increase in the number of these tales, starting in the year 1000, enables us to analyze their forms and their objectives.

TWO

DREAMING OF THE DEAD

Beginning in the first centuries, the Christian culture encountered and attempted to resolve the problem of the dead, particularly the question of the supposed return of some of the dead. As we have just seen, Saint Augustine clearly defined the church's attitude on the subject. At the same time, throughout the early Middle Ages, documents of ecclesiastical origin were little concerned with ghosts. But this changed after the eleventh century, in particular due to the appearance at that time of autobiographical tales of ghosts. These tales enable us to come as close as possible to the innermost attitudes of the people of the Middle Ages (or of some of them) with regard to the dead. Such tales are found in Christian literature beginning in the first centuries but increased in number after the year 1000 due to several factors: a general renewal (as Georg Misch has shown) of autobiographical writing; the development of what Michel Zink has called "literary subjectivity" (or the recognition of the status of author and of the legitimacy of the "I" in literature); the valuing of the personal dream in the consciousness of the self; and the development of the *memoria* of one's natural and spiritual kin. Written by monks and clerics and also, beginning in the thirteenth century, by literate laymen, autobiographical tales take us to the heart of the "work of mourning" and of the ambivalence of those who were in the clutches simultaneously of the obsessive remembrance of deceased loved ones and of the will to forget them.

Between the eleventh and the fifteenth centuries, three types of autobiographical ghost tales were written. In some cases the author tells not of a true apparition but rather of a feeling of an invisible presence very close by. In other cases, rare and limited to mystical literature (beginning in the thirteenth century), we read of a conscious vision of the dead, a vision experienced in a moment of ecstasy. Most often throughout the period in question, the autobiographical ghost tale is a tale of a dream.

The Visible and the Invisible

Written at the beginning of the eleventh century, the account of the Saxon bishop Thietmar of Merseburg was undoubtedly the first to give so many details on apparitions of the dead and to enable a precise comparison between autobiographical tales and tales that the author related through hearsay. He wrote his chronicle between 1009 and 1018. It is a considerable work, one to which historians are indebted for a large part of their knowledge of the Holy Roman Empire. Thietmar belonged to the very high aristocracy of the Germanic Empire. For several generations the history of his family was joined with the destiny of Saxony. He became the bishop of Merseburg in 1009. As "Bishop of the Empire" (Reichbischof) and also a great scholar, he was both an actor in and an interpreter of the political history of the empire. In addition to the pivotal events that he describes in painstaking detail—the reigns of emperors, military campaigns, episcopal successions, etc.—he includes other, quite different tales, the usefulness of which he considers to be just as great and whose truth he himself can attest to. Thus in Book I he tells of the military campaign of Henry I in Mecklenburg and Pomerania in 926. Two of Thietmar's great-grandfathers were participants, before they both were killed during the battle of Lenzen, marking the reconquest of the town of Walsleben, which the Slavs had seized and burned. Mentioning this town, which had a place in his family's memory, and noting its destruction under the blows of the pagans causes Thietmar to veer off to another subject, which leads, through an association of ideas, to an entire series of ghost stories.[1]

So that no Christian would doubt, as the pagans did, that the dead would be resurrected at the end of time, Thietmar, on the faith of the accounts he collected, tells what happened in Walsleben after the town was rebuilt. A mob of dead people appeared, in the cemetery, before the curate of the region. A dead woman, whom the priest recognized, told of the priest's imminent death. To this tale, which tells of already distant events, Thietmar immediately adds a more recent story that he himself had heard in Magdeburg when he was living there (between 987 and 1002). He considers this tale "perfectly consistent with regard to vision and sounds" with the earlier story. One night the watchmen of the church of the merchants see in the distance, in the cemetery, some small lights above the candles, and they hear two men singing matins and lauds. When the watchmen draw closer, they no longer see anything. Struck by the strangeness of the tale, the next day Thietmar tells it to his niece Bridget, who was the abbess of the monastery of Saint Laurent and who was confined to her bed. Far from being surprised by the story, Bridget in turn tells him how the bishop Baudry of Utrecht (918–975) had reconstructed and reconsecrated in Deventer an ancient church that had been destroyed and how he had relegated it to a priest. At dawn one day, in the church and the cemetery, the priest found dead people who were celebrating mass and singing. Following the orders of the bishop, the priest spent a second night in the church, but the dead chased him away. The third night the priest armed himself with relics and holy water and forced himself to remain awake; but at the usual hour the dead captured him and placed him on top of the altar, where they burned him to death. The bishop ordered a fast lasting three days for the salvation of the priest's soul. Bridget adds that she could tell many other similar tales, for "if the day belongs to the living, the night is given to the dead."

Thietmar derived a religious lesson from all these stories, a lesson that was intended for the "illiterate and the Slavs" who, in his opinion, believed that the soul did not survive after the death of the body. For him these accounts, which echoed the Scriptures and Book IV of Gregory the Great's *Dialogues*, proved that the soul survived after death and awaited the final resurrection. People, he explains, exist between the angels and the animals. For if the former are completely spiritual and immortal, and the latter completely corporeal and mortal, people have a mortal body but an immortal soul, which the death of the body did not affect. Without Thietmar being aware of it, his tales show something else as well: that the dead came to announce the imminent death of someone; that time belonged in part to the dead; and that the dead were ready at any moment to take over the places that the living had temporarily vacated—a town destroyed during a military incursion or an abandoned church. The dead were at home among ruins, and they fiercely defended the place they had conquered. It was thus essential that clerics delimit, with the sprinkling of holy water, the respective locales of the living and the dead. The year 1000 marked the invasion of ghosts but also the redoubled efforts of the living to reject them.

In Thietmar's tales the dead usually manifest themselves through generally anonymous sounds or apparitions (in one instance a female parishioner was recognized). In other cases the relationship between the dead person and the living is more personal, and names are provided. These other tales fulfill more political functions and reveal the important place that Thietmar occupied in the imperial aristocracy, his familial ties, and the "memorial structure" that underlies his entire chronicle.[2]

In 981 the archbishop Adalbert of Magdeburg, who had just died, appears to the faithful Walter to say that he is unhappy with the choice of his successor, Ochtricus, who is guilty of professional misconduct. Walter tells Thietmar of the apparition.[3] Ochtricus dies soon afterward, but before this, Thietmar's brother, Husward, has a vision of the deceased provost Athelken, who comes to voice his reproaches to the archbishop.[4] This is not all: in 1012, Walter's dead mother appears to her daughter to announce the impending death of the archbishop of Magdeburg, Thaginus, and his replacement by Walter. Before becoming archbishop, Walter reminds his sister of the promise she had made to him in the event that he should die before she did: to respect his charitable bequest of the domain of Olvenstedt, in order to ensure his salvation.[5]

The accession to power, the devolution of property, the memory of the deceased—the dead played a role in all successions. Those among them who, through their former functions, watched over the future of the episcopal seat of Magdeburg appeared whenever there was a change in the office. Even if the election caused only a slight problem— the risk of an unworthy successor or the reversal of some property promised to the church—the dead irrupted in the dreams of the living, thwarted their ambitions, awakened their bad consciences, and provided fodder for their tales.

However, in contrast to all these tales based on oral testimonies reported by the bishop Thietmar of Merseburg, is the unique account of the bishop's personal experience.[6] This account is remarkable in its even more precise attention to details. Thietmar was in his domain of Rottmersleben on December 18, 1012, a Friday, when at the first crowing of the rooster, a light filled the church and he heard a groaning. Questioning some old men, he learned that a similar phenomenon had already occurred several times and had announced a death. In fact, the death of his niece Liutgarde soon confirmed the prognostic, and afterward Thietmar and his companion several times heard at night, while everyone else was sleeping, a noise that sounded like a tree falling; he even heard "the dead who were speaking to each other," and this was always the sign of an imminent death in the domain. It is noteworthy that in this single autobiographical tale, the dead person remained invisible; the person was manifest not through an image, even an oneiric one, but by a light, by a strange sound that had nothing human about it, or by the rustling of inaudible voices. The bishop, along with all the inhabitants of his domain, watched for and interpreted these noises and whisperings; the bishop wrote of the strange sensation he experienced on the approach of what he believed to have been the presence of a dead person (each noise, the growling of an animal or the sudden falling of a pile of wood, perhaps causing him to jump). For him, in a world where everything was a sign and demanded to be decoded, the invisible arrival of the dead was a reality that announced the imminent death of someone close to him.

This type of autobiographical ghost tale seems to have been quite rare. We can, however, connect it to the much later tale that the emperor Charles IV (1355–1378) himself told, in Latin, of a troubled night spent in his castle in Prague.[7] His room was in the old section of the castle. His companion Buschko was in another bed in the same room, which, in spite of the darkness of the night, was made quite bright by the fire that burned in the fireplace and the many candles that were lit. All the doors and windows were closed. The two men had barely fallen asleep when the sound of footsteps in the room woke them. The emperor ordered his companion to get up, but the man saw nothing unusual; before going back to bed, he stirred the fire, relit the candles, and drank from a cup of wine that he then set down next to a large candlestick. But once again the emperor heard someone coming and going, although he saw no one in the room. Then all of a sudden the cup that Buschko had set down was thrown, as if by an invisible hand, against the wall above Buschko's bed and fell into the middle of the room. The two men, seized with panic, crossed themselves. The next day they found the cup still on the ground and showed it to their servants.

In his account Charles IV next makes a great effort to prove the truth of his experience and to convince his listeners or readers that he was not dreaming. In this autobiographical tale it is especially noteworthy that the emperor says he saw no ghost, only the mysterious throwing of the cup. Yet in two manuscripts of the *Vita Caroli*—which were written in German around 1470–1480 and accompany this story, which is unchanged—there are miniatures representing the emperor in his bed, in the bedroom of the Prague castle, during that troubled night (illus. 7 and 8).[8] In both cases the illustrations change the tale in two ways. Whereas Charles IV insisted that he and his companion were awake, the illustrations show them asleep. The drawings therefore portray the emperor dreaming, both to make clearer his confrontation with a spirit and to conform to a literary tradition, that of the dreams of rulers. At the same time the illustrations visibly portray the spirit that haunts the room, in the form of a small man. In one of the two miniatures this human figure is completely nude, in conformity with many representations of the souls of the dead, and it is crossing its hands in a gesture that is found elsewhere and that seems to me to be the sign of a request. The artist interpreted the emperor's tale as the classic visit of a soul who is in purgatory and who comes to request suffrages. In the second miniature the soul is not nude but is wearing a doublet. It makes the same gesture with its hands.

Whereas the autobiographical tale gives no visible form to the spirit, the illustrations, though representing a dream, are characterized by the function of objectivization, comparable to the function of reported tales: the murky sensation of a presence is transformed into an affirmation of the quite visible apparition of a dead person having all the corporeal characteristics of a living one.

Ecstatic Visions of the Dead

Beginning in the thirteenth century, visionary and mystical literature produced very different autobiographical ghost tales. Their authors were clearly identified. They were sometimes men, such as the Dominican Robert of Uzès, who, at the end of the century, wrote down the "visions" and the "words" that had been revealed to him. He described the ecstatic states in which he found himself when, in the cloisters or in the church of Avignon, he was deep in prayer and contemplation. On these occasions, he said, the souls of his relatives were manifest to him either, if they were blessed, in the aerial form "of a white sheet containing dry wood" or, if they were enduring purgatory, as "black, on reed spikes like roasting meat"; in each instance the "spirit of the Lord" spoke to him, clarified the vision, and informed him of the respective status of those souls.[9] Significantly, Robert insisted that these dead did not appear to him in a dream but while he was in a state of exceptional spiritual excitation, beyond the abilities of ordinary people.

Such ecstatic states were found above all in the convents, particularly in Germany. The most striking case is unquestionably that of Gertrude, who entered the convent—of more or less Cistercian obedience—of Helfta in 1261, at the age of five. She spent her life there, afflicted with illnesses and great suffering, and died in 1301 or 1302 without ever having become abbess. There she met and came under the influence of several women mystics well-known for their visions: the abbess Gertrude of Hackerborn (d. 1291), the nun Mechtilde of Hackerborn (d. 1298), and the Beguine Mechtilde of Magdeburg. Even though Gertrude of Helfta did not herself write down the revelations she received during great physical suffering, she dictated them in such a way that we can still discuss them here as autobiographical writings. Gertrude titled her collection of revelations *Herald,* for she considered her book to be the herald of the Lord, who was speaking in a certain way through her mouth. The fifth and final book (it was completed after her death) presents a continuous series of tales of the apparitions of the souls of the deceased.[10] The systematic form of this collection of tales should be noted, for it indicates a conscious organization. The deceased are classified according to their social rank: the first twelve entries deal with recently deceased nuns from the convent; the next five tales tell of the apparitions of lay brothers; and only later does she relate, in order, the tales of someone near to her, of relatives of members of the community, of a deceased knight, of a poor woman, and of yet another dead woman. Gertrude never says that she dreamed of these souls: she saw them and spoke to them in an ecstatic state, in the midst of a violent light, while they often seemed to her very closely and corporeally associated (on the heart or in the breast, she says several times) with Christ or the Virgin. The reason for these apparitions' visits was generally that the deceased women and men had not expiated all of their sins; through prayers and the sacrifice of the host, requested of a priest, Gertrude then labored for their deliverance.

Such tales of apparitions of the dead experienced while the recipient was in a wakeful state are characteristic of this visionary and mystical literature. Even when they are autobiographical tales, this literature most frequently avoids speaking of dreams, which were related to a more common experience and were not, like ecstatic vision, signs of election. The same is true in the reported tales that also flourished in this visionary literature. We see this, for example, in the collection of visions attributed to the Dominican sisters of Unterlinden in Colmar at the turn of the thirteenth century. Here the sisters' visions are reported in succession. Quite often a dead sister or sometimes a Dominican brother appears to a sister who was once an acquaintance. Each time the conditions of the apparition are specified, and each time we are told that the visionary was awake.[11] Significantly, only two tales of dreams are mentioned; in one of them, it is the devil who appears "in the guise of a recently deceased matron,"[12] and in the other, the sister awakens to experience the same vision a second time, now in a *"manifest"* state.[13] It cannot be emphasized enough that the conscious vision in this type of monastic and mystical tale enjoyed a much more favorable status than did the dream.[14]

Dreaming of the Dead

Unlike the tales we have just noted, most autobiographical tales of ghosts were accounts of dreams. There even existed a close connection between the oneiric experience and a recourse to autobiography. The autobiography and tales of dreams could be developed in the Christian literature of the second Middle Ages only by breaking away from the suspicion that traditionally weighed on both genres. What was under fire with regard to dreams was the recognition of the subject, of his or her autonomy, of the unconscious that was liberated during sleep, of the admission of the inadmissible impulses and desires of the sleeping body.[15] Throughout the first millennium the "I" reflected on itself and expressed itself using models of behavior and a concept of identity whose point of reference was outside the individual subject. When the first Christians were summoned by their inquisitors to reveal their identities, they stubbornly responded to each of their questions: "I am a Christian!"[16] "Christian" was their true name as well as their title as members of the new faith. The same was true for the monks in later centuries: their gestures, prayers, and songs existed and had meaning only within the context of the liturgical practices of the entire monastic community, which itself was considered to be in communion with the angelic choruses. According to Cassian and Saint Benedict, the novice who uttered his final vows made a complete gift to God of his person, his mind, and his body: "from that day he knows he no longer even has power over his own body."[17] Such conditions did not favor the autobiographical telling of the monk's experiences and particularly of his dreams. For a long time the cleric or the literate monk had confidence more readily in a written or even an oral tradition, in authorities (those of the Bible or the church fathers), in narrative models that established a requisite chain of "trustworthy" witnesses. The same held true for tales of ghosts: rather than noting one's own dreams, one would reproduce in writing the tales passed on by an *auctoritas*—an "authorized" text or person—whose necessary mediation intervened between the individual and the mysteries of the hereafter.

Throughout the early Middle Ages great suspicions weighed upon dreams. Just as the elevation of dreams went hand in hand with that of the subject in the twelfth century, during the early Middle Ages both dreams and their subject were objects of repression. One of the reasons was that the dream gave direct access to the revelation of hidden truths about the hereafter, without the mediation or the control of any ecclesiastical authority. This explains the weapon that the clerical culture deployed against the temptations of an excessive valuing of dreams: their diabolization. Thus the reinterpretation of ancient classifications enabled one to give primary importance to the assumed origin of dreams rather than to their form or their meanings. Now, if it was accepted that saints or kings could be the beneficiaries of dreams of divine origin, the common mortal fell easy prey, especially during sleep, to "diabolical illusions." This is the meaning of the fundamental opposition that existed, throughout the Middle Ages, between "true" dreams and "false" ones: the former were justified by the verity of their objects (the saint who appeared in a dream was really a saint, and the prophecy revealed in a dream was truly of divine origin and would be verified), whereas the latter were invalidated by the falsity of their assumed author. If the devil did in fact exist, in dreams he revealed only pure illusions that exploited the Christian, leading to his downfall. This explains the bias in favor of conscious visions reported by witnesses beyond suspicion: in contrast to the individual appropriation of the supernatural through dreams, the conscious vision guaranteed a "clear" vision, sheltered from the nocturnal intrigues of the devil and from the guilty complacency of sleep and the body. The accounts of authorized mediators built a barrier against diabolical temptations.

Christian Autobiography and Ghosts

In the first millennium, therefore, there were few autobiographical accounts of dreams of ghosts. The first and one of the most famous is the dream of Saint Perpetua while she was imprisoned shortly before being martyred in 203, near Carthage. Her young brother Dinocratus, who had died at the age of seven, appeared to her; he was dressed in rags, and on his face was the canker that had caused his death. He seemed to want to drink from a well whose coping was too high for him. Perpetua understood that her brother was being punished in the hereafter and that she was to help him. A few days later, after having prayed for him, she again dreamed of her brother and this time understood, from his blissful appearance, that he was saved.[18] Ambrose of Milan (c. 339–397) also describes, with great emotion, the dream in which his dead brother Satyrus appeared to him. The dead man's expression was so clear that Ambrose believed he had seen the very soul of his brother, but it was only an illusion: the oneiric image was simply the fruit of Ambrose's mind tormented by pain.[19] Much later we encounter the same occurrence in the apparition of the abbess Hathumod of Gandersheim (d. 874) to her brother the monk Agius of Corvey, who wrote her vita two years later. Agius's account is in the form of a poem, following the tradition of the ancient genre of the *consolatio*, which Boethius had reintroduced into Christian literature.[20] In a dream, Agius conversed with his sister about monastic rule and the management of the monastery, which was being overseen at that time by their sister, the abbess Gerberga. Agius begged Hathumod to appear to him frequently in order to console him on her disappearance. He implored her to show him her *imago*, both in his dreams and when he was awake. But significantly, he did not describe such a conscious vision.

With the monastic renewal of the autobiography in the eleventh and twelfth centuries, we begin to encounter a substantial number of tales of personal dreams and, when the occasion arose, of dreams of ghosts.

With good reason the monk Otloh of Saint Emmeram (c. 1010–c. 1070) is considered to be one of the principal voices in the rise of monastic interest in introspection in the middle of the tenth century. He expresses this preoccupation above all in the form of visionary literature. The attention he pays, looking beyond outward appearances, to the hidden meaning of his destiny is also used in the reform of monasticism, in which he was an important participant.[21] Born in the diocese of Freising, of an undoubtedly noble family, at the age of seven he entered the monastery school of Tegernsee, where he decided to become a monk, against his parents' wishes. At fourteen he earned, through his talents as a scribe, the distinction of being sent to the monasteries of Hersfeld and Amorbach and to the court of the bishop of Wurzburg before returning to Tegernsee. Forced to flee to the abbey of Saint Emmeram in Ratisbon, he took his final monastic vows there at the age of twenty. It was in this monastery that he met one of the great reformist figures of contemporary monasticism, William of Hirsau (d. 1091), whose cause he embraced fully.[22] His actions turned many against him, and he was forced into exile from 1062 to 1067–1068 at the abbey of Fulda (which also participated in the reformist movement, but within the Cluniac obedience). He then went back to Saint Emmeram, which he never left again.

In his various books, Otloh returns several times to the vicissitudes of his inner battles and his conversion. Even though he expresses himself using the great models of Christian literature—primarily the tale of the conversion of Saint Jerome and the tales of diabolical temptations inspired by Saint Cassian and the *Lives* of "the Fathers of the Desert"— there is no reason to doubt the personal nature of his experience or his sincerity, especially in his autobiographical *Liber de tentationibus suis et scriptis*, in which he expresses the dilemma of the monk who wants to read both the pagan authors and the Bible. Several sections of this autobiography are repeated in *De doctrina spirituali* and in the first four tales of the *Liber visionum*, written around five years before Otloh's death.[23]

It is this last collection of tales of visions that we must consider in greater detail. The work opens with a prologue in which Otloh emphasizes the usefulness of visions for the edification of Christians. Through visions, God admonished Otloh when he had not yet sufficiently improved himself. Moreover, he is only, he says, following the example of the Scriptures and of Book IV of Gregory the Great's *Dialogues*. These visions are sometimes peaceful or agitated dreams (*per somnia quieta vel inquieta*), but sometimes the visions are perceived in a wakeful state. Otloh, following a rather well-known narrative scheme, often shows how a conscious vision sometimes confirms a dream, which is more subject to doubt.

Only the first four tales (out of twenty-three) are truly autobiographical. But as a whole, they represent close to a third of the work. All four are tales of dreams. They deal with different stages in Otloh's life: the first two dreams occurred during his childhood and while he was still in Tegernsee (thus before 1032); the third concerns his conflict with the archpriest Werinher and his departure for Saint Emmeran; the fourth is a nightmare he had in 1055 when he was ill and in open opposition to his abbot. In these dreams divine, angelic, or diabolical manifestations alternate, but there is never any mention of ghosts. We can at least notice, once again, the very strong connection between dreams and autobiography.

This connection is confirmed if we consider fifteen other reported tales, which are mostly tales of visions perceived in a state of wakefulness.[24] Otloh says that he collected these tales directly from trustworthy sources, whom he makes every effort to name.[25] Most often the tales concern a monk who learns, by means of a supernatural revelation, that he is soon to die or that dead people he once knew are enduring punishments in the afterlife due to their opposition to monastic reform. Seven tales also deal, directly or indirectly, with ghosts.

None of these ghost tales are autobiographical, and dreams are involved in only two cases; for the most part the reported tale imposes the objectivization of the conscious vision. In all cases the ideological function of these tales is clear: ghosts are mobilized in the service of church reform. Discussing the first two tales (Visions 6 and 7), Otloh says they are "similar," although the first describes the resurrection of a dead woman and the second the apparitions of dead people.[26] Both tales are aimed at the lay aristocracy guilty of usurping ecclesiastical property. In the first case a dead servant woman (who is quickly resuscitated) presses the "tribunal" Adalric, in the name of her also deceased parents, to return a *curia* to the church; the *curia* was usurped by Adalric's father, Ruotpold, who is enduring all sorts of torture in the afterworld. In the following tale two brothers on horseback encounter "a large cavalcade flying in the air." A proud knight steps forward and asks them, on behalf of their dead father, to return a domain the father had stolen from the monastery. Otherwise their father, they themselves, and their descendants would be damned. The burning lance the knight holds out to the two brothers is the *signum*, the proof of the truth of the vision. The two brothers comply and soon become monks. One of the watchwords of the reform—restitution to the monasteries of property that had been stolen from them—is all the better illustrated by these two tales, since Otloh says he heard the second one from a brother who himself had heard it directly from the primary agent of the reform in the middle of the century: Pope Leo IX (1049–1054).[27]

The following two tales (Visions 8 and 9) are also connected, and they are clearly aimed at a second object of reform: the internal life of the monasteries. Otloh obtained them from the same source, a relative, a monk from Tegernsee. They both involve the monastery's abbot, Ellingerus, who was guilty of poor administration.[28] Otloh's source had heard lamentations and cries in the church (presumably those of dead monks) announcing the burning of the monastery. The abbot had not listened to the monk and had neglected to find a safe place for the church treasure and the books, which were destroyed in the fire. Then this guilty abbot fell ill, and he paid no better attention to the admonitions of Duriagus, a cleric who had spent his life in and had died at the monastery. Duriagus appeared to the abbot in a dream, attached him to a column, and beat him with canes.

Finally, three tales (Visions 12, 16, and 17) illustrate the urgency of the moral reform of Christians in general and demonstrate the effectiveness of prayers for the dead.[29] During the octave of the Epiphany, Otloh encountered a penitent at the gate of the monastery; when he was a child, this person had, with his lies, induced his father to commit perjury.[30] For the entire year that followed his father's death, and then on Christmas Day, "that night when many souls deserve to find final rest," the father had appeared to his son in a dream (in somnis), then in a wakeful state (aperte)—this second vision serving to confirm the first—to beg his son to help him escape his torments. The son did penance, and Otloh warned against the consequences of perjury. Another tale was told to Otloh by a monk from Fulda: a brother accidently drowned, but the cellarer, who had presumptuously concluded that he had committed suicide, had him buried outside the community's cemetery. The dead man appeared to the cellarer to remind him that only God has the power to judge.

Finally, Otloh relates a tale he received from a source whose name he has forgotten; he nevertheless is clear on both the meaning (sensum) and the tenor (sermonem) of the tale, which he relates for the edification of those who will read it. Empress Theophano (d. 991), the wife of Otto II, should have earned eternal damnation for having introduced the luxury of the Byzantine court into Germany. She nevertheless appeared to a nun to ask the nun to help her through her prayers. Otloh claims not to know what the nun finally did, which causes concern regarding the fate of the empress in the hereafter.

This last case shows particularly well the degree to which the tale of conscious visions was a social object. This was due to the oral—then written—transmission that gave birth to it; but this was also due to the diffusion of a tale within the social space in which it was intended to circulate and even, in some cases, to become a means of political propaganda. This is another important difference between the tale of a conscious vision and the autobiographical tale of a dream, whose significance and uses frequently remained confined within the intimate circle of relatives and others close to the dreamer-writer. Another famous monastic autobiography written at the beginning of the twelfth century illustrates this point perfectly.

The monk Guibert of Nogent (c. 1055–c. 1125) had taken the Confessions of Saint Augustine as an exemplary model. But that model was not what inspired him to speak of his childhood dreams, and it especially was not what caused him to speak of them in the way he chose to do. Already advancing in years when he wrote De vita sua, in it he tells of two dreams he had when he was a child. In these dreams, the origin of which he attributes to the devil, he saw terrifying images of dead people.[31] In one case he specifies that he had once seen the men, whom he does not name, die by the sword, or by some other means, or that he had heard

the story of their deaths. He is certainly recounting an authentic nightmare that perhaps resulted from witnessing a traumatic sight or hearing
a tale of violence that made such a strong impression on him as a child
that he never forgot it. In his second childhood dream, he heard voices,
and then a dead man (who had undoubtedly drowned in the public baths,
a place for troubling sexual seductions), accompanied by a demon, appeared to him.[32] Here too the dead person is not named, and the dream
perhaps followed a drowning that the child had heard about.[33] Since today, much more so than in Guibert's time, the psychology and the development of the personality of children are fully accepted concepts, how
can we deny the impact of violent images on the mind, the nightmares,
and the lasting memories of the child Guibert?

In addition to his own childhood dreams, Guibert relates a long
dream of his mother's.[34] If this tale is not strictly autobiographical, it
comes very close to being so, as we shall see. Moreover, it is not a true
tale of an apparition but rather the tale of an oneiric voyage into the
hereafter. Because of this, it belongs to another narrative tradition, one
that is found more frequently than tales of apparitions in the strict sense.
Guibert is not recounting the only dream his mother had (she supposedly
also dreamed of the Virgin Mary protecting her son). Guibert brings a
very specific interest to these dreams, due to his deep affection for his
mother: although he never mentions the name, it is clear that she was to
him what Saint Monica was to her son Saint Augustine. Guibert's mother
was a specialist in dreams and their interpretation. Those who knew her
best—her son, his tutor, and other pious women in the region—recognized that she had a true "knowledge of dreams," independent of any
control or any mediation on the part of clerics; comparing the content
of dreams (hers as well as those of others) and the facts of external reality,
she revealed oneiric portents (portenta) and told people the best way to
act. This is exactly what she does for herself when she derives the meaning and the lessons from her longest dream.

This dream occurred one Sunday night in the summer, at the hour
of matins (two details that guarantee the celestial origin and truth of the
event). The mother was stretched out on a narrow bench in an uncom-
fortable, mortifying position, which prepared her body for the supernatural experience that would follow. Once asleep, she first feels her soul
leave her body, then it is led through a colonnade that leads to the opening of a well. Some "phantom human shapes . . . [whose] hair seemed to
be eaten by worms" come out of the well and try to tempt her soul into
it: these are the damned, and the well is the opening to hell. But from

behind her comes a voice that orders the phantoms not to touch her trembling soul.[35] Having overcome this trial, which qualifies her for loftier revelations, she sees her dead husband, next to the well where she is leaning. He appears as the young man (*juvenis*) he was at the time of his death.

She asks him a series of questions. Is his name indeed Evrard? Guibert has Evrard deny this, perhaps to avoid having his mother's dream associated with a ritual evocation of the dead, with an act of necromancy. But above all, Guibert comments, "a spirit can only answer another spirit in a manner befitting a spirit," and it would be absurd to think that spirits address each other in the afterlife using their earthly names; in addition, if they kept their names, they would recognize in the hereafter only those people they had known on earth. Guibert, as a loyal disciple of Augustine, wanted to keep a distance between the society of the living and the "spiritual" world of the dead—especially since the idea of a limitless sociability in the hereafter, without any relation to the closed circle of one's acquaintances below, was contradicted by the message in many other contemporary tales: the dead recognize each other only insofar as they knew each other while they were alive. For the same reason, they almost always appear only to their relatives and friends back on earth. Therefore Guibert of Nogent may be insisting on the opposite occurrence because he knows that the position he is defending is in the minority.

Where does Guibert's dead father reside? Evrard answers his widow by saying that he lives in a "place" not far from "where they [stand]." It thus appears that the location of the encounter is a sort of antechamber to hell (at the bottom of the well) and that the "place" where Evrard, who is not damned, endures great suffering is a sort of "purgatory" that has yet neither its configuration nor its name.[36]

What condition is he in? Evrard shows her terrible wounds on his arm and side, and his wife also sees a little child standing next to him. The child is crying unbearably. Guibert explains the child's presence: during the first seven years of their marriage, Guibert's parents had not been able to consummate their vows due to an act of witchcraft. Evrard, giving in to the pressures of his youth and of "evil counselors" and wanting to assure himself of his virility, had sexual relations with a loose woman (*muliercula*), whom he made pregnant. The child of their sin died the same day it was born, without having been baptized, and this is why the child is being punished, perhaps even damned. At least the "experiment" (this is the term Guibert uses) was conclusive for Evrard: he was able to go back to his wife, who gave him several legitimate children, one of whom was Guibert. But the wound on the ghost Evrard's side signifies that he broke his conjugal vows (is this an allusion to Eve's being born out of Adam's side?), and the child's crying adds even more to his suffering.

Do the prayers, masses, and alms his widow offers for his salvation comfort him? He answers yes and in particular suggests that she seek the prayers of a religious woman, Liutgarde, who lives near Guibert's mother. It is likely that praying for the dead was a social function, a specialty that the region recognized in that pious woman, just as the role of interpreter of dreams fell to Guibert's mother.

When Guibert's mother finishes her conversation with her husband, a new sight awaits her: she recognizes, kneeling on a board placed on the edge of the well, the knight Renaud of Beauvais and then one of Guibert's brothers, both of whom are blowing on the fire that is to devour them in hell. Neither of the two is dead yet, but Guibert's mother's morning vision is a presage to their imminent deaths and their damnation: the same day, at noon, Renaud would be assassinated, and then Guibert's brother, guilty of blaspheming, would soon die. She next sees the "mere shadow" (*speciem umbraticam*) of a dead old woman led by two coal-black demons. This woman was a very close friend to Guibert's mother; they had lived together and had promised each other that the first to die would appear to the other to let her know about her fate in the hereafter. This woman's continual mortifications and two premonitory visions she had had before dying might have suggested that she would experience a better fate. Once dead, she had also appeared to another person in thanks for having soothed her pain. However, if we are to believe Guibert's mother's dream, the woman seemed at that point to be drawn toward hell.

Nothing marks the end of the dream, the return of Guibert's mother's soul into her body. But she wastes no time in interpreting her dream and making the necessary decisions. The death at noon, that same day, of the knight Renaud confirmed the truth of the vision. Similarly, she was not surprised by the dream of the child who was wailing; she was in fact aware that her husband had had an illegitimate child with another woman and that the child had died without being baptized. All her attention is given to her husband because she has remained his faithful spouse after his death and because of all the dead people, or those condemned to death, who appeared to her, he alone was capable of being freed from his torments. Like the doctors of the time, she decides to take care of her husband's suffering soul, the torment symbolized by the wound on his side and by the cries of the child, "by setting like against like"—by herself taking on the responsibility of a small child whose incessant crying, caused by the devil, will keep her awake every night. This suffering from the crying of a child will enable her to deliver Evrard from the unbearable cries of the little phantom. Philippe Ariès has wondered whether Guibert's "child" truly existed in the Middle Ages, and we indeed see here the degree to which a little child is only an instrument for the use of adults: Guibert owes his being born to the "experimental" birth of the bastard child; this child is tormented because of a sin he did not commit, because he had been deprived, through no fault of his own, of the grace of baptism. His fate seems quite harsh. It is only at the end of the century that any mention is made of a limbo for children, of the painless yet eternal waiting place reserved for children who died without being baptized and who were, for that reason, deprived forever from access to heaven. Finally, the quite living "double" of that phantom (a substitute for Guibert next to his mother) is only the tool, through his cries, for the mortification of the pious woman (just as a hairshirt or severe discipline would be). Like the changelings in folklore, children were interchangeable in order to satisfy the expectations of adults, to heal the body,[37] or to save the soul.

Even though Guibert is not recounting a dream that he himself might have had but instead a dream experienced by his mother, who told it to him, the autobiographical bent is obvious. One might even say that it is still Guibert who is dreaming, through his mother. The dream is of other dead—the father, the brother, those close to Guibert—but above all the dream is of himself, in the guise of a little substitute child. Ghosts and the memory of dead parents serve another function here, one characteristic of the times and particularly of this author: the discovery of the self, the search for one's identity.

The Penitential Dream

In the thirteenth century, autobiographical writing developed and expanded, feeding on the new practices of introspection and penance imposed on Christians by the Fourth Lateran Council (1215) and by the apostolate of the mendicant orders. The Dominican Thomas of Cantimpré recalls how his father, visiting some hermits in the Holy Land, made a vow to pledge Thomas to the priesthood so that he could celebrate mass for his father's salvation when the father died.[38] When the father finally dies and Thomas neglects his duty, in a dream he sees Christ—but not his father—appearing to him and reproaching him while showing him the wounds of the Passion. In this unique autobiographical tale, Christ is substituted for the father, whom one would expect to have appeared; for this religious man, Christ is the supreme authority figure, a figure stronger than the image of his earthly father.

We again see the obsession with sin and purity, but in an even more exacerbated form, in the autobiography of the hermit Peter Morone (who in 1294, though for only a few months, was to become Pope Celestine V), known by the title "Coelestiana." This obsession occupies the entire text and in particular the hermit's tales of dreams, when he aspires to a moral law that dictates his own behavior. In his dreams this law takes on the faces of the dead people closest to him, such as the father abbot who, before dying, asked Peter to pray for the abbot. Appearing to Peter in a dream, the father abbot holds him by the cowl of his habit and orders him to say mass even though Peter considers himself unworthy to do so.[39]

Laymen: The First Writings

Finally, in the thirteenth century educated laymen also took up their pens, spoke about themselves, and described their dreams. The first source in France of this lay "literary subjectivity" was Jean, sire de Joinville, the very dear friend of Saint Louis. After the death (1270) and the canonization (1298) of the king, Joinville dedicated *Livre des saintes paroles et des bons faits de notre saint roi Louis* to his memory. Based on an earlier narrative, written in 1272, of the life of the king, this work was commissioned by Jeanne of Navarre (the wife of Saint Louis's grandson Philip the Fair, under whose reign the king was canonized) and was offered in 1309 to Saint Louis's great-grandson, Louis X the Stubborn. Although the work was completed, Joinville added one more story, that of one of his own dreams in which the saintly king, whose dear friend he had been, appeared to him:

> Now I must tell you some things about St. Louis which will be to his honour, and which I saw in my sleep. It seemed to me, then, in my dream, that I saw him in front of my chapel at Joinville, and he was, I thought, wonderfully gay and light of heart; and I, too, was happy to see him in my castle, and I said to him:

"Sir, when you leave, I will entertain you in a house I have in a village of mine called Chevillon." He answered me with a laugh: "My Lord of Joinville, by the faith I owe you, I have no wish to leave this place so soon."[40]

Michel Zink has brilliantly analyzed this dream within the logic of subjective writing and of Joinville's personal relationship with the memory of his departed royal friend. Joinville had two dreams of the king. The first occurred during Lent of 1267, while the king was still alive. Saint Louis appeared to him wearing a vermeil cloak, the premonitory sign of the crusade of Tunis, which was in fact carried out the next morning and during which Louis IX would die prematurely, a martyr. The second dream occurred when the king was already dead. In it is a reference to the chapel where Joinville had an altar erected in honor of the new saint following his canonization in 1298. Therefore Joinville dreamed, at the earliest, some thirty years after the death of the king. In the meantime he had been pushed aside by the entourage of Louis IX's successors, in particular by Philip the Fair, and he was forgotten during the distribution of relics after the canonization.[41] All of this made him quite bitter and directly explains his dream. By contrast, he was struck by the happiness and the laughter of his dead friend, who offered reassurances of wanting to remain close to him. According to Michel Zink, the names Chevillon and Joinville are, for the old seneschal, the symbolic expression of his desire to connect himself—to pin together, to join together—with what remained of Saint Louis: the king's lively and joyous image, which he saw in his dream, and the king's body, which he would like once again to touch as in the past but the possession of which (in the form of relics) was denied him.

Such tales show well what a ghost meant to an educated person in the Middle Ages, including a layman capable of writing about and questioning the meaning of his own dreams. The ghost was born of the still smoldering and unburied memory of someone close and beloved—a child, a father, a sister, a brother, the spiritual "father" of the monastic family, a very dear and venerated friend, such as Saint Louis was for Joinville—who departed too soon and too suddenly. Using the strategy of an illusory presence, the dream temporarily filled the void created by the death. Coming as close as they can to the most intimate affective experiences of the people of the past, historians discover a familiar, or at least understandable, relationship to the dead. As regards a "belief in ghosts," historians encounter the experience of mourning and the *memoria*, the painful work, in large part unconscious, of separation. To conclude, let us analyze a later tale, told by a Florentine layman of the fifteenth century, that sums up all the characteristics the previous tales have enabled us to assemble.

The Nightmare of Giovanni Morelli

Giovanni di Pagolo Morelli was a rich Florentine merchant. He began to keep his "journal" in 1393, at the age of twenty-two, and he continued to write in it intermittently until 1421; he died in 1444, at the age of seventy-two.[42] Following the conventions of the genre of *ricordi*, this "record book," written in Italian, begins by glorifying the ancestors of the author's lineage. Then Giovanni Morelli talks about his parents and about the dual tragedy of which he sees himself the victim and which in large part explains his desire to write of his life: he never knew his father, who died when Giovanni was not yet two years old, and his mother, who quickly remarried, abandoned him. In his eyes she was the epitome of the typical "cruel mother," a true scourge for young Florentines of the Quattrocento, children who were so often the victims of their mothers' hasty remarriages.[43] Then, as we read, new blows of fate strike Giovanni: the successive deaths of his grandfather and his elder sister, then a thwarted love affair. In 1396 he records his marriage and later the births of four children. The eldest, Alberto, is a sickly child, but when he is very young easily learns Latin and the psalms as well as the commercial techniques necessary for the merchant that he would be called on to become. It is for him that Giovanni starts writing again in 1403, at the age of thirty-one. For Alberto, he wants to be the attentive father that he himself never had. He intends to write down advice for Alberto to read later in life in case Giovanni, like his own father, happens to die prematurely—advice on how to behave in society, deal with representatives of the city, make "friends and relations" (an essential issue for all Florentine nobles and rich merchants) if need be by using the power provided by money, and obtain the services of a wise counselor and "keep him always present in your mind." An "excellent man [who is] sage and old and without vice," this counselor was to be a true tutor and even a substitute for the real father should he happen to die.

But once again Giovanni is dogged by misfortune. On June 5, 1406, Alberto dies, at the age of nine, after nineteen days of terrible suffering. Giovanni notes all the details of his dying and his final gestures.[44] The child gives himself up to God several times and to the Virgin, whose image (the *tavola*) he kisses, and he says his prayers very devoutly. However, he does not receive the last rites, and his father, while hoping that God might pardon the sins of such a young child, begins to doubt. Giovanni repents for his own negligence and also fears for his own life, as if the death of his son were the premonitory sign of his imminent death. The whole family goes into mourning: the house is abandoned for a month (the time of the "trental," requiem masses said for the one who is dead); for the whole summer no one goes into the boy's room, which the father continues to avoid for six full months in order not to be struck by too intense a suffering. He attempts, without truly succeeding, to erase the mental "image" of his son from his thoughts, except when he prays for Alberto. "I cannot," he writes, "nor can even his mother forget. Instead we continually have his image before our eyes, remember his ways, his conditions, words and acts, day and night, at lunch and dinner, inside and out, sleeping and awake, at the villa and in Florence." Their pain is transformed into a sort of accusation against their dead son, as if Alberto were taking some sadistic joy in torturing his surviving parents: "We think he is holding a knife that is stabbing us in the heart."[45]

On the first anniversary of the death, Giovanni indulges in a quasi-ritual evocation of the dead boy, a sort of private session of necromancy.[46] Very explicitly, Giovanni wants to "communicate to his blessed soul some refreshment [*refrigero*: there appears, here again, the old notion of *refrigerium* promised to souls in purgatory] or at least some memory of me, [his] afflicted and suffering father." *Ricordanza*: the dead, like the living, must remember. The father's pain is rendered even greater by the fact that through his own fault, his son died without receiving the last rites. Giovanni could not accept that Alberto was going to die, and he also thought that God would pardon such a young child.[47] A year later he becomes aware that his son's piety at the time he died was insufficient, that the "good Christian death," even for a child, assumes that the rites chosen by the church would be carried out. Because the "rite of passage" remained incomplete, Giovanni is haunted by the image of his son. Exactly one year after the death of his son, at the exact hour that Alberto died, he therefore seeks to exorcise the phantom through a ritual of his own invention.

When the moment arrives he puts on a penitential robe: a nightshirt that leaves his knees exposed, with a halter (*coreggia*) around his neck. At the very instant (*in quest'ora et in questo punto*) of his son's death exactly one year earlier, he grasps the *tavola* that the child kissed and that represents a crucifixion with Saint John the Evangelist and the Virgin Mary. He covers it with kisses and, while continuing to pray, alternately stares at each of the holy figures. The material image of devotion is the support for a reflection or contemplation—*immaginare e ragguardare*—intended, says Giovanni, "to dispose my soul and body and all my sentiments with more fervor and love."[48] In the midst of uncontrollable sobbing, the miserable father prays to Christ, the Virgin Mary, Saint John the Evangelist, Saint Catherine of Alexandria, and also Mary Magdalene, "who by the merit of the worthy words and works of your most delectable apostle Magdalene, through which she merited the grace of the resurrection of Lazarus her brother." He says, "If it were possible, I would desire to again have his body alive on earth." Giovanni would at least like to be sure that God is going to receive the boy by his side in heaven; as haunted as the father is by the image of his son, he thus doubts that this has already happened.

Having completed his painful prayer, Giovanni goes to bed. But he is unable to fall asleep and turns over and over in his bed. He understands that "the devil full of envy" (*lo invidioso Nimico*) is assailing him to show him the vanity of his prayer and to convince him that the soul of his son is but a chimera—*che l'anima fusse niente o un poco di fiato*. All of the remorse of the father takes on the voice of the devil, who reminds him of the course of his miserable life year by year beginning with the premature death of his father, his abandonment by his cruel mother, the beatings by his schoolmaster, his awaiting of his son when his wife was pregnant, and the birth, the childhood, and finally the premature death of Alberto. In the torments of insomnia, the enemy reveals the terrible explanation for the death of the son: it is Giovanni, the father, who is responsible for it, for Giovanni loved Alberto too little, treating him like an outsider, even refusing him the kisses that would have made him sense his father's affection,[49] and neglecting to have him confess at the time of his death.

Giovanni finally falls asleep. He sleeps for an hour, then has a dream. This dream is "true," guaranteed by the inspiration of God and of several saints (his patron saint, John the Baptist, as well as Saint Anthony, a patron saint of Florence, Saint Benedict, Saint Francis, and Saint Catherine, to whom Giovanni had prayed earlier). It is through this dream that he becomes certain that Alberto is ultimately saved. The dream comprises two parts. In the first, the dreamer sees himself in his house in Settimello, in the country. Plagued by the image of Alberto, he decides to climb Monte Morello (which bears his family name). The higher he climbs, the more his pain gives way to the memories of the happy times when Alberto was alive. However, he sees a bird (as big as a parrot, with completely white feathers, eyes of fire, a golden beak, and green feet) fly away and land on different trees. The bird's cry becomes increasingly somber; it picks at its feet until they bleed, then falls from a branch while a sow, which a pig had just befouled, passes over it and covers it with excrement. But Giovanni sees a young girl dressed all in white (una donzella bianchissima) coming closer, holding a wheel in her left hand and a palm leaf in her right: it is Saint Catherine, who, with her wheel, cuts the sow in pieces. Then a cloud of birds circle around her, and one of them, like the one he had seen earlier, lights on the hand of the saint. The bird immediately takes on the form of a "spirit" (e divenuto ispirito), on whose head the saint places her hand. The spirit is like a "white angel" who turns, full of joy, toward Giovanni; then the father, in the face of the angel, recognizes the features of his sweet son (il mio dolce figliuolo). "Figliuolo mio! Alberto mio!" he cries out, and he wants to embrace his son, but his efforts are in vain because spirits—he soon learns—are immaterial. "Be patient and do not seek the impossible" (Abbiate pazienzia e non cercate lo impossibile), his son tells him. A dialogue between the father and the son then takes place. Alberto reassures and thanks Giovanni: as a result of the prayers that Giovanni addressed to God, his son has "gone to heaven." But Giovanni wants to know more. Is it true that Alberto died because of the sins of his father? Will Giovanni be consoled by his other sons for the death of his eldest son, and will he have other children? Will he be pardoned by God for having neglected the sacraments? Will he be prosperous? Will he live a long time? Alberto's spirit reassures him regarding his role in his son's death and on all other points gives him the best reasons to hope; Alberto assures him in particular that he will live to be old (which indeed happens). Then the vision evaporates, and Giovanni wakes up, full of joy.

This extraordinary tales shows perfectly how a cultivated layman at the end of the Middle Ages was able to confide to the intimacy of his record book the painful and anguishing experience of his mourning and the precise analysis of his own dreams. The entire Christian afterlife is present in this long tale: God, Christ, the Virgin Mary, and the saints to whom Giovanni vows a particular devotion. On the other side, incarnating his bad conscience, are the face and the voice of Satan. Between the two is the dead child, whose memory, day and night, haunts the father, who accuses himself of not having loved his son enough and of having perhaps compromised his son's salvation. This man was not fundamentally different from us, and we can well understand his unhappiness and the images that haunted him. Thanks to him, we can grasp what ghosts truly were: they existed only through the strength of the imagination of the living, of the relatives who could not accept the unexpected and premature death of a child or someone else dear to them; they felt guilty for an unfortunate destiny or for the lack of concern they showed while there was still time to do so. The father saw the son as if he were alive; Giovanni wanted to take his son in his arms but understood that the distance between them was uncrossable, for the ghost was only an image in a dream. At the end of a year, to the day, the child was saved; the "labor of mourning" was finally completed thanks to the internalization of a temporal rhythm that had long been part of the liturgy of the dead: the anniversary marked the end of the obsessive return of the deceased, signifying his separation from those close to him, the liberation of the living.

Such a document gives the strongest impression of veracity. The modern reader feels sympathetic, in the primary sense of that term, toward Giovanni, the tormented father whose trial seems so credible, so believable, to us. The authenticity of the feelings expressed is undeniable, even though the historian, always concerned with identifying the common places of the ambient culture, notes that the most personal experience, in order to express itself, is subject to the appropriate features of Christian orthodoxy and to the temporal rhythm of the liturgy. But let us above all stress that Giovanni Morelli says he dreamed of his dead son. At no time does he talk about a vision he might have had while awake. This detail becomes significant when we compare this tale to many other autobiographical and oneiric tales of ghosts, as opposed to the much larger mass of reported tales of a conscious vision.

THREE

THE INVASION OF GHOSTS

In contrast to the autobiographical ghost tales was a rather considerable mass of ghost tales that were related from the written or, most often, oral account of a named or anonymous source. But these tales can hardly be grouped together in the same narrative genre. Here too, we need to be alert to the forms of the narration to which the content and the specific functions of the written tale are closely connected. Granted, any ordering of "narrative genres" is necessarily arbitrary, since they more often overlap than fit within rigid boundaries. Although a given genre might have been found in a specific period in time, several genres generally coexisted within the same period. In a schematic way, let us nevertheless distinguish three major types of ghost tales.

1. The *miracula* were often anonymous tales, gathered into collections that were found exclusively in ecclesiastical establishments (sanctuaries, monasteries); their function was to enhance the reputation of those establishments through the telling of miraculous events that had occurred there or that were associated with the local saint. Thus this is essentially a hagiographical genre, prevalent beginning in the first centuries of Christianity and culminating, so far as our purpose is concerned, in the twelfth century.

2. The *mirabilia* were tales of wonders that, unlike miracles, were not immediately related to the divine power or glory of a saint but originated from the astonished observation of curiosities in nature or in the human sphere. In medieval compilations of tales of marvels, the author's hand is much more noticeable. The author was generally not a monk but was a cleric immersed in the world and culture of laypeople. The shining moment of this literature, which was written in Latin but which has more than one trait in common with literature written in the vernacular, was the turn of the twelfth century.

3. Beginning in the first half of the thirteenth century and lasting until the end of the Middle Ages, preachers, both secular and predominantly religious figures of the mendicant orders, distributed *exempla* by the thousands. These tales also dealt with supernatural occurrences but, unlike the *miracula*, they did not place these occurrences in a specific location; on the contrary, these tales derived a moral lesson from the reported event, which was understood to be a universal occurrence. The collections of *exempla*, notably those that are presented in alphabetical order, were used in a preaching technique whose effectiveness depended largely on the stereotypical nature of the tales, unlike the claimed uniqueness of the *mirabilia*.

There can be no suggestion of locking into such a typology. We would then fail to recognize the existence of many tales that might be considered as falling between one or another genre. Other written documents are even more clearly beyond such classifications, such as, at the end of the Middle Ages, the long accounts of interrogations of ghosts, which were true exorcism proceedings.

Finally, we will examine in more detail the images of ghosts. No illustrations are related to an autobiographical tale (no medieval illuminator or painter, it seems, represented a ghost that supposedly appeared to him or her). In their unique way, illustrations therefore fulfilled the same function as reported tales of visions. And in no case can these representations be reduced to the status of mere illustrations of the ghost tales.

In Praise of the Present

All these documents not only were more numerous after the turn of the year 1000 but also were brand-new. From that time until the twelfth century, several of the authors of these documents emphatically insisted on one characteristic: the novelty of such tales. Granted, there is a *topos* here. For a very long time, Christian authors were amazed to encounter the "novelty" of various phenomena, since the unusual was considered to be an indication of a perturbation in the social or cosmic order, even to be a sign that the end of the world was at hand. In his time Gregory the Great had already noted the increase in revelations concerning the souls of the dead, and in this he had seen an eschatological sign.[1] However, such notations multiplied beginning in the eleventh century. They might have taken on the same significance, tied to the eschatological expectations of the authors and their surroundings. In other cases, such notations indicated an acute observation of a veritable renewal of the tales that were in fashion, those that were listened to and passed on most readily, those that appeared worthy of being transcribed, whereas this had not been the case in earlier times. Thus an awareness of the value of the contemporary began to be formed in the minds of monks and clerics who were able, perhaps for the first time, to pull themselves out from under the weight of traditions (so fundamental in the Christian culture) and out from under a reading of history directed exclusively toward waiting for the end of the world.

At the turn of the year 1000, Thietmar of Merseburg—the first of our authors to provide a large number of ghost tales—insisted on the contemporary nature of the apparitions he was relating, "these events having occurred in the most recent times which are our own."[2] But it was above all in the twelfth century that we encounter the most explicit judgments. Several authors emphasized the novelty and the increase in the number of apparitions of the dead, changes that they rightly attributed to the rise of the cult of the dead. These "modern examples," says the monk Guibert of Nogent, reveal the "status of souls" in the hereafter.[3] The abbot of Cluny, Peter the Venerable, was indignant that, thanks to the writings of the ancients, people knew well so many things that had happened "five hundred or one thousand years ago" but knew nothing of what "occurs today": no book mentioned the present. He wanted to remedy this omission by telling about contemporary "miracles," notably about revelations of the deceased. The dead, with God's permission, appeared to the living in order to induce them to confess their sins and in order to solicit suffrages.[4]

At the end of the twelfth century the English chronicler William of Newburgh also contemplated the wonders that abounded in his time. He felt it was his duty to report them in writing, just as an educated person compared the present age to that of the ancients. And this effort of comparison left him with no doubt: ghosts did not seem to be more abundant in his time because people were speaking of them more often; indeed, their wanderings were a new phenomenon!

> That cadavers of the dead, borne by I know not what spirit, leave their tombs to wander among the living, terrorizing them and annihilate them, then return to their tombs which open by themselves before them, is a fact that would be difficult to accept if in

our age numerous examples didn't prove it and if accounts did not abound. If such facts did occur in the past, it is surprising that we find no trace of them in the books of the Ancients, who did however put great effort into setting memorable things down in writing. Since they never failed to note even the smallest details, how could I let pass in silence something that, when by chance it occurs in this century, evokes so much astonishment and horror? Moreover, if I wanted to write about everything of this sort that as I have learned has occurred in our time, my task would be much too great and weighty.[5]

There are few such fascinating accounts of the completely new attention paid to the value of the current time by the educated of the twelfth century (here the author is a secular canon and not a monk, who would have undoubtedly been more sensitive to tradition). The tales of apparitions of the dead could not escape the curiosity of such authors, tales they transcribed right after having heard them, while noting, as so many guarantees of authenticity and as if to invite their readers and listeners to verify the facts, the quite recent date of those facts and the familiar names of people and places.

Monastic Visions

Monastic literature—sermons, lives of saints, letters, chronicles, and of course, collections of miracles—played a principal role in the increase in the number of ghost stories in the eleventh and twelfth centuries. The *miracula* tell of all sorts of perturbations in the order of Creation through the will of the Creator. The stories might tell of the healing of a sick person or the resurrection of a dead person, as well as of a sign that appeared in the sky, a vision or an apparition of a saint, the devil, or a deceased person. People (saints and monks), objects (relics), and places (abbeys) are respectively the most frequent agents, sources, and venues of miracles, due to their privileged relationship with God.[6] The growing number of tales in this grouping of monastic texts that deal only with apparitions of the dead is above all linked to the increasingly determining role that the monks played in the commemoration of the dead: the dead returned to demand "suffrages" of the monks, whose work would free the dead from the torments they were enduring in the hereafter. These tales also participated in the contemporary monastic reform movement, in particular at Cluny.

The geographic diversity and the variety of narrative traditions entice us to widen the scope of our observations to Germany, Italy, and France. The inquiry is wide-reaching and cannot claim to be exhaustive. But it is possible to indicate a few strong points, to stress the places that, like Cluny, functioned as true "laboratories" for narrative traditions relating to ghosts and also to question the absence of such tales in other places.

A few isolated tales enable us to illustrate the diversity of the geographical origins and of the functions of such tales. Here, for example, from German Switzerland, is a tale of a female ghost—the case of a female ghost being extremely rare—set within a hagiographical vita. According to the *Vita S. Wiboradae* (written around 976 by Ekkehard of Saint Gall some fifty years after the death of the saint), Wiborada saw and heard her deceased servant ask her to be careful to supervise the servant's replacement, who was responsible for cleaning the chalices before mass. The saint was believed to have taken advantage of the encounter to ask the dead woman the date of her own death.[7] Often the lesson had a more general social significance, as in the surprising tale of the dream that the abbot Robert of Mozat had at the time of the construction of the basilica of Clermont and of the manufacturing of a gold relicary statue (a *majestas*) of the Virgin and child. This tale was written down around 946 by the deacon Arnaud.[8] In his dream the abbot Robert sees the workshop where the goldsmith Aleaume and his brother are finishing the precious statue; into the workshop comes the bishop Stephan II of Clermont, led by Robert's dead predecessor, the abbot Drucbert of Mozat. Drucbert is addressed as *patronus:* he is a "good" ghost, almost a saint. He is amazed at the *novitas* of the statue and questions the bishop about the place where it is to be put. Drucbert in fact belongs to the earlier generation that did not know of such three-dimensional gold statues, quite close to pagan idols. The dead man's falsely naive question is therefore the occasion for the bishop to explain and to justify a new form of worship and a new object of devotion. Thus the dead abbot gives this cultural innovation the support of his *auctoritas*, that of a being from the hereafter, a quasi-saint and an ancestor. Here the ghost is fulfilling the function of legitimation.

Let us cite another example, this time from Spain. The "great miracle" reported in the last third of the eleventh century by the *Chronicle of Iria* in

Galicia tells of the apparition of King Sancho (who died after being poisoned by one of his traitorous vassals) to his widow, the queen Godo.[9] The document is of episcopal and not monastic origin, but it also involves the monastery of San Estéban de Ribas de Sil, which benefited from royal largesse. The protagonists meet again after death, not as king and queen but as husband (vir) and wife (uxor sua). Godo weeps over the fate of her late husband, fasts for forty days, and distributes alms, as any widow worthy of that name was supposed to do. The only token of the remarkable status of the donor—the fur that she gave to a poor priest for the salvation of her husband and that her husband, at the time of a second apparition, appeared wearing—was deposited as a relic in San Estéban de Ribas de Sil.

All these tales are independent of one other. They do not form a series, as is discovered in other monasteries. But elsewhere it is the absence of ghost tales that is striking and that must therefore also be explained.

Two of the most powerful monasteries of Christendom claimed to possess the body of Saint Benedict. One of these was Fleury-sur-Loire (where, from the end of the ninth century to the beginning of the twelfth, no fewer than five monks in succession—Adrevald, Aimoin, André, Ralph Tortaire, and Hugh of Saint Mary—continually pursued the writing of an exceptional book of miracles). The other one was Monte Cassino (where three monks in a row—Leo, Guy, and above all Peter the Deacon—wrote the chronicle of the monastery between the second half of the eleventh century and the first half of the twelfth century). In the miracles of Fleury, the only supernatural apparitions are those of Saint Benedict; no ordinary dead person, no monk or dead abbot, had the privilege of appearing to the living monks.[10] The situation is hardly more favorable in the chronicle of Monte Cassino: there too, Saint Benedict tends to claim the monopoly of apparitions (to the point of showing himself surrounded by the "multitude of dead monks").[11] One might therefore assume that in those abbeys that were completely devoted to the cult of such a great saint, the monks had scarcely any interest in more common tales of visions and apparitions. In other places, on the contrary, where notably monastic commemoration could be connected to the community of dead monks without favoring such a great patron or founding saint, where the demands of ecclesiastical reform invested ghosts—as messengers from the afterworld—with a sure ideological function, tales of ghosts were able to increase and be compiled much more effectively.

The Rome-Cluny Axis

The tracts and letters of Peter Damian (1007–1072), documents that were written in the same period but in Italy, include other reported tales of ghosts. It is not the austere hermit of Fonte Avellana who is expressing himself in these writings but rather, after 1057, the cardinal-bishop of Ostia, the champion of church reform, the admirer and ardent defender of Cluny.[12] Peter Damian spared no effort in bringing about the universal reform desired in Rome: he writes to them all—pope, emperor, bishops, abbots, simple monks—to judge, condemn, or advise, frequently using concrete examples to illustrate his argument, tales whose authenticity he guarantees. Thus he speaks of ghosts in a letter addressed to a certain monk B. to convince the monk of the necessity of a complete penance before death,[13] and in two pamphlets sent to the abbot Desiderius of Monte Cassino he deals specifically with suffrages for the dead.[14] Eight tales are of particular interest to us. They fit into the complete range of the premonitory visions of the judgment that follows death, visions of souls in hell, apparitions of the Virgin (whose cult Peter Damian worked diligently to expand), and apparitions of the devil, not to mention other edifying miracles. Peter Damian always insists on the proximity of these tales in time, for they are contemporary (*nostris temporibus*), and in space, for they are mostly Italian (*nostris regionibus*). Most important, he gathered them himself from the accounts of trustworthy sources whose names and titles he provides: a certain hermit, a monk (i.e., his disciple and friend, the monk John), a certain bishop friend (he says he heard the tale from Rainaud, the bishop of Cumae, who had himself heard it from Bishop Umberto of Saint Ruffina). Finally, in 1063 his travels to France enabled him to collect several tales directly from the abbot Hugh of Cluny, whom he admired unreservedly.[15]

Three lessons can be derived from these eight tales, all of which are ghost stories or are related to ghost stories. First of all, they systematically illustrate the value of the three types of suffrages from which the dead can benefit: masses, prayers, and almsgiving.[16] Regarding masses, the wife of a miner buried in the collapse of a mine has a mass said every day for the salvation of the soul of her husband, who she believes is dead. After a year has gone by, he is discovered alive; a little bird, digging a passageway through the rocks, brought him food every day, except on the day when, due to a storm, his wife was prevented from having the Eucharist celebrated (this tale was quite successful: it is found among the writings of Guibert of Nogent, Peter the Venerable, and Jacobus da

Voragine). Regarding prayers, a widow hires a priest to say prayers for the salvation of her husband in exchange for daily contributions. But this bad priest does nothing. One day she has a chicken, some bread, and some wine taken to him by her dishonest servant girl, who, having consumed everything on the way, "prays to God to feed the dead man in heaven." The next day the husband appears to his widow in a dream to thank her for heaping "food" on him for the first time the day before. The moral of the story is in accord with Peter Damian's demands for reform: it is better to pray for the dead than to pay simoniacal priests to do so. As for almsgiving, the same tale shows that it is better to give to the poor than to unworthy priests. From that time began the opportune innovation of the monasteries in the region: in addition to the usual charity, the abbots henceforth received three poor people at their tables. Also, the celebration of the memory of the "dearly departed" was extended from the day of the anniversary of the death to the entire octave that followed. The intensification of the *memoria* of the dead went hand in hand with that of the charity shown to the poor. The monks were the great providers of "food": some material, to benefit the poor, and other spiritual, to benefit the dead. Such was the role of monks in that society, and such was the basis of their economy.

These tales were also intended to convince others that in the afterlife, the Virgin Mary was the primary helper of souls. Several ghosts came back to assert as much. For example, the Roman woman Marozia, dead for about a year, came back to tell her goddaughter that the Virgin had delivered her that very day, on the Feast of the Assumption of Mary. The bishop Rainaud of Cumae also told Peter Damian that a dead man had appeared to Rainaud's godson and had led him in a dream to a gathering of saints where he had seen the Virgin, who judged and absolved the patrician John. The same bishop also told Peter Damian that the Virgin pulled a priest from the clutches of the devil at the very moment of his personal judgment. Indeed, although the priest had neglected the daily service and the services for the saints, he had always performed the service for the dead. The funeral service had therefore become the most important part of the priests' duties, the part that, when all hope seemed in vain, enabled them in extremis to be saved. The bishop, however, did not know whether that dead priest returned to tell of his adventure himself.[17]

The final lesson was that the living and the dead are united. On the one hand, the individual contractual ties that people establish before death remain in effect after death and underlie apparitions of the dead.

On the other hand, the prayers that monks offer for the dead represent a superior form of solidarity, which encompasses all others and goes beyond them through its effectiveness. It is remarkable that Peter Damian evokes the contractual solidarities of the lay society: here it is not the father who appears to his son or the brother to his brother, following ties of kinship, but it is the husband who appears to his wife, or the godmother to her goddaughter, or the godfather to his godson. Thus we implicitly discover a great theme of Gregorian reform, to which Peter Damian more than others eagerly attached his name: the encompassing of lay society within the symbolic networks controlled by the church, whether through the baptism of children and the role of godfathers and godmothers or through a stricter definition of a Christian marriage—exogamous, exclusive, and stable. In this way the Christian family was considered to be a primary cell for prayer, of which each member would reap the benefits after death. This represents a fundamental structure in tales of apparitions, one that we will see again in most later tales.

However, the universal solidarity instituted by monastic prayer for the dead dominated any individual contractual bond. The letter addressed to monk B. shows this eloquently by recounting what Martin, a hermit of the Camaldolese, said to Peter Damian: a monk who had sinned in excess obtained the agreement of another monk, whose "close friend" he had become, to share the very hard penance that he had been given. The *amicitia* survived the death of this helpful monk, full of virtue. A few days later the second monk appeared to his friend in a dream. "Things are bad," he tells him, "because of you!" Indeed, he had died before completing the entire penance, which, through the contract, had become his own, as if he himself had committed the sins. We see well the limits in this society of what today we call individual responsibility: guilt was more an objective than subjective notion, a burden that could be shared and transferred among "friends." This was moreover the reason for the effectiveness of suffrages for the dead. Suffrages were based on a system of equivalency, of compensation and of exchange with the living: for so many additional prayers, the one who was benefiting from them received that many fewer punishments in the afterlife.

The model for suffrages for the dead, the model that underlies all of Peter Damian's observations, is Cluniac. Peter Damian not only was successful in defending the cause of Cluny at the Council of Chalon in 1063, not only was tied through friendship to the abbot Hugh of Cluny (1049–1109), but also was quite specifically convinced of the merits of the Cluniac liturgy of the dead and of the establishment of the Feast of the Dead on November 2, the day after All Saints' Day. This Cluniac innovation, which dates from around 1030, soon extended to all of Christendom.[18] Peter Damian went so far as to write the *Life of Saint Odilo*, in which he follows word for word, or very nearly, Jotsuald, the first hagiographer of the abbot Odilo, in his famous tale of the origin of the feast day: a Sicilian hermit heard some demons, who were bustling about in the flames of Etna, bewail the fact that the prayers, alms, and masses of the Cluniac monks pulled reprobate souls too quickly from their torment. Informed of this vision, the abbot Odilo instituted the Feast Day of the Dead. Soon an apparition of the dead pope Benedict, freed from the punishment of the hereafter through the suffrages of the Cluniacs, confirmed the validity of that initiative.[19] Peter Damian himself requested in writing of the abbot Hugh that he be able to benefit after his death from the suffrages of Cluny: he wanted not only to be admitted into the community of prayer of the Cluniac monks but also to benefit from the prayers of the monasteries affiliated with the great abbey.[20]

Marmoutier: The Community of Monks

An anonymous collection of miracles compiled at the Benedictine abbey of Marmoutier, near Tours, between 1137 and the end of the century, encourages useful comparisons with other narrative series.[21] This collection was evidently intended to be used within the monastery: for the most part only monks, including three abbots in succession, are noted in it, though it sometimes mentions people who had strong ties to the community and who had died a short time before or were still alive at the time the collection was written down. The scribe twice insists on the contemporary nature of his tales.[22] Within the walls of the monastery, these tales must have been known and accepted by everyone, to the point of making it unnecessary to mention any "trustworthy" informants. However, the scribe does specify his intentions aimed at posterity.[23] He wants to warn the monks against any negligence in the spiritual services they owe to their dead brothers,[24] at the risk of being the targets of their revenge.[25]

The collection is made up of sixteen tales.[26] No fewer than six relate apparitions of the dead. The other tales compose two distinct groups, which are important to identify in order to understand the category in which the tales that are of primary interest to us are found. Seven tales relate not the return of a dead person but the moment of the death throes, or the passing of a monk whom confession frees in extremis from hell, or of a monk to whom the patron of the monastery, Saint Martin, appears to announce that he is to die, or to whom the saint appears even to pull his soul away from the devil. One also reads of a monk whose brothers see his soul, in the form of a small child or a dove, leave his body at the moment of his death.[27] In the second group, three tales deal with miraculous events from which the entire monastery benefited.[28]

Through such a collection of visions and miracles, the monastery represented itself as a group of individuals (who before and after death must account for a singular destiny) and as a community of the living and the dead. The monastery was a spiritual "family," united in daily concerns (acquiring land, building up the treasure, harvesting the crops, stocking the kitchens), grouped around its tutelary saints (above all Saint Martin but also Saint Benedict, Saint Fulgentius, and Saint Corentin) and completely directed toward a concern with death. The six ghost tales tie together these two complementary relationships, between the individual and the monastic community and between material goods and spiritual benefits.

The tales do not all have the same structure or the same function. Some talk about dreams, but most tell of a conscious vision. In all cases, however, the tales are reported, not autobiographical. In three of them, the story is rather simple: a dead person appears to a living person to ask for suffrages or to assign the task of requesting suffrages from all the monks. The goal of the apparition is always the same: to claim the right (*jus*) of the dead to benefit from the spiritual suffrages of the living.[29]

Let us take, for example, the story of the priest Herveus, who, after a tumultuous, successful life in the world, came to seek salvation among the monks of Marmoutier.[30] He gives them all his property, including the notes for the debts still owed him. Before dying, he specifies when each of the debts is scheduled to be paid back to the monks. He also comes to an agreement with his "godfather and friend," who owes him sixty pounds. Although no one else knows about this debt, the dying priest does not require his friend to swear to pay the debt but requests only "a holy kiss of faith and of peace" by which the friend pledges to pay the debt to the monks in one year. The priest then dies, and the monks, anticipating the reimbursement, fulfill their *debitum fraternitatis* with their prayers. But at the end of a year, the debtor purposefully fails to pay back his debt, and the monks stop praying for the dead priest, who becomes concerned and appears, wearing a monastic habit, to the chaplain of the church on the road to Tours. The priest makes the chaplain a messenger to the debtor to urge him to pay back his debt. The debtor refuses, but on the very same day, stricken with a great pain that he interprets as a punishment, he calls back the chaplain, whom he sends to tell the monks that he will pay back his debt to them, and he makes a gift of his person and all his property to the monastery. The dual messenger function (*internuntius*) of the chaplain (on behalf of the dead man to the debtor, then on behalf of the debtor to the monks) highlights the importance of the relationship that joins the three types of agents in the tale. This relationship underlies the conversion of people (the two friends in succession) and of property (the debt, then the entire charitable donation), a process carried out to ensure the salvation of souls and the benefit of the monastic economy.

Two other tales specify the conditions for the functioning of solidarity between the living and the dead. The first deals with two monks who before being brothers in religion are brothers through blood (*germani*).[31] Their spiritual kinship is added to their natural kinship: they are only that much more united when the hazards of life (one of them, on the orders of the abbot, leaves for a monastery in England) and then of death (the monk in England dies, far from his brother, who stayed at Marmoutier) separate them. The very day of his death the monk appears to his brother in a dream three times, requesting that his brother ask the abbot to have prayers said for him. But once consulted, the *custos* of the abbey says that it is not customary for monks to pray for a brother whose *kalenda*, that is, the day of his death, chosen as the anniversary date of his liturgical commemoration, is unknown. That same day the rumor spreads in the monastery that a messenger monk (*nuntius*) has just arrived bearing a note announcing the brother's death, which occurred on the same date as that very day. Considering the distance traveled by the messenger, the monks estimate that the brother must have died one year ago to the day. To find out more, they go in search of the messenger, but he cannot be found. In fact it was the dead man himself who returned to confirm the truth of his brother's three dreams and to signify that he died that very day and not a year ago. The lesson is clear: the strength of the spiritual kinship of the monks (possibly reinforced by the natural kinship of the brothers) abolishes all distance and any amount of time. The spiritual family of the monks escapes any constraints of geography, just as the cyclical time of the monks—"calendaric" time completely ordered toward the celebration of the "anniversary" (of the deaths) of the brothers—is never ending.

The last tale illustrates the sociological limits of the monastic "family."[32] Every year the archdeacon and provost of Clermont would visit Marmoutier and make a contribution to the monks of "treasures, silk clothing, and goods." This time he asks abbot William to keep him at the monastery, where he quickly becomes the sacristan. But this former secular cleric has not yet taken on the collective memory of the monks: on All Saints' Day he has a vision in the church of three *personae* (one in the middle, taller than the other two) followed by an uncountable procession of former abbots and monks, among whom he can identify no dead person of his acquaintance. He asks them to tell him who they are, and he learns that the first three figures are Saint Martin and, on either side, Saint Fulgentius and Saint Corentin. He also learns that the abbot Odo in that same year of 1137 was to join the cohort of dead abbots. This tale shows the necessity of the long apprenticeship in the funerary memory of the monks. The collective recitation of the names in the necrology was supposed to help, just as were, more modestly, the tales of ghosts themselves. But the tales certainly illustrate only part of the monastic memory.[33] Missing from the list are all the aristocratic families that, at Marmoutier and elsewhere, exchanged charitable donations for an inscription in the obituary and the assurance of prayers and masses after their deaths.[34] The Clunaic tales of the abbot Peter the Venerable, however, exhibit a greater openness to apparitions of the dead lay aristocracy.

Cluny: Monks and Nobles

The eighth abbot of Cluny (from 1122 to his death in 1156), Peter the Venerable is the author of a collection of tales of miracles, *De miraculis*, which, among other contributions, provides quite valuable information regarding apparitions of the dead.[35] Born around 1092–1094 into a noble family of Auvergne, he was destined from a very young age for a monastic life: first an oblate at Sauxillanges and then a monk (in 1109 the abbot of Cluny, Hugh the Great, heard his final vows), he became prior of Vézelay, then of Domène. His election as abbot of Cluny enabled the resolution of the very serious crisis that the order had just experienced under the abbacy of Pons de Melgueil, who, removed from office in 1122, died in 1126 after attempting to regain control of the monastery by force. From that time Peter was able to devote himself to the restoration of regular observance and of the material stability of Cluny; the general chapter of 1132 and the *Statuta* of 1146–1147 were the important stages of this reformative activity. His writings also testify to this will for reform:

he wrote a great number of letters and three polemical and doctrinal treatises against heretics (*Contra Petrobrusianos*), Jews (*Aversus Judaeos*), and Moslems (*Contra Sarracenos*).

As for *De miraculis*, it is a collection of sixty tales of miracles gathered into two books of twenty-eight and thirty-two chapters respectively. Peter supposedly conceived the project in 1127, after things had settled down following the aftermath of the abbacy of Pons. At the end of that crisis, which had shaken the authority of the abbot as well as the power and the prestige of the order, Peter intended to convince the monks and the world of the excellence of Cluny and of the high place for miracles from God and to clarify, using doctrinal commentaries, the beliefs of the monks and of the faithful. This doctrinal point of view leads us not to translate *miracula* as "marvels," as D. Bouthillier and J.-P. Torrell propose, but as "miracles," even though this means stressing how, in the twelfth century, this term had a broader meaning than the one we normally attribute to it today.[36] Granted, the *miracula* were, like "marvels," extraordinary events, but their meaning for monks and clerics of the time was understandable only with reference to divine will. The monks and clerics had no doubt as to the unequivocal nature of the miracle. We will see, on the contrary, that if their contemporaries indeed had a certain concept of the marvelous, they did not so easily assign it an origin and a reason.

For the most part the *miracula* Peter the Venerable describes are visions. In consideration of the dignity of Christ, the work opens with eucharistic miracles. Next follows a large number of celestial visions of Christ, the Virgin Mary, angels, etc. But there is an even greater number of diabolical visions: the attacks of the devil against Cluny are in fact proof of the holiness of the monastery. Midway between celestial and diabolical visions, Peter the Venerable also offers ten tales of apparitions of the dead. He thus fixes himself in the Cluniac tradition of the memory of the dead, a tradition founded by Odilo and pursued by Saint Hugh.[37]

In every case, Peter claims to be speaking of recent miracles, the tales of which (nine times out of ten) he collected directly from trustworthy sources at Cluny itself or during his travels. Although the order of the collection is intentionally chronological, the dates do not indicate the order in which the events occurred but—Peter admits this himself—the order in which he collected the accounts. In 1135 he wrote a first draft, which was to become part of the first book of the work. On his return from his voyage to Spain in 1142, he recast it and added new tales. Most of the second book was written later, between 1145 and 1156. During this writing, which lasted more than twenty years, the tales of apparitions of the dead were distributed into three groups, and their contemporary character was increasingly asserted.

The first five tales (Book I, chapters 10, 11, 23, 24, 26) were written around 1135. They deal with relatively old apparitions (supposedly occurring from fifty-five to twelve years earlier).[38] Peter appealed to informants, monks or priests, whose integrity he guarantees but whom he names expressly in only two cases (chapters 23 and 26).

The following two tales (Book I, chapters 27 and 28) were written during and immediately after Peter's trip to Spain in 1141–1142. The first apparition had just occurred when Peter learned of it in the diocese of Lyon. He wrote it down a few months later in Spain, where he also learned of another apparition, an older but locally famous one, the tale of which he was fortunate enough to hear directly from the visionary. He immediately wrote down the story.[39]

The last three tales deal with apparitions that occurred in 1145 and 1149. Peter also wrote them down without delay.[40]

The apparitions that Peter the Venerable describes are either dreams or visions perceived in a wakeful state. Peter constantly reiterates his distrust of dreams, which are propitious to the illusions of the devil. He therefore agrees to relate only the oneiric apparitions for which he can provide all the guarantees of authenticity: either because the nobility and holiness of the informant leaves no room for suspicion,[41] or because his informant personally experienced the dream,[42] or finally because he is describing his own dream. The seven conscious visions do not require as many guarantees: none are autobiographical, and only once is the informant the beneficiary of the vision.[43]

It is enlightening, once again, to distinguish clearly the single autobiographical tale, which is a dream, from the reported tales, which are mostly tales of conscious visions. The personal dream that Peter relates occurred during a trip to Rome at the beginning of Advent in 1145. Peter agrees to describe it, he says, because he himself can give all the necessary guarantees of its truth.[44] Just as he is leaving Cluny, Peter the Venerable learns of the death of the prior of Charlieu, William of Roanne, a man of great merit. Peter strongly suspects that William was poisoned by his own monks, who had rebelled against the discipline he wanted to impose on them. During Peter's first night in Rome, he sees the dead prior in a dream. All the while aware that he is dreaming, he sees himself embrace the prior and hears himself question William about the death. The dead man confirms the abbot's suspicions concerning the cause of his death and the identity of the murderer. Peter wakes up and makes an effort to etch into his memory what he has just dreamed. He then falls back to sleep, and the identical dream recurs, which, Peter the Venerable comments, proves that it is true. This time the dead man's tale moves the dreamer so much that he wakes up with his eyes and cheeks wet with tears. Once back at Cluny, Peter the Venerable makes the criminal appear before the chapter of the monks and condemns him to perpetual banishment. In the sketchy analysis that Peter proposes of his dream, we see him connect his oneiric experience to the diurnal agony he had experienced regarding the fate of his friend. The dream confirmed his fears and his suspicions. But the recurrence of the dream was not enough to convince Peter of the truth of oneiric images without more material proof. Usually a conscious vision that followed a dream confirmed the dream. In this autobiographical tale, the second dream filled the same function of authentication.

Unlike this autobiographical tale of a dream, the tales of apparitions reported by Peter the Venerable are characterized by a more complex structure than seen in other collections of *miracula*. Indeed, the apparition connects three if not four types of actors: not only the dead person and the recipient of the apparition but also, among the living, the one who was ultimately intended for the apparition and, among the dead, other deceased to whom the dead person gives the news or who appear at the dead person's side. This ternary or quaternary structure of the tale is explained by Cluny's function as a privileged location for the dead in search of suffrages: the dead person makes the recipient of the apparition the messenger (*nuntius*) to the abbot and the community of Cluny. The structure is also explained by the inclusion of the lay aristocracy in the tales.[45] Through the intervention of the beneficiary, the dead person asks relatives and heirs to do whatever is necessary to ensure the dead person's salvation. The advantage of this complex structure is a very great suppleness when the dead person's request comes up against the resistance of the living: if the recipient is reluctant to convey the dead person's message, the deceased on a second occasion may appear directly to the intended person. In a reverse scenario, if the intended person refuses to hear the message of the intermediary, the dead person might ask the messenger to organize the suffrages.[46]

Whether dead or alive, almost all the figures named by Peter the Venerable were known in other circumstances: they truly lived in the times and the conditions that are well-known to us through the rich archives preserved for Cluny and its region. Thus these tales lend themselves particularly well to an attempt to write a social history of the imaginary. Indeed, the death of someone did not end the natural or spiritual relationships that the living maintained, but on the contrary, the death reactivated them in remembrance. In this regard Peter the Venerable's tales provide a model that can be compared with other narrative collections, as will be shown later.

To ensure the salvation of the soul of a dead person or persons by means of suffrages—prayers, masses, almsgiving—that the dead come back to request is the primary function of all apparitions. In Peter the Venerable's opinion, apparitions confirmed Cluny's vocation to save souls in purgatory from their agony in the hereafter. Ever since Cluny organized the liturgy for the commemoration of the dead—by instituting, around 1030, the Day of the Dead on November 2—Cluniac customs required a monk to whom a deceased person appeared in a dream, particularly if the dead person was a relative or someone the monk once knew, to inform the community so that salutary masses might be celebrated for that person.[47] Apparitions also enabled the refutation of the arguments of those who "deny or doubt that ecclesiastical services are useful to the dead faithful," arguments that threatened the entire foundation of the Cluniac economy. The strongest opposition came from the heretic disciples of Peter of Bruys (the Petrobrusians), whom Peter the Venerable mentions in De miraculis[48] and whose criticism of the cult of the dead he systematically refutes in Contra Petrobrusianos: not only do the good works of the living benefit the dead, but also the good works of the dead benefit the living, those of the living benefit the living, and those of the dead aid the dead.[49] How might the dead be useful to the living? The tales of De miraculis never present the dead as intercessors to God on behalf of the living. However, a dead person might give a living person useful advice and announce an imminent death. In Christian society a dead person could provide no greater service than to invite a living person to prepare for death. The same tales also show how a dead person who appeared could be useful to another dead person who did not appear (such as the lord of Beaujeu, Guichard), by asking for suffrages for the other dead person as well. Indirectly, Peter the Venerable's ghost tales fulfilled still other functions.[50] By telling all the reasons they were tormented in the hereafter, the dead tended to strengthen the social order as the abbot of Cluny dreamed of it: without murder or theft and with knights who respected clerics, who did not violate the consecrated walls of the cemeteries, who protected the poor, and who righted the wrongs they had done the weak. In other words, the dream of a society without "unjust war,"[51] a society in which knights would dream only of leaving for the Crusades or on a pilgrimage to Rome, unless—better yet—they were to become monks. The tale of an apparition that Peter heard in Spain again illustrates another function of his ghost tales. It constitutes a sizable piece of the politico-financial strategy of the abbot of Cluny. Twenty-eight years earlier, in 1114, Peter the Venerable's source, Peter Engelbert, had received the apparition of his servant Sancho, who had died four months earlier. Peter Engelbert asked him, as well as a second dead person who suddenly appeared at the window, for news of several dead people, including King Alfonso VI of Leon-Castilla, who had died in 1109. Peter Engelbert thus learned that the king had experienced great torments in the hereafter but that the prayers of the Cluniac monks had delivered him from his agony. Peter the Venerable heard this tale in Najera in the spring of 1142 and immediately wrote it down, for he now possessed a weighty argument in the negotiations he was to enter several months later in Salamanca with King Alfonso VII, the grandson of the dead king. Peter wanted to persuade the king to honor the arrangement made by his predecessors Ferdinand I, and then Alfonso VI himself, to pay annual dues to Cluny. On July 29, 1142, the abbot of Cluny obtained satisfaction. We might assume that Peter took great joy in informing Alfonso VII that the king's dead grandfather owed his salvation to the prayers of Cluny! The king's generosity was simply the rightful payment for the suffrages of the monks.[52]

The promotion of the liturgy of the dead and, consequently, the material and spiritual development of the great abbey, from Burgundy to as far as Spain, were the reasons for writing down, gathering, and distributing these *miracula*. To that end the author's subjective point of view, except when he was invoked as a guarantee of the authenticity of a tale, gave way before the assumed objectivity of the related event. Indeed, no doubt was to weigh on the truth of the apparition. The tales were in no case to cause the slightest suspicion that they might be diabolically connected to dreams. In their socialized form—to the ends of monastic "propaganda" of the apostolate—most of these ghost tales thus describe an apparition perceived in a wakeful state.

In certain cases one might theorize that a true dream was transformed into a conscious apparition in the "socialized" version of the tale. But beyond the fact that this hypothesis is impossible to prove (we would have to have several successive versions of the same tale), it seems useless to me. Once established and accepted by all, couldn't the narrative schema of the apparition of a dead person before a conscious living person by itself engender new tales, independent of any previous oneiric

experience? Nor can Peter the Venerable be suspected of having wit-
tingly forged "false" tales of apparitions. Quite to the contrary, he was
adamant about reporting only what he held to be definitely established.
The narrative schema was a horizon of belief that enabled the gathering
and the shaping of all tales that conformed to the desired end: the promotion of the Cluniac liturgy of the dead. Thus throughout a complex
social transmission—by word of mouth, between sources, from author
to audience—these tales took on the form of *miracula*, the form that, at
this time, was best suited to their believability and their effectiveness.
They were not mere apothegms whose figured meanings would have
been independent of any objective situation. Nor was the author content
to suggest that these supernatural manifestations were only likely and
not true. He believed he was reporting *true* stories.

Granted, the tales are not true according to our own criteria: we do
not "believe" in such ghosts. But they were true for him, for his readers,
for his monk and lay listeners, both because the entire religious culture
of the time pushed to admit this truth and because those who said so
could not lie, and above all because the highly controlled transmission
of the tale was the best assurance of its credibility. These stories of conscious visions were "true" because they were believed to be true. In this
regard Peter the Venerable's tales represent a successful narrative and
ideological model, the culmination of a long monastic tradition (we have
followed it since the time of Gregory the Great) that never ceased,
throughout the centuries and while adapting to social evolutions, to re-
fine its forms and functions.

Unlike the autobiographical tales that made a breakthrough in the
twelfth century, the *miracula* were anchored in a much older hagiographical tradition. But the genre was transformed at the same time; it was
incarnated into systematic collections, and its function changed from
glorifying the local saint to exalting more widely the monastery or the
monastic order. However, the "concern with the self" was introduced into
several collections of miracles, for example in that of Peter the Venerable,
who not only reports tales he heard but also mentions, at least once, his
personal oneiric experience. In contrast, an anonymous collection such
as that of Marmoutier bears the imprint of no outstanding personality. In
all these tales, as varied as they are, the ghost is someone close to the
living person to whom the apparition appears. The ghost is linked to
the living person through natural kinship, spiritual kinship, proximity of
dwelling places, or the material and spiritual services exchanged by
monks and the lay aristocracy. Within this framework the ghost implores

suffrages and tells of the dire consequences of sin. Therefore, the miraculous apparition is the bearer of a moral lesson; it became the instrument of ecclesiastical reform or even strengthened a true political agenda.

Under such conditions we can understand the extraordinary success of such tales. Forgotten are the former hesitations of the church fathers with regard to ghosts! The greatest monasteries promoted the tales and collected them. The autobiographical dream, the translation of a unique and intimate experience, thus remained in the minority. What was most fitting to these tales was the conscious vision of an objective third party, a vision guaranteed by a chain of indubitable sources (preferably monks). These tales, like other objects (the treasure, relics, land), made up the patrimony of the monastery, giving them an almost juridical value of truth.

Through what paradox could the tales of conscious visions appear truer than the personal tales of dreams? The autobiographical tale of a dream and the reported tale of an apparition perceived in a wakeful state belonged to two different orders of truth. The first related to the intimate truth of the subject face-to-face with the divine, to what the subject alone was able to express of a personal experience. For a long time the dream, in order to be taken into consideration, had to be that of a saint, a monk, or a king. The second type of tale owed its status as an authenticated story to its very distribution, to its social uses, to the authority of those who transmitted it and put it down in writing. In a society firmly based on the authority of the "authorized" tradition of the church and its consecrated figures—clerics and monks as holders of tradition, as writers, and as mediators with the divine—such tales were beyond suspicion.

FOUR

THE MARVELOUS DEAD

Mirabilia: The Marvelous

Although tales of apparitions of the dead found a systematic form of expression and an explicit ideological finality in the monastic *miracula*, ghosts were also present in a different type of tale: the *mirabilia*, or tales of marvels. It is necessary to point out the difference between the *miracula* and the *mirabilia* even though the two notions, whose names have the same etymological root, often overlap and even though both refer to the same idea of a wondrous event. The distinction is made clear by an author from the beginning of the thirteenth century, an expert in the matter: Gervase of Tilbury.[1] For Gervase, *miracula* and *mirabilia* both had the ability to evoke *admiratio*, a wonderment for something new, rare, or unheard of. But *miracula* consisted of a suspension of the natural order (*praeter naturam*) through the will of the Creator (such as the Virgin Mary's pregnancy, the resurrection of Lazarus, or a miraculous healing), whereas *mirabilia*, even if they did not contradict the natural order, amazed the beholder, who did not understand what caused them. One does not understand why the salamander is unharmed by fire, why a volcano like Etna burns endlessly without being consumed by the heat, why the flesh of a peacock does not decay. In other words, these were two types of apparently analogous phenomena that differed in their relationship to the order of Creation and that evoked quite different attitudes: the miracle invited one to rely on one's faith, to accept the total power of God, who was upsetting the order that he himself had established. Human reason could only bow before such phenomena. On the other hand, the marvelous aroused the *curiositas* of the human mind, the search for hidden natural causes, ones that would someday be unveiled and understood.

The development of the latter attitude at the turn of the twelfth century must be seen as an early form of the scientific spirit that valued inquiry (*inquisitio*), true accounts of the facts, and even experimentation (*experimentum*).[2] This approach was applied in a very broad field, to stones and to plants, to history and to geography, as well as to manifestations of spirits, fairies, and the dead.

Like Gervase of Tilbury, William of Newburgh defined the *mira et prodigiosa* ("marvelous and wondrous things"),[3] but less by their rarity than by their having a "hidden reason" (*occultam rationem*). Referring to Saint Augustine, William reasoned that if God was the single Creator, he had "distributed" forces and powers that, with his permission, the angels (good and bad) and the people might use to produce amazing things. Some were only diabolical "phantasms," but others were "true," such as those fossilized stones in which could be seen the forms of two dogs and a toad wearing a golden chain around its neck. The reassuring mention of "God's permission" at the source of these phenomena was a commonplace of ecclesiastical literature anytime the supernatural was at issue. But we should stress the new contemporariness of the formula at the turn of the twelfth century. Once the all-powerfulness of the Creator was accepted as unquestioned, the Creator was relegated to the rather passive role of spectator of the marvels of the world. Suddenly, even though the *mirabilia* were placed in the service of a religious or moral lesson, they were seductive above all by their stupefying character and their ability to unveil the unsuspected realities of geography, zoology, or history. As for the educated people, the scholars, they henceforth had the ability to judge and use nature without the risk of attacking God.

The literature of *mirabilia* is particularly well represented in the Anglo-Norman realm. The court of the Plantagenets, much more than that of the Capetians, cultivated a taste for oral traditions and folklore and supported the clerics who gathered them. For in that kingdom, in that time, the most diverse languages and traditions crossed paths—Angevin, Norman, English, Welsh, and even Irish—objects of curiosity and of comparison. Is it not the diversity of cultures that hones the minds of men and women? And in addition to this literature in the Latin language was literature in the young vernacular, in the courtly novels and the "Matter of Britain." This came out of the same court milieus and was produced by clerics who also went into the service of princes and shared the interests of the aristocracy for the oral traditions of folklore, marvelous legends, and fantastic tales. Several works in Old French (for example, *Amadas et Idoine* and *Perlesvaus*) take up the fantastic motif of the haunted cemetery—the *âtre périlleux* ["perilous cemetery"]—or of the chapel in which a dead knight, lying in rest, rises up in his coffin at the approach of the hero. Their fictional content and versified form distinguish these works, but their themes are found in the Latin *mirabilia* and even, for some, in the *exempla* of the preachers.[4]

All these tales introduce two novelties into our work. On the one hand, they portray individual apparitions of the dead from lay milieus, which the clerical literature had largely ignored up to that time; the tales are also connected to narrative traditions chosen precisely because of their unfamiliar characters that did not fit into normal clerical categories. On the other hand, it is in the literature of *mirabilia* that the collective apparitions of the dead, already mentioned in certain tales of miracles, make a forceful entrance under the hitherto unknown name of "Hellequin's hunt."

The "Secularization" of Tales

Let us distinguish three generations of sources that are found around the turn of the twelfth century. The first is that of "historians" who were still monks, such as William of Malmesbury (1096–1142) and Geoffrey of Monmouth (c. 1100–1155), who became bishop of Saint Asaph. They considered themselves the heirs of Bede the Venerable and intended to pursue the great tradition of the historiography of England, fed on ancient references (the legend of Troy and the eponymous hero Brutus) and Celtic legends.[5] William of Malmesbury is the author of the *Gesta regum Anglorum*, written around 1125, which has often disconcerted modern historians with the juxtaposition of two attitudes that today appear contradictory: sometimes, in the manner of Bede from the seventh century, there is a rigorous criticism of historical accounts and sometimes an extreme "credulity" toward tales of marvels.[6] Indeed, in William's eyes, wonders were the signs of a hidden order of nature and of time, but they were no less "true" than events that came out of what we call history. Their function was not, like the *miracula* reported by Bede, to demonstrate the superiority of Christianity or the holiness of a certain figure.[7] The amazement they inspired was enough to justify their place in the chronicle. For example, trusting the faith of a source that he himself questioned, the historian reports how demons recently snatched the body of the witch of Berkeley from the church where she had been mistakenly buried. We do not have here, he says, a "celestial miracle, but an infernal wonder," which only someone who has not read the fourth book of the *Dialogues* of Gregory the Great would deem "unbelievable."[8] However, William also castigates the "foolishness" and the "credulity" of the English who maintain that the "spirits" of King Alfred, abandoning the king's cadaver, wander around at night near houses and, more generally, that demons bring the dead back to life and make them run around.[9] Those are only, he believes, illusions provoked by demons. However, as proof of their passage, the deceased can leave a physical mark on the body of the one to whom they appear.[10]

We already know of the canon William of Newburgh's (1136–1198) interest, seen in the final book of his history of England (*Historia rerum anglicarum*), in "memorable things that have occurred in abundance in our time": meteorological wonders, famine and epidemics, a fatal accident during the digging of a well, a popular revolt in London in 1196, a rain of blood in 1198, and especially "the wondrous thing that occurred in the same period in the county of Buckingham"—a ghost story that he follows, along with three other similar stories concerning Yorkshire, at the very north of England. These four tales form a little collection whose coherence William stresses before continuing with his chronicle.[11]

In all four cases William emphasizes the recent nature of the events that his sources, generally men of the church, have related to him. Whereas the first story took place in Buckinghamshire, the three others occurred in the north of England: in the castle of Anant in Yorkshire and even farther north in the abbey of Melrose and in Berwick on the Tweed, on the Scottish border. The ghosts are very different from those mentioned by Peter the Venerable. For example, they are not the souls in torment who humbly return to solicit suffrages from the living but are evil-minded dead, like those described in the Scandinavian sagas: "pestilential monsters," according to the chronicler. They terrorize their relatives and the entire neighborhood, make dogs howl at night, and are accused of corrupting the air, of causing epidemics, and even of drinking people's blood. Two of them are explicitly called vampires (*sanguisuga*), and when their graves are opened, they are found stained with blood; the cadavers are all swollen, the faces florid, the shrouds torn apart. The chronicler also puts great effort into describing the behavior of the local people (*popularis opinio*) and into contrasting it to the behavior praised by the ecclesiastical hierarchy. Locally, that hierarchy appears distraught and hesitant. In the first tale the archdeacon Stephen (William of Newburgh's informant) is questioned by the population about the means to be used to get rid of the monster; in doubt, Stephen writes to the bishop Hugh of Lincoln, reputed for his holiness, to ask his advice. In the final tale the local clergy gathers and deliberates for a long time. In every case the solution finally proposed by the clerics consists of opening the tomb and placing a written prescription for absolution on the dead person's chest. In contrast, the clerics consider "indecent and unworthy" the method used by the residents and, above all, by the "young" who are able to overcome their terror: in a group (up to ten people), they go to the cemetery, dig up the cadaver, chop it into pieces, and burn everything on a pyre outside the village. Beforehand one of them cut out the heart, for its presence would have prevented the cadaver from burning. In the last tale we even see the young people overtake the clergy, so much do they doubt the efficacy of the less rigorous methods these men propose. Although he himself was a canon, William of Newburgh passes no negative judgment on the radical methods of the residents; as an author hungry for *mirabilia*, he is content to describe their actions with amazement, and he admits that they have given the village back its peaceful nights and its pure air.

The "Court Clerics"

It was primarily the "court clerics" who valued tales of marvels. The most important among them—Walter Map, Giraldus Cambrensis, and Gervase of Tilbury—were members, at least at certain times, of the entourage of King Henry II Plantagenet and his sons.[12] They were not monks but were secular clerics endowed with scholarly or university titles and with a few prebends. None of them achieved the highest functions of the ecclesiastical hierarchy. They owed their social position to the benevolence of the prince they were serving and not to the authority of the church. Walter Map was of Welsh origin, born in 1130–1135 on the English side of the Wye, in the south of Hereford. After studying in Paris, he entered the service of the diocese bishop, Gerard Foliot, and then of King Henry II starting around 1170. As archdeacon of Oxford, canon of Saint Paul of London, he served in particular the crown prince Henry. But the prince died in 1183, and the king in turn died in 1189, destroying Map's ambitions. With no more success than that of his compatriot Giraldus, he did not manage to reach the Welsh episcopal seat of Saint David. He died in 1209–1210, at an exceptionally old age for his time. His *De nugis curialium* (On courtiers' trifles), undoubtedly written around 1181–1182,[13] has not survived in its original format, assuming there was one. The work does not fit within a very well defined literary genre: it derives from a collection of *mirabilia* but appears to parody the genre of the "Mirrors for Princes." It is a satire of the court, of religious orders (in particular the Cistercians), of the society of the time, and it makes use of a multitude of fables and tales of wonders taken sometimes from classical culture (the author claims to imitate Valerius Maximus and abundantly cites Horace and Ovid) and sometimes from local oral traditions.[14] Thus Map devotes several chapters to the apparitions of "fantastic" beings, which he interprets in diabolical terms: *"fantasma* is derived from *fantasia,* i.e., a passing apparition for the appearances which occasionally devils make to some by their own power (first receiving leave of God), pass by with or without doing harm."[15] For example, in a tournament a mysterious knight suddenly arrives and for a whole day defeats all the opponents he confronts. But when he is finally killed and stripped of his weapons and armor, no one recognizes him. Most often these apparitions deal with fairies who, like Melusina, marry mortals, to whom they give many children before disappearing. In this collection is the story of the "sons of the dead woman." The woman's husband had just buried her when he notices her dancing with some other women. He pulls her out of the circle and couples with her, and they have many children, whose descendants still lived in the time of Walter Map. The story would be incredible, he writes, if the "sons of the dead woman" did not provide the living proof of the truth of the fact. In the language of this author and his contemporaries, the adjective "fantastic" only partially covers what the word evokes for us when we speak, for example, of "fantastic" literature or films. The realm of the latter consists of the irruption of the supernatural into the daily course of life. In the Middle Ages too, the word expressed the maximum intensification of the marvelous. But unlike *mirabilia,* the *fantasticus* remained imprinted with a value judgment because it bore the weight of the old suspicion of diabolical illusions, of which dreams, above all, were the instruments.[16]

Giraldus Cambrensis (or de Barri) (1146–1223) was born of a Norman father and a Welsh mother.[17] Thus he too was a native of the borders of the kingdom of England and Wales. His maternal uncle David FitzGerald, who became bishop of Saint David, sent him to study in Paris. Having returned to Wales, he became the archdeacon of Brecon and from that time ardently hoped to succeed his uncle on the episcopal seat of Saint David, which he wanted to have raised to the rank of an archbishopric. His constantly thwarted ambition (in 1176, 1198, and 1215) haunted his dreams and formed the focus of his autobiographical writings (*De rebus a se gestis* in 1208, *De invectionibus* in 1216). He wrote more than ten other works, always strictly linked to his own experiences. Having entered the service of the princes Henry and then John, in 1185 he visited Ireland, which he describes in the *Topographia Hibernica*, dedicated to Henry II, and the conquest of which in 1169 he recounts in the *Expugnacio Hibernica*, dedicated to Richard the Lion-Hearted. On the occasion of the preaching of the Crusades in 1188, Giraldus accompanied the archbishop of Canterbury to Wales; he wrote two works based on this voyage—*Itinerarium Kambriae* (1191) and *Descriptio Kambriae* (1194). In neither of these works does he systematically deal with apparitions of the dead. But the regions he visited were not unfamiliar with ghosts. In his account of the conquest of Ireland, Giraldus was so struck by the propensity of the inhabitants to speak of their visions and dreams that he decided to insert a small report on the matter into his narrative. First there are a few requisite ancient references: Valerius Maximus relates that in a dream, a Greek man sees his friend whom an innkeeper had killed and who came to ask him to avenge the death; after the poet Simonides buried a drowning victim, the dead man appears to him in a dream to warn him of the danger he would risk in taking to the sea the next day. But Giraldus is primarily eager to give recent examples: in a dream on the eve of a military campaign during the conquest of Ireland, Giraldus's half-brother Walter de Barri sees his dead stepmother (Giraldus's own mother), who dissuades him from setting out. He tells his dream to his father, who advises him to follow the advice of his dead stepmother; but Walter does not heed this "true" dream, and he is killed in battle that very day. In other cases, however, dreams are deceptive, and it is better not to trust in them.[18] In *De invectionibus*, Giraldus gathers no fewer than thirty-one oneiric visions, all of which concern him, either because he himself dreamed them or because others had dreamed of him in them: in every one of these visions he finds the confirmation of his moral excellence, which strengthens him in his desire to pursue his career. Thus, a ghost who appears in a dream to a canon of Saint David is a dead monk whose status in the hereafter is pitiful but who says he is consoled by the idea that Giraldus's situation is soon to improve. As soon as this dream is reported to him, Giraldus interprets it without the slightest hesitation: it is his career that is going to improve; he will become archbishop![19]

Gervase of Tilbury also belonged to the circle of clerics who were curious about everything Henry the Younger surrounded himself with.

Gervase even dedicated *Liber facetiarum*, undoubtedly somewhat similar to Walter Map's *De nugis curialium*, to the young prince.[20] But his training was rather juridical and therefore Italian: he studied civil and canon law in Bologna. Following the death of his first protector in 1183 he entered into the service of the nephew of the king of England, the Emperor Otto IV of Brunswick, whom he represented as marshal of the kingdom of Arles. He was also a judge in Sicily and a superior judge of the county of Provence. In 1211 he dedicated to the emperor *Otia imperialia* ("Imperial Diversions"), a group of *mirabilia* collected during his travels in the Anglo-Norman realm and then in Provence, in the Pyrenees, in the Alps, and in Italy. The topographical marvelous plays an essential role throughout the work, which notably deals with the dead: near Arles, the bodies buried in the Aliscamps are privileged not to lay open to "diabolical illusions";[21] in Pouzzoles, in Campania, the bishop prays for a year to free a soul from purgatory, which is most likely located in the nearby Vesuvius.[22] Certain unique apparitions of the dead also catch the attention of Gervase of Tilbury, ghosts such as the one in the story "of the dead man who killed his widow."[23] In the county of Arles the knight William of Mostiers had made his wife swear on her life not to marry any other man should he happen to die. After becoming a widow, she honors her promise for several years, then gives in to the pressure of her friends who assure her that "a dead man doesn't have the power to do harm." Returning from the church where the second marriage was blessed, these women, seated, circle around the bride. But suddenly she screams out: "Miserable woman that I am! I have violated the trust of my marriage and here is my husband who is going to kill me with a mortar." The dead man is visible to her alone, but everyone sees the mortar that an invisible hand raises and then crashes down on the woman's head, shattering her skull and spilling her brains. For Gervase, the marvelous trait of this tale is the image of the mortar that seems to move by itself through the air while the cries of the woman affirm that the dead man is indeed there. But the normative character of the tale and the instrument of punishment are no less important: the dead man (stricter than the church at the time) takes a position against the remarrying of widows, and to enforce this prohibition, he uses a kitchen instrument, a mortar, as a lethal weapon.[24] At the beginning of the fourteenth century the *charivari*—extreme noise—also loudly denounced remarriages through the din of casseroles and pans, of kitchen utensils diverted from their normal functions.

The Ghost of Beaucaire

The longest of the "marvelous" tales compiled by Gervase of Tilbury tells of the repeated apparitions of a dead young man to his young cousin, in Beaucaire, between the month of July and September 29, 1211.[25] The recent event had caused quite a stir; the marshal of the imperial court of the kingdom of Arles immediately became aware of it and even became personally involved in conversations with the dead man. Through his long tale, Gervase intended to convince those who doubted that the dead could return to provide revelations to the living. There was not, therefore, unanimous belief in this area. The author also wanted, through the voice of the dead man, to confirm both faith in general and, more specifically, the Christian representations of the hereafter. The tale thus leans toward a lesson in theology and also toward political prophecy. In fact, Gervase of Tilbury forewarned his imperial reader, Otto IV, that he was sending, at the same time that he sent this public report on the apparitions of the dead man, a secret report on revelations that concerned the emperor more directly. Although this second text has never been found (if it ever truly existed), the mention of secret revelations intended only for the ruler bears witness, at the beginning of the thirteenth century, to the important role assigned to the occult, astrology, and political prophecy in the ideology of the nascent state.[26]

The dead man's first name was William. A young man of a good family from Apt, he was exiled to Beaucaire to the home of his uncle because of violent acts committed in the town where he was born. In Beaucaire he died following a brawl. Such a violent and premature death caused him to become a ghost. But he died a perfect Christian, armed with the sacraments of the church (penance and last rites) and after pardoning his killer. His apparitions begin three to five days following his death, and the person to whom he appears is his young cousin, an eleven-year-old virgin. The young girl's being singled out is explained by the intense and chaste love of young people. According to a *topos* of many tales of apparitions, she had asked the dying man to appear to her after his death, if he could, to inform her of his condition in the hereafter. His apparition is therefore awaited, and the young girl is keeping a vigil in her room, her lamp lit, when her dead cousin manifests himself to her visibly, naked but covered with rags. She is afraid, but he reassures her and begins a conversation. In the adjoining room the girl's parents hear only the words of their daughter, and when they arrive on the threshold of her room, concerned and armed with the sign of the cross, they cannot see the dead man, who immediately leaves his cousin.

Seven days later he appears to her again while her parents have gone to pray for him at the monastery of Saint Michel-de-Frigolet. He begins to feel the first beneficial effects of this pious act, even though he is still accompanied by a horned devil, which the young girl chases away with holy water.

In a few days news of the apparitions spreads, and the neighbors come running. Henceforth the young girl is used as a medium by people wanting to question the dead man through his intermediary. First a layman, a friend of Gervase himself and a knight of Saint Gilles, puts the spirit to the test by verifying whether the ghost knows of the charitable deed the knight had just done in secret to aid a poor person.

A second person is a cleric. Such apparitions, which upset the entire neighborhood and then the whole town, did not long remain the sole privilege of laypeople. The clergy soon claimed them. Through the intermediacy of the young girl, the prior of Tarascon assails the dead man with questions but does not see him (the prior even comes very close to stepping on his foot!). The dead man, according to his cousin, is now accompanied by Saint Michael, and he has been wearing his own clothes ever since his aunt gave them to the poor. He complains again of the suffering caused him by a sword belt of fire, but his suffering is ended when the belt, which he had borrowed from a citizen of Apt, is returned to its rightful owner. Thus once again the symbolic and numerical equivalency between good acts carried out on earth on behalf of the dead person and diminished torments in the hereafter is affirmed, as is the strict correspondence between material objects (clothing, a belt) and their imaginary doubles (the clothing and the sword belt of the dead man).

In the days that follow, the young girl continues to converse with the dead man on behalf of the prior and then of educated men who are not named. A threshold is crossed when a priest, "educated, a good religious man fearing God," obtains permission from the dead man to speak with him directly without an intermediary: the debate then rages up to the "arcana of the divine plan" in a continuous series of brief questions and answers that make up a sort of *inquisitio*, of which Gervase of Tilbury, who writes under the priest's dictation, is the scribe. Later the bishop William of Orange, not being able to come himself, has an entire questionnaire sent through a messenger, the contents of which the dead man guesses in advance.

Most of the ghost's revelations deal with the future of souls after death. As a point of comparison or confirmation, reference is made more than once to the *Dialogues* of Gregory the Great, but without any sense of inferiority. On the delicate question of the stay of the damned and the elect between death and the Last Judgment, Gervase of Tilbury, not being able to find explicit information in Gregory's work, is inclined to follow the revelations of the dead man, who, on these issues, "knows more through experience."

The dead man first confirms the horror of death. The word itself is unbearable to him, and the spirit implores the young girl to speak of it only euphemistically, using the word "passing." Clearly, before the efflorescence of the macabre and the horror of death, there were some limits to the "tame death" of which Philippe Ariès has spoken. The dead man remembers his death throes: he saw good and bad angels fight over his soul until the former carried it away. This battle thus takes the place of an individual judgment of the soul: no mention is made of an intervention by Christ or even the Virgin Mary. After death, the soul wanders for four or five days, which is about the time it took for the ghost to appear to his cousin. We therefore see again here the wandering of souls that the *armariés* of Montaillou affirmed and that contrasts with the idea of an immediate entrance into purgatory. But in Beaucaire this wandering lasts only a few days, not until the following All Saints' Day. The hereafter described by the dead man of Beaucaire presents still other unique characteristics.

At the end of a few days, the souls of those who are neither saints nor damned go to purgatory, thus designated as a noun at the beginning of the thirteenth century. This purgatory is aerial, which might correspond to one of the localizations of purgatory that were sometimes suggested, but which above all, in the logic of this particular tale, designates purgatory as a temporary place. In fact, the dead man mentions two other temporary aerial locales: for the damned, an "aerial" hell, a prelude to a subterranean hell that will follow Judgment Day; for the righteous, the "Bosom of Abraham," conceived as an aerial paradise preceding the "judicial paradise," after the Last Judgment, when the saints will have retrieved their glorious bodies and acquired a complete vision of God.

In several ways this cosmology of the afterworld is different from that which the church was then attempting to impose. There were not three principal places in the hereafter but five. The idea of a sort of purgatory for saints and of progressive access, even for them, to beatific vision was to be found again in the great debates that, in the same region a century later, would stir up the pontifical court in Avignon. But the words of the dead man of Beaucaire did not take the form of a doctrine that claimed to be definitive. The ghost freely offers approximations, since he sometimes asserts that purgatory is far from paradise and sometimes that it is near both paradise and hell.

Speaking from his own experience, he describes the status of souls in the aerial purgatory. This "place" is subject to a time analogous to earthly time, with alternating days and nights (but the nights there are not as dark as those on earth) and with a sabbatical rest between Saturday evening and Sunday evening. Saint Michael Day (September 30) is also a day of rest. The name of Saint Michael does not designate a specific angel but a function of protection of souls in purgatory: to everyone his "Saint Michael." The Saint Michael of the dead William whispers to the ghost the answers he is to give to the young girl or to the priest. As in the *Dialogues* of Gregory the Great, the purgatorial fire is a corporeal fire, even though the spirit that endures it is incorporeal. The ghost does not have a true body, only—and we can recognize the Augustinian influence here—an "image of a body" (*effigiem corporis*), although he is not completely insensitive to bodily activity and contact: he cannot bear the weight of the stole that the priest seeks to place on his shoulders.

In purgatory, souls experience a progressive relief, hastened by prayers, almsgiving, and masses offered by the living and also by the sprinkling of holy water. As we have seen, the transformations in the appearance of the ghost in the course of his apparitions indicate an improvement in his condition due to the beneficial effects of suffrages.

The ghost strongly insists on his superhuman faculties of sight, if not of foresight. Souls see everything that takes place on earth (the ghost saw the prior enter the town of Beaucaire and drink with the schoolmaster). They even delve into the hearts of the living (but William refuses to betray his cousin's secrets to the prior). They foresee future events (thus the dead man can, through the mediation of his cousin, forewarn his uncle and that uncle's son of the plot their enemies are hatching against them in Avignon). Souls observe the arrival of other souls, who advance toward them (but they do not recognize those arriving souls whom they did not know on earth). They see each other in the aerial purgatory but do not recognize each other unless they already knew each other on earth. They witness the torment of damned souls and the happiness of the blessed, whom they accompany in songs to the glory of God. Nor are they deprived of the vision of God and the Virgin Mary, whom they will see in all clarity only after they have left purgatory or after the Last Judgment.

The ghost stays very close to the living, most often without their knowledge. But strong with divine authorization, he can appear simultaneously in two places and in different modes. One day he visits in a dream and awakens the priest, who is napping on one side of the Rhone, at the very moment when, in Beaucaire, the ghost appears to his conscious cousin to warn her that the priest, whom he says he forewarned through another spirit, will arrive late. In fact it is the ghost himself who appeared simultaneously in two distinct places, but he hides this fact from his cousin so as not to denounce the priest, who had dozed off.

He is not content just to reveal the mysteries of the hereafter. Even though he says he prefers to talk of spiritual things rather than corporeal things, he makes judgments on the society of the living. Underneath his words the moral order peeks through when he forewarns his cousin, whose exclusive love he requests, that he will cease to appear to her if she loses her virginity. This demand expresses the charismatic value that folklore attributed to the virginity of girls. Perhaps it also has a deeper affective resonance, by expressing, through the voice of the dead man, the secret wish of the young girl to remain faithful to the one who ignited the first sparks of love in her.

How might we judge the entire document in light of the beliefs and doctrines of the church at the time? Henri Bresc sees heresy poking through when the ghost says that the priest's stole is "the bond of the devil" (vinculum diaboli).[27] But the expression does not connect the priest to the devil (which would be sacrilegious); it signifies, on the contrary, that the priest has the power to bind the devil with his stole. The ghost is, moreover, of irreproachable orthodoxy: when the priest asks him what he thinks of the persecution (occurring at that time and rather close by) of the Albigensians, he answers that nothing could please God more and that the flames of the pyres are nothing compared with those that await heretics in hell.[28] He himself displays a generous knowledge of the cult of the saints, of ex-votos, of guardian angels, of the apotropaic use of wooden crosses, and of holy water kept in houses: he describes in detail the practices and objects that historians of "popular religion" often find mentioned only in later periods. Even more original is what he says about the patron saints who assist each Christian individually: since there does not seem to be any privileged connection between a patron saint and a person's first name (which seems rather to have been chosen from among the local saints), the ghost recommends that each person discover the identity of his or her celestial patron in order to be able to solicit favors; he has his uncle and his uncle's son told to solicit respectively Saint William and Saint Bénézet (the builder of the Avignon bridge).

Gervase of Tilbury's tale, in the form of a rigid interrogation, presents a familial news item that, at the mercy of a rumor that spread, became a social event. In a single narrative it joins together the presentation of heterogeneous, but not contradictory, practices and beliefs: some are of clearly scholarly origin, such as the explicit reference to Gregory the Great or the idea of a gradual beatific vision, whereas others appear to be "popular," such as the value accorded to the virginity of girls and the idea of the wandering of souls—concepts that the church would do its utmost, between the thirteenth and the fourteenth centuries, to reject. Much of the interest of this tale lies in the ghost's hesitations when he speaks, notably when he is asked to localize purgatory: his hesitation betrays, perhaps, clashes between levels of culture but also, undoubtedly, the persistent suppleness of various purgatorial representations, including among the educated (beginning with Gervase of Tilbury) at the beginning of the thirteenth century. However, the most important aspect of the tale is the role of the eleven-year-old girl. There is no reason to doubt the truth of her experience, told to us in Latin by an educated man. But Gervase's tale says much about the trauma of the girl, shaken by the sudden loss of the young cousin whom she adored and to whom, most likely, she had promised herself. In her mental anguish, she pursues the dialogue that his sudden and bloody death had interrupted. But in that society, death could not remain a "private" affair: the public rumor mill immediately took over, and preestablished roles were spontaneously distributed. The child was invested with the function of medium, and her vaticinations, first reserved for the circle of neighbors, were soon gathered up and exploited by the clerics. One cleric even managed to take her place in order to adequately translate truths from beyond the grave. Throughout all this time Gervase remained listening, seduced by the marvel and eager for predictions, which he took great pains to communicate to his master, the emperor.

Thus the folkloric marvelous could be changed into a political marvelous and the tale joined with another tradition, that of revelations intended for rulers of this world—kings, emperors, the pope. Visions of the hereafter, prophecies, and apparitions of Christ or of angels played essential roles in this realm. At the end of the Middle Ages, ghosts too were listened to more attentively.

FIVE

HELLEQUIN'S HUNT

Tales of *mirabilia* did not deal only with apparitions of individual ghosts. Such tales are even more interesting when one notes how they readily included the folkloric traditions of the hosts of the dead. In fact, the twelfth century marked the first appearance in these texts of the term "Hellequin's hunt," found in diverse forms to the present day. Its earliest mention can be attributed to an Anglo-Norman monk, Orderic Vitalis (1075–1142).

The Account of Orderic Vitalis

Orderic was the son of a cleric from Orleans who had entered into the service of a Norman nobleman living, after the conquest of England, in the region of Mercia, on the border of Wales. It was here that Orderic was born and spent his early childhood. When he was ten, his father, who had maintained ties with Normandy, sent him as an oblate to the abbey of Saint Evroult, in the diocese of Lisieux, where he would spend the rest of his life. In Orderic's time the abbey was an important link in the monastic reform that was occurring in Normandy under the influence of the abbey of Fécamp (reformed by William of Volpiano) and of Cluny; in 1132 Orderic was himself sent to Cluny, which was then under the abbacy of Peter the Venerable.[1] Saint Evroult was struggling for its independence from the two powers that were threatening it: the bishop of Lisieux and the seigneurs of the region, in particular the fearsome lord Robert of Bellême.

At Saint Evroult Orderic undertook to write the thirteen books of his *Ecclesiastical History*, a monumental history of the Normans. In his mind, this work was to be for the Normans what Bede's *Ecclesiastical History* was for the English.[2] Orderic compiled written documents, but with the third book he collected primarily contemporary oral accounts. His informants were the monks of Saint Evroult and also nobles and knights from the region, people whom he considered the best resources for the Norman memory, people in the best position to tell him about the conquests, the sieges, the battles, the alliances, and the successions that made up the focus of his narrative.[3] In the history of the Normans, was it not the duke and the nobles who played the primary roles? He also called on his own memories.[4] He wrote most of his work between 1123 and 1137 and most of Book VIII, which is of immediate interest to us, between 1133 and 1135.[5]

In Chapter XVI of Book VIII, and again at the beginning of Chapter XVIII, Orderic dwells on Robert of Bellême's misdeeds, which occurred around forty-five years earlier. Robert of Bellême was an evil lord—*nequissimus, pessimus,* says Orderic—whose cruelty was equaled only by that of his mother, Mabel (she had her prisoners assassinated). Robert of Bellême was the sworn enemy of the protector of Saint Evroult, Hugh of Grandmesnil, whom he besieged in Courcy in 1091. It is within this context, in the same year and in the same region, that the apparition of Hellequin's hunt is mentioned.[6]

Orderic heard the tale directly from the witness, a young priest named Walchelin, who served the church of Bonneval, which belonged to Saint Aubin of Angers. During the night of January 1, 1091, he was returning from a visit he had paid to a sick member of his parish when, alone and far from any dwelling, he heard the din of a "great army," which he assumed belonged to Robert of Bellême en route for the siege of Courcy. The night was clear; the priest was young, courageous, and strong. He sought shelter among four medlar trees, ready to defend himself, if necessary. At that moment there appeared before him a giant man who was armed with a mace and who ordered him to remain where he was and watch the procession of the "army" (*exercitus*), which was coming in successive waves.

The first group was the most ill-assorted. It formed a "great crowd on foot," with beasts of burden laden with clothing and every kind of furnishing and household goods, like robbers bending under the weight of their plunder. The people hurried along, lamenting, and among them the priest recognized some of his neighbors who had recently died. Then came a band of bearers (*turma vespillionum*), whom the giant joined; they were carrying, two men each, some fifty biers on which sat dwarfs with unusually large heads the shape of barrels (*dolium*). Two Ethiopians—

black demons—were carrying an enormous tree trunk, on which a wretched man, bound and wailing in pain, was being tortured; a fearful demon, sitting on the trunk, was goading his back and sides with red-hot spurs. Walchelin recognized the poor man: two years earlier, the man had killed the priest Stephen and had died without completing his penance for his crime. Next came a troop of women on horseback, riding on sidesaddles covered with burning nails; the wind unremittingly lifted them several feet from the saddles, then dropped them, painfully, back on to the sharp points; their breasts were pierced with the nails heated in the fire, which caused them to shriek out, bewailing their sins. These women, among whom Walchelin recognized several noblewomen, had lived lives of debauchery and ostentation.

The terrified priest then saw a "great troop of clergy and monks," led by bishops and abbots with pastoral staffs. The clergy and bishops were wearing black caps, and the monks and abbots wore black cowls. They lamented and begged Walchelin, whom they called by name, to pray for them. The priest was shocked to find among them men whom he had held in great esteem before their deaths: notably the bishop Hugh of Lisieux (d. 1077) and the abbots Mainer of Saint Evroult (d. 1089) and Gerbert of Saint Wandrille. But only God could know people's hearts and decide to subject sinners to the various purifications of the "purgatorial fire."

Even more frightening was the next group, which earned the longest and most specific description: the "army of knights" (*exercitus militum*), dressed all in black and spitting fire. All of them rode on huge horses, carrying various weapons and black standards, as if heading off to battle. The priest recognized, among others, Richard of Bienfaite and Baldwin of Meules, who were the sons of the count Gilbert of Brionne and who were both "recently" deceased, and Landry, "vicomte and advocate" of Orbec, who had died within the year and who shouted at Walchelin, bidding him to take a message to the count's wife. But the others told Walchelin not to listen to this liar, a corrupt, merciless parvenu.

After several thousand knights had passed, Walchelin realized that he was undoubtedly witnessing Hellequin's "rabble" (*familia Herlechini*); he had heard that many people had seen the group, but he had not believed his informants and had even made fun of them. He feared he would not be believed either if he did not bring back some certain proof (*certum specimen*) of his vision. Thus he decided to capture one of the black horses that went by without a rider. The first escaped him. He blocked the path of the second, which stopped as if to allow him to climb on it and which exhaled from its nostrils a cloud of steam the size of an oak tree. The priest put his foot into the stirrup and took hold of the reins, but he immediately felt an intense burning on his foot, and his hand became indescribably cold. As he let the animal go because of the pain, four knights burst forth, accused him of trying to steal their property, and ordered him to follow them. But the fourth rider intervened: he wanted to give Walchelin a message for his wife and sons. Walchelin answered that he did not know the fourth rider. The knight introduced himself: he was William of Glos, the son of the deceased Barnon of Glos, the former steward of William of Breteuil and of the latter's father, the earl William of Hereford. The principal crime of William of Glos was usury; he had fraudulently acquired and willed to his own heirs a mill that he had held as collateral for a loan that he knew could not be repaid. As punishment, he carried a burning mill-shaft in his mouth, "heavier than the castle of Rouen." Walchelin was to go ask his wife, Beatrice, and his son Roger to help him by restoring the mill to the legitimate heirs. But the priest refused to recognize the dead man. William of Glos was dead, he said; if he told the son and the widow that he had seen William of Glos, wouldn't they think him a madman? The dead man then listed the "signs" that ultimately convinced the priest, who listened to the message he was to convey. But Walchelin had second thoughts. He did not want to be the messenger of a criminal. In a terrible rage, the man took the priest by the neck with a burning hand that left an indelible mark, the *signum* of the authenticity of the apparition. William let Walchelin go when the priest invoked the mother of God and when another knight appeared, brandishing a sword and accusing the four others of wanting to kill his brother.

The new arrival revealed his identity: he was Walchelin's own brother, Robert, the son of Ralph the Fair. The knight reminded Walchelin of many childhood events they had shared, thus revealing many *signa* to him. The priest remembered very well, but he refused to admit it. His brother accused him of obstinancy and ingratitude: after the death of their parents, wasn't it Robert who had enabled him to go study in France? Walchelin burst into tears and finally agreed to recognize his brother. Robert told Walchelin that because he had sought to steal the property of the dead *(res nostra)*—something no one had ever attempted to do before—he would have to share their punishments. But because Walchelin had sung mass that very day, he would be saved. The dead man's punishment consisted of carrying burning weapons that were very heavy. Robert told Walchelin that the day he had been ordained a priest and said his first mass, in England, their dead father, Ralph, had been freed from his torments. Robert too, similarly, had been relieved of the shield that had tortured him. He was still carrying his incandescent sword but hoped to be rid of it within the year. When his brother asked him why his spurs were covered with a mass of congealed blood, the knight answered that it was not blood but was fire that seemed "heavier" than the Mont Saint Michel to him and that was his punishment for the haste with which he had spilled blood in his lifetime. Finally, forced to end their conversation in order to join the army of the dead, he implored his brother to remember him and to help him, through prayers and alms-giving, to ensure his release one year from the next Palm Sunday.[7] Walchelin, he said, should turn over a new leaf as well, for the priest was to die before long. For three days Walchelin was not to tell anyone what he had seen and heard. On these final words, the knight disappeared.

For a week the priest was gravely ill. When he was better he told his tale to the bishop Gilbert of Lisieux, who had personally cared for him. Walchelin lived another fifteen years or so, which enabled Orderic Vitalis to question him and to see the horrible burn mark left by the hand of the dead knight. Orderic says he faithfully transcribed the priest's account for the edification of his readers. He then resumes the tale of the siege of Courcy at the point he had left off.

This first written account of Hellequin's hunt has inspired many commentaries.[8] Its insertion in Orderic's chronicle invites us to see it as one of those *mirabilia* of which the Anglo-Norman clerics were so fond. The very name "Hellequin's hunt," the detail of the four medlar trees,[9] and the role of the young priest as a "messenger of souls" sketch the folkloric content of the document. But this text is foremost a product of the scholarly culture of that time—through its author and its language, through its classic listing of the infernal tortures that are found on the tympanum of Conques, and also through its narrative structure, whose coherence does not appear to me to have been enhanced even though it reinforces its ideological significance. Indeed, remarkably, the entire procession of the dead is made up of three large groupings that can easily be connected to the trifunctional schema of the society as had been defined by the clerics of the north of France since the end of the tenth century.[10] But, no less remarkably, the "three orders" here receive unequal treatment, as much in the amplitude of their descriptions as in Walchelin's attitude toward the different types of dead.

The first group is the most heterogeneous. They are the dead who belong to the third function: the troop (*turba, turma, cohors, agmen*) of ordinary folk who are on foot, the simple anonymous men and women (even if they are noble) who were all attached to material possessions (to the point of stealing them), to pleasures of the flesh, and to useful objects of daily life (bags, utensils, pots). No mention is made of any communication between these dead and Walchelin, who is content only to recognize some of them.

Next comes the much more coherent but more briefly mentioned group, which corresponds to the first order of society: that of monks and clerics. Their troop (*agmen*), which is anonymous with three possible exceptions, presents the opposite, black-clad image of the *turba* of the blessed and luminous monks who ordinarily appeared within the monastery walls. Even though some of these dead recognize and name Walchelin, he does not communicate with them either.

The "army of knights" (*exercitus militum, cohors, agmen, phalangis*) is completely different. It is a socially homogeneous group (even though a parvenu has slid into its ranks) and homogeneous also in the emblematic signs (horses, weapons, standards) of its function in society. It is the only group that is described as *exercitus*, a word that appears elsewhere only to designate the whole procession of the dead. One might even ask whether the expression *familia Herlechini* might not rather be applied to this group, by analogy with Robert of Bellême's warrior troop, also called *familia*, the "hunt" of knights grouped around their leader. In any event, this group certainly holds the privileged attention of Orderic Vitalis, who simultaneously stresses the knights' crimes and punishments and also the conditions of their redemption. Walchelin communicates only with those among the dead knights who separate themselves from the anonymous troop. But the dialogue does not take shape without difficulty, and on this point the narrative displays a subtle gradation.

The viscount Landry wants very much to assign Walchelin a mission. But Walchelin, who is not of low birth and seems to share the dead knights' prejudices toward this parvenu, does not respond to his entreaties.

William of Glos is no luckier, for Walchelin is even more evasive with him, and after agreeing to listen to his request, Walchelin breaks all ties with him.

The only knight with whom Walchelin ultimately communicates is his own brother Robert. Ties of blood, the duty of a spiritual gift in return for the services rendered by Robert while he was alive, and the proof given showing that masses free the deceased from their torments authorized a relationship of exchange between the dead man and the living one.

We can thus see the true difficulty of the lesson that Orderic Vitalis assigns to his tale to "edify" his readers: the endless procession of dead people, whom one assumes are heading toward a final punishment (though this is not said explicitly), presents, in accordance with the schema of the three orders, a complete social typology of crimes and punishments, on both sides of death. But if there are many dead to implore suffrages from the living, the conditions in which the living can answer them efficaciously are quite limited. The solidarity of natural kinship appears to give some hope of salvation only to a single dead man: Walchelin is solicited by his dead brother in his capacity as a priest but also and primarily in his position as the dead man's brother, since they had the same father.

The military part of the troop attracts the most attention, due to the social origin of the two main protagonists. More generally, the other accounts we will examine indicate that the troop of the dead is most often an *army* of the dead (*exercitus mortuorum*), a sort of infernal double of the feudal army. Even here Hellequin's hunt echoes the malignant troop of the lord of Bellême. Described in detail by the reformer monk Orderic Vitalis, the fantastic spectacle of the punishments endured by the rapacious, thieving, and murderous knights belongs to the entire apparatus put in place by the church at that time to impose the Truce of God and even the Peace of God.[11] The damned knights symbolize a savagery that the church was striving to eradicate or to channel—through institutions of peace, through crusades, through curses and miracles,[12] through the explicitness of the restrictive notion of "just war," and with the sanctioning of Saint Bernard, through enrollment into the good "militia" of the military orders. An awareness of the tradition of Hellequin's hunt does indeed throw new light onto the famous *In Praise of the New Knighthood* (written between 1129 and 1136), in which Bernard of Clairvaux plays on the homophony of the words *militia* and *malitia*. The knights of the times he is describing—with their *furor*, their deadly weapons, their harnesses, their insignia, their taste for women (whom they resemble with their long hair)—clearly mirrored the phantoms of Hellequin's hunt. Whether they committed a mortal sin by killing someone close to them or whether they themselves died in battle, they were the game of the devil: were they not going to participate in the ride of the damned? The only way to get rid of these "criminals and impious, rapists and sacrilegious, homicides, perjurers, adulterers" and to enable them at the same time to bring about their own salvation was to enroll them among the Knights Templar, forced into monastic discipline—with shaved heads, without women, and without the fallacious pleasures of the hunt.[13] Undoubtedly, in the twelfth century there was a relationship between the increasing prevalence of the furious army of the dead and all the contemporary measures being taken to rein in the feudal system and to limit its wars and devastation.

How Ancient Is the "Wild Hunt"?

Most historians and folklorists who have charted the tradition of Hellequin's hunt and the "Wild Hunt" up through contemporary folklore have insisted on its very long history. In the military character of this collective apparition and in the mythical figure of its leader, Hellequin, scholars have wanted to find a relic of the second Indo-European function or even an echo of the juvenile and warring associations (*Männerbünde*) that the ancient Germans were thought to have known.[14] There is no doubt that the name Hellequin (or Herlequin or Helething), which appeared first in Normandy and then in England, is of Germanic origin and refers to the army (*Heer*) and to the assembly of free men (*thing*), of those alone who bore arms.[15] Nor can we doubt that written texts at the beginning of the twelfth century recorded—belatedly perhaps—much more ancient oral traditions. But what is important to the historian is not so much the age of a tradition as the currency of its uses. We will attempt to locate more ancient accounts of the army of the dead, primarily to show how few there were and how allusive they were in comparison with the bulk of otherwise precise accounts that appeared after the twelfth century. Especially begging interpretation is the transformation of the documents, the sign of a more general ideological and social mutation.

The earliest mention of Hellequin's hunt is a rather obscure allusion made by Tacitus in the *Germania* concerning the *Harii* who fought at night while taking on the appearance of an army of ghosts. During the early Middle Ages the harvest remained thin. In the seventh century a Greek author, Damaskios of Damascus, asserted that at the time of the siege of Rome by Attila two centuries earlier, the spirits of the dead warriors (or rather the "images of their souls": *éidcla îcn psuchcn*) continued to fight for three days and three nights with even more ardor than did the living men.[16] In the West, Saint Augustine, in *The City of God*, described the confrontation of two armies of demons that left an accumulation of bodies and horses on the battlefield, a presage to the battle that men were soon to wage.[17] A few centuries later, in his *History of the Lombards*, Paul the

Deacon (c. 720–c. 787) recorded the reports, at the time of the plague of Justinian in the fifth century, of the "murmur of an army" heard accompanying the scourge.[18]

Once again the year 1000 marked a turning point. Accounts continued to establish a link between these apparitions and the real wars of the living or to associate the troop of the dead with that of "evil spirits." But the accounts were much more abundant and richer than before. Several types of apparitions were combined: sometimes there was a sort of procession of the penitent dead, an army of pitiful shadows that raised its lamentations and begged for prayers; sometimes, more fearful, the furious army traveled through the air in the din of weapons, horses, and dogs. The same author (Raoul Glaber) mentions them in succession; another (in a miracle of Saint Foi of Sélestat) manages to connect them. And often the army of the dead is not described explicitly but is evoked only in the background of an individual apparition.[19] It was not rare for a dead individual to separate from the troop of the dead (as was seen in the tale of Orderic Vitalis) in order to carry on a dialogue alone with the beneficiary of the apparition. Let us now examine these accounts.

The Elect and the Damned

Raoul Glaber began writing his *Historiae* at the abbey of Saint Bénigne of Dijon in 1028 and continued writing it until just before his death at Cluny in 1049.[20] The entire work is filled with tales of wonders, demoniacal or celestial apparitions, and descriptions of collective disasters—famine, incursions of the Saracens—in which historians of the romantic period heard the echo of the "terrors of the year 1000," compensated by the fully hopeful image of a Christendom covering itself with a "white mantle of churches."[21] In those troubled times, at dawn on the Sunday of the octave of Pentecost (Trinity Sunday), after lauds, we read that Vulferius, who was a monk of the diocese of Langres and was a doctor in his monastery, suddenly sees the church, where he is praying alone, filled with a procession of serious men wearing white robes and purple stoles. The one who is leading them, carrying a cross in his hand, claims to be "the bishop of many peoples" *(multarum plebium)*.[22] These men say that during the night, unbeknownst to the monks, they attended matins and lauds. The bishop immediately begins to celebrate Trinity Mass on the altar of the martyr Saint Maurice. Answering the monk's questions, the dead men reveal that they are Christians killed by the Saracens in the defense of their faith. Through their deaths, they merited the place of the blessed; traveling through Vulferius's region, where other men are to join them, they are headed toward this place. When mass is finished, the bishop gives the kiss of peace to his assistants and gestures to the monk to follow him. And since they all immediately disappear, Vulferius understands that he will not live for long, which was in fact what occurred. Five months later, in December, Vulferius goes to Auxerre to take care of some monks who are ill. He wants to see the patients the very evening he arrives, but the other monks insist that he wait until the next day. Soon his death throes begin, punctuated by two visions of the Virgin, who confirms that he has received the grace to see what few men have seen and that consequently he must die. But she grants him her protection in this trial. Indeed, on the third night the bells announce the death of Vulferius while devils attempt in vain to take his soul.

In Book V Raoul Glaber describes once again repeated apparitions of demons and other wonders that do not leave much hope for the survival of those who have witnessed them. He takes a local example that he dates around twenty-five years before the time he is writing. Near Tonnerre, the priest Frotterius, one Sunday after dinner, looks out his window and sees an army of men on horseback going off to battle (*acies equitum veluti in prelium pergentes*), coming from the north and heading west. He calls to them in vain to ask them for some explanation; his very voice seems to speed up their disappearance, and he is seized by such terror that he cannot contain his tears. He dies within the year, and those who heard the story believed that the apparition was a presage. The following year, the invasion of King Henry I (in 1015) did in fact cause many deaths in the region.

These two tales of collective apparitions contrast almost term to term. In the first, the dead are blessed, former religious figures who, in spite of themselves, battled infidels and underwent martyrdom. This is why they are associated with Saint Maurice, a soldier and martyr. In the second tale, the dead are knights who are going into battle; they come from the north (which is not a good omen) and travel quickly outside and not within the consecrated place of the church. Far from explaining their condition, they refuse all communication with the living man who calls to them: they form an army of the damned. There is, however, a common trait between these two collective apparitions. The first follows the massacre brought about by the Saracen incursions, and the second announces the massacres that will be caused by the invasion of the Capetians. The accounts represent two extreme poles of war: on the one end, the war for one's faith, which led to martyrdom and was concretely accomplished in the Crusades; and on the other end, the bloody war that Christians waged among themselves at the risk of being damned. War was a sign in which the past and the future, terrestrial life and salvation, history and eschatology, were all connected.[23] An opening into the afterlife, the apparition revealed the symbolic meanings of the event: an obstacle to the political project of the chronicler, the establishment of the *pax christiana*. War—the just and the unjust—was mentioned by means of the vision, for the values of war and of peace depended on the transcendent meaning of "history" as Raoul Glaber understood it.

Tainted Souls

Between 1108 and 1138 or 1155 at the earliest, the tale of an apparition in Alsace—an apparition of two different troops of dead—was added to a manuscript of the *Book of Miracles of Saint Foi of Conques*, which had been undertaken at the beginning of the eleventh century. This apparition concerns the monastery of Saint Foi of Sélestat, which originally had ties with the distant abbey in the Rouergue.[24] This tale might be considered the "myth of the origin" of a title of donation that, in 1095, established the land wealth of the Alsatian monastery. We can easily understand why the monks wrote down and divulged this "myth," which gave their community an illustrious origin and guaranteed it protections in the future. But the tale's function did not stop there, since the story also concerns the ascent of the Hohenstaufen family to the imperial throne. As often happened (for example, as in the tales of Peter the Venerable), the ghost tale was the crossroads of various interests, both lay and ecclesiastical.

The monastery's powerful protectors who intervene in the tale are four brothers of high nobility: Frederick of Buren (1079–1105), the duke of Swabia and the son-in-law of the emperor Henry IV; the bishop of Strasbourg, Otto (d. 1100); another brother, Walter; and finally the count Conrad, who died in 1094. When Frederick, Otto, and Conrad go on a pilgrimage to Santiago de Compostela, they stop at Conques, where they are welcomed "into the fraternity and the participation of all the (spiritual) goods" of the monks. The monks pray for their noble visitors, who in turn generously repay the monastery. Once back home, the three brothers decide to bequeath to Conques the church that they themselves and their mother, the countess Hildegard, had recently built (in 1087) in honor of the Holy Sepulcher. At the request of the founders, the abbot of Conques, Bego (1087–1108), sends a monk by the name of Bertramnus to Alsace to establish the new community. A second monk, Stephen, soon joins him. But for more than two years, in an empty monastery, the monks know only hunger, thirst, and cold, to the point of wanting to abandon everything and return to Conques. It is then that the miracle takes place, through the intercession of Saint Foi, to whom reversals of fortune were familiar.[25] Within the logic of the tale, the apparition probably occurred in 1094–1095, after the death of the countess Hildegard and her son the count Conrad but before 1095, the date of the title of the surviving brothers' donation benefiting the monastery.

A knight by the name of Walter of Diebolsheim, a former vassal of count Conrad's, often did penance at night outside the monastery, wearing a hair shirt and no shoes, while the monks sang matins inside the church. One night he is pulled out of his prayers by the vision of two different groups of figures: in a courtyard composed of cloisters and the workshops of the monastery, he sees a large group of pilgrims arrive dressed in white and holding a bell and a sack; on the "public road" that passed below the monastery, he sees a crowd of riders whose horses and clothing are entirely red. Assuming that the first group, the Whites, are true pilgrims, he shows them the entrance to the monastery, and one of them calls him by name. A direct dialogue begins: Walter asks the White one who he is to dare to give the knight an order. The other answers that he is Walter's dead master, the count Conrad; he reminds the knight how, when he was alive, he favored Walter, more than all his other vassals, with his kindness. Stupefied, Walter drops to the ground.[26] Then the dead man reassures the knight and gives Walter the proof (*signum*) that he is not a "phantom" (*fantasma*) and that he is talking to his vassal with God's permission: the proof is the common memory of a hunt in winter. This *signum* also enables Walter to be believed by Conrad's three brothers. By virtue of his vassalic oath (*per fidei sacramentum*) and in exchange for the past good deeds of his lord, the knight must in fact accept the mission that the dead man assigns him with regard to the brothers. Death does not end vassalic obligations; the living vassal must continue to obey the orders of his dead master and lend assistance, if only through his prayers.

Walter must ask the bishop Otto of Strasbourg, whose prayers and almsgiving will help Conrad in the hereafter, to give Conrad's share of his inheritance to Saint Foi. The recollection, in the guise of *signa*, of two memories will convince the bishop that Walter is not lying.[27] And a prediction is added to these proofs: before dying, the bishop will complete a pilgrimage to Jerusalem and will return after two years. If between now and then he has given the monastery the property that Conrad wants him to, he will die in a state of grace; otherwise, he might well leave this world sooner than anticipated. We know that Otto in fact participated in the First Crusade at the call of Pope Urban II and that he died shortly afterward, in 1100.[28]

Walter must also warn another brother, whose name is also Walter, against his taste for clothes, horses, and costly weapons. Of all the brothers, this Walter might well be the first to follow Conrad into death, and he must be prepared for it. We know that this brother died before 1105.

Most important, the knight Walter was to find the third brother, the duke Frederick, for of all the brothers, he would survive and would be the sole heir (superstitem et heredem) of the lineage (familia). As a signum, Walter was to remind him that at the moment he entered into the court of the emperor with his brother Conrad, the two brothers had told each other a secret known only to them. And Walter was to transmit the following prediction to him: his lineage (progenies) was the richest and was destined for glory; his descendants would become kings of the Romans and emperors. We know that in fact a son of Frederick of Buren, Conrad III, in 1138 became the first king of the Staufen dynasty and that the nephew of Conrad III, Frederick III of Swabia, became king in 1152 and acceded to the empire in 1155 under the name of Frederick I Barbarossa. But Conrad specified the conditions under which this dynastic destiny was going to be accomplished: Frederick was to protect the church of Saint Foi, which he had founded with his brothers, and guarantee its freedom. By giving the church the brothers' common property (commune predium), Frederick would ensure the future of his lineage and would simultaneously enable his dead brother to avoid hell.

Before following the orders of his lord, Walter wanted to know more about the Whites and the Reds. Conrad continues: the Whites are the souls of those who lived chastely and did penance for their crimes on earth; they went in pilgrimage into the house of Saint Foi and earned her help through the gifts they offered her. They have escaped the tortures of hell,[29] but they do not yet enjoy eternal rest. They are moving toward perfect happiness, led by Saint Foi; Conrad shows Walter the luminous outline of Saint Foi, leaning at the entrance to the monastery, which the Whites are preparing to enter. The Reds, destined on the contrary to the infernal flames, are those people who disregarded divine and human laws and died in battle or without having done penance. If Conrad had not benefited from the help that Saint Foi lavished on him in exchange for the gift of that church, he would not be following the Whites but would be in torture with the Reds. The Reds are going "as far as Nivelles, in the mountain of Hell."[30]

Immediately afterward, the dead man disappears. Left alone, Walter marks with two stones the place where Conrad appeared to him. But since he tells no one where those stones are located, no one knows where the apparition occurred. Didn't the narrator (a monk) fear some act of necromancy in this place? Shortly afterward, the surviving brothers meet to divide up their inheritance. The monks, who still know nothing about the apparition, are ready to be satisfied with a mill, a garden, a field, and a small woods. Each of the brothers is already receiving the oaths of fidelity from the knights and peasants who belong to his share, when the knight Walter comes to find each one separately to inform him of the apparition of his brother, as well as of the proofs and predictions that concern him. Immediately, recognizing the "signs" and crying over their dead brother, the brothers put all their property back together and give all the land and men (predium et homines) to Saint Foi for the salvation of the souls of their brother and of their ancestors and for the redemption of their own sins. Thus the monks did not receive the meager share that was at first intended for them, but thanks to the miraculous intervention of Saint Foi, "they became rich and possessed everything." The cartulary of Conques contains the title of donation, dated July 23, 1095, which lists all the property left to the monks and mentions among the reasons for the action the death of Conrad and his mother.[31]

To ensure the individual salvation of a dead man, to justify retrospectively the ascent of a dynasty, and to legitimize the material protection owed a church—these were the three, tightly overlapping functions of this tale, which, with the help of a myth, expounds an older deed dating some decades earlier. Equally important is the use this unique tale makes of images that were widespread in other places: for example, the structural contrast (by social type, clothing, color, place, and destination) of two different groups of dead people, those who will surely be damned and those who, like Conrad, are the elect in power. Like the tale of Raoul Glaber a century earlier, this story depicts the imposed collective division of souls right after death, but here the division is less radical. It does not entirely anticipate that of the Last Judgment, since the Whites' salvation, even if ensured, is not yet completely achieved. Nor is a collective division exactly the same as the individual judgment that decides the fate of each soul at the moment of death. One might say of the Whites, like Conrad, that they are going through a sort of strange "purgatory," both itinerant and without trials, quite different from the fixed and closed

1 The ghost of Samuel:
a diabolical interpretation.
Guyart des Moulins, *Bible
historiale* (Paris, first quarter
of the fifteenth century).
New York, Pierpont Morgan
Library, MS M394, fol. 127 v.

2 The ghost of Samuel: as a
resurrected body. *Gumbertsbibel*
(Germany, before 1195).
Erlangen, Universitätsbibliothek,
MS 1, fol. 82 v.

· diuiel. il tent mõ ſeſgent pmanablem̃
du ſuſatenier ſamuel ſel la.b.ꝛhyſt. xxv.

Cel temps ſaſſembleꝛt les phi
liſtiens a batuille encõtre iſrl:
Lois diſt achis a dauid: Tu et
tes lõmes vendꝛes auec moy
en la batuille encõtre iſrl.⁊ ie

3 The ghost of Samuel: the dead man appearing as if alive. Guyart des Moulins, *Bible historiale* (France, c. 1291–1294). London, British Library, MS Harley 4381, fol. 127.

4 The ghost of Samuel: as a phantom. *Kayserchronik* (Bavaria, c. 1375–1380). New York, Pierpont Morgan Library, MS M769, fol. 172.

5, 6 The ghost of Samuel: the living-dead. *Tickhill Psalter* (England, early fourteenth century). New York Public Library, Spencer Collection, MS 26, fols. 43 and 42 v.

5

6

7

nam pozurui ar smesta a w

8

7 Emperor Charles IV's dream: the spirit in the image of a living man (Germany, c. 1470–1480).
Vienna, Österreichische Nationalbibliothek, MS 581, fol. 21 v.

8 Emperor Charles IV's dream: a representation of the soul (Germany, c. 1470–1480). Vienna,
Österreichische Nationalbibliothek, MS Ser. N. 2618, fol. 18 v.

9 The invisible spirit of Gui de Corvo (Simon Marmion?, Flanders, 1474). Malibu, J. Paul Getty
Museum, MS 31, fol. 7.

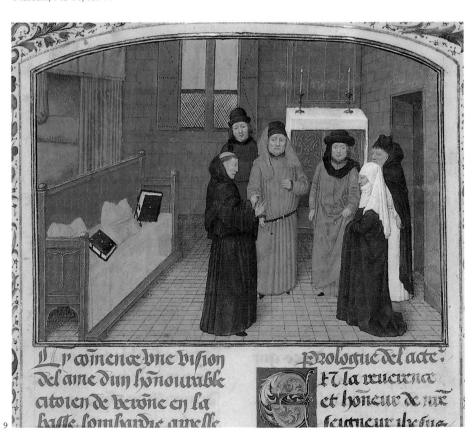

10 King Arthur
diabolized
(Otranto, mosaic,
c. 1170).

11 The charivari
in *Roman de Fauvel*
(Paris, 1316).
Paris, B.N.,
MS Fr. 146,
fol. 34.

12 Hellequin
on horseback
and coffins.
Paris, B.N.,
MS Fr. 146,
fol. 34 v.

13 Hellequin
and the cart
of the dead.
Paris, B.N.,
MS Fr. 146,
fol. 34 v.

14 The charivari
in *Roman de Fauvel*.
Paris, B.N.,
MS Fr. 146,
fol. 36 v.

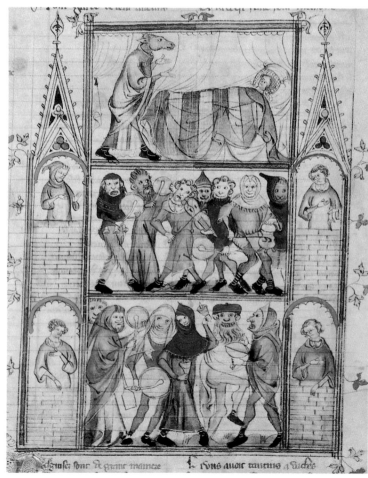

12

13

14

LXCHO VIIII.

Hnf quid ubi fcar. Nocaufme cofpofe dicitr. Quam phuf elbcne. Pacefe efte uolena fbetpi.

Per faecto daur faedf. Tulefrint quaf luftgar faetha...

GREGORIVS

fogruraruf. uer In
hluf prachmonu
prfedio luxar
aeffacineurfetm
urbetm miffif di
fciruluf fuif Con

15 A miracle of Saint Benedict: the dead young monk (1071).
The Vatican, Apostolic Library, MS Vat. Lat. 1202, fol. 57 r.

16 Second miracle of Saint Benedict: the two dead nuns (1071).
The Vatican, Apostolic Library, MS Vat. Lat. 1202, fol. 57 r.

17 Second miracle of Saint Benedict: the two dead nuns (Eleventh century).
Abbey of Saint Benoît-sur-Loire, capital.

18 The apparition of the dead prior to the sacristan Hubert. Gautier of Coincy, *Miracles de Notre Dame* (Paris, 1330–1334). Paris, B.N., MS Nouv. acq. fr. 24541, fol. 60 v.

19 The apparition of the dead prior to the sacristan Hubert. Gautier of Coincy, *Miracles de Notre Dame* (France, early fourteenth century). Paris, B.N., MS Fr. 22920, fol. 105.

20 The pilgrim and the dead: a representation of the soul as a nude figure. Guillaume de Diguilleville, *Pèlerinage de vie humaine* (fifteenth century). Paris, Bibliothèque de l'Arsenal, MS 5071, fol. 80 v.

19

18

20

21

21 The pilgrim and the dead:
the dead as phantoms.
Guillaume de Diguilleville,
Pèlerinage de vie humaine
(fourteenth century).
Oxford, Bodleian Library,
MS Douce 300, fol. 115.

22 The pilgrim and the dead:
the dead as phantoms.
Guillaume de Diguilleville,
Pèlerinage de vie humaine
(fourteenth century). Paris,
B.N., MS Fr. 823, fol. 89.

23 The pilgrim and the dead:
the dead in a macabre
representation. Guillaume de
Diguilleville, *Pèlerinage de vie
humaine* (fourteenth century).
Paris, B.N., MS Fr. 376, fol. 83.

22

23

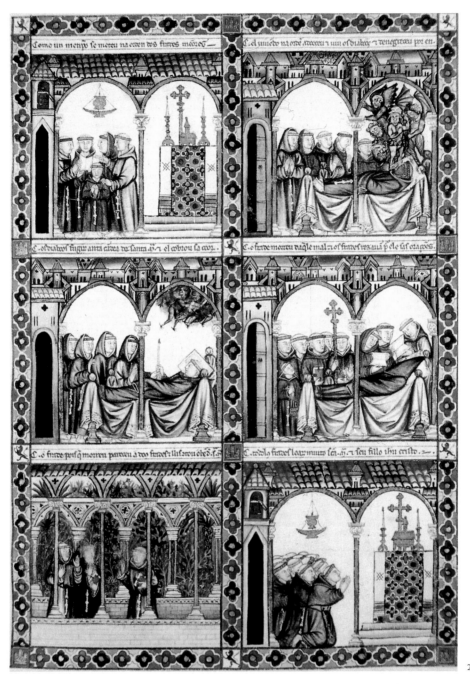

24 The apparition of the dead Minorite brother to his brothers. Alfonso X the Wise, *Cantigas de Santa Maria* (c. 1272). *Cantiga* CXXIII. Escorial, MS TI1, fol. 136.

25

25 A phantom telling a father about the death of his son. Alfonso X the Wise,
Cantigas de Santa Maria (c. 1272). *Cantiga* LXXII. Escorial, MS TI1, fol. 80.

singulos dies ⬥
Nisi conuersi fueritis gla
dium suum uibrauit arcū
suum tetendit ⁊ parauit
illum ⬥
Et in eo parauit uasa
mortis sagittas suas arden
tib; effecdit ⬥
Ecce parturiit iniustitiam
concepit dolorē ⁊ peperit ini
quitatem ⬥
Lacum aperuit ⁊ effodit
eum ⁊ incidit in foueam
quā fecit ⬥
Conuertetur dolor eius
in caput eius ⁊ in uerticē

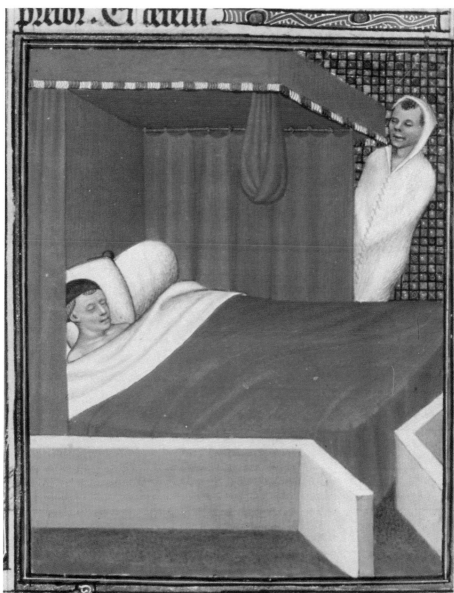

26 The phantom of a damned man? *Livre d'heures à l'usage de Rouen* (fifteenth century). Paris, B.N., MS Lat. 1178, fol. 107 v.

27 Tingoccio appearing to his friend Meuccio: a macabre representation. Boccaccio, *Decameron*, VII, 10 (fifteenth century). Paris, Bibliothèque de l'Arsenal, MS 5070, fol. 273.

28 The drowned man appearing to the poet Simonides. Boccaccio, *De casibus virorum illustrium* (fifteenth century). Paris, Bibliothèque de l'Arsenal, MS 5193, fol. 76 v.

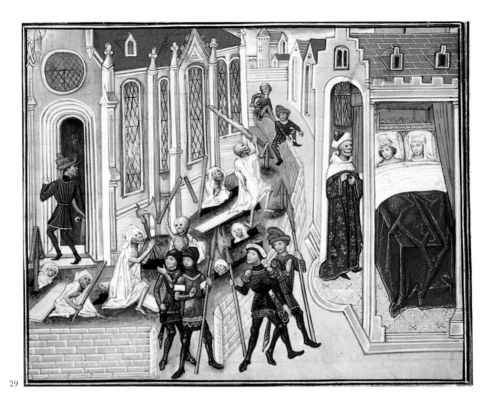

29

30 detail

29 The dead in the cemetery and the apparition of the dead friend. Jacobus da Voragine, *Légende dorée* (fifteenth century). Mâcon, Bibliothèque municipale, MS 3, fol. 25 v.

30 Recumbent figure: a ghost of stone? Würzburg, Marienkapelle. Tomb sculpture of the knight Konrad von Schaumberg, 1499.

30

place of tortures that would dominate ideas of purgatory at the end of the century. An analogous distinction between two troops of dead, the Reds and the Whites, is found at the beginning of the thirteenth century in the work of Gervase of Tilbury. In the bishopric of Turin was an abbey that sheltered the relics of Saint Constantine and the martyrs of the Theban legion (undoubtedly, Gervase is speaking of Saint Maurice); in the shadow of a mountain, every year on the saint's feast day, pilgrims witnessed the appearance of a double procession of figures, some dressed all in white and others all in red. If a pilgrim climbed the mountain, the vision disappeared.[32] In the most ancient classifications of colors, red and white, along with black, play a fundamental role. But the symbolism of colors, subject to interpretations that have varied throughout history, does not follow an immutable code. Here, these two colors most likely designate two types of saints and not the damned; the martyrs are in red.

Other contemporary tales speak only of a single troop of dead, sometimes in a positive light but most often negatively. The criteria of the division are openly ideological: the cohort of saintly monks is contrasted with the furious army of pillaging knights.

The Procession of the Elect, the Ride of the Damned

The apparition of the troop of the elect was related most often in monastic tales: the blessed who appeared were monks, and they appeared to other monks to assure the living of their happiness and to warn against infractions of the monastic rule. "Mirrors" of the monks, these texts had the function of self-justification. This explains their place in monastic hagiography and *miracula*, for example at the beginning of the twelfth century in the *Life of Bernard of Tiron*, the prior of Saint Savin, in Poitou. In the church of that monastery, where he prays alone at night, he sees a "multitude of monks white as snow" who gather in a chapter, which he joins. One of the dead, who is the leader of the others, informs him that nineteen monks of the community are going to have to die and that they must prepare themselves for this. Bernard goes to warn them and tells one of them (who assumes Bernard simply had a bad dream) that he will be the first to die, which does in fact happen and thus proves the truth of the apparition.[33] The last of the *miracula* of Marmoutier, dated from 1137, is comparable: having only recently become a monk, the former archdeacon of Clermont sees, appearing before him in the church during the night of the Feast of All Saints, the three patron saints of the monastery (Martin, Fulgentius, and Corentin), as well as a procession of dead monks, arranged according to the chronological order of their deaths. The monk recognizes some of them. The dead sing hymns for the dead with him, then tell him of the coming death of the abbot Odo. The monk hastens to awaken the other monks, notably Garnier, who will succeed Odo, and some of them hear and see the procession before it disappears.[34]

In contrast, most tales depict the ride of a troop of the future damned. At the beginning of the twelfth century, Orderic Vitalis's account of Hellequin's hunt was far from unique. Although initially the army of the dead generally did not have a specific name, at the end of the century this was no longer true. Often this army was evoked only briefly, in reference to the misfortunes of the century or to the traps of the devil or in comparison with other wonders. When the army of the dead was mentioned for itself, it was the object of more circumstantial descriptions. Very quickly it also became a literary theme.

Paradoxically, the literary form of the most ancient tale (even older by a few years than Orderic Vitalis's account) is undoubtedly the farthest from the written forms of a tradition passed on orally. It indeed belongs to the genre of *mirabilia*, but to those that derive their subjects from the mythology of the ancients as much as from the traditions of folklore. Around 1125 William of Malmesbury used those traditions in the guise of an ancient fable. He included in his *Gesta regum Anglorum* the most ancient version known of the tale titled the "Venus d'Ille" (since made famous by Mérimée's story), which he strangely links to an apparition of the troop of the dead.[35] The story is supposed to take place in ancient Rome: during a ball game a young groom places his wedding ring on the finger of a statue of Venus. But the goddess keeps the ring and prevents the young man from consummating his marriage. Following the advice of a necromancer priest, Palumbus, the young man goes to a crossroads, where he witnesses the heterogeneous procession of a troop of horsemen and foot soldiers led by Venus, who is riding a mule and dressed to look like a prostitute. The demons who surround her, and who themselves bow to the constraints of the conjuration of the priest Palumbus, force Venus to give back the ring. As for the necromancer Palumbus, he was later put to death by the Roman people. From this tale one might think that the explicit diabolization of the nocturnal procession goes hand in hand with the literary reworking of the theme.

Other texts allow a better approach to the oral traditions of the time. At the time of the conquest of Ireland in 1169, during the siege of Osraighe, the English army, resting at night, was attacked by thousands of warriors, who filled the sky with the din of their weapons. These *phantasma*, explains Giraldus Cambrensis, often accompanied military expeditions to Ireland.[36] In England itself, the Anglo-Saxon chronicle of the abbey of Peterborough, near Northampton, relates the history of the country from the invasion of the Saxons under the leadership of Cerdic (in 496).[37] The exploits of one king in each period form the principal axis of the tale. Thus in 1127 King Henry I gave the abbey of Peterborough, whose abbot had died in 1125, to his relative Henry of Poitou, who was already directing the Cluniac abbey of Saint Jean d'Angély. The chronicler doesn't have harsh enough words to criticize the greed of this prelate, who accumulated several ecclesiastical titles and demonstrated duplicity both toward the king and toward the abbot of Cluny, Peter the Venerable. Henry of Poitou, says the chronicler monk, was to the abbey of Peterborough what a "drone is to a beehive." After his arrival at the abbey, on Sexagesima Sunday (February 6, 1127), in the deer-park of Peterborough and in the forests between that "town" and Stamford, many people and monks that night heard and saw hunters, twenty or perhaps thirty, black and big and hideous, on horseback or on goats (or rams), blowing their horns and accompanied by a pack of black, loathsome dogs with huge eyes. This lasted throughout Lent and Easter, and no one knew when it would end. But the chronicle answers that question: in 1132, the king, finally understanding the perfidiousness of Henry of Poitou, took the abbey away from him, banished him from the land, and named a new abbot, Martin, whose behavior was exemplary. Let us note here, for the first time, the theme of the hunt and also the connection between a lapse in royal power and the apparition of the "Wild Hunt." The more often royal power, for better or worse, made its presence known—and this would increasingly be the case in twelfth-century England—the more the troop of dead hunters or warriors tended to be identified with the feudal monarchy in the reverse mode of an infernal royalty.

In the very same years, but on the continent, the chronicle of the bishops of Mans recorded the calamities, wars, and famines that crushed the inhabitants of that region. In 1135 an "unbelievable wonder" occurred that testified, according to the chronicler, to the countless traps of the enemy. The house of the prevost Nicholas is haunted by a spirit—a "faun," says the cleric in Latin—who plays tricks on the inhabitants, makes noise, moves dishes around, and tangles up the thread that Nicholas's wife has prepared to do her needlework. Conjured by a priest, the spirit gives his name but without showing himself: he is Garnier, Nicholas's dead brother, and he asks his relatives to free him through masses and almsgiving to the poor. These suffrages will separate him from the "evil troops" that have accompanied him and who seek to introduce evil into the house.[38] In this text the troop of dead (or demons?) itself is not described; as often happens, it is only evoked in the shadows, behind the face, or the voice, of the single dead person who manifests himself.[39]

In Germany the most explicit text in this period comes from the chronicle of Ekkehard of Aura in Franconia. In its final pages the chronicle relates the conflict between the priesthood and the empire until the Concordat of Worms in 1122 and the death of the emperor Henry V in 1125 (the date when the text abruptly stops). Once again, ecclesiastical and political turbulence is accompanied by wonders and signs: bad weather (storms in the diocese of Trèves and in Saxony, shooting stars), accidents (a tower of the abbey of Fulda collapses), troublesome or terrifying visions. Strange phenomena, to our eyes completely unrelated, are noted and placed end to end. In 1120, in Saxony, on several nights in a row, watchmen see an incandescent man cross a field separating two fortresses.[40] In 1123, revolts break out in Saxony, then throughout all of Germany; troops of robbers on horseback invade villages and churches, despoil the peasants, and set fire to and steal the food reserves, provoking famine and scarcity. Shortly afterward, in the diocese of Worms, residents for several days see a "highly armed multitude of wandering horsemen" leaving in troops *(turmas)* from a mountain and returning to it at the hour of nones. Bearing the sign of the cross, the people question a member of the troop *(persona)*, who assures them that the horsemen are not phantoms *(fantasmata,* illusions of the devil) or real knights *(milites)* but are the souls of knights recently killed in battle. The weapons, the clothes, and the horses, which were the instruments of their sins, are now the incandescent instruments of their torment. The count Emicho (killed in battle in 1117) appears among the people and tells them that their prayers and almsgiving can redeem him.[41] These fantastic horsemen were the doubles of the quite real horde of robber knights.

In all of these accounts, the fantastic troop does not bear a particular name. On the other hand, close to a half century after Orderic Vitalis's account and, once again, in the Anglo-Norman realm, the name "Hellequin's hunt" reappears. Its quite localized appearances are undoubtedly explained by the Anglo-Saxon and then Scandinavian population of these regions. But we owe them to the clerics who deemed these local traditions worthy of appearing in their Latin texts. Those who, more than others, could see the interest in these appearances were monks and especially Franco-Norman, Anglo-Norman, or Anglo-Welsh clerics, men on geographic borders and witnesses to the diversity of ethnicities and languages, some of them connected to the most brilliant, the most variegated, and also the most contested court of the time, that of the Plantagenets.

Political Uses of Hellequin's Hunt

In 1175, in a letter addressed to the chaplains of the Anglo-Norman court, Peter of Blois—a theologian, archdeacon of Bath, and adviser to the king—lambasts the clerics of the court (*curiales*) who dream only of worldly ambition. Pursuing them with his irony, he calls them "the martyrs of the century, worldly professors, disciples of the court, knights of Herlevinus"; unlike the true martyrs, who gain the kingdom of heaven, these "martrys," in their tribulations, are led to hell. The *curiales*, according to the archdeacon, resemble the wandering army of the damned. The metaphor seems to have been common: Walter Map develops it in two chapters of his *De nugis curialium*.[42] From the outset Walter Map associates the constant moving around of the court of Henry II to the wandering of Hellequin's hunt (*cetus et phalanges Herlethingi*); "in them many persons were seen alive who were known to have died." It even seems that the court of Henry II was substituted for the fantastic army, since that army had disappeared after the first year of the reign of the king (1154–1155). Before that, Hellequin's hunt was "famous" in England, and it had also been seen in the borderlands of Wales and of Hereford; some in Brittany (like Walchelin, according to Orderic Vitalis) had even risked their lives trying to seize the horses of the dead. But Walter Map's text is interesting primarily because it proposes an explanation of the name "Hellequin's hunt," gives a face to its eponymous chief, and above all, reveals a true myth of the origin of the hunt, which goes back to the Celtic origins of the population of Great Britain.[43] The name of the hunt is believed to have come from that of the king of the very ancient Britons, King Herla, who had concluded a pact with the king of the dwarfs (the "Pygmies," says our author), that is, the dead.[44] The dwarf king invites himself to Herla's wedding to the daughter of the king of the Franks and, on this occasion, gives his host lavish gifts. A year later Herla goes into a cave where he discovers the magnificent palace of the dwarf, who is celebrating his own wedding and who lets Herla leave loaded down with gifts: "horses, dogs, hawks, and every appliance of the best for hunting or fowling." The king of the dwarfs also presents Herla with the gift of a small bloodhound (the English name translates well the Latin appellation, *canis sanguinarius*, which expresses the cruelty of the animal). Herla is to carry it on his horse and he and those with him are to take care not to dismount before the dog does; if they do, they risk being turned into dust. When Herla emerges from the cave he learns, by questioning a shepherd, that two centuries have passed since his departure, whereas he believed he had been gone only three days. A new population, the Saxons, now occupy the land of the Britons. He is condemned to wander forever with his army, since the dog will never jump to the ground. According to Walter Map, his wandering, which is his punishment for having made a pact with the king of the dead, foreshadows the tribulations of the court of Henry II.

In this tale, in which several folkloric motifs are easily identifiable (such as the difference in the passing of time on earth and in the hereafter),[45] the theme of the pact between the living and the dead stands out. This is essential to the tale, since Walter Map sees the acceptance of the pact as King Herla's fundamental error and the reason for his punishment. This agreement suggests a diabolical pact, but Walter Map does not call it that, and on the contrary, he preserves the ambivalence of the tale. King Herla's error resides above all in the imbalance of the exchange: the dwarf, through his increased gifts, ruins the reciprocal relationship that he himself proposed. Without expecting any gift in return, the giver doubles his offering: he crushes the other man with his gifts. King Herla is literally paralyzed by the generosity of his partner, to the point of no longer being able to get down from his horse. This is what condemns him to the wandering of the dead.

The unbalanced exchange between Herla and the dwarf, and its consequences, allow us better to understand other perilous situations in which an exchange between the living and the dead proves impossible. This is the case in Orderic Vitalis's tale when Walchelin tries to take a horse belonging to the dead; for this mistake he should have died and been taken away by the dead. At the beginning of the thirteenth century, Gervase of Tilbury confirms that in England and Brittany, this misdeed cost the lives of some men who were too rash and greedy. Only a relationship of perfect reciprocity, in which a spiritual countergift responds to a material gift, can have beneficial effects: Walchelin, by saying salutary masses for his dead brother, paid off his debt to his brother, who, while alive, had paid for his studies in France. The exchange was then perfect, and it saved the living man, who survived this encounter with the dead, as well as the dead one, whose torment ceased at the end of a year. But we can also understand the social conditions of this: if the sacrifice of mass and prayers alone enabled the metamorphosis of material goods into spiritual goods, the mediation of the church, which had the monopoly over such an operation, was necessarily going to be involved in all relations between the living and the dead.

In the course of the thirteenth century, the geographical area in which Hellequin's hunt is mentioned extends toward the east of France and Italy. The circulation of information in the educated milieus may in part explain this spread. But the name, like the phenomenon, must have existed before its recognition by the learned culture. The name experienced transformations, which aroused a growing etymological curiosity in clerics. In the diocese of Beauvais, the Cistercian Helinand of Froidmont (d. 1230)—a former secular cleric, an indirect disciple of Abelard, a trouvère and poet of death—gave in his autobiography (*De cognitione sua*) a very precise treatment of Hellequin's hunt.[46] He introduces it into a passage on the knowledge that people want to have of their destiny after death. To this end the *Moralia* of Gregory the Great, the *De consideratione* of Saint Bernard, but also the works of pagan authors were useful to him. However, in his opinion, Virgil was wrong to claim that dead heroes appear to the living in the clothes they once wore and that they remain concerned about the horses, weapons, and chariots they owned in this life. Virgil would thus be at the origin of the error, shared at that time by the "people" (*vulgus*), concerning Hellequin's hunt (*familia Hellequini*). This is followed by two tales that Helinand heard from informants very close to him.

The bishop Henry of Orleans, the brother of the bishop of Beauvais, often told of a marvelous thing (*rem valde mirabilem*) that he had heard directly from his informant, a canon of Orleans named John. This man had ordered a cleric in his service, Noel, to accompany the archdeacon Burchard of Pisy to Rome. Noel was to protect the archdeacon and keep his accounts. Before parting, Noel makes a pact with John: the first one to die will appear to the other (*socius*) within thirty days, not to frighten him but to warn him and to inform him of the dead man's condition. As the two travelers approach Rome, they begin to fight about money, and Noel promises himself to the devil by uttering a curse. The same day, while crossing a river, he drowns. The following night John is resting awake in his bed, the lamp lit because of his nocturnal terrors, when Noel abruptly appears before him wearing a very beautiful cape the color of lead to protect him against the rain. John is surprised to see him back from his trip so soon, but Noel reveals that he is dead and that he is enduring very great torments for promising himself to the devil shortly before drowning accidently. Without this sin, the only one he committed since his last confession, he would have avoided these torments. The cape he is wearing weighs on him more than if he were carrying "the tower of Parma" on his shoulders, but its beauty symbolizes the hope of pardon (*spes veniae*) that his last confession offers him. John promises to help him but first asks if he is a member of the *militia Hellequini*. Noel denies this, telling him that that troop has recently ended its journey, "for it has completed its penance." Before disappearing as he had come, the dead man points out that the popular appellation *Hellequinus* is incorrect and that it is *Karlequinus*, from the name of the king "Charles Quint," who has long atoned for his sins and whom the intercession of Saint Denis has recently freed.

Helinand heard the second tale from his paternal uncle, Hellebaud, the former chamberman of the dead archbishop of Reims, Henry. While his uncle and a servant are riding in the direction of Arras on the orders of the archbishop, they encounter in a forest, on the stroke of noon, in a din of horses, weapons, and war cries, a multitude of souls of the dead and demons. The two men hear them say that the provost of Arques henceforth belongs to them and that soon they will also have the archbishop of Reims. Carrying the sign of the cross, Hellebaud and his companion approach the woods, but the "shadows" disappear, and the men can no longer make out their words, only the confused noises of weapons and horses. Once back in Reims, they find the archbishop in very bad condition: he dies within fifteen days, and his soul is taken away by evil spirits. In the troop, the horses ridden by the souls of the dead are none other than demons who have taken on that shape, and the heavy weapons carried by the souls are the weight of their sins.

The interest of these two tales goes well beyond the two points that Helinand of Froidmont intends to demonstrate. Granted, the clothing and the horses of the dead are not those they possessed while they were alive but are rather the symbols of the torments that the demons were inflicting upon them. The scholarly rationalization of the name of the hunt comes from the homophony of Hellequin and Charles Quint. The mention of Saint Denis suggests a vague reference to the Carolingians, whose torments in the hereafter had been described by many visions for a long time.[47] As in the tale of Walter Map, the wandering of Hellequin's hunt is supposed to have ended recently. Is this a narrative convention that consists of relegating folkloric traditions to a completed past (just as today we speak of traditions that are supposed to have disappeared after the war of 1914–18)? Or should we see here the indication of an objective evolution of belief? In Helinand's case, the mention of this disappearance agrees with the idea that Hellequin's hunt, rather than an army of the damned, is a sort of itinerant purgatory. In fact, ambivalence characterizes this troop, which, although infernal, sometimes still offers some hope for salvation to its dead souls. Didn't the "birth of purgatory" at the end of the twelfth century actually hasten the diabolization of the troop of dead—or even convince some that it had disappeared, since in its penitential function, it henceforth had no reason to exist?

At approximately the same time and in the same Cistercian milieu, the monk Herbert of Clairvaux, abbot of Mores in the Jura (d. 1190), made room for Hellequin's hunt in his *Book of Miracles*.[48] Zachary, a brother in the monastery of Vauluisant (in the Yonne), often told of the vision that he had had in his youth and that had made him decide to enter the monastery. He was a young peasant, armed with a bow, guarding the harvest at night. He encounters a woman out in the field, whom he believes he recognizes, and then a sort of man (*quasi homo*), whom he takes for a thief. The woman tells him that he is going to see the *familia Herlequini*, and in an unbearable din, there in fact appears, moving through the air without touching the ground, a "fantastic" multitude of "blacksmiths, metal workers, carpenters, stonecutters, tanners, weavers, and fullers, and men of all the other mechanical trades," subjected to terrible torments. One of them, who is carrying a ram on his shoulders, comes toward the young man, whom he forbids to say a single word and to whom he reveals his identity: he is Zachary's old friend (*sodalis tuus, familiariter in amicitia iunctus*), and he asks Zachary to return to a poor widow the ram he stole from her. Then he will be freed from his torment. Before disappearing with the other dead, he reveals "many other things" to the peasant. This relationship of reciprocity between a living person and a dead one is now familiar to us. Similarly, the prohibition (here, on speech) and even the flight in the air recall the misadventures of King Herla, condemned with his companions never again to touch the ground.[49] Completely original, on the other hand, is the "third function" of this Hellequin's hunt, the possibility of which Orderic Vitalis was content only to mention. The visionary himself is a simple country policeman, and in the troop of the dead he does not see horses, dogs, or knights but only artisans tortured by the tools they used when they were alive, like the damned sculpted on the tympanum of Conques.[50] These unfortunate people do not appear to be reproached for any specific sin: are the "mechanical arts" in principle condemnable?

For the church, the true danger came nonetheless from the "second function"; it was this group, with its favorite violent activities, that monopolized the imaginary of the furious army. This group was related above all to war, but we have also encountered the theme of hunting. Here, finally, is the tournament: in the twelfth section—devoted to the dead—of his *Dialogus miraculorum* (around 1223), the Cistercian Caesarius of Heisterbach cites the account of a monk of Villers, in Brabant; he successively describes the "tournament of the demons" that a servant of the count of Lootz was supposed to have witnessed at the place where a bloody battle had taken place the day before, and he also notes the "tournament of the dead" (*tornamentum mortuorum*) in which a priest claimed to have seen, right out in a field at night, a confrontation between knights who had recently died.[51]

Hellequin or Arthur? The Diabolization of the Troop of the Dead

At the beginning of the thirteenth century, Gervase of Tilbury included in his collection of *mirabilia* many tales of collective apparitions of the dead: in Catalonia was a rock whose summit was flat and where, at noon, mysterious knights confronted one another. If the viewer moved closer, the vision disappeared.[52] In Sicily, ever since antiquity, Etna was considered to be the mouth of hell. At the beginning of the eleventh century a hermit, settled on the slopes of the volcano, heard demons complain that the prayers of Cluny took away souls they were torturing in the fire. According to Gervase of Tilbury, the "people," the "natives," said that "in our time," "Arthur the Great" appeared there. A young stable boy of the bishop of Catania, after chasing a runaway horse on the steep paths and in the gorges of the mountain, discovers a fabulous plateau and then a palace, where Arthur, seated on a royal throne, is waiting for him. Arthur inquires about the reasons for the visit and then returns the horse and gives many presents for the bishop of Catania. He also explains to the young man that he is living in this subterranean palace to take care of the wounds that he received from his nephew Mordred and the duke of the Saxons, Childeric, wounds that reopen every year.[53]

Beginning in the twelfth century, the Arthurian legend spread to

Italy, particularly to the south of the peninsula and as far as Sicily, under the influence of the Norman knights.[54] The figure of King Arthur in the mosaic flooring of around 1170 in the cathedral of Otranto gives evidence of this (illus. 10). King Arthur, identified by an inscription (rex Artus), is wearing a crown and holding a sort of mace. His right arm is raised, and he is riding a goat. Around this figure are a naked man, who appears to be watching the scene, a feline, who is standing in front of the goat, and a dog (?), which is crushing a man. The scene is placed between that of the expulsion of Adam and Eve from earthly paradise and those of the sacrifice of Cain and Abel and of Abel's murder by his brother. Highly diverse interpretations of this representation of Arthur have been proposed. Notably, critics have wanted to see a positive character in it, in accordance with the good fortune of Arthur's palace in the tale of Gervase of Tilbury; the proximity between the mosaic of King Arthur and the sacrifice of Abel could be used in a defense of this hypothesis.[55] But such a notion disregards rather easily the very negative connotation of the animal that Arthur is riding (the same animal that the king of the dwarfs rides in Walter Map's tale), as well as the neighboring scenes in the mosaic and other contemporary tales concerning the legendary king.[56] In 1223 the Cistercian Caesarius of Heisterbach told of two tales, explicitly qualified as mirabilia, one of which he heard from a canon of Bologna and the other from two abbots of the primarily Italian court of the emperor Frederick II.[57] A servant of the bishop of Palermo is looking on the slopes of Etna (mons Gyber) for a horse that has escaped. He encounters an old man, who tells him that his lord, King Arthur, is keeping the horse in the mountain of fire. The old man bids the servant to tell the bishop to come to Arthur's court in fourteen days or risk a severe punishment. On his return, the servant informs his master, who laughs at the story and does not obey. On the given day the bishop dies. According to the second tale, some men hear, on the slopes of Etna, voices of demons who are preparing a fire in which to burn the soul of the duke Bertolphe, who just died. Caesarius (implicitly contradicting the Life of Odilo of Cluny) asserts that Etna is the "mouth of Hell" and not "Purgatory," for only reprobates go there, men such as the king of the Goths, Theodoric, according to the Dialogues of Gregory the Great (IV, 30). The confrontation between these two tales is interesting. In the first, Arthur is the king of death, like the king of the dwarfs in Walter Map's tale. And the bishop of Palermo was supposed to have gone to the court of King Arthur in Etna, just as Herla agreed to go to the subterranean palace of the dwarf king; without a doubt the bishop would then have brought back his horse, but at the risk of also being condemned to perpetual wandering. In the second tale, Arthur's name is not uttered, but the volcano is the same: here emerges the old tradition of infernal Etna, bending the interpretation of the tale in a negative direction and preparing for Arthur's association with the devil.

Arthur, the ambivalent king of the dead (in Otranto, in the collection of Gervase of Tilbury, and again in Caesarius of Heisterbach's first tale), is thus progressively diabolized (in Caesarius's second tale) just as Hellequin's hunt takes on an increasingly negative connotation. Favoring this double evolution, several accounts explicitly connect or even confuse the names of Hellequin and Arthur. To the Englishman Gervase of Tilbury, the story of the runaway horse of the bishop of Catania recalls the tales of apparitions of Hellequin's hunt heard in Brittany and in England. In Great and "Small" Britain, he says, the guards of the forests say that at noon or at the beginning of the night, when the moon is full, it is very common to see and hear a crowd of hunters, with their dogs and their horns; the hunters call themselves, according to these witnesses, the *societas ou familia Arturi*. The substitution of the name Arthur for that of Hellequin is obvious. Arthur, like Herla in Walter Map's tale, was believed to have been the "king of the very ancient Britons."[58] The association is even clearer in a mid-thirteenth-century *exemplum* by the Dominican preacher from Lyon, Stephen of Bourbon (d. 1261).[59] The names of the two figures this time are joined to each other and are associated with the theme of the subterranean kingdom. But the ideological framework of the tale is quite different from the ones presented by Walter Map and Gervase of Tilbury. The pleasure of the tale was succeeded by the scholastic demonstration, the ambivalence of the *mirabilia* by the desire to give all phenomena an unequivocal and diabolical meaning that the *exemplum* of the sermon had as its function to impose. In the credence that the people (*vulgus*), the peasants (*rustici*), and especially the old women (*vetulae*) gave to dreams, the preacher (who was also an inquisitor) perceived the "ancient superstition" and the remnants of paganism under the influence of the illusions of the enemy. Indeed, in order better to trick simple souls, the demons sometimes took on the appearance of knights who were seen hunting or participating in tournaments in the *familia Allequini vel Arturi*. Stephen of Bourbon heard that a peasant in the Jura, who was carrying a log in the moonlight on the slopes of Mont-Chat, saw a pack of dogs and a troop of hunters on horseback and on foot; he followed them as far as a magnificent palace, that of "King Arthur." There knights and ladies were dancing, playing, and feasting. He was led into the bedroom of one of the ladies, who was incredibly beautiful. He fell asleep in her bed but in the morning woke up lying on his log, "well tricked by the devils." Another peasant encountered the same troop of horsemen, who were turning toward each other and asking: "Does this hood suit me well?" The hood or the cape is the specific dress of the dead and the instrument of their torment.[60] But in Stephen of Bourbon's tale, the dead are more than ever confused with demons. The ostentation and revelries in their palace are no longer the attributes of the marvelous tale but are dangerous diabolical *fantasmata* that, in the early morning, vanish like dreams.

Hellequin, Herla, and Arthur are the names of the same mythical character, the king of the dead, who sometimes, at night in the forests or on the main road, rode at the head of his furious troop and who sometimes reigned in his subterranean palace on the border of Wales, in Etna, or on Mont-Chat, attracting the living by a practice of gift-giving in which life and death were at stake. But in a half century, the preachers, trained in scholastic theology, followed the court clerics so fond of *mirabilia*. They managed to substitute the devil for the king of the dead. Even though they did not totally rule out the possibility that the furious troop might have a penitential aspect (and might offer to some of its members a hope of salvation), Hellequin's hunt was increasingly detached from the both material and imaginary world that governed the economy of suffrages for the souls in purgatory. One of the great theologians of his generation, William of Auvergne, the bishop of Paris, indicates this evolution as well as these hesitations, when he is the first to propose, in his *De universo* (On the universe of creatures), written between 1231 and 1236, a true theory of Hellequin's hunt.[61] He seems to hesitate between two interpretations: were they souls in purgatory, or were they evil spirits[62] who at night took on the appearance (*similitudines*) of knights "that in French one calls *hellequin* and in Spanish the *ancient army* (*exercitus antiquus*)"?[63] In all cases the witnesses did not see real horses, real weapons, a real ride, but only "signs" intended to terrify the bad and to evoke suffrages for the souls of the dead. These apparitions preferably occurred at crossroads, for those places, due to the number of people of all sorts that passed through them, were more "polluted" than the fields (theology was aware of ecology!). In these sordid places, the living were shown the true punishments endured by the evil in the hereafter, the causes of their punishments, and the suffrages they needed. In the place of purgatory (*locus purgatorii*), which William of Auvergne asserted was a single place and an "earthly habitation," expiatory punishments were adapted to the sins for which the dead did not do penance in their lifetime. God allowed these apparitions so that those who abused weapons (*abusores armorum*) and committed murder and robbery would see with terror the punishments of those who in their time acted in the same way. We cannot define any better the ideological function that the church assigned to Hellequin's hunt in this moral mirror that it held up to those for whom violence was a trade.

To this end, William of Auvergne establishes an explicit connection between the troop of the dead and purgatory, as if the former periodically came out of the latter. But we may wonder in particular whether the development of the doctrine of purgatory as a specific and fixed place for the individual expiation of souls in the hereafter ruined the possibility of a "purgatorial" itinerancy. Thus only the following alternatives remained: either the definitive disappearance of Hellequin's hunt (this is what Walter Map and Helinand of Froidmont claimed) or its complete diabolization. The containment in purgatory of individual souls in agony was contrasted with the furious and undaunted army of "evil spirits."

Thus in the thirteenth century, a religious and moral interpretation of the theme of Hellequin's hunt triumphed. In earlier tales, the theme participated simultaneously in secular strategies for power and in monarchic ideology. At Saint Foi of Sélestat, alongside the confirmation of a monastic foundation, it was related to the retrospective expression of a political prophecy to the benefit of the Hohenstaufen. In the Anglo-Saxon chronicle of Peterborough, the apparition of the furious troop accompanies King Henry I's unfortunate choice of an unworthy abbot. For the king's adviser, Peter of Blois, Hellequin's hunt was a metaphor for the royal court, aimed against the corrupt *curiales*. In Walter Map's tale, the dynasty of the Plantagenets is situated in the succession of Briton, then Saxon, kingdoms of England. According to Gervase of Tilbury, the foresters of the king witness apparitions of the *familia Arturi* in such a way that the legendary king and the real king seem to rule in tandem and dispute sovereignty over the same hunting grounds. Indeed, the mythical power of the king of the dead reinforced the legitimacy and the efficacy of the living king's power over the jealously guarded space of the forest. To protect his forests and his exclusive hunting rights, the king could take advantage of the terror that Hellequin's hunt inspired in his subjects.

In the *exempla*, on the contrary, the only king with whom Hellequin-Arthur is associated is the devil, the ruler of hell. The framework of reference is no longer monarchic ideology but moral theology—penitential attitudes and the anguish of the "death of the self" that preachers and confessors, along the lines of the Fourth Lateran Council (1215), attempted to inculcate in the "Christian people." Finally, at the beginning of the fourteenth century in Paris, during the troubled years of the end of the reign of Philip the Fair, moral satire, political ideology, and the folkloric ritual of the charivari joined together in the literary form of the *Roman de Fauvel* to evoke Hellequin, the king of the dead and of disguise.

SIX

THE IMAGINARY TAMED?

A New Speech

At the beginning of the thirteenth century, all of Christendom was smitten with a "new speech."[1] It came to life with a multitude of "parliaments" (from the parliament of the king to the most modest "parlor of the bourgeois") and places devoted to verbal exchanges, to judicial debates, to bargaining, to scholarly disputes in the universities, and to public declarations of the word of God. The preachers' pulpits (made of stone both inside and outside churches or of wood, able to be moved onto the public square or into the middle of a field) were one of the principal meeting places and formed the symbol of this blossoming new speech. Christianity, the religion of the Word, thus made new ties with the source of its most profound inspiration, but within a world transformed by urban growth, by the development and the rising population of the cities. It was at this time that a true "Christian people," which was something other than a vague reference to the mass of the baptized, took shape and assumed a visage, perhaps for the first time: vast crowds of laypeople felt they had something to say in the church and trembled at the watchwords of the moral reform and of the return to the apostolic ideal. The seductions of real speech led more than one of them into heresy. In fact, in order to respond to those aspirations and to refute the heretics, new religious orders were organized and encouraged: the Mendicants. The principal ones were the minor orders (the Franciscans) and the preachers (the Dominicans). These orders were a sort of hybrid between the secular clergy (they shared a mission vis-à-vis laypeople, and they competed against that clergy on its own territory) and former monks (they too led a conventual life, but one without the constraints of being permanently cloistered). Their milieu of choice was the city, urban society, the university. Their primary weapon was speech, the sermon.

Beginning in the thirteenth century with the Mendicants, or under their influence, preaching underwent profound quantitative and qualitative transformations. The written vestiges of this are considerable—sermons that have been preserved number in the hundreds of thousands—even though they represent only a very small and fixed part of all that was uttered. The rhetoric of the sermon became systematic in order to become increasingly effective; it imposed a strict plan, invariable divisions, and the requisite trilogy of its arguments. The "authorities" (auctoritates), drawn from the Bible or the Christian authors, stated all the facets (even if they were contradictory) of authorized tradition. But that tradition, pitted against disbelievers and heretics, begged to be proven; this was the role of the "reasons" (rationes), which came directly out of the university dialectic in which the brothers had been trained. Finally, the "examples" (exempla) illustrated—in the form of short and concrete tales, fables, or short stories—the advantages, to the Christian, of righteous behavior.[2]

The exempla were not always clearly distinguished from the miracula, which we have already encountered. Moreover, the vocabulary itself underwent several fluctuations, as is seen in the title of the early-thirteenth-century Dialogus miraculorum, by Caesarius of Heisterbach. Caesarius was a Cistercian monk who was addressing the novices of his monastery (he was officially responsible for them). Although his work is a collection of tales (along the lines of any collection of exempla), it is also, in the tradition of the Dialogues of Gregory the Great, an exchange of edifying discussions between a master and his student. But the work was immediately used by other preachers, both secular and Mendicant, as one of the primary sources of exempla to pad sermons addressed to laypeople and no longer just to monks.

One must nevertheless keep in mind a distinction between miracula and exempla. From the point of view of form, the exempla were usually shorter, and they abandoned specific references to precisely named people or places; they intended to portray only human types and universally experienced situations. With the exempla, the narrative material also lost its variety and was subjected to unchangeable, repetitive structures, which were thereby all the easier to memorize and were therefore more efficacious when addressed to an illiterate audience. Massive, systematic, repetitive—the new preaching appeared as an enormous machine to be used to convert souls. Situated between the written and the oral, the literature of the *exempla* was one of the principal cogs of that machine. These tales were gathered by the hundreds into thematic or alphabetical collections with tables of contents or indexes. They were intellectual techniques that are included among the decisive innovations of the scholastic age.

The goal of the *exemplum* was the individual salvation of all of the Christians who made up the audience gathered at the foot of the pulpit. The necessary horizon of preaching in general and of the *exempla* in particular was therefore death, the individual judgment of the sinner at the moment of death, the joys or the tribulations of the hereafter, and at the end of time, the Last Judgment and the resurrection of the dead. Terrifying or calming, death and the dead were equally and very concretely present in a large number of tales to give hope (by showing, with supporting examples, that up until one's final breath, it was never too late to repent one's sins) or to invoke fear (by describing, in vivid detail, the horror of infernal punishments). Ghosts therefore had their place in the *exempla*. In fact, they were most abundant there. In this sense, as well, the *exempla* that portrayed ghosts differed from the *miracula* that made use of the same themes: the *miracula* aimed above all to reinforce the liturgy of the dead, and the *exempla* sought instead to prepare Christians to die well.

However, in the *exempla*, ghosts appeared as they did in the miraculous tales of Peter the Venerable, and they made the same requests of the living. But they also had unprecedented traits. In the *exempla*, all of lay society was included, the dead as well as the living. Knights and monks were still the primary agents, but simple folk increasingly made their presence known—men of the towns and the fields, women and men, and of course, the Mendicant brothers. Relatively less mention was made of the wild army. Attention was concentrated instead on the individual dead person, on his or her requests made of close relatives or the parish priest for masses, prayers, and alms. The place the dead person came from was made clear: in most cases it was purgatory, which was, from that time on, well individualized and localized. Wasn't one of the functions of the third place in the hereafter, according to Jacques Le Goff, "the imprisonment of ghosts"?[3] It is true that purgatory put an end to uncertain wanderings. In a time when the municipal and royal authorities were concerned with the increase in the number of homeless vagabonds, purgatory gave suffering souls a fixed place of residence. If it was scarcely reassuring to see them, at least one knew with almost complete certainty where they came from. The wanderings of ghosts were therefore channeled but not denied, since never had ghosts, or at least the texts that mentioned them, been so large in number.

This increase in the number of tales of ghosts in search of suffrages was on a par with the intensification and the spread in lay society of liturgical and more generally cultual practices governing the relationships between the living and the dead. The Cluniac liturgical model was then replaced by a Mendicant model. In the former the monks, through their prayers, ensured the salvation of noble benefactors in exchange for charitable donations of land approved by the family of the deceased (*laudatio parentum*). In the second model the deceased made their own wills, in a testament brought before a notary, leaving sums of money intended to buy, in as many churches as possible, the greatest number of masses likely to hasten a definitive escape from purgatory. On the one hand were the land, the liturgy of the monks, and the collective will of the aristocratic lineage. On the other hand were the will of the individual, the role of money and the bourgeoisie, the Mendicant orders, and what Jacques Chiffoleau has called the "accounting of the hereafter": the register, by double entry, of masses and of the years of purgatory that the masses enabled one to avoid. The framework of all these practices was the local community of the living and the dead, the parish, the inseparable couple of the church and the cemetery at the very center of the town or the neighborhood. Within this framework new relationships were born in the face of death. When one could not rely on a line of ancestors (the lines that made the nobility), one associated with neighbors, people like oneself, within the framework of one's trade, the parish, the community of residents, or the zone of influence of a Mendicant monastery. One of the important goals of the charities and confraternities of assistance and prayer was to ensure, equally to all their members, after death, worthy funerals and then the suffrages necessary for the souls' salvation.

These, then, were the figures who, at the beginning of the thirteenth century, were swarming in the *exempla*, in particular those who told stories of ghosts. Since we cannot possibly look at them all, let us focus on a few to demonstrate not only the evolution of the genre but also the limits of its influence.

The Cistercian Contribution

The Cistercians belonged simultaneously to both the ancient and the new worlds. Thus their tales appear to straddle two genres: the *miracula* and the *exempla*. Their status as monks, their liturgy, and their spirituality of death connected them to the Cluniacs, with whom, however, they often clashed. But since they belonged to a still young order, one better anchored in a monetary economy, and since they were informed from within their barns of all the tales that their lay brothers and salaried manual workers were telling them, they provided a link between the world of the cloisters and the village or sometimes even the urban society.

The Cistercian homiletics paved a wide path for the preaching of the Mendicant orders, as can be seen abundantly in the ghost tales of the time. In Saint Bernard's own writings,[4] then in the *Lives* of the founder of Clairvaux, the dead, such as the sister of Saint Malachi and many dead monks, appeared everywhere.[5] The apparitions of the ordinary dead, monks or laypeople, increased above all in the Cistercian collections at the turn of the twelfth century: the *Exordium magnum* (Great Cistercian exordium) by Conrad of Eberbach,[6] the *Liber miraculorum* by Herbert of Clairvaux,[7] the unpublished manuscript of the abbey of Beaupré,[8] and the *Liber miraculorum* of the monastery of Himmerod.[9] The work that undoubtedly crowns this narrative production is that of the Rhenish Cistercian Caesarius of Heisterbach, who transcribed a good sixty or so *exempla* concerning ghosts.

Caesarius was born in Cologne around 1180. A student of the cathedral school of that city, he converted and completed a pilgrimage to the Marian sanctuary of Rocamadour before becoming a monk in Heisterbach in 1199. The donning of the habit, like his devotion to the Virgin (who is very present in his writings), was a personal choice, made when he was twenty years old. In a sign of the times, there is a noticeable difference between this monastic "vocation" and the destiny that was set out in advance for Otloh of Saint Emmeran, Guibert of Nogent, or Peter the Venerable, oblates raised from a very young age within the walls of a monastery. Very soon Caesarius became the teacher of the novices of Heisterbach. He was inspired by this experience to write his principal work, *Dialogus miraculorum* (written between 1219 and 1223), a fictitious dialogue between a *magister* (himself) and a *novicius*. In 1227 he became prior, which earned him the right to accompany the abbot often on visits to other abbeys (Marienstatt, Eberbach, and Himmerod in the Eifel) and on voyages (to the Netherlands) and thus enabled him to learn much by reading and listening, which is apparent in his many sermons. He died around 1240, leaving an important and diverse collection of written works, of which we will mention here only the *exempla* concerning ghosts.[10]

Most of the tales in *Dialogus miraculorum* were intended for the instruction of novices, for individual or group reading, or for future preaching. Out of 746 chapters and an almost equal number of tales, the collection includes fifty ghost tales. A dozen similar and sometimes identical tales are found, moreover, in the Dominical sermons or in the psalms sermons that Caesarius wrote starting in 1225.[11]

In the prologue to *Dialogus miraculorum*, the author explains that he is reporting "true miracles that occur in our time and every day." Here, then, is the "everyday miracle." It is not a matter of succumbing to the unforeseeable charm of the marvelous, or even of celebrating the extraordinary miracles that occurred in a particular monastery, but of revealing the permanent signs that guide all those who know how to recognize them onto the path to salvation. It is the "exemplary" value that defines the "miracle," as this Cistercian states in his primarily didactic and doctrinal work. The book sets out twelve "distinctions" that mark the ideal course of the Christian, from the "merits" acquired through conversion and penance (the first six distinctions) to the "retributions" gained after death (the following six distinctions). Each tale is cited and commented on by the "master" at the request of the "novice."

Tales of ghosts represent about 6.6 percent of the work. As is normal, we find three-fifths of them in the twelfth and last distinction, since ghosts were the principal means that the living had of knowing "the suffering and the glory of the dead." The dead return from three different places, henceforth clearly distinguished in the geography of the afterworld: paradise, hell, and in the very large majority of the tales, purgatory. The preponderance of souls in purgatory is explained by their transitory status and by the reasons for their apparitions: they do not simply aim to inform the living about the realities of the afterworld, to announce the imminent deaths of the living, or to forewarn the living of the punishments in the hereafter. Souls in purgatory, and they alone, are able to improve their fate with the help of prayers, almsgiving, and especially masses celebrated by the living, acts that are unnecessary for the elect and useless for the damned. For Caesarius of Heisterbach, the dead who solicit suffrages can therefore come only from purgatory, even if, distraught by the horrible torments they endure there, they erroneously call it "the pit of Hell."[12] The Cistercian master does not hesitate to contradict the dead themselves, not only those who say they are returning from hell but also those who claim that almsgiving provides the most useful suffrages; according to Caesarius, the mass is even more efficacious.[13]

Regarding tales of ghosts, only one written source—a Cistercian col-lection of tales of visions—is cited.[14] All other tales came from oral sources, gathered directly by Caesarius from abbots, monks, and nuns belonging to the order. Most were obtained locally (from the valley of the Rhine, Flanders), but others, due to Caesarius's own travels and to information reported by his abbot concerning the general chapter, deal with more distant homes of the order, in particular Cîteaux and Clair-vaux, the cradle of the Cistercians.[15]

Caesarius introduces himself as the author of the work: he is the *scriptor*, not exactly what we would call an author (since medieval writing was a work of compilation) but certainly a more important role than that of a simple scribe. He uses the first person to say that it is indeed he who gathered and transcribed the tales, then composed the work. It is also he who is hiding behind the *magister* leading the dialogue. But here the autobiographical nature of the book ceases. Unlike Peter the Venerable, Caesarius never mentions an apparition of which he himself was the ben-eficiary. This was a characteristic trait of the *exemplum*, a tale that claimed to be completely objective. Although it was essential that the author in-tervene in the first person in order to give all guarantees as to the "authen-tic" transmission of the tale (saying "I heard," *audivi*, or "I read," *legi*), it was also appropriate that the tale describe an action that might have been carried out by any Christian. The credibility and the efficacy of the *exem-plum* depended on this: the *exemplum* was a cultural object that was to be shared regardless of any differences in status, nationality, or language. All people, whatever they might have been or wherever they might have lived, were to be able to learn from it and use it to their benefit. The internal logic was therefore completely different from that which pre-vailed in the *miracula* of Peter the Venerable: the personal dream he re-lates in the first person is a unique and localized experience, not repro-ducible, one that affirms *hic et nunc* the legitimacy of the abbot and of the order he incarnates. That kind of autobiographical dream had no place in Caesarius of Heisterbach's work: all the tales of apparitions related the vision of a third party. Thus they were most often conscious visions and not dreams. Faithful to ecclesiastical tradition, Caesarius was wary of dreams, those "vain musings" of the *visio phantastica* that, it was always feared, may have been inspired by the devil.[16] People spoke of their dreams when it was appropriate to tell about personal experience. But people spoke of the visions of others when reporting an oral tradition to be weighed on the scale of social values.

In this collection, it is primarily dead monks who appear, and monks are even more prevalent among the living who receive the apparitions. For the most part, the apparitions fit into the mold of the spiritual kinship of the Cistercian order. For the monks, the apparitions were a family affair. Out of this came the preponderance of a simple narrative structure: a dead monk appears directly to his former abbot, without going (as did the dead knights in the tales of Peter the Venerable) through the intermediacy of a messenger (*nuntius, internuntius*) who was required to ask for the necessary masses.

Compared with the miracles of Marmoutier or Cluny, the Cistercian collection is exceptional in the strong participation of women and, more precisely, of nuns in the exchange between the living and the dead. In the two earlier monastic collections I have just mentioned, not one woman is included among the dead or even among the living who are beneficiaries of the apparitions. In the stories of Caesarius of Heisterbach, however, the reader is struck by the presence of about one dead woman for every four dead men and of a large number of Cistercian nuns among the visionaries. This feminization of the participants in an apparition is due to the weight of the "second order"—the female branch—at Cîteaux. It announced the *cura feminarum* of the Mendicants. This tendency was even more evident in the Rhineland and in Flanders in the role of the cloistered nuns, the Beguines, and the local recluses, well-known in the twelfth century for their visionary experiences. This is illustrated particularly well by Sister Acselina, called a "saint" (*beata*) and mentioned in three different chapters as the beneficiary of four apparitions of the dead.[17] A dead prior of Clairvaux, believed to be in heaven, reveals to her that he went to purgatory for having acquired monastery property through "avarice." On the contrary, the holiness of the abbess Ermentrude of Ditkirgen, in Bonn, earned her the right to be admitted to heaven immediately at her death; she nevertheless appears to Acselina after thirty days to render thanks for the sister's devotion to the Eleven Thousand Holy Virgins of Cologne. Sister Acselina had much affection for her "spiritual sister" in the order, and when the latter was about to die, Acselina made the abbess promise to appear to her to inform her of Ermentrude's fate in the afterworld; this is what the dead woman did in revealing to Acselina that she was saved. Finally, when the monk David, of holy reputation, dies in another monastery of the order, his shirt is given to Sister Acselina. Soon afterward the dead man appears to her to tell her that this shirt would be more useful to the monk Gerard Waschart. After receiving it, Gerard in turn shares it with his brother

Frederic, a monk of Heisterbach, where the relic continued to manifest its thaumaturgic powers.

Unlike the tales of Marmoutier, these stories were not confined within the walls of the monastery. They widely involved the lay population (about 30 percent of the dead are laypeople) because the monks and the cloistered nuns continued to maintain ties with their natural families even after death, ties that the monastic family did not abolish, even though the monastery tended to be substituted for the familial home. A "noble adolescent" who had become a convert in Clairvaux was sent onto a farm to watch the sheep; out in a field, he receives the apparition of his dead cousin, who begs him to ask the abbot for three masses on his cousin's behalf.[18] When, during Lent, the abbot of Heisterbach visits the monastery of the cloistered Cistercian nuns of Nazareth, a young sister who died eight years earlier among the Benedictine nuns of Bredehorn in Frisia appears to him in a dream to beg his help. She has been abandoned by her entire earthly family: her father, her mother, her maternal aunt who became a nun of Nazareth, her cousin (a Cistercian in Syon), and her two other maternal aunts, both married. Nor has the dead nun benefited from the prayers of her sisters in religion, that is, from the Benedictine nuns. The suffrages ordered by the Cistercian abbot were thus intended to palliate the double failings of the natural family and the spiritual family. And Caesarius concludes with a note on the supremacy of the monks of the White Order over the monks of the Black Order, who neglect their own dead.[19]

There was an openness to the lay world as well because the Cistercian monasteries (like Cluny already) maintained relationships of every kind with the aristocracy of the region. But most of the dead nobles or knights who appear in *Dialogus miraculorum* have nothing to hope from the living: the dead are damned and return only to warn the living against the infernal punishments that they too are bringing upon themselves. The dead are not, as they were for Peter the Venerable, traditional or potential donors. Well-established in the monetary and merchant economy of their time, the Cistercian monasteries no longer depended as much on the charitable donations of the nobility in order to grow and prosper. The nobles could be considered for what they were: vile warrior sinners and thieves. Count William of Julich well deserved the terrible fate he endured after his death: the devil in person informs his vassal Walter of this, and then the damned one sadly confirms it when he appears to a recluse nun. But not all nobles were so evil: the father of the same Walter is pulled from the clutches of the devil at the end of twenty-one years through the persistent prayers of his widow (she lost an eye due to her crying!) and of his son Theodoric, a Cistercian monk whom the furious devil calls "bald and lousy."[20]

Two reasons in particular justified the unenviable fate of men of war in the hereafter: the violence they committed against the poor and the weak, and the practice of tournaments. The former reason generally left some hope for the dead man, under the condition that his heirs consented to return the ill-gotten property. As in the tales of Peter the Venerable, this type of apparition reintroduced the role of the *nuntius*, the intermediary between the dead and the living. Unnecessary within the walls of the monastery, this intermediary function once again became important as soon as the relationship between the living and the dead included laypeople. The dead man assigns his messenger the task of pleading his case to his children so that they themselves will agree to go to the abbot of the monastery to request the precious suffrages, as in the tale that Caesarius heard from the monk John of Heisterbach, who himself heard it from his father Erkinbert, a citizen of Andernach. This man sees the dead knight Frederic of Kelle riding on a black war-horse, out of whose nostrils shoot flames and smoke. The dead knight asks Erkinbert to go to his sons to implore them to return the sheepskin that he stole from a poor widow and that he is wearing at that moment. But the sons refuse, abandoning their father to his eternal torment.[21] The fate of another dead knight who became rich through usury and who bequeathed his ill-gotten gains to his son is no more enviable. One night he kicks loudly at the door to his house while crying out his name (which Caesarius is very careful not to repeat) and claiming he is the master of the house. The son's servant looks through the keyhole and recognizes the dead man, but he responds hypocritically that his master is dead and that he will not open the door. Weary of the fight, the dead knight leaves after he hangs on the door some fish he brought for his son. In the morning the son discovers that this "infernal food cooked in the sulfurous flames" has changed into toads and snakes.[22] Few other texts show as well as this one does, even in the words used (*fortiter pulsans*), how impulsive the return of the father's image is against all the son's efforts at defense.[23]

Damnation without appeal also threatened knights who were killed in tournaments and who continued, beyond death, to clash in great numbers. On this topic Caesarius takes up the metaphor Saint Bernard used but in a more literal sense: these knights are the "militia of the devil." The theme is not unlike that of the "army of the dead," in the violence and the collective nature of most of these apparitions and in the times and places in which they occur—at night, on the edge of a forest, on the large road, or across a field. Few men survived such apparitions. Just such a "fantastic" tournament (not of real bodies, Caesarius specifies, but of images invoked by the devil) is seen on the banks of the Moselle in 1223; witnesses recognize among the dead jousters the count Louis de Lootz and his brothers Arnold and Henry, followed by the knights Thierry Heiger and Henry of Limbach.[24] Another time, at nightfall in a field, a priest hears the din of a "very great tournament of the dead" who call out: "Walter of Milene, Walter of Milene." A knight by that name had died not long ago. The priest protects himself until dawn by tracing circles around himself each time the apparition takes place.[25]

In Caesarius of Heisterbach's tales, all of lay society is present. The whole motley and sinful little world of the town comes to life: "priests' wives," bourgeois, usurers, thieves, and also secular priests or canons. The portrait the author paints of them is not always negative: he can recognize forms of devotion among simple women, devotion that he cites as examples. Thus we see the moving conjugal piety of the wife of the usurer of Liège: refusing to despair of the improbable salvation of her husband, she manages to have his body, which was deprived of a Christian burial, interred in the cemetery where she has herself walled up as a recluse. For seven years she prays endlessly for the soul of her husband, until he appears to her dressed poorly and asks her to carry on. Another seven years pass, and he appears to her all dressed in white, definitely saved.[26] The growing attraction of the large city of Cologne, located quite close to Heisterbach, was noticeable. One citizen of this city, whenever he was alone, recited the Ave Maria. After his death he appears to his niece; he is covered from his head to his feet with the letters of the Hail Mary.[27] This type of tale passed, without a single word being changed, into the *exempla* of the Mendicants.

The Preaching Machine: The Mendicant Orders

After the Cistercians, the amount of narrative material accumulated by members of the Mendicant orders became so great that it cannot be measured. It also increasingly withdrew from any specific sociological or local anchoring. Though the brothers of a preacher's order remained favored informants for him, the protagonists of their stories belonged to all social categories, to all age groups, and to both sexes: knights, artisans, usurers, gullible peasants, old superstitious women, and young co-quettes. Moreover, certain collections of sermons adopted an *ad status* classification—depending on the socioprofessional group—in the search for a better adequation of the word of the church and of new social realities. Similarly, there was no theme that this word avoided broaching: the entire life of ordinary men—married life, working life, transactions at the marketplace, escapades at the bordel, etc.—provided fodder for preaching and for striking home a moral lesson. Within the thick fabric of ordinary social relations, the omnipresent mass of ghost tales was inserted into the sermons of the Mendicants. Granted, the preachers spoke of ghosts primarily with regard to a preparation for death or the uncertainties of dying and of what came next.[28] But ghosts cropped up elsewhere still, quick to surge forth at the best times of life to remind people, when they least expected it, that everything had an end and that they always had to be ready to die.

Let us look at *Liber exemplorum,* written in the middle of the thirteenth century by an anonymous English Franciscan from the provinces of Ire-land. The work is divided into two parts of very unequal size. The first (60 chapters) contains *exempla* concerning "higher things": Christ, the Vir-gin, angels. In it are two ghost tales intended to recall the Virgin's power of intercession after death.[29] The second part (152 chapters) deals with "lesser things," that is, with daily life examined according to a list of vices classified in alphabetical order. Now there was no realm in which ghosts were not useful for putting the living back on the right path: they had only to appear once, and everything was put in order! Thanks to them, a preoccupation with death would no longer leave a young woman guilty of *acedia* (negligence in her religious duties) or a drunk drowned in *gula* (the vice of impenitent eaters and drinkers). Here are two examples.[30] Seven years earlier, while the author of the collection was carrying out his functions as a lector in the convent of Cork, a widow was murdered in her bedroom during the night by a burglar. A few days later she ap-pears to her sister, who is thirty years old, and tells the sister, in English, that she is horribly burned because on feast days she used to leave the church before communion: "for that I hoede out er the un(de)git." The Franciscan translates: *Quia exivi ante communionem.* He explains to the good woman *(muliercula)* the meaning of her dead sister's words: when the priest takes the body of Christ during mass, he does so for all the people in the parish, who must therefore be present without exception. A similar scene, with the same actors, enables the preacher, a bit later, to speak of the violence committed against innocent people and their property: the assassinated widow appears a second time to her sister, whom she dissuades from seeking revenge against her murderers. She says she has the protection of a boxer (*pugilltor*) who can avenge her if he wants. She agrees to give the name of the boxer, Nazareus, but her sister still does not understand. This sister, called *ydiota*, goes to see the Franciscan, who explains to her that her sister's defender is none other than Christ. And he also gives a little sermon on divine justice and mercy.

In the same period, in Flanders, the Dominican Thomas of Cantimpré compiled a huge work, *Bonum universale de apibus*, which resembles both a collection of *exempla* and a moral encyclopedia.[31] The metaphor of bees that makes up the title of the work is well justified: the work is like a hive, with compartments in which each cell collects a new tale. It is also composed of two unequal parts: one concerns the *prelati*, ecclesiastics (twenty-five chapters); the other, "other men" (fifty-seven chapters). Each chapter in turn deals with dozens of points, each illustrated by several *exempla*. As one would expect, the issue of "suffrages for the dead" is found in a large number of ghost stories. What is new is the enlargement of the notion and of the list of suffrages; added to the traditional trilogy of prayers, almsgiving, and masses, under as many new headings, are tears, fasting, vigil and affliction, and the restitution of ill-gotten property, this to prepare—like the septenaries of vices, of virtues, or of the gifts of the Holy Spirit—a new septenary of suffrages for the dead.[32] Thinking of the dead was no longer an activity limited in time, contained within a liturgical ceremony; it had to accompany all the daily activities of ordinary people and thus contribute to altering attitudes of bodily piety, increasingly marked by tears and macerations as well as by reflection on the fragility of human life, on sin, and on penance.

Let us also note how ghost tales reinforced the economic implications of penance and, ironically, contributed to the criticism evoked by the growing importance of money in spiritual matters. This can be seen in the *exemplum* that tells of an affair that, in its time, caused quite a stir in Ulster. The brother Dunekan, who was witness to the story, told it to the brother Robert of Dodington, who repeated it in a sermon. A master of a house buys the salvation of his recently deceased son with money and is sold indulgences by a Franciscan brother for a few deniers and a quantity of wine (the *biberagium*, comparable to what was originally the "bed and breakfast" charitably offered to a poor traveler). The affair is concluded, and the following night, "the spirit of the son" appears, flooded in light, to his sleeping father to reveal that he is saved. The father awakens the entire household, including the Franciscan, who repents for having sold such precious goods when he thought he was selling only the wind. He wants to buy them back, but their new owner does not want to return them.[33] The *exemplum* is ambiguous: it castigates the greed of certain religious figures, but it also demonstrates the efficacy of indulgences and almsgiving for the liberation of souls in purgatory.

For his part, Thomas of Cantimpré presents the *restitutio* of ill-gotten goods—usurious notes and abusive loans—as a means of freeing the dead from their torments. A Dominican tells Thomas the tale of his father, who died before being able to pay the shoesmith who had shod his horse. The dead man appeared to his servant; holding an incandescent horseshoe in his hand, he begs the servant to go find his Dominican son and then his widow so that they will pay back his debt.[34]

The repetition of the same motifs or the same *exempla* from one collection or from one sermon to another, like their insertion in recurrent systems of classification and demonstration, tended increasingly to eat away at the unique traits and the element of surprise that each tale might conceal. The apparition of a dead person, which so many writings present as a stupefying and frightening phenomenon, was no longer anything but a scenography in which each role was known in advance and whose unfolding led back, most of the time, to the same schema. We can sum up this type of story as follows: a dead relative who does not seem very proud of himself appears to a conscious or, more rarely, sleeping *quidam*. The dead relative speaks in a direct style. "Fear nothing," he says, "I have not come to harm you. I am enduring terrible torments in purgatory and I have come to ask you to hasten my liberation through masses, prayers, and almsgiving." The living person, convinced by some "sign" of the truth of the apparition, agrees to do whatever is necessary, and soon the resplendent dead person appears a second time to show that he is saved and to thank the living relative.

The banalization of tales of apparitions of the dead was not an isolated phenomenon. It was a response to a general strategy whose goal was to create a Christian mode of edifying familiarity with death and with the dead, a mode orchestrated, moreover, by the increased ritualization of funeral services, by the valuating of the space of the cemetery as a holy place in the heart of the community of the living, by participation in the burial services of the dead, and within the privileged classes, by the daily reading of the book of hours. The confraternities' celebration of the memory of dead confreres and the increase, by the hundreds, of masses for the dead indicate the same tendency. Two tales, reproduced in dozens of copies, seem to me, within the framework of this massive ideology of Christian death, to have a paradigmatic value. Let us entitle them "The Promise of the Two Friends" and "The Passing through the Cemetery."

The first narrative type borrows the ancient theme of the two friends who promise each other that the first one to die will appear to the other to reveal the dead one's "condition" in the afterworld. The pact specifically aims to provoke an apparition, which is therefore desired and in principle even expected.[35] Caesarius of Heisterbach takes up this type of tale in at least four accounts, though the social status of the protagonists vary: two clerics, two monks, two nuns, and a knight and his daughter.[36] In other collections the same tale concerns a schoolmaster and his pupil or two students.[37] Elsewhere it serves as an opening structure for the theme of lovers who swear to find each other again in spite of death.[38] In fact, the theme goes far beyond *exempla* alone. The continuator of the anonymous *Chronicle of the Dominican of Colmar* (1308–1314) claims to have obtained such a story from the surviving friend, a vagabond by the name of Sererius, who was believed to have told his adventure to a woman from Soultzmat, herself an informant of the Dominican chronicler. The dead man had promised to appear to Sererius on the thirtieth day following his death. On the given day, Sererius enters the tavern of a village, drinks heavily, and as in the stories of a pact with the devil, forgets his promise. The dead man goes into an inhabited house in the area and calls to a peasant passing by: "Go to the tavern and tell Sererius that his friend is waiting for him in this house to inform him, as promised, of the condition of the faithful and the unfaithful dead." Terrified by the news, Sererius replies that he refuses to "hear the words of the dead." An hour later, at twilight, the ghost sends another peasant. This time Sererius becomes angry: "I don't want him to speak to me and I don't want to answer him!" A few days later, while looking for a bridge to cross a river without getting his feet wet, he sees a troop of men on horseback approaching him and recognizes dead knights, killed in combat. They all cross the river in silence, with the exception of one, who makes his way toward him: it is his friend. Sererius wants to flee, but the other persuades him not to go and, threatening to kill him, forces him to listen.[39]

The countless tales of apparitions linked to the parish cemetery constitute another major type. This type comes from the crucial role the cemetery played, especially in the central Middle Ages, in the symbolic structuring of the space of the living. Preachers continued to repeat that one could go across a cemetery at night without fear if one prayed for the dead who rested there, that those dead were grateful to pious people, and that, when the time came, the dead would come to the aid of the living. An example is the story of the priest who regularly prayed for the dead each time he went across the cemetery. One night he hears the dead conclude his own prayer with "amen, amen."[40] In another story a knight often goes to pray in the cemetery; one day his enemies chase him into the cemetery, and the dead stand up outside their graves to lend him aid.[41] However, the dead might also chastise the living who neglected to pray for them or threaten to take with them those of the living who infringed on the rules of morality. A well-known story tells of a bishop who allegedly forbade a simple priest from celebrating mass for the dead, who then threatened to punish the bishop severely.[42] In an equally famous *exemplum* a drunkard, going across a cemetery one night, stumbles on a skull. He loses his temper: "What are you lying there for like that, you miserable head of a dead man? Come home with me; you'll share my supper."[43] The skull answers that he accepts the invitation and that he will follow the drunkard; terrified, the man locks himself in his house. After knocking violently on the door (*ostium pulsans*, the expression is the same as in Caesarius of Heisterbach's tale of the dead father who took fish to his son), the dead man is told that the master is not there. "I know well that he is there," the dead man insists, "like it or not, I'm coming in." The drunk man (who suddenly regains all his senses!) has the door opened and sees enter "the miserable figure of a dead man, presenting the terrible spectacle of bones and rotting flesh." Following the narrative schema of a mutual invitation between a living person and a dead one (as in the encounter, in Walter Map's tale, between King Herla and the king of the dwarfs), the dead man invites the drunk to come see him a week later. The fantastic tale pierces from underneath the *exemplum*, and the terror of the dead is freely expressed in this gruesome figure, which is already characteristic of the macabre.

To conclude, let us pause at the odd work by Rudolf von Schlettstadt, prior of the Dominican convent of that town after 1288. This is a compilation of fifty-six anecdotes that were told in that region at the time. The work is difficult to characterize, and the title, *Historiae memorabiles*, was given by the modern publisher. In fact it is both a regional chronicle filled with rumors and imaginary facts and a collection of *exempla* that could be used from the pulpit. Some twenty or so tales deal with the persecution of Jews, notably the great pogrom of Franconia in 1298, sprinkled with tales of ostensible desecrations of hosts and legendary ritual murders of Christian children by Jews. Six tales refer to ghosts, each more fantastic than the one before.[44] A bishop of Lübeck rises from his grave and chases his unworthy successor from his church, beating the man with a candelabra; a thieving knight, Swigerus, recognizes in the wild army the double of his flayed war-horse. The lord Berthold of Staufen visits his sister in Basel, a widow of the bourgeois Peter Schaller. Schaller appears to Berthold in his room just in time and enables him to escape from the devil, who is metamorphosed into a woman. A dishonest officer, Henry of Rheinau, is riding with his son-in-law; his horse suddenly swerves, he cries to his companion to get away, and he falls onto the ground, his hand horribly burned. Later he would say he had been attacked by three dead men, whom his son-in-law did not see: Eberhard of Habsburg, the bourgeois Henry of Orschwiller, and the knight Henry, who was killed in battle. Finally, two tales deal with a rich canon and provost of the cathedral of Basel, Thierry of Spechbach, who accumulates ecclesiastical benefits and is fond of the good life and women. During the visit of his prebends he spends the night in the home of one of his vicars. Having eaten a good meal and taken a nice nap until eleven o'clock, he "wakes up, goes to relieve himself, and goes back to bed leaving the window open in order to enjoy the serenity of the sky and the air." The window opens up onto the cemetery, where he suddenly notices a crowd of men who are dancing with torches and singing a humble lament in German, a warning addressed to him. In the manuscript the musical score is transcribed with the notes as well as the words.[45]

Later the provost dies, an old man, without having turned over a new leaf. A few days after his death a guardian of the cathedral sees, in a dream, his soul tortured by demons on a tall column protected by razors. This time it is the dead provost's turn to sing, but in Latin because he was a cleric. Once again, the manuscript reproduces the notes of the song, which the guardian remembers so well that he is able to sing it to the canons:

> We who are on uncovered ground,
> Voices sounding in the desert,
> We the desert, we deserted,
> We who are sure of our suffering.[46]

The "desert" of death is, for the anonymous troop of souls in purgatory, the loss of ties of kinship that they cannot reconnect between themselves or with the living.

Rudolf von Schlettstadt's tales are known only through a sixteenth-century manuscript copied by the count of Zimmern and used in part by his nephew in *Chronicle of Zimmern,* written in German. In it one again finds the stories of the thieving knight Swigerus, of the lord Berthold of Staufen, and of the provost Thierry of Spechbach, the spectator of the dance of the dead *(Totentanz)* in the cemetery.[47] This later reception of the tale confirms that the macabre at the end of the Middle Ages—with, in one case, fleshless and putrid bodies and, in the other, the dance of the dead—simultaneously prolonged and surpassed the visibly different representation that the Mendicant preachers of the thirteenth century sought to impose. Indeed, the *exempla* of the thirteenth and fourteenth centuries, for the most part, insisted neither on the terror inspired by ghosts nor on the horror of death itself. Rather, by distilling a minimum of fright, they stated the arithmetic of merits, suffrages, and punishment, and they recalled the lessons that the dead could give to the living to incite the latter to calculate their chances of escaping hell and of shortening their time in purgatory.

Tales therefore became somewhat warped depending on the type of works in which they were found. Likewise they underwent alterations in time and space. The relative uniformization throughout Europe of the Christian culture in the final centuries of the Middle Ages is a phenomenon of primary importance. But it should mask neither sociocultural nor regional differences. Marginal compared with the urban centers of power and culture, certain regions more easily escaped the clutches of Mendicant preaching and the apostolic efforts that came out of the Fourth Lateran Council of 1215. The domestication of ghosts remained imperfect there, as can be seen a century later in three regions that were separated by great distances but all of which experienced—more superficially or at a later date—the imposition of the official culture's influence: the Ariège region of the Pyrenees, Yorkshire at the extreme north of the kingdom of England, and Brittany.

The Wandering Souls of Montaillou

We are indebted to the Inquisition register of Jacques Fournier, bishop of Pamiers in Ariège, for our knowledge of ghosts in that region at the beginning of the fourteenth century.[48] But we are also indebted to people who were invested locally with the power to see the dead and to communicate with them. These were the *armariés,* or "messengers of souls." One of the most reputed among them was Arnaud Gélis, alias Bouteiller, of Mas Saint Antonin. Arnaud was a canon's servant, a sort of sacristan who, strong in the revelations he obtained from the dead, guided families in mourning—especially women—toward priests who said masses for the dead. Arnaud earned a little food and drink or small sums of money for his services. Pressed by the judge, he admitted having been the beneficiary of some twenty apparitions, all experienced in a wakeful state. The dead people he saw one-on-one were known to him, and he could therefore name them. Many were canons (Hugh of Durfort, Hugh of Rous, Athon of Unzent, Pierre Durand, etc.) who, only recently dead, continued to call on his services and engaged him to have masses said for them. He also served as mediator in family matters left in suspension after the death of a relative. A dead woman named Barcelona engaged him to reconcile her son-in-law William of Loubens with her daughter, who had fled to the home of her brother Arnaud of Calmelles, in Pamiers, but the daughter wanted nothing to do with William. Arnaud also went to Brune of Escosse to tell her, on behalf of her dead daughter, Barcelona, widow of Pons Faure, that she must give up her silken blouses. Sometimes Arnaud saw many more than one dead person at a time: when the soul of Pons Bru appeared to him at harvest time, it seemed to be accompanied by a hundred other souls who were wandering back from the church of Saint Martin de Juillac.

Arnaud was not the only one to make a profession out of seeing the dead. There were also female *armariés*, such as Arnaude Rives of Belcaïre and Raimonde, the daughter of Pons Hugon de La Force. Raimonde was Arnaud Gélis's own cousin, and Arnaud was able to make use of her revelations. She often saw the dead and spoke to them. She sometimes would go away for three or four days to "be with the dead" and came back all saddened: here we recognize the "shamanic" model of the voyage to the dead, a model also at work among the *benandanti* of Frioul and whose form, diabolized by the church, would become the witches' Sabbath.[49] In the course of her travels, Raimonde saw Arnaud's parents, who gave her messages to give to their son. His mother, Rousse, wanted him to give a good veil as a gift to a poor old woman, and his father, Raimond Gélis, asked his son to pay back a debt that he himself had not had time to pay.

Although all the witnesses questioned by the inquisitor emphasized the privileged role of the *armariés*, they also all admitted that the dead, endowed with a body, although invisible, were everywhere. One risked running into them if, while walking, one stuck one's arms or legs out too quickly. The peasants of Montaillou did not really adopt the ecclesiastical representation of purgatory, born a century earlier. A single dead man evoked his suffering in the "purgatorial fire," but he was a canon of Pamiers, Pierre Durand. The others wandered "over hill and dale" in the immediate proximity of the village, on paths and around houses. They preferred to visit churches in which they had been parishioners, cemeteries where they had been buried, and places where their families prayed and maintained oil lamps for them. Only the damned were led by demons into the ravines. As for Jews, it was not known whether they went to a "place of rest"; perhaps they too went to heaven, but for the time being it was certain that they did not enter into churches. On All Saints' Day, bands of souls together went to the "place of rest," peaceful and without punishment, an earthly antechamber of the heaven that would open to them at the Last Judgment.

In contrast to the church's "vertical" representations of the afterworld—from hell to heaven going through purgatory—a "horizontal folklore," according to Emmanuel Le Roy Ladurie's expression, was subscribed to by the peasants of Montaillou. This kept the familiar dead right next to the living and kept them from torments and the dislocation of a distant purgatory. But the villagers stated their beliefs without a spirit of contradiction, content to repeat what, they believed, had always been said in their valleys. Moreover, as the role of Arnaud Gélis shows so well, all these various beliefs coexisted rather well, at least until the arrival of the inquisitors.

The "Spirits" of Yorkshire

Around 1400 an anonymous monk from the Cistercian abbey of Byland, located in the county of York at the extreme north of England, consulted a manuscript more than two centuries old from the library of his monastery and noticed that in two places, a few folios were missing. The prestige of the works that the manuscript contained (works by Cicero and, more recently, by Honorius Augustodunensis) did not dissuade him from adding, in his own hand, a dozen stories—"ghost stories"—that he himself had heard told in the region.[50] The presence on the adjoining folios of works of rhetoric and of a collection of commonplaces dealing with penance suggests that the Cistercian intended to use these tales as *exempla*. But in all evidence, he above all gave in to a fascination with extraordinary and truly fantastic stories.[51] All the tales deal with recent local facts, of which the monk was not the direct witness but which were told to him by word of mouth. The narration is rooted in a known landscape, whose places are near and named: the neighboring Cistercian abbey of Rielvaux, the village of Ampleforth, the city of York, etc. The monk of Byland declares himself concerned with reporting exactly either public rumor (*dicitur, referunt aliqui*) or the testimony of the "ancients" (*veteres, seniores, antiqui*). But unlike the authors of *exempla*, he cites no informant by name. He does not seek to give an ecclesiastical guarantee to his tales, and the tales are therefore perhaps only that much freer with regard to official cultural models. He is also careful not to give any moral commentary.[52]

Out of twelve tales, eleven deal with apparitions of the dead.[53] They do not present a single narrative structure. Some resemble the *miracula* or the *exempla* already encountered, with the distinct roles of the dead person, of the beneficiary, and sometimes of the one for whom the apparition was intended. In a "wondrous" case (*mirabile dictu*)—that of a woman who carries a spirit on her back[54]—there is no narrative development. In other cases, on the contrary, the tale goes through many exciting developments.[55]

The apparitions are always perceived in a wakeful state, never in a dream. They are individual apparitions that frequently occur, as in other collections, against the background of a troop of dead; in one case fifteen invisible spirits, thirty in another case, accompany the spirit that alone manifests itself.[56] In another tale, a parade of dead men on the backs of animals recalls the troop that appeared to Walchelin in Orderic Vitalis's tale. Richard Rountre of Cleveland goes on a pilgrimage to Santiago with a group of pilgrims. They stop for the night on the edge of the royal road and organize guard duty because of "nocturnal terrors"; when it is his turn to watch, Richard sees a crowd of dead go by making a lot of noise and showing their *mortuaria*, that is, the horses, sheep, cattle, and other animals that were offered to the church at the time of their funerals.[57]

On the whole, the reasons and goals of the apparitions conformed with the usual schemas of ecclesiastical ideology. Spirits manifested themselves because of sins that had not been expiated: murders (including that of a pregnant woman), thefts (of spoons, of six deniers, or of hay to fatten a cow dishonestly), perjury, extraction of an inheritance, the concubinage of a priest, or the death of a newborn that had not been baptized (which recalls the case of the adulterine half-brother of Guibert of Nogent). Several had been excommunicated while they were alive and had died without reconciling with the church. They are the souls in purgatory whom the living "conjure up" ritually to tell their "name," the "cause" (of their apparition), and the "remedy" (that they need) (*nomen, causam, remedium*). This "remedy" is usually "absolution" by a priest. Clerics therefore also intervene, but essentially in their capacities as the final recipients of the apparition and as those qualified to say masses for the salvation of the dead.

In spite of these rather common traits, this collection of tales stands out from most of the contemporary *exempla* because of its fantastic character. Only the tales told by William of Newburgh two centuries earlier, in exactly the same region, Yorkshire, show similar traits regarding the modes of apparitions of ghosts and the means used by the living to rid themselves of the ghosts. In these tales it is never a question of "souls of purgatory" but of very corporeal "spirits" that rise out of their graves, spill out of the cemetery, and terrorize the villagers, who easily recognize them and attack them with equal violence. These "spirits" (*spiritus*) usually appear in a human form, but some are subject to surprising metamorphoses: one of them, a former "mercenary" from Rielvaux, appears in the form of a horse that rears up, then as a haystack with a light in its middle, and finally "in the shape of a man" who proposes that the living man carry his sack of beans (legumes that are traditionally associated with death) for him, but not beyond a waterfall, a sort of symbolic border that he refuses to cross.[58] Another dead man, who was excommunicated, appears to the tailor Snowball in the form of a crow flying as if it were going to die and shooting out sparks. Violently knocking into the man, it wounds him cruelly and makes him fall from his horse. The same spirit then reappears in the form of a dog that is wearing a chain around its neck but that is capable of speaking like a man to beg Snowball to ask suffrages of a priest for him. When he again appears, it is in the form of a goat that groans while saying "ah! ah! ah!"; it falls to the ground and then gets up in the form of a very tall man. Throughout the tale, two other spirits turn around Snowball. He does not see them but learns from the first spirit that one of them, his wife's murderer, looks like a steer without eyes or mouth or ears (he cannot communicate with the living and will therefore be neither exorcised nor saved), whereas the other, in the form of a hunter sounding his horn (which evokes the "Wild Hunt"), is a dead religious figure whom only a child who has not yet reached puberty (the privilege of virginity) would be able to conjure.[59]

Even when they come expressly to request suffrages, these spirits are purposely aggressive, dangerous, and feared. The wound that the crow inflicts on Snowball is a form of blackmail: the spirit will not reveal the magical means to heal it (by rubbing it with a certain sandstone that

Snowball would find under a flat rock in a waterfall) until Snowball brings him absolution from a priest. In Kilburn, the spirit of Robert, son of Robert of Boltebi, escapes from the cemetery at night, terrorizes the inhabitants, and makes dogs howl.[60] The spirit of the former curate of Kirkby, Jacques Tankerlay, returns one night to gouge out one of his ex-mistress's eyes.[61] In Ampleforth, an anonymous spirit follows William of Bradforth four nights in a row, crying out three times "how! how! how!"; his terrible voice resonates like an echo in the mountains, throwing William's horrified dog into the legs of its master.[62] Again in Ampleforth the spirit of the sister of Adam of Lond is the cause of "nocturnal fears and the terror of people of the village."[63] In Cleveland the spirit of a dead man who was excommunicated follows a man for twenty-four miles and, not able to have himself "conjured" by another witness, throws the living man over a hedge.[64]

Most of these dead are named. They are all men (with one exception), and all are laymen (with the exception of a curate and a canon). All the beneficiaries of the apparitions are also laymen, inhabitants of the same villages but rarely very close relatives. In a word, the system of natural or spiritual kinship, so important in the other collections of stories, here largely gives way to relationships of neighborhood and to a community of inhabitants.

Two tales nevertheless shed an original light on kinship relationships. During his pilgrimage to Santiago, Richard Rountre sees a troop of dead men, then notices a newborn baby that leaves the troop and rolls to his feet in a stocking. The little spirit explains to him that it is his aborted son and that the midwives buried it in one of its mother's stockings without baptizing the baby. The father clothes the child in his own shirt and gives the newborn a name while invoking the Holy Trinity. The baby immediately jumps up, full of joy from this recognition of kinship, a sort of wild emergency baptism taking the place of a postmortem baptism. The paternal gesture recalls the practice, widespread at that time, of "sanctuaries of grace" where babies who died before being baptized were brought in the hope that they could be resuscitated for just an instant, for just enough time to baptize them.[65]

The last tale illustrates another aspect of kinship: the conflict, in the figure of the wife, between marriage and kinship, between the lineage of the woman's husband and sons on the one hand and her own family heritage on the other. The sister of Adam of Lond (thus identified with reference to her patrilineage) gave her brother deeds belonging to her husband. When she dies, Adam evicts his brother-in-law and his nephews

145

from their property, "that is, a *toft* and *croft* with their dependencies in Ampleforth and a bit of land in Heslerton with its dependencies." But the dead woman appears to William Trower to beg him to ask Adam to give back the deeds and the land, or else she will not be able to "rest in peace until Judgment Day." Adam refuses. The following night, William "leads" the dead woman directly into Adam's room. Since Adam refuses to change his mind, his sister warns him that he will replace her in her torments when he dies. The story was told that Adam of Lond's son, most likely to shorten the trials of his father in the afterworld, ended up giving partial satisfaction to the legitimate heir.

Although tales always spoke of "spirits," those spirits had an extraordinary "corporeity." The woman who brings a spirit to her house on her back "digs her fingers deeply into the flesh of the spirit, as if the flesh of that same spirit were a putrid phantasm, and not solid."[66] When the tailor Snowball uses his sword to strike the spirit that assumed the form of a crow, he seems to hear the sound of a pillow being struck (under the same circumstances, a tale of Caesarius of Heisterbach mentions a similar noise). Those spirits were so concrete that the living could take hold of them (*comprehendere*), carry them, and fight with them. Young Robert Foxton manages to hold a spirit at the exit of the cemetery against the door of the church (*kirkestile*) until the curate, alerted by the other youths of the village (*juvenes*), arrives to conjure it.[67] Spirits spoke, but with the strange voices of ventriloquists: one spoke "from within its guts and not with its tongue, like in an empty jug."[68] Looking through the mouth of the spirit that is speaking to him, Snowball contemplates the "insides" of the spirit, which "forms its words in its intestines and does not speak with its tongue."[69]

All the witnesses sought to end the nocturnal returns of these spirits. The usual means was to obtain duly remunerated absolution from a priest: to deliver the spirit that appeared to him, Snowball pays five sous to have the spirit's excommunication lifted by the priest of York who first pronounced it. Absolution is written on a note, and Snowball strives not to "defame the bones" of the spirit, that is, not to reveal its name or the cause of its torments. He then has 180 masses lasting two or three days said for the dead man by all the religious Mendicants of the town. Finally, he returns to Ampleforth to bury the note of absolution in the grave. His goal is both, it would seem, to preserve the secret of this strange "confession" and to signify to the spirit that it is liberated from its punishment. During this time the spirit, "lying on its back," observes him without his knowledge. Nor does Snowball see the demons that torment the spirit all the more feverishly, since they know that their prey will soon escape them. The legitimacy of this procedure in three acts is confirmed by several canons and by a noble confessor, the brother Richard of Pickering. It was the same method that the clergy of the region, following the testimony of William of Newburgh, had extolled two centuries earlier. But we also see enduring until around 1400 a more expedient method, which was not exclusively that of the young villagers. It was, in fact, the abbot and the convent of Bellelande that ordered the exhumation from their cemetery of the body of the curate of Kirkby (who had returned to gouge out one of his ex-mistress's eyes), not to burn it (as in the tales of William of Newburgh) but to throw it, with its coffin, into the pond of Gormyre.

Thus the monk-scribe was indeed the interpreter of village tales. He sought neither to illustrate the spiritual affinities of a community of monks, nor to demonstrate to aristocratic lineages associated with the monastery the effectiveness of monastic suffrages for the dead, nor finally to impose on the faithful edifying and ready-made *exempla*. Rather he was writing a sort of ethnological work before its time, seduced by the *mirabilia* of his land, recording the beliefs and the practices in which the teachings of the church were inextricably mixed with traditions that easily recall the sagas of northern Europe.

A Breton Ghost

The last account we will look at here is too isolated to offer the value of proof. It nonetheless serves as an interesting possible comparison with the tales of the monk from Byland. It is an *exemplum* in French, taken from a collection of sermon manuscripts from the beginning of the fifteenth century.[70] The story takes place in Brittany. A baker who recently died returns at night to lend a strong hand to his wife and children by kneading the bread dough with them and by encouraging them to work. His family flees while the neighbors run over to see the "marvel." They chase the dead man away by making a lot of noise, but he soon returns and throws stones at them. Avoiding the paths, he arrives covered in mud up to his thighs, which adds even more to his terrifying appearance. The people ask if he is "a dead man or an evil spirit." They finally decide to open the grave, where they find the dead man "covered with mud up to his knees and his thighs, just as they had seen him go along the path." The first time they fill up the grave, but that is not enough to prevent the dead man from returning. They therefore decide to break his legs, which ends his wanderings.

As Hervé Martin, who discovered and published this unique text, writes, we are here far from the usual *exempla*, in which the souls in purgatory implore suffrages from those close to them. Here there is no question of masses, almsgiving, and prayers, or of purgatory, or of the slightest blessing. By acting physically on the cadaver, the villagers hope to fix the dead man in the grave. Everything occurs as if the ghost and the cadaver are one, as if the former brought into the grave the mud that soiled him. This ghost is an evil-minded dead man very similar to the ghosts of Yorkshire at the same time, and he endures an equally violent treatment at the hands of the local population. In both cases we can admit the persistence, in spite of the action of the church (it is a preacher who informs us of this tale), "of a very archaic belief in the survival of the double." We can also see in it the use, to distance the evil-minded dead, of ritual practices very different from those of the church: certain clerics disavowed them, but others, still in the fifteenth century, admired their "marvelous" character.

In the margins of the central core of western Christendom there coexisted beliefs and practices that the unification of ecclesiastical structures had not yet reached but that the "preaching machine" (of which the inquisitorial procedure was also an aspect) was in the process of absorbing. This is what we learn in part from such documents. Differences from the norms appeared in the absence of a dominant discourse, which gradually and in all places spread out. They came out of more ancient and tenacious cultural strata, some even earlier than Christianity. But for all that, they were not passive "remnants" of old paganisms. Centuries passed by, enabling a progressive and mutual impregnation of influences. In a very short time, witch trials would be unleashed, and already the inquisitors were worried. But in the fifteenth century, the "wildest" folkloric traditions remained tolerable, continuing to whet the curiosity of more than one cleric.

SEVEN

THE DEAD AND POWER

Three long tales stand out from all others due to their length, which reaches those of true small treatises, and to their form, which is that of long dialogues with a ghost, who is required to respond to a series of systematic questions. The questions and answers bear on the status of the dead person in particular and on the dead in general and their fate in the hereafter. These dialogues echo the great contemporary debates on those themes. In this regard they demonstrate an insertion of theological reflection into a narrative genre. Their interest lies in the diversity of the points of view expressed, over a long period of time, since these texts spread out from the beginning of the thirteenth century to the first half of the fifteenth century. Finally, the particular audience for these texts—which are offered to the emperor or to the pope—enables us to emphasize the political function of ghost tales. The first of these tales has already been analyzed among the *mirabilia* compiled by Gervase of Tilbury and intended for Emperor Otto IV of Brunswick at the beginning of the thirteenth century. Longer than the other ghost tales of this author, this one also has a different structure and destination; it represents an elementary form of the genre, one that is both narrative and didactic, as echoed by two other "tracts," toward which we now direct our attention.

The Spirit of Gui de Corvo

Around a century after Gervase of Tilbury, in 1324 or 1325, Johannes Gobi, prior of the Dominicans of Alès, presented to Pope John XXII, at court in Avignon, the account of an affair that was rather comparable to the story of the ghost of Beaucaire. He himself had just been implicated in the affair. Indeed, between December 27 (the feast day of Saint John the Baptist) and the Epiphany of the same year, he himself led the questioning of the spirit of Gui de Corvo, a citizen of Alès who had died the preceding December 16. Since that time the invisible spirit had haunted the bedroom of his widow. Writing for the pope, Johannes Gobi drafted a short version of the event; he spoke in the first person and explained how he questioned the "invisible voice" of the spirit and gathered the ghost's answers.[1] Some ten years later his tale was developed into a long version in which the prior is named in the third person. Johannes Gobi is not necessarily the author of this second version, which might have been reworked by another Dominican. Encountering enormous success, this version was translated from the Latin into many European vernacular languages and was even embellished at least once with illustrations. It is even possible, as the conclusion of the long version explicitly suggests, that this amplified text appeared in 1334 within the context of the Avignon debates on beatific vision.[2]

Johannes Gobi questions the spirit on three occasions. During the night of December 27 he asks an initial series of thirty questions, to which the spirit is compelled immediately to respond. The second interrogation takes place on the eve of the Epiphany, but it is shorter, since this time Johannes Gobi fails to beseech the spirit to obey him: after eight questions, the spirit slips away into a current of air. They meet again one last time the next day. This time their roles seem reversed, and the spirit, revived, denounces the evil preachers and the dissolute lives of couples (is this an admission of his own sins?) and requests three hundred masses for himself and for his wife. Subsequently, since the spirit no longer manifests himself, Johannes Gobi assumes that he must have left purgatory and, at Easter, been admitted into heaven.

The conjuration ritual carried out by the prior includes some extravagant precautions. Forewarned by the widow, when Johannes Gobi goes to the premises, he is accompanied by a master in theology, a lector in philosophy from the convent, and a notary to draw up an official report. Ordered by the mayor of the city, an escort of two hundred armed men accompany him and guard all points of access to the house (the men are spread out three-by-three in honor of the Trinity). Each man is required to give his confession, the prior says a requiem mass, then all parts of the house are sprinkled with holy water. At midnight the sound of a broom is heard, and the horrified widow recognizes the arrival of the invisible spirit of her husband. On the advice of the prior, she asks him to admit who he is. That done, Johannes Gobi begins speaking to force the spirit to submit to the prior's will and respond to all his questions.

Some of the questions aim only to verify that the ghost is a "good" spirit: it must recognize, for example, that the prior is carrying the body of Christ hidden on his person (an evil spirit would have struggled not to respond). The most original questions bear on the places of the hereafter. For the spirit, purgatory is double *(duplex est purgatorium)*: it endures alternately as common purgatory, during the day, in the center of the earth, and as individual purgatory, at night, in the earthly place where he once sinned, that is, his own bedroom. In the end the church did not retain such a dual concept of purgatory, but the notion was not foreign to the Dominican scholasticism of Albert the Great and of the *Supplement* that the pupils of Thomas Aquinas added to the *Summa theologica* of their master.[3] A Dominican himself, Johannes Gobi could not have been unaware of that current. Whatever the case may have been, compared with the assertions of the ghost of Beaucaire a century earlier, those of the spirit of the citizen of Alès are much more consistent with the eminently more settled teachings of the church: the system of three principal places (hell, purgatory, and heaven) was well recognized.

The spirit's other answers also support henceforth well-established ideas: the corporeal fire that incorporeal beings endure in purgatory, the usefulness of suffrages for the dead, the assistance of angels. Obviously, the text composed by Johannes Gobi and enlarged later was not only the tale of a wondrous occurrence. It was above all a doctrinal argument, a demonstration presented in the unexpected form of a dialogue with the spirit of a dead man, a sort of theological *disputatio* on the hereafter, on the remission of punishment, and on salvation.

The goal of the opuscule was thus not exactly the same as that of the long "marvelous" tale by Gervase of Tilbury. Gervase was undoubtedly more fascinated by wonders and by the prophetic and political value of the revelations of the dead person. But similarities are noticeable if we consider the two principal protagonists: the eleven-year-old girl and the widow. The woman—who, on December 27, goes with her women friends and neighbors to the prior of the preachers of Alès to request his help—is a widow shaken up by the very recent death of her husband and by her strong feeling of guilt following a sin committed with him, in the conjugal bed where the spirit now comes to terrify her every night. The text does not reveal the nature of the sin, which was protected by the secrecy of confession but which certainly involved the sexual behavior of the couple, unless it was a matter of an infanticide. The couple admitted their sin in penance, but neither the husband, before his death, nor the wife expiated it. The obsessive nocturnal returns even have psychosomatic effects on the widow: when she senses that the spirit is passing right next to her, she screams and falls down in a faint. She is truly possessed, not by the devil but by the spirit of her dead husband, a phantasm of her own remorse. By conjuring the spirit, the Dominican is therefore exorcising the wife. This is represented marvelously in a miniature attributed to Simon Marmion in a manuscript of the French version of the dialogue (illus. 9).[4] Forming a circle in the bedroom around the place where the spirit is believed to stand, the widow and the other witnesses stare at the empty center of the room, at the place where the invisible spirit is supposed to be. In the background, someone is leaning to the side in an attempt to see the ghost, but there is nothing to see! Only the Dominican is not looking at this central spot: his eyes are focused on the face of the wife, indicating well the true place of the obsession. The conjuration and the masses free the spirit, who thus gains purgatory. But when Johannes Gobi, to conclude, implores the widow henceforth to lead a holy life, she is the one whom he wants above all to free from the weight of her sin and from her feeling of guilt.

The Grandfather of Arndt Buschmann

A century later we find another opuscule some forty pages long written in Middle German.[5] It tells, in great detail, of the repeated apparitions of a dead man, Heinrich, to his grandson Arndt between November 11, 1437, and Ascension Day, 1438. Arndt Buschmann himself is believed to have written this text, following the ghost's orders, after entering the order of the Premonstratensians and learning to write. In 1450 Arndt was to have presented his account to Pope Nicholas V during a jubilee pilgrimage to Rome. However, even though there is no reason to doubt that a Rhenish peasant was the author of this text, it is likely that he did not write it or, at least, that he did not write it alone. Moreover, a Latin version of the text, attributed to the Dominican John of Essen (1444), soon came into circulation. Another indication is the use, throughout the German version, of the third person, with three exceptions.[6] The hand of a cleric was most probably behind this peasant, who presents himself as illiterate[7] and who mentions many contacts with priests (the curate of his parish of Meiderich, a priest in Cologne). We must also point out obvious influences from other tales of visions, beginning with the *Dispute* between Johannes Gobi and the spirit of Gui de Corvo, the text of which had been available in Latin and also in German for a century. Several of the questions that Arndt asks the spirit of his grandfather seem to come directly from the earlier text. How can the spirit speak, since he does not have a corporeal tongue? Why was that spirit, rather than another one, granted permission to appear? Why is Arndt, rather than someone else, the beneficiary of the apparition? In which order of society is it better to live to escape the punishments of the hereafter?[8] Johannes Gobi had already asked similar questions of the invisible ghost of Alès.

What we know about autobiographical tales of apparitions also induces us to be cautious: all those we have seen so far involve a dream. Here, on the contrary, Arndt is always awake when he sees his dead grandfather. The first time he even sees his grandfather in the form of a dog, following a type of apparition also witnessed in one of the tales of the monk of Byland. And in this latter case the tale emanates from an oral tradition culled by the monk in the neighboring villages, certainly not from the personal experience of the scribe.

For twenty-six weeks, Heinrich Buschmann, who died forty years earlier (this delay between death and the time of the apparition is unusually long), appears fourteen times to his grandson. These apparitions can be divided into two periods. In the first, up until around the tenth apparition at the end of the winter, Arndt attempts to find the means to conjure the spirit of Heinrich and, in order to hasten his liberation from purgatory (*vegevur*), to have him admit the sins that were the reason for his punishment. Then the dialogue between the living man and the dead man can have free rein until Heinrich's definitive liberation.

At the time of the second apparition, on December 5 (the feast day of Saint Benedict), Arndt conjures the dead man following the counsel of a priest, John of Dinslaken. Heinrich trades the form of a dog for that of a tall, old man dressed in gray. To relieve the dead man, Arndt undertakes two trips in a row to Cologne, where he has thirty masses said for his grandfather's salvation. He also goes on a pilgrimage to Aix-la-Chapelle accompanied by the brother of the curate of his village. In all his travels, he comes up against the traps of an evil spirit who attempts to prevent the liberation of the dead man. On the contrary, a good spirit, who appears to Arndt in the guise of a man dressed all in white, spares him no amount of aid. For example, this spirit enables him to recover money that was stolen from him and that he had intended to use to have masses said for his grandfather. In the meantime, seeing him without resources, the dean John agrees to say five masses for the price of four!

After the eleventh apparition, the dialogue with the dead man becomes increasingly more concise. It bears either on the status of souls in purgatory in general (on the effectiveness of suffrages for the dead, the relationships between the body and the spirit, the most condemnable sins, the confession of sins and salvation) or on the particular fate of Heinrich and other dead people named by Arndt or even on the future of Arndt himself. Then Heinrich explains why he is appearing only now to his grandson: he had bequeathed to his son Bernt, Arndt's father, a sum of money that was supposed to have been devoted to his salvation. But Bernt died too soon to be able to ensure Heinrich's liberation. Moreover, Heinrich's other children, induced by an evil spirit, had diverted the entire inheritance, thereby neglecting his salvation. Heinrich thus had to wait to be able to speak to his grandson.

Heinrich also explains that greed is the primary reason for his present punishments. Through greed, he opposed his son's marriage to a girl without means (and he was proven wrong, since the girl's father subsequently became rich). He also diverted for his own profit the charitable bequest of a dying man. Being young and poor to the point of considering emigrating and fearing he would have to beg, he did not hesitate to work on Sunday. He lived in debauchery between the age of twenty and his marriage at thirty years old, and this is why he first appeared in the form of a dog. Until his death at the age of eighty-eight, he neglected to kneel before the Blessed Sacrament.

Arndt obtains information concerning the fate of several other dead people, some in purgatory, such as his other grandfather, and some in hell. One of Heinrich's nieces is in purgatory, even though she indulged in sorcery (wichgelien). She invoked the "white ladies or holy Holde," who live underground in wild places and who, on Thursday nights, visit houses that are cleaned in their honor and where a meal has been prepared for them. She said and did this with the curate's blessing, and both of them, in Heinrich's opinion, did so in good faith but were misled by evil spirits; this is why they were admitted into purgatory and did not go to hell. The Holde were in fact demons who used the gullibility of simple folk, whose children they killed if these folk resisted them. One might be tempted to see in this surprising document written in the vernacular a firsthand account of folkloric beliefs at the end of the Middle Ages. One must, however, again be cautious, since the influence of scholarly demonology is so obvious: under the name of Holde are easily found the traditional denunciations issued from the Canon Episcopi (tenth century) and the echoes of scholastic literature on sorcery (notably, regarding children, of De universo by William of Auvergne).

Finally Arndt questions the dead man about his own fate and about the future. To what place in the hereafter will he go when he dies? Will his punishment be lessened because he took care of Heinrich's salvation? Will he be able to play the viol without committing a sin? Must he take holy orders to ensure his salvation? The dead man demonstrates tolerance and realism: it is not one's condition that saves, but personal merits, and it is not through music that one is damned, if one plays with good intentions. How long will the world exist? When will the Antichrist be born? This time the dead man admits his inability to answer questions that are among the secrets of God.

Throughout these conversations, from one apparition to the next, the dead man's condition gradually improves. Between two apparitions he is even allowed to appear before the face of the Lord, and he returns from that radiating a light so intense that Arndt loses sight in one eye. After the definitive disappearance of the dead man, who is henceforth saved and who orders Arndt to publish the revelations, the grandson fully recovers his sight. The tale ends with the citation of witnesses who, in the village of Meiderich, can confirm the facts: the members of the Buschmann family, servants, and the brother of the curate who accompanied Arndt to Aix-la-Chapelle.

The Discernment of Spirits

The two long tales in dialogue form that we have just summed up share more than one point in common, points they also share with the long tale of the ghost of Beaucaire as told by Gervase of Tilbury: the length of the text, the repetition of the apparitions for a fairly lengthy time (as long as six months in the last case), the both narrative and didactic form of the document, and the author's involvement in the unfolding of the facts, either as a visionary, as an exorcist, or as a scribe taking dictation from one of his witnesses. In all three cases, a true local fact likely existed in the background. This consisted, at least in the first two cases, of the traumatism brought on by the abrupt loss of someone dear and, in all the cases, of the rumor that swirled around a fact that was perhaps minor but that enabled an entire community—the parish of Meiderich, the towns of Beaucaire or Alès—to take hold of the event. What was important, from then on, was putting the story down in writing, which necessarily demanded clerical mediation and an inevitable bending of the form and the meaning of the text: the dead person, representative of the afterworld, became the spokesperson of the moral law. To the apparition's witness, who would be the first to transmit the message, the dead person recommended maintaining respect for Christian morality (for example, respect for Sunday rest) and carrying out pious works. Among these three accounts, over two centuries, it is not surprising that the questions and the answers were blended and in some instances were even reproduced almost identically. Indeed, as much as in the *exempla*, ghosts became the instruments of an ecclesiastical policy of moral and religious indoctrination, which here found its narrative outlet but which was also supported by an entire theoretical literature in full bloom.

The central concept of that literature was *discretio spiritum*, the discernment of spirits, an idea that derived its justification from one of the charismas listed by Saint Paul (1 Cor. 12:10) but that historically experienced increasing success between the end of the fourteenth century and the seventeenth century, in the great era of sorcery and demonology. Among the first important works, several came from imperial lands, in particular from the University of Vienna, where Henry of Langenstein (or of Hesse), who wrote *De discretione spiritum* and who died in 1397, once taught. The comparable works of Nicolas of Dinkelsbuhl and Henry of Friemar were also extremely influential.[9] The Council of Constance of 1415 resulted in new controversies evoked by the revelations of Bridget of Sweden. On this occasion Jean Gerson, representing the University of Paris, wrote his *De probatione spiritum*, which followed his *De distinctione verarum visionum a falsis* (1401).[10] In it he demonstrates a traditional distrust of dreams as much as of the revelations of women. Since there were strong similarities between the manifestations of different sorts of spirits, both good and evil, he draws up a list of the virtues that good visionaries should demonstrate: thus *discretio*, that is, moderation, in eating incites one to beware of the so-called visionaries who glorify themselves for not eating at all.[11] More generally, cases of visions and apparitions needed to be submitted to a rigorous—typically scholastic—grilling of six questions: *Quis? Quid? Quare? Cui? Qualiter? Unde?* For the rank of people, the status of a priest, university positions, and, likewise, the written and duly authenticated accounts of revelations, counted among the best guarantees of the truth of those tales.

Another treatise concerns ghosts more directly: *Tractatus de animabus exutis a corporibus* by James of Juterborg or of Paradise, who taught at the University of Cracrow, became abbot of the Cistercian abbey of Paradise, and died in Erfurt in 1465. This treatise is sometimes associated in ancient editions with Johannes Gobi's opuscule on the revelations of the spirit of Gui de Corvo.[12] From the outset the author notes that the souls of the dead do not always manifest themselves visibly but reveal themselves by throwing stones and pots that break and by overturning stools, to the terror of people who soon flee their houses. "Bumps, throwing, whistling, sneezing, groaning, cries, wailing, clapping" manifest the invisible presence of the soul that the living will have to question. The author takes up his pen to reassure the faithful, to invite them to aid the souls of the dead, and to incite them to do penance themselves. His treatise demonstrates, from beginning to end, a perfect integration of ghosts into the official religious system of the time. James of Paradise even stresses that apparitions of the dead characterize Christianity exclusively: among the Saracens and the Jews, only demons appear. Thus purgatory was an invention of the Latin Church. The concrete procedures through which one enters into contact with the souls of the dead in particular captured the author's attention. Words do not mislead: he speaks of "the experimentation," the "ceremony," and the "questioning" to which souls must be subjected. He admits to marginally deriving his models from the Scriptures but more from the tradition of the church, from *miracula*, and from *exempla*. Many citations indeed run through his treatise, where Gregory the Great resides alongside the scholastics (Thomas Aquinas, Peter of Tarentaise) and Aristotle's *Ethics*. The ritual he describes recalls to the smallest detail the one that Johannes Gobi says he used in Alès: four or five priests, having confessed and having said their mass, go to the place where the spirit habitually appears. They first assure themselves that "all superstitious inquiry ceases": any uncontrolled act that might recall ancient necromancy must disappear, to be replaced by an ecclesiastical ceremony that resembled necromancy greatly but that alone was legitimate. The word "exorcism" is not used: that rite and the official role of the exorcist did not yet have the identity they would later acquire.[13] A candle that was blessed at the time of the preceding feast of the purification (Candlemas) is brought, holy water is sprinkled, and the sign of the cross is made; the censer is swung while "the seven psalms or the gospel of John" is sung. "The stole does not seem useless," specifies James of Paradise. Didn't the ghost of Beaucaire call it "the bond of the devil"? There then follows a humble prayer intended to implore God to enable the spirit to reveal, without wronging those present, "who he is, why he has come and what he wants," that is, with very few differences, to answer the questions asked of the ghosts of Byland: *Nomen? Causam? Remedium?* After the prayer is the conjuration, whose formulary the author gives.

> We immediately beg you through Jesus Christ, you spirit, to say who you are, and if there is one among us to whom you wish to respond, to name him or point him out with a sign: "Is it this one, N.?" "Or perhaps that one, N.?" And so forth, while naming everyone else present, for it is understood that he will not respond to each one of them. If a voice or a noise is heard when someone is named, it is that person who is to question him, by asking him of which man he is the soul, why he has come, what he wants, if he wishes suffrages, either in masses or in alms. And how many masses? Six, ten, twenty, thirty, one hundred? Said by which priests? Regulars or seculars? Or in fasting; what kind? How much? By whom? As for almsgiving, to the profit of whom should they be given? In hospices or in leprosaria? Or to other beggars and poor? And what sign will he give of his liberation?

The author notes, however, that such an ecclesiastical ceremony is not always necessary for the revelations of the souls of the deceased. Within the domestic and familial framework there was a place for a direct manifestation "of the dead husband to his wife, or vice versa, of the father to his son, or vice versa, of the mother to her daughter, or vice versa, of the brother to the brother, etc." He therefore emphasizes the importance of kinship relationships, which we have already seen in tales of all sorts. Yet, wherever all ecclesiastical guarantees were not gathered together, it was necessary to call on other criteria to ensure the "truth" of the apparition. Supported by scriptural examples (the Annunciation, the dreams of Daniel), in the case of the visit of a good spirit, the fear that struck the witness did not last long. The formal connection between the appearance and the being (between *species* and *res*) was also a good sign: a good dead person kept his or her voice and appearance as a person, whereas an evil spirit readily changed into a lion, a bear, a frog, a snake, a black cat, a dog, or a black shadow. Only a white dove was positive. Finally, the words and gestures of a spirit were signs that did not lie: if they contravened faith and morality, one was dealing with an evil spirit.

In all the procedures, the maniacal concern with detail enabled the clerics to become masters of the supernatural and to reduce the ambivalence of its meanings. The results allow us to measure the path traveled since Saint Augustine. It was no longer a matter of denying the possibility that the dead visited the living: even though our authors admitted the rarity of visible apparitions, they ended up giving the revelations of the dead not only the guarantee of the Scriptures and of the later narrative and doctrinal tradition but also that of the entire ecclesiastical apparatus. Purgatory, indulgences, and series of masses were an integral part of the economic machine that supported the church at the end of the Middle Ages. Ghosts were one of the cogs in that machine. Clerics were no longer content simply to record and reproduce the tales they gathered; as licensed necromancers (they did not use that name), they solicited the revelations of the dead, with a concern for an integrated management of souls on earth and in the hereafter and for their own benefit, the material and spiritual aspects of which were always closely connected. They did not do this without anguish, however, for the signals were never completely certain, and the enemy was lying in wait for a sign of the slightest weakness. The obsession with the demoniacal and with sorcery, which would characterize the beginnings of modern time, was already apparent everywhere.

The Powerful and the Dead

The long dialogues that we have been discussing not only displayed a common form and theme but also were intended or even offered to a pope or an emperor. Thus they can be included in another series, one that we have already seen several times: that of the revelations of the dead concerning a ruler, whether as the beneficiary,[14] the deceased, or the one for whom the vision was intended.

The tradition for this is very old. We can find it as far back as the evocation of Samuel by the medium of Endor at the request of King Saul. During the early Middle Ages the great "political" visions of the hereafter increased in number; they were based on the model of *Visio Wettini*, which was attributed to the monk Heito of Reichenau (824) and which described the torments that Charlemagne endured beyond the grave. Shortly afterward, *Visio Rotcharii* revealed, on the contrary, that the emperor was henceforth saved. The same type of visions flourished again in the Ottonian era.[15] At the end of the Middle Ages, rulers paid more attention to prophetic literature and to the "revelations" of the mystic visionaries such as Bridget of Sweden (1373) and Catherine of Siena (1380).[16] In the meantime we must also mention the millenarian legends relating to the "hidden king" whose death was put in doubt and to the "Emperor of the Last Days," whose salutary return or reincarnation in a new ruler was ardently expected. Thus, with the sudden death of Emperor Frederick Barbarossa during the Third Crusade of 1190, prophecies began to circulate. And when Frederick II became emperor thirty years later, the Joachite milieu and the Imperial party, who were hostile to the Roman pontiff, saw him as the "Emperor of the Last Days," who was going to chastise the corrupt church and bring about the kingdom of the spirit.[17]

Usually, tales of apparitions of dead kings neither presented such depth nor had such repercussions. In their narrative structure and content, they are scarcely distinguishable from tales of the ordinary dead: we have seen this in the "great miracle" reported in the last third of the eleventh century by the *Chronicle of Iria*, in Galicia, on the subject of the apparition of the dead king Sancho to his widow, Queen Godo. The strictly royal nature of such tales is found later and in other locations: in the kingdom of the Capetians, in that of the Plantagenets, and wherever monarchic power and ideology enjoyed the most significant progress. Shortly after the death of the king of France, Philip Augustus (1223), the *Visiones Philippi* was circulated; this work assured the people that the king, benefiting from the protection of Saint Denis, patron of the dynasty and of the royal necropolis, had gone to heaven. At the exact hour that the king had died, another dying man—very far away, in Italy—was said to have benefited from the apparition of Saint Denis accompanied by the king, dressed in white and preceded by angels. This tale, immediately transmitted by the chroniclers (Guillaume le Breton, Philippe Mouskés) and the preachers connected to the dynasty, originated in the abbey of Saint Denis and in the immediate entourage of the king.[18] The Dominican Stephen of Bourbon obtained a version of it directly from the dead king's sister, Sibyl of Beaujeu. In this *exemplum* the Dominican insists on the words of Saint Denis: the king was saved because while he was alive, he always "honored the saints and their feast days, honored and took under his care churches and holy places, and protected religious people."[19] An entire political program and a hagiographical sketch are contained in this short tale! If one believes the king's sister (or the Dominican), Philip was such a perfect king that it was scarcely necessary to pray for his soul: the king very nearly became a saint, an ideal that his grandson, Saint Louis, would attain.

Indeed, Louis appeared in a dream of his faithful companion Joinville, even though the king was already dead (since 1270) and canonized (in 1298). The oneirical apparition and the autobiographical tale of it that Joinville leaves behind, the *Book* that celebrates the memory of their friendship, the relics that Joinville cannot bear to be deprived of, and the statue that he promises to erect by himself are so many "places of memory" established for the glory of the holy king.

Some tales fulfilled even more explicit political and dynastic functions. The ghost tale then acquired an efficacy that, in at least two cases, was beyond any doubt. When, in the spring of 1142, Peter the Venerable encountered King Alfonso VII in Salamanca, he was able to relate a ghost's revelations regarding the dead grandfather of the king, King Alfonso VI of Leon-Castilla. Since that king had been freed from his torments in the afterworld thanks to the prayers of the Cluniac monks, the abbot was able to demand that the current king pay his debts to the abbey. An agreement along those lines was in fact concluded on July 29 of the same year. In Alsace the apparition of the dead count Conrad of Staufen to his vassal Walter had an analogous function and efficacy. The dead man asks his messenger to request of his brothers the duke Frederick of Buren and the bishop Otto of Strasbourg to give a generous donation to the church of Saint Foi. A deed of donation dated July 23, 1095, proves that his mission was successful. This long tale is associated, moreover, with a dynastic prophecy by announcing that the descendants of the duke would be kings and emperors; this prediction came true in 1138 (with the advent of Conrad III) and in 1152 and 1155 (when Frederick III of Swabia in turn became king and then emperor under the name of Frederick I).

In still other cases, ghost tales that were intended for rulers had the function of a "Mirror of the Prince." Wasn't the legend of Hellequin's hunt, so prized at the English court, supposed to suggest to the king that he reform his government? The chronicle of the abbey of Peterborough established an explicit link between the apparition of the fantastic troop and the unfortunate naming by the king of a corrupt abbot in 1127. At the court of the Plantagenets, the evocation of Hellequin's hunt traditionally served the ends of political satire: in 1175 the king's adviser, Peter of Blois, compared the perverted *curiales* to the "knights of Herlevinus." For his part, Walter Map saw in the leader of Hellequin's hunt a legendary king of the "very ancient Britons," Herla, and he noted that the apparitions of the troop of the dead had ceased since the first year of the reign of Henry II Plantagenet in 1155. For Map, the court of England was substituted for the ancient army of the dead, and a curse weighed on the court, a curse that the king could avoid only by reforming his own *familia*.

These tales that, in various capacities, put revelations of ghosts in the service of monarchic power resemble and at the same time differ from the three tales by Gervase of Tilbury, Johannes Gobi, and Arndt Buschmann. All three of these, in one way or another, were addressed to rulers. Gervase of Tilbury in 1214–1215 not only dedicated his *Otia imperialia* to Emperor Otto IV of Brunswick but also claimed to have addressed to the emperor a particular and secret report on the apparition of the ghost of Beaucaire: "I am sending to you by a faithful messenger, in secret enclosure, that by which, *serenissime* Prince, you will give satisfaction to God and that in which you displease Him, as I have heard from his mouth [of the ghost], so that you will rejoice in this good disposition and that the bad [disposition] will make you undertake a meditation of penance and that by setting yourself to progress in the good, you will hasten to avoid evil or to remedy it."[20] The duty of penance for a conquered emperor, exiled in his distant domain of Brunswick and sensing the approach of death (he died in 1218), does not have just one individual dimension. The insistent allusions to the Albigensian Crusade, which had just been completed and to which the ghost referred when he said that God approved the massacre of the heretics, and likewise the rest of the text, which explains how the count Raymond V of Toulouse was excommunicated for having committed a sacrilege,[21] show that such a tale sought to appeal to the emperor so that he would be concerned with Christian reform.

It was not to the king or to the emperor but to the pope that Johannes Gobi and Arndt Buschmann both addressed versions of their long tales of apparitions. In 1325, before the consistory gathered in Avignon, the Dominican read a brief account of his dialogue with the ghost of Alès. Only two manuscripts have preserved this shorter version of the *Dialogue*, whereas the later long version was much more widely distributed. It likely appeared ten years later alongside the quarrel about beatific vision, in which Pope John XXII was implicated. As for the peasant Arndt Buschmann, who in 1437–1438 received the revelations of his dead grandfather Heinrich, he acted on the orders of Heinrich when he joined the Premonstratensian Order and wrote down the tale of his visions before offering his opuscule to Pope Nicholas V in 1450 in Rome. These three long revelations thus join the genre, characteristic of the end of the Middle Ages, of prophetic accounts addressed to the pope or to rulers to encourage their efforts in the moral and political *reformatio* of their kingdom and of Christianity. In this regard one might add still other ghost tales in which recourse to allegory is typical of the political literature of that period. This is the case in *Epître lamentable et consolatoire*, of 1396, addressed to the king of England, Richard II, by "an old solitary man of the Celestines of Paris," who was none other than Philippe de Mézières. Richard had just married Isabella, the eldest daughter of the king of France, Charles VI, and the army of the Crusades had been crushed by the Turks in Nicopolis. Philippe de Mézières turned to Richard II to implore him to put an end to the war with France and to the Great Schism—an appeal Philippe had already made in vain in 1389 in his major work, *Le Songe du vieil pèlerin*. This time as well, *Epître* ends with a vision: one of the stricken crusaders, Jean de Blézy, appears to the author. The crusader is in the dress of a pilgrim, covered with blood, with a large wound on his left side, and he reveals to the "old solitary man" that on the eve of the battle, the camp of the king of Hungary was visited by a mysterious lady, Discipline de Chevalerie, "the mother of victories," followed by the figure of a dog (a hunting dog lying down), an allegory of *Obedience double*. But almost immediately a hurricane disfigured the lady, an annunciatory sign of the disaster that the Christians would meet the next day. Before disappearing, the knight, a true "living" dead person, requests aid for all the "Christian prisoners, in this world and in the other."[22]

Since the twelfth century (with *Policraticus*, by John of Salisbury, the first work of the genre), the political thought of the Middle Ages was expressed in theoretical works that assumed, depending on the case, a more or less didactical or philosophical character. We see this especially after the thirteenth century when the scholastic theoreticians—Thomas Aquinas, Giles of Rome—began to draw inspiration from Aristotle's *Politics*. But "politics" in the Middle Ages was something else again: it was not conceived without manipulating the emblems and rituals that marked the sacred nature of power and of the sovereign and without paying attention to revelations from the other world, which confirmed the king in his authority and predicted his destiny (following the ambiguous model of Saul appealing to the medium of Endor). Alongside the tutelary saints with which each dynasty surrounded itself, alongside angels, or alongside Christ, who appeared on the battlefield, ghosts had their role to play in this medieval manner of conceiving politics. This is also seen at the beginning of the fourteenth century in *Le Roman de Fauvel*, in which the king of the dead, Hellequin, leads a diabolical charivari that could well have been intended for the king of France.

The Charivari of Fauvel

The first mention of the ritual of the charivari, which is also the first precise description of it, is found in a literary work from the end of the Middle Ages, *Le Roman de Fauvel.* This novel in verse form (3,280 flat octo-syllabic verses in two books) was written between 1310 and 1314 by Gervais du Bus, a notary at the royal chancery. One of the preserved manuscripts (B.N., MS fr. 146) in addition includes some interpolations that were added in 1316 and that are believed to have been written by a certain Chaillou de Pesstain or Raoul Chaillou, a bailiff in various prov-inces and then an investigator of the reform—an official connected, as was Gervais du Bus, to the court of the king. The description of the chari-vari is contained in the longest of these interpolations of 1316. This pas-sage is all the more significant in that the description in verse is illustrated with four color drawings (illus. 11 to 14) and is accompanied by "silly songs," along with musical notations, whose lyrics have double meanings with an obscene content. Also included is the *lai des Hellequines,* which belongs instead to courtly lyrics:

> En ce dous temps d'esté, tout droit ou mois de may
> Qu'amours met par pensé maint cuer en grant esmay
> Firent les Herlequines ce descor dous et gay.

> [In this mild time of summer, right in the month of May,
> when the thought of love brings dismay to many a heart,
> the Erlking's ladies composed this sweet and gay descort.][23]

All of this, then, composes a sort of "complete" document, simultane-ously textual, musical, and illustrated. Furthermore, the strictly ritual di-mension doubles as a "mythical" dimension, since the din of the *chalivali* is compared by the poet to the wild irruption of Hellequin's hunt. The leader of the dead is represented in two of the drawings as a giant wearing the wings of birds facing forward on his head and leading, on foot or on horseback, the parade of masks.

The eponymous hero of the novel, Fauvel, is an allegorical horse whose name is derived from the initials of the French words for six vices: *Flatterie* [Flattery], *Avarice* [Greed], *Vilenie* [Pettiness], *Variété* [Vacillation], *Envie* [Envy], *Lâcheté* [Sloth]. Fauvel is held responsible for having *bestourné* the order of the world and of the kingdom: it is the theme of the world turned upside down. The disorder is primarily political, since the hero is *torché*, that is, flattered, and is followed in his madness by the king, the pope, and the nobles. In the second book Fauvel, installed in his palace, decides to marry Fortune, who declines his advances and throws him into the arms of Vainglory. From this union, placed under such bad signs, countless "new *fauveaus*" are born who dishonor the most beautiful land in the world. But that land, hopes the author, will finally be saved by the "lily of virginity." The interpolation that interests us comes at the time of the marriage *à main senestre* [left-handed, maladroit] of Fauvel and Vainglory: scarcely have the newlyweds retired to their bedroom when there bursts forth the most incredible charivari that has ever been seen "par les quarrefours/De la ville par mi les rues":

> Onc chalivali si parfaiz
> Par desguiser, par diz, par faiz,
> Ne fu com cil en toutes choses.

> [In disguises, words, and deeds,
> In every way, no charivari had ever been
> so perfect as this one.]

[translation from Rosenberg and Tischler, *The Monophonic Songs in the Roman de Fauvel*]

The description and the illustrations that are interspersed between the lines particularly emphasize disguises and masks: some of those who contest Fauvel's marriage have turned their clothes *devant derrière* [backward] or have dressed themselves in a sack or a monk's habit. Pretending to be drunk, they create a din with kitchen utensils that they strike against each other (pans, hooks, grills, copper pots, tubs). Others, who have sewn cow udders on themselves, ring bells or play other percussion instruments: drums, cymbals, rattles. A cart also arrives on which is mounted an *engin de roes de charetes* [wheeled cart] whose spokes knock together while turning against six iron rods, making a noise of thunder. Other men are wearing *barboeres*, that is, they are masked like "savages." Indeed the images reveal, within an urban framework in which spectators are at their windows, the irruption of bestial or diabolical masks, and certain characters are disguised as women. The text specifies this: they shout, make obscene gestures ("Li un moutret son cul au vent" [one of them shows his bare ass]), break doors and windows, and throw salt or manure. Then, on two points, the ritual takes on an explicitly funeral connotation:

Avec eus portoient deux bieres,
Où il avoit gent trop avable
Pour chanter la chançon au deable.

[They carry two coffins with them,
In which there were those too capable
Of singing a song to the devil.]
[my translation]

Indeed the image shows Hellequin on horseback and four figures in front of him carrying two "coffins" containing the heads of men and women set into niches recalling reliquaries. The viewer of the image may, understandably, think of heads of the dead and more specifically of the damned ("capable of singing a song to the devil"), especially since one of the heads is black and displays a macabre row of teeth.[24]

Right after them comes the leader of the troop of the dead:

Il y ravoit un grand jaiant
Qui aloit trop forment braiant;
Vestu ert de son broissequin (= d'un drap);
Je croi que c'estoit Hellequin,
Et tuit li autre sa mesnie,
Qui le suivent toute enragie.

[There was a huge giant
Who came in screaming;
He was wearing his sheet;
I believe it was Hellequin
And all the rest of his hunt,
Who followed him in a great fury.]
[my translation]

The description that follows insists on the skinniness of his *roncin* [nag], which implies that this fantastic, ghostlike knight is coming home from exile:

Aussi com si venist d'essil

[As if he were coming back from exile]

But the poet concludes that the vigor of the charivari was not enough to turn Fauvel away from carrying out his matrimonial plans and from "honoring his wife." We must remember, moreover, that charivaris did not really aim so much to prevent contested marriages as to seize, for the benefit of a group of youths, the opportunity to finish up the night in a tavern.

Indeed this justly famous passage has for a long time enabled historians and folklorists to wonder about the origins and functions of the charivari ritual, especially when—particularly well noted in France from the end of the Middle Ages—it protested an ill-matched union. This above all involved cases in which a widower remarried a young girl, who was then taken from the "pool" of potential wives from which the young men of the same village or neighboring villages might have made a claim.[25]

However, a specialist in medieval literature, Nancy F. Regalado, has pointed out that the specific nature of the literary document must be taken into account.[26] Disagreeing with the preceding interpretations, she denies the possibility of a direct ethnological reading of *Fauvel.* Moreover, refuting the hypotheses of Carlo Ginzburg,[27] she notes that this description of the charivari is the only one that makes explicit reference to Hellequin. Since the first account at the beginning of the twelfth century (that of Orderic Vitalis), the motif of Hellequin's hunt became a literary theme that aimed to provoke laughter rather than fear. We see this, among other places, in the thirteenth-century *Jeu de la feuillée* by Adam de la Halle, in which Crokesos, the envoy of the "king Hellekin," irrupts onto the scene in a noise of bells.[28] The culminating point of this evolution was in the *commedia dell'arte* with the association of Hellequin and Harlequin. Under these conditions it is risky to see in the interpolation of *Fauvel,* as Carlo Ginzburg proposes, the confluence between a folkloric "ritual" and a "myth" that dates much earlier and that relates to the collective return of the dead. For Nancy Regalado, on the contrary, *Fauvel* is simply a combination of literary themes whose only goal is to reinforce the moral satire and the instruction of the prince, which are also the novel's true purposes. For her, *Le Roman de Fauvel* "is not a mirror of the real, but a Mirror of the Prince."

Indeed, nothing authorizes us to speculate on the Indo-European (or even more ancient) origins of Hellequin's hunt. Within the context of the formation of feudalism and of the church's opposition to feudal war, we have, on the contrary, proposed a historical interpretation of Hellequin's hunt. Similarly, we must take into account the historical context and the unique nature of the historical account that makes up *Le Roman de Fauvel.*

Nancy Regalado goes in this direction, but it seems to me that we can both add to and go beyond her demonstration.

We can add to it, for *Le Roman de Fauvel* is not—if we pay close attention to what is known by contemporary ethnology—the only place the troop of the dead and the charivari are encountered together. Its literary motif is sustained by beliefs that ethnologists often glean on-site.[29] The charivari in the case of a remarriage reveals the sunken face of the deceased spouse (in general, the widower's wife), whom the leaders of the charivari seek to appease. Having the responsibility for the control of matrimonial alliances and therefore for an essential part of the reproduction of the social group, the young people are the mediators between the generations, between the living and the dead. Their ritual practices aim not only at *a* dead person, whom it was appropriate to definitively separate from her former spouse, but also—as Carlo Ginzburg has noted—at *all* the dead of the community. By disguising themselves and creating an infernal din, the young men seem to imitate the collective return of the dead, of which Hellequin's hunt is the strongest literary expression. However, it seems to me more correct to speak not of mimicry but of a ritual homology between two forms of transgression: the one that the dead themselves commit by crossing the limits between life and death in a reverse direction, and the one that the masks and disguises represent in abolishing the fundamental distinctions, of Christian anthropology, between male and female, human and beast, and human and demons.[30] In this way, through the masks and disguises of the charivari, like the carnival, the young people *evoke* the dead more than imitate them, so that they will come to protest the "difficult joining" of an ill-suited union or one contrary to social or moral norms. Granted, the historian touches, once again, on only one tale, which is, moreover, taken here in a compelling literary form. But in the background of this tale nothing prevents us from hearing the echo of true ritual practices that were perhaps new in their time.

It is nonetheless necessary to return to the precise context of the account, as Nancy Regalado is right to invite us to do. It seems that we can go even farther in this direction. Elizabeth A. R. Brown, a historian of the reign of Philip the Fair, suggests relating the literary description of the charivari given in *Fauvel* to the critical situation that ruled at the court of the king of France in the same years.[31] Philip the Fair died on November 29, 1314, the same year that Gervais du Bus, a member of the royal chancery, completed his satirical novel. The three sons of the king subsequently reigned—Louis X (1314–1316), Philip V (1317–1322), and

Charles IV (1322–1328)—[32]whereas their sister Isabella married the king of England, Edward II. In the spring of 1314, a few months before the death of the old king Philip, who was already quite weakened, Isabella informed her father of the scandalous behavior of two of her sisters-in-law, Margaret (the wife of the future Louis X) and Blanche (the wife of the future Charles IV). Both were caught committing adultery with two young knights of the king's entourage. They admitted that their adultery had been going on for three years. The two knights (two brothers, a fact that added to the scandalous nature of the crime) were flayed; the two princesses' heads were shaved, and the women were locked up in Château-Gaillard. The king's third daughter-in-law, Jeanne of Burgundy (the sister of Blanche) was found guilty of complicity but was not imprisoned. At issue in this scandal was not only conjugal morality. The outrage committed against the ruler, cuckolded by his wife as in the courtly romances, was doubled, in the case of the daughters-in-law, by a possible corruption of the royal blood and by a terrible danger for the legitimacy of the dynastic succession. Finally, the absence of male heirs for the three sons of Philip the Fair, and the choice in 1328 of their cousin Philip VI of Valois to succeed Charles IV, cast aside any doubts that might have weighed upon a dynastic succession in a direct line.[33]

Le Roman de Fauvel (1314) and its interpolation concerning the charivari (1316) were exactly contemporary to this scandal, which upset the very same milieu in which Gervais du Bus and Chaillou de Pesstain worked. Given the political and satirical dimension of their work, we thus cannot rule out the idea that the literary charivari was also a way to criticize, using cloaked words that were still understood by all, the adultery of the princesses and the blindness of their husbands. The birth of the many little "fauveaus" from the ill-fated union of Fauvel and Vainglory showed well the danger in not watching over the relationships of the wife of a future king. The satire enabled this danger to be brought up by assigning the king of the dead, Hellequin, the task of conducting the charivari right under the windows of the palace.

EIGHT

TIME, SPACE, AND SOCIETY

Ghost tales—whether conveyed by word of mouth, put down in writing, reconveyed by preachers from the pulpit, included in treatises to enjoy a more scholarly distribution and reach the highest spheres of Christianity, or entered into letters or works intended for the king—fulfilled a complete range of functions. They expressed and, at the same time, shaped the various modalities of beliefs in the return of the dead or in purgatorial punishments. They aimed to impose a morality and norms of behavior. Some of them even participated fully in the rise of political ideology.

More widely, beyond the central figure of the ghost and the explicit message delivered by the ghost's revelations, the plots of the tales in their entirety were heavy with meaning that, due to the tales' repetition in similar forms, ultimately shaped the listeners' or readers' views of the world. In this way, through their massive distribution, the tales also fulfilled a cognitive function by inducing and confirming the representations of spatiotemporal structures (between the here-and-now and the hereafter) or social structures in which the dead, as well as the living, were involved. The same was true—as we will see in conclusion—of representations of the human figure (the relationships between the soul and the body) and of how the invisible was perceived and represented.

Individual Time and Collective Time

Ghost tales abounded with references to time and space. Several temporal logics came into play: the individual time particular to a certain dead person (the date of death, the time that had elapsed since then) combined with collective times (notably liturgical), which placed value on certain days of the year, days of the week, or hours of the day. Moreover, the time of the dead, as imagined by the living, was necessarily double: it participated both in the earthly world into which the dead person burst forth and in the hereafter from which the dead person came (notably purgatory). These two facets of time were examined side by side and sometimes even entered into a proportional relationship (it was said, for example, that a thousand years on earth were the equivalent of three days spent in the purgatorial fire).[1] This is what enabled the actions of the living to work in favor of the dead, since the years of indulgence acquired by the living shortened by an equal or proportional number of years the duration of the punishments endured by the dead person in purgatory.[2] This "purgatorial time" enabled a broader notion of the chronological amount of time that might pass before a dead person was likely to appear on earth—from, on the one hand, the moment of death and the individual judgment of the person's soul to, on the other hand, in the more or less long term, the moment of the soul's liberation toward heaven. These time spans, finally, were inscribed in a longer-term eschatological perspective whose end—in the two meanings of the term—was the resurrection of the dead and the Last Judgment.

As a general rule, a dead person was expected to appear shortly after death. The person was, one might say, still very "warm" in the memories of those who had known him or her. The time of ghosts was the time of living memory, of the mourning of those near, and of the conflicts that a succession engendered among them. This time ran out with the stock of masses provided for by the testator. It lasted a few months, perhaps a year, rarely more. Many ghost tales therefore stress the recent nature of the death, specifying the time that has passed since the death. The case of Heinrich Buschmann, who appears to his grandson Arndt "forty years less twelve weeks" after his death, is the exception that confirms the rule. Thanks to the series of tales of miracles or *exempla*, we can propose a few coded elements. In the *miracula* of Peter the Venerable, the amount of time between a death and an apparition varied from a few years and even six years after death (I, chaps. XI and XXIV) to four or two months (I, chaps. XXVII and XXVIII) and even a few days (I, chaps. X and XXVI, and II, chap. XXVI). The apparition of which the author himself was the beneficiary in a dream must have occurred immediately after the death (II, chap. XXV). Among the *exempla* of Caesarius of Heisterbach, five describe a period of a few years. Two indicate periods of ten and seven years. Another talks about a first apparition at the end of a year and a second one a year later. In five other tales the time is thirty days. Five other apparitions occur after twenty, seven, or only four days or even after "a few days." Finally, three apparitions take place the day after the death, the very same night, or "immediately afterwards." In most cases the apparition thus occurs in the midst of mourning and highlights the complete void that the death has created among the living.

Starting from the date of the death, the liturgical time of prayers and masses for the dead person was celebrated for three, seven, or thirty days (the trental) and at the "head of the year" (on the anniversary of the death), resulting in a number of apparitions. Thus the monks of Marmoutier understandably thought that one of their brothers, who had died in England, appeared on the date of his *kalenda*, that is, on the anniversary of his death as inscribed on the "roll" of the dead, whereas he had actually died that same day and not a year earlier. The dead returned at different times after the prayers and masses from which they benefited directly, in order to attest to the efficacy of those suffrages, to ask the living for an additional effort, and to thank them for their help before disappearing forever.

The Calendar of the Dead

This time frame, which was unique to the dead person and which depended completely on the date of death, intersected with the collective time of the living, that of the calendar and feast days, the days of the week, and the division between daytime and nighttime activities. Tradition has it that Odilo, the abbot of Cluny, moved the Day of the Dead to November 2, the day after All Saints' Day.[3] The celebration of the Day of the Dead has been well documented starting around 1030.[4] But there were still other commemorative days that were intended for specific categories of dead or that followed more ancient or local liturgical customs. The church, by establishing February 22 as the date for the Chair of Saint Peter or the Holy See, was likely attempting to eradicate the Roman *parentalia* and the custom of offering libations on graves. Making November 2 a commemorative feast day must have had, among other reasons, an analogous function of moving from spring to fall the principal moment of the Christian celebration of the dead.[5] At Cluny itself the dead relatives of the monks were commemorated on February 3 and July 6, on the octave of the Holy Apostles Peter and Paul. On the Thursday of the octave of Pentecost and on Saint Michael's Day (September 29), the monks prayed for the brothers who were resting in the cemetery. At

Chaise Dieu the dead were celebrated on January 14. The Dominicans prayed especially for the fathers and mothers of the brothers on February 4.[6]

Interestingly, it does not seem to me that these commemorative days served as privileged anchoring points for apparitions of the dead. Regarding November 2, apparitions were even less forced to bend to the constraints of the calendar, since that date was relatively recent. But all the dead were celebrated on November 2 (and, to a lesser degree, on other feast days), whereas apparitions mostly concerned specific dead people. Moreover, it was indeed on All Saints' Day (as was said in Montaillou) or on Saint Michael's Day (according to the testimony of the ghost of Beaucaire) that the dead were freed from their punishments and left the surroundings of the living for good. In sum, the time of apparitions depended principally on an individual logic (the day of the death, which fixed the term of suffrages to thirty days or to a year) or on more ancient calendrical rhythms, which the liturgy of the church only partially resumed. If there was indeed a time of the year that, according to our medieval tales, attracted ghosts, it was Christmas and the Twelve Days (from Christmas to the Epiphany) and, more widely, winter, the dark part of the year.

According to Orderic Vitalis, it was during the night of January 1, 1091, that the curate Walchelin encountered Hellequin's hunt on his way home. At the beginning of the fourteenth century, in Montaillou, the *armarié* Arnaud Gélis also strove to be precise: he noted that he saw that very year, five days after Christmas, the soul of Barcelona of Pamiers, the mother of Arnaud of Calmelles. There is most likely a link between these apparitions, especially collective apparitions, and the winter solstice, which encouraged the return of the dead.[7] In the Roman world the calends of January, along with their masquerades, which had long been condemned by the church, had similar meanings.[8] But we must above all take into account the reasons explicitly advanced by our authors. These reasons are very clear in the tale, told to Otloh of Saint Emmeran, of the apparitions of the informant's dead father. This father "appeared to the son frequently during the year following his death," to beg his son to use prayers to pull him from the torments of the afterworld. But the son proved to be negligent, and the father appeared again "at the time of the following Christmas." And the dead man himself explains the choice of this holiday to his son: on that night, he says, the souls relieved by the prayers of the living can rest (*anime requiem habere merentur*). But he, through the negligence of his son, was able to obtain only one small hour of rest, just the time necessary to come and complain to his son of his suffering.[9] Two temporal logics thus intersect here: that of the remembrance of the specific dead person, from the death to the anniversary, and that of the collective remembrance of all the dead in general. At Christmas the souls of the dead, freed for a moment from their torment, can visit the living.

Other tales mention more broadly the entire Christmas season, if not the day of the Nativity itself. Thietmar of Merseburg cites the specific date of December 18 (but perhaps it was actually January 18, 1012) for the noisy manifestations of the ghosts he witnessed in his own home. When the dead made repeated apparitions, Christmas and the turn of the new year were the pivots for their revelations: according to Johannes Gobi, the spirit of Gui de Corvo was manifest to his widow and then to Johannes Gobi himself between the second day after Christmas (the feast of Saint John the Baptist, on December 27) and the Epiphany. They waited for him on Easter, but he no longer showed himself, a sign that he had left purgatory at the end of winter. As for Heinrich Buschmann, his apparitions (fourteen in all) spread out between November 11 and the day of the Ascension, that is, exactly during the entire winter portion of the year. The choice of this period must have a folkloric explanation: November 11, Saint Martin's, indeed marked the beginning of what Claude Gaignebet calls "popular winter,"[10] the day when the bear and the wild man came out of their caves, which symbolized the land of the dead. On Ascension, the soul of Heinrich rose to heaven in the footsteps of Christ. That is why on Pentecost, Arndt expected a new apparition of Heinrich, who did not show himself.

The grandson's disappointed expectation is easily explained, for many tales of apparitions focus on Pentecost, the movable holiday in the spring. Raoul Glaber reported that the monk Vulferius of Moutiers Saint Jean saw his church fill up with blessed dead at daybreak on the Sunday of the octave of Pentecost (the first Sunday after Pentecost), that is, the day of the Feast of the Trinity. Martyrs of the Christian faith who had fallen under the blows of the Saracens, these dead were thus symbolically associated with the glory of the church.[11] This commemorative day had an ancient funereal character. According to tradition, a holiday for all the dead faithful had originally been celebrated the day after Pentecost, before Odilo of Cluny moved the day to November 2. The *Rule* of Isidore of Seville fixed the commemoration of the dead brothers resting in the monastic cemetery to the day after the octave of Pentecost.[12] The transfer to November might be explained by the fact that in autumn, the monks had more provisions to accommodate the influx of poor into the monastery: the poor were considered to be substitutes for the dead, and the material food they were given symbolized spiritual "food," that is, the suffrages that shortened the trials of the dead.[13] However, the original holiday did not disappear. At Saint Bénigne of Dijon, the monks prayed for the dead in "the second holy day (that is, Monday) of that week of the octave of Pentecost, namely the Holy Trinity." At matins, twelve poor people ate their fill of bread and meat, then all the poor who arrived received bread and wine. At Cluny itself the abbot Hugh made Thursday a holiday for the dead resting in the cemetery of the brothers. On that day, he specified, the bells were to ring at vespers "as on All Saints' Day," and twelve poor people would be fed in the monastery. For the military aristocracy, whose place we have seen in the Cluniac tales of apparitions, Pentecost was the great holiday of knighthood, that of the collective dubbing of young warriors. The ritual of entering into knighthood was a rite of passage, thus a sort of symbolic death through which the young man "died" in his first "state" to be "reborn" into the order of knighthood under the direction of his elders and the invocation of the lineal ancestors.[14] On this occasion the new knights indulged in war games, notably in the tournament, but the clerics avidly denounced the violence of these rituals, and many ghost tales in fact feature knights who met a violent and untimely death in a tournament.

The Week of the Dead

A good many ghost tales also provide specifics regarding the days of the week. Following a long tradition, the dead lived like the living, according to the rhythm of the week, and on the seventh day they had the leisure to rest. In Judaism as well, the Sabbath of the dead temporarily ended the torments of the damned souls.[15] Quite naturally, Sunday was chosen for the repose of the Christian dead. Inspired undoubtedly by the apocryphal *Visio Pauli*, the *Voyage of Saint Brendan* asserts that Judas, condemned to hell, intermittently enjoyed a bit of repose on a nearby island. Judas explains to his visitors that he remains there in peace from Saturday evening to Sunday evening, during the two weeks of the Christmas season, during Marian holidays, and at Easter and Pentecost but that all the rest of the time, including during the other big holidays, he is tortured endlessly in hell.[16] Gervase of Tilbury and Stephen of Bourbon reported a Sicilian legend according to which the souls tortured in the fire of Etna enjoyed a rest from Saturday night through Sunday night, before once again suffering during the whole week.[17] Such legends accompanied a liturgical innovation noted as of the eleventh century by Raoul Glaber and Peter Damian.[18] Since the dead are again delivered to their torments during Sunday night, it is preferable to pray for them at that time. This is what the liturgists Jean Beleth, Sicard of Cremona, and William Durand also asserted in the twelfth and thirteenth centuries.[19] Confessors (such as Thomas of Chobham) and preachers (such as Johannes Gobi) assumed responsibility for spreading this devotion, by setting aside Monday as the day for a procession through the cemetery, for the benediction of the graves, and for the celebration of masses for the dead.[20]

Day and Night

The different times of the twenty-four-hour day were not irrelevant to ghosts either. "Just as the day belongs to the living, the night is conceded to the dead," according to Thietmar of Merseburg's niece Bridget, who is citing the bishop of Utrecht.[21] With very rare exceptions, the dead appeared at night, not only in dreams, as was fitting, but also, quite often, to those who were fully awake—at nightfall, in moonlight,[22] at midnight, or even in the second half of the night, at the tenth or eleventh hour after dinner,[23] after matins (especially in dreams that, at this hour, were supposed to be the truest).[24] The ghosts of Byland indicated such preferences: one of them "was used to leaving his grave at night" in order to terrorize the neighborhood.[25] However, some ghosts appeared at dawn: it was at that time, says Thietmar, that on Friday, December 18, at first cockcrow, the church was filled with a bright light, and a loud growling announced the arrival of the dead.[26] Although some apparitions were manifest to conscious people at noon,[27] these cases were rare.

Why at night? Traditionally, the darkness suited the most disturbing supernatural manifestations, those of the devil and of demons and those of ghosts, who suffered in places little different from hell. But we must be careful not to dramatize too greatly the medieval fear of the night. In the Middle Ages one could savor the calm of a beautiful night without fear, as did the provost of the church of Basel, who, after a copious meal and a brief nap until the eleventh hour of the night, woke up, went to relieve himself, and then went back to bed, leaving open the window that faced the cemetery in order to be able to contemplate the serenity of the sky and the air.[28] The provost's nonchalance added even more to his sins, for it was indeed true that "nocturnal terrors" served to reinforce the Christian's duties. Fears were inscribed in the ideological program of what Jean Delumeau has called "the Christianity of fear."[29] When the monk of Byland describes the bivouac of a group of pilgrims who were going from Yorkshire to Santiago de Compostela, he illustrates perfectly the common attitudes toward night: "They spent the night in a forest near the royal road. Each one of them took a turn watching for part of the night because of their fear of the night (*propter timorem nocturnum*) and the others slept feeling more secure."[30] Clerics grafted a theological explanation onto this common fear of the night, a fear that the dead Heinrich Buschmann, questioned by his grandson Arndt, echos:

> "Why do you appear to me at night rather than during the day?" and the spirit responds: "As long as I cannot go to God, I remain in the night, and this is why I appear more often at night than in the day."[31]

The earthly night, propitious to the most disturbing apparitions, was as black as sin; it was also as black as the darkness of the afterworld that it prolonged on earth, the darkness inhabited by the souls deprived of the illumination of the vision of God.

Where Did Ghosts Come From?

Just as ghosts participated in two contiguous continuums of time, they also could be found in three distinct places: the location of the grave where the cadaver was decomposing, the imaginary place where the soul of the dead person was thought to exist temporarily (in principle, purgatory) or permanently (hell or heaven), and finally, the earthly place where a living person was witness to the apparition of a dead person or of the troop of the dead. These three places were tightly connected to each other.

The separation of the soul and the body at the moment of death explained how the dead person could appear independently of the cadaver, sometimes even quite far from it. In tales most consistent with ecclesiastical reflection—which defined the apparition as a pure image and which claimed to eject all "concern" with the body—the dead person appeared anywhere, depending on "God's permission." Moreover, the model was ancient, since in the Old Testament, Samuel, who was buried in Ramah (1 Sam. 15), appeared in Endor (1 Sam. 28). It was in Rome that Peter the Venerable saw the apparition, in a dream, of the spirit of the prior William, who had just died, poisoned in Charlieu. At Marmoutier a monk had the vision of his brother, who had died that very day in England. Spirits, explained the clerics, were not subject to the weight of earthly bodies or to the constraints of space and time. The spirit of the young man from Apt, of whom Gervase of Tilbury speaks, even had the gift of ubiquity: he appeared, at the same moment, both to a priest who was taking a nap on the left bank of the Rhone and to his young cousin who was in Beaucaire, on the right bank. Not all ghosts, however, were so easily freed from their grave sites. Many appeared in the cemetery, near their tombs, or could be appeased only by intervening physically on their cadavers, as in Yorkshire or Brittany.

The imaginary stay of the dead person in the hereafter and the earthly place of the apparition also maintained complex relationships. The doctrine of purgatory, understood to be a specific place in the hereafter, took a very long time to be formed. Ghost tales testify to these gropings, sometimes even quite belatedly. In the middle of the twelfth century, a dead person asserted that the prayers of the monks had enabled him to leave the "purgatorial fire," where he had endured horrible torment, and that he was then in the *refrigerium*, where he was enjoying even greater beatitude while awaiting the Last Judgment.[32] According to this tale, in which the notion of purgatory is still sought out (which was completely normal for that time), the soul successively experienced a transitory expiation in the "purgatorial fire," and then, by virtue of a distinct historical tradition that notably went back to Tertullian, the soul went through a "cooling," a foretaste of the complete blessedness of the elect.[33] Beginning in the thirteenth century, in conformity with the ecclesiastical doctrine that had just "invented" purgatory, it was said that in general the soul escaped from purgatory, where it endured punishments, to appear for a few moments to a living person likely to help it benefit from suffrages. But even at that time, many tales were far from conforming to that schema. A damned soul could even return from hell, although in principle it had nothing left to expect from the living.[34] Furthermore, "purgatory" was not always named as such, for the function of our tales of apparitions was not to describe the geography of the different places of the hereafter (as does the *Vision of Tnugdal* or the tale of *Saint Patrick's Purgatory*) but was to present the torments of the souls in purgatory in order to solicit suffrages from the living. Finally, these notions were subject, even after 1200, to variations that were not always concerned with "official" doctrines. For a long time the old Gregorian idea of an expiation

179

of souls *on earth* was maintained. It was not rare for the dead person to return to the "scenes of the crime." "Where we have committed our infractions, there we must pay the punishments due for our infractions," declares a ghost cited by Peter the Venerable.[35] The dead also haunted the places that were familiar to them. For example, the "Chronicle of Petershausen" (1156), near Constance, cites the astonishment of a brother when he encounters the recently deceased monk Bernard in the monastery. The dead man explains that God, as a punishment, caused him to travel "through and watch over all the corners of the cloister."[36] But let us remember that the idea of wandering, even the idea of a purgatory on earth, could be combined with other representations. Still, in the fourteenth century, the spirit of Gui de Corvo of Alès claimed to spend his days in the "common Purgatory" in the center of the earth and his nights in his "individual Purgatory," in his widow's bedroom. According to the ghost of Beaucaire, on the contrary, the souls of the deceased wandered on earth until the third or fourth day after their deaths, before entering into an "aerial Purgatory." The peasants of Montaillou also indulged in a not very orthodox tinkering that replaced the harshness of purgatory with the wandering of souls and then with a "place of rest" in complete peace. Not until Heinrich Buschmann, in the Rhineland of the first half of the fifteenth century, did a ghost speak somewhat "correctly" of purgatory (*vegevure*). But that same ghost remained unique when he described the progression of the souls freed from purgatory as they moved, in stages, toward celestial paradise, through the nine angelic choirs. According to the dead man, one of Arndt's friends who had recently died spent only seven hours in purgatory before rising to the third choir of the angels. A widow was already in the eighth choir, right next to the Virgin.[37] When Arndt is concerned about knowing the fate reserved for him ("Will I go to Purgatory or to Heaven?"), his grandfather tells him that he will first spend ten days "in the same place where Jesus Christ led Adam and Eve and the people of their kind when he took them from Hell while waiting to lead them to Heaven."[38] The originality of this text comes from the localization, between purgatory and paradise, of a sort of antechamber to paradise, a place where Adam and Eve and the righteous of the Old Testament were believed to have gone after being pulled by Christ from "Hell"—or, rather, from the limbo of the patriarchs.[39]

Thus the revelations that the dead themselves made concerning the places in the hereafter led to a nuancing of the more coherent and stable image of purgatory as given by the theoreticians, theologians, and preachers in their concern with imposing the new doctrine. These variations and hesitations allow us to understand better the eagerness of the clerics to instill a normalized representation of the places in the hereafter. If we indeed see how the terminology of purgatory was gradually imposed, how the location itself tended to find its place and its duration, other possibilities seem to have existed for a long time.[40] The tales are useful in that they offer a more diverse and fluid image of medieval representations of the hereafter, at the meeting point of the writings of clerics and the oral traditions of laypeople.

Inside and Outside

Even more important to the living than the places where the dead came from were the places where the living encountered the dead. Tales portray several typical places, which may be classified depending on whether the apparition was individual or collective, oneiric or perceived in a wakeful state.

On the one hand was the house, including the bedroom and the bed—a superb place for oneiric apparitions. This was also the place for many apparitions that occurred when the beneficiary was awake, at least so long as the dead person appeared alone and was distinguishable and identifiable. Apparitions of the troop of the dead did not occur in this domestic space: their domain was the exterior wild spaces, which included haunted houses, since these houses had been deserted by their inhabitants for a long time. The theme (well noted already in antiquity) of the haunted house has run through Christian literature from the *Vita Germani* by Constantius of Lyons (fifth century) to the sermons in German of Geiler von Kaysersberg.[41]

Most often, however, the individual dead person returned to his or her own house, to appear to a member of the family. Tales sketch an entire domestic geography of an apparition. In the middle is the bed, where the dreamer or the one who, in half-sleep or even completely awake, lies resting and suddenly sees a dead relative. When the spirit of Gui de Corvo comes to disturb the nights of his widow, the bed is in the middle of the scene, even though the woman is not lying on it. But the tale designates the bed as the location of the unspeakable sin that the couple committed and as the place that is undoubtedly familiar with the visits of the dead man. In the bedroom, according to other tales, the fireplace recalls the fire of the punishment after death, but the cold dead person might also seek to warm up in front of the fireplace by turning over the coals, in a gesture of familiarity.[42]

The concrete limits of the house—the door, the threshold, the edge of the window—also played a remarkable role. The contrast between the interior (*intus*) and the exterior (*foris*) was a fundamental schema of medieval ideology. Here it was a matter of separating, even of protecting, the living who were *inside* from the dead and the evil spirits who were *outside* and whom the living wanted to repel. In an *exemplum* by Caesarius of Heisterbach, the door remains closed to the dead master of the house, in spite of his pounding and calling.[43] The threshold of the door delimited the intimate space of the apparition: let another living person appear on the threshold, and that person would see nothing or would, by his or her presence alone, chase the ghost away.[44] Some people, sheltered by the walls of their houses, observed through their windows the passing of the furious troop of the dead[45] or the dance of the dead in a cemetery.[46] Conversely, in a miracle from Peter the Venerable, a dead person leans on the outside edge of a window in order to intrude on the dialogue that, inside the house, pits Peter Engelbert against his dead servant Sancho.[47]

In the monasteries, according to tales of oneiric apparitions, the interior space was centered on the monks' dormitory and the bed of the brother. Apparitions that occurred to someone in a wakeful state were also most often nocturnal and more often occurred in the church: in the torpor of matins, a monk was suddenly seized by the return of a dead brother. Another place that encouraged monastic apparitions was the cloisters, which the *Cantigas* of Alfonso the Wise describe and illustrate with regard to the apparition of a dead monk to two of his brothers. It was also in the cloisters, of the cathedral of Pamiers, that the *armarié* Arnaud Gélis often encountered the dead canons of that church.[48]

The Cemetery

The cemetery was one of the places most favorable to apparitions. From the year 1000 to the eighteenth century, the proximity of the space of the living to the space of the dead was a major feature of the history of traditional societies and mentalities of Europe. At the end of the ancien régime, the cemeteries of the cities were emptied of their bones and were relocated to the outskirts of the cities.[49] But before then, at the dawn of the Europe of lords and villages, the cemetery sometimes preceded the establishment of a village. The dead grouped the living around them: "it was around the dead that the labor of their descendants was assembled," writes Robert Fossier.[50] This can be represented by concentric circles, as can still be seen in so many European villages. In the center is found the parish church, and then crowded around it are the tombs of the cemetery (but in the period I am discussing, the graves were undifferentiated, and the consecrated land of the cemetery was marked at best with one large cross for all the dead); the cemetery was enclosed by a wall, and the bishop, during his parish visits, constantly reminded his parishioners that they should maintain this wall to separate the holy space from the profane space and to prevent their animals from wandering among the graves. Also excluded from the "Christian land" were the unbaptized (Jews), children who died without being baptized (they were to have a "corner" to themselves, the earthly equivalent of the limbo of children in the hereafter), and suicides, who were thrown into a ditch or into the flow of a river. Beyond the cemetery extended the rest of the village and, even farther, following the classic opposition of the *ager* and the *saltus*, the cultivated land bordered by a forest.

Between the church and the village, the cemetery was therefore an intermediary place, and it played a mediating role: the living had to go through it constantly, not only when they went to church or returned from church but also when they went from one end of the village to the other or, in town, from one quarter to another. They went by it, traveled through it, and attended to leisure or mercantile activities in it, activities that apparently had little relationship to death or the dead.[51] At least this was the opinion of theologians and preachers, whose opinion sometimes differed from that of the simple curates. In particular the church constantly castigated dancing in churches and cemeteries as being "pagan," "superstitious," "or indecent." But can we not see in these prohibitions the sign of a competition between two types of behavior, each of which, in its own way, sanctified the space of the dead? In the face of church rituals, the young dancers stomping in rhythm on the ground of the dead communicated with their dead relatives and their ancestors. They danced in the cemeteries as the dead themselves were believed to dance during the night and just as the "danse macabre" occurred in them, as was sometimes portrayed on the walls of the nearby church or in the ossuary of the cemetery.[52] Thus the cemetery was an oneiric and fantastic place, as is seen in the vernacular literature in the recurrent theme of the *âtre périlleux* besieged by evil spirits who want to ravish an innocent soul there.[53]

Certain tales of miracles specify the configuration of the cemetery, a framework for the apparitions of the dead. According to Peter the Venerable, a young monk from Cluny is led by his dead uncle, the former prior Achard, from his bed, through the main cloisters of the abbey and the cloisters of the infirmary, to the door of the cemetery. There the dead monk and his nephew find themselves in the midst of a countless group of dead monks gathered in a chapter. In the middle of the cemetery shines a lantern of the dead, "out of respect for the faithful who rest there." A "great venerable judge" rules over the cemetery, resplendent with light, and Achard, prostrate on the ground, has to beg his pardon for being late. At the end of the gathering, the procession of dead monks leaves the cemetery through another door by going through a large fire—some more quickly, others more slowly.[54] Thus we find here, on earth and in the space of the cemetery of the abbey where the monks had lived, images of the judgment and of a fire that one went through to be "purged" of one's sins.

The Wild Boundaries of the Land

Outside the inhabited places, individual apparitions were much more rare. A dead person might, for example, have appeared in the middle of a field, but that was rather unusual.[55] But it was in a field near a castle that the dead knights pursued their infernal tournament.[56] Farther, the wild places, the "ravines and the underbrush," were traversed, in Ariège, by the wandering souls of the dead.[57] The borders of the territory (the kingdom, the parish) were propitious to apparitions of the troop of the dead, of Hellequin's hunt. According to Walter Map, it was on the border of Wales, in the province of Hereford, that the fantastic troop of King Herla, the king of the dead, was seen for the last time. The Welsh claimed to have seen the king plunge into the Wye, the river that marks the border of England.[58] The bodies of suicides were also thrown into a river, thereby depriving them of a Christian burial,[59] and it was a river that marked, for a ghost of Yorkshire, an uncrossable boundary.[60] Sometimes a river was the border between the land of the living and the land of the dead, and sometimes a river led to the dead or belonged to the dead, as in the tale, already mentioned, of the adventure of the tailor Snowball.[61]

The large road (*via strata*) played an important role in many apparitions of the army of the dead. According to Orderic Vitalis, the din of the horses, chariots, and dogs announced from afar the arrival of Hellequin's hunt, and the curate Walchelin had only enough time to hide under the trees and in the bushes that lined the road (*procul a calle*). The latter tale stresses the desolate nature of the place: the curate had gone that night to assist a sick person "at the farthest end of his parish," and he was coming back "alone" and "far from any human dwelling."[62] The road guided the wandering of the dead and gave their troop its rhythm. It also led them toward a more definitive stay: in the tale of Saint Foi of Sélestat, the knight Walter sees the troop of Reds, who are heading north into the infernal "mountain of Nivelles," go by on the large road, whereas the Whites are promised to paradise.

Road intersections were traditionally marked by a fear of evil forces. In crossroads, people carried out divinatory practices, among other things, which were denounced throughout the early Middle Ages.[63] Sometimes sinners who had died excommunicated, such as certain usurers, were buried in intersections.[64] In the thirteenth century, the bishop of Paris, William of Auvergne, explained that crossroads were places polluted by excessive use and that this was why diabolical illusions and phantoms of tournamenting knights were encountered there. The bishop of Paris (an ecologist before his time) noted that these phenomena did not occur in the fields, which were "very clean" places.[65]

All these tales of apparitions help us to understand that neither space nor time was given a priori and that neither was neutral. Societies have never ceased to construct space and time as fundamental frames of reference for beliefs and actions. Times and spaces are invested with the values of the societies that use them and ponder them. Among other material or symbolic means, the imaginary movements of the dead were used by people to ponder social spaces and times and to master these concepts to their own benefit.

The Tale of an Apparition: A Bond of Social Relationships

Relationships between the living and the dead were formed on the spatiotemporal line of the tale. In spite of the diversity of the tales and of the narrative genres, these relationships present recurrent structures. The simplest directly contrasts a living person and a dead one, as in the autobiographical tales of dreams. In other cases the beneficiary of the apparition is only the messenger—called the *nuntius* (Peter the Venerable) or the *internuntius* (Marmoutier)—of the dead person to the final target of the apparition. In Montaillou, the role of the messenger of the souls, or the *armarié*, was a lasting function recognized by the local society. In the monastic *miracula* or the *exempla* of the preachers, another role, and not one of the least important, was occupied by the church, since it was to the church—in the person of the abbot of the monastery, the prior of the Mendicant convent, or the parish priest—that the recipient of the apparition had to appeal to celebrate the masses requested by the dead person.

Connected to those who assumed the above-mentioned roles, who were implicated by the fact of the apparition itself, were those people who were involved in the transmission of the tale. The beneficiary of the apparition might have reported the facts to the cleric, who then wrote them down. In other cases the priest responsible for saying the masses for the dead person bore witness to the apparition that was reported to him; then his tale was written down. In still other cases the informant only reported an anonymous rumor to the author. An apparition therefore never involved just two actors, a dead person and a living one, but an entire chain of witnesses, intermediaries, informants, scribes, preachers, and listeners; more than a distinct supernatural event, the apparition was a cultural object that was developed socially depending on its circulation. Under these conditions we should note everything that connected those involved in the tale as well as in its transmission and reception. The relative status of the beneficiary, the intended recipient, and the informant was never arbitrary. Quite to the contrary, the apparition flowed within the framework of earlier relationships, between people whom the death of a relative had once again brought closer: affective relationships; social relationships of friendship or neighborhood, of a common community of inhabitants; and above all, relationships of natural and/or spiritual kinship. The dead, says Gervase of Tilbury, appear *confinibus et amicis*, to relatives and friends.[66] At the time when Robert of Uzes, according to his own admission, "was praying for those of his blood," he had a vision of the torment endured by the souls of his relatives.[67] But we must be careful not to think that relationships of kinship were always strong before an apparition. Apparitions contributed to making those relationships exist, to giving them new life by enabling the one who saw, recognized, and named a dead relative to say, for example, that the dead person was his son, his brother, his vassal, or even his "brother" in religion.

Kinship: Alliance

Apparitions frequently portrayed an alliance that had been broken by the death of one of the people involved. They concentrated attention on the survivor, usually on a woman, for texts seem to focus only on the cases in which the husband was dead. In principle, female ghosts should be as numerous as male ghosts in our tales, since for the church, the salvation of the souls of women was as important as that of the souls of men. Demographic reasons alone (young wives survived their older husbands in greater numbers) cannot explain such an imbalance, which was undoubtedly connected more to the preeminence of the man in the devolution of inheritances and, notably, of the share earmarked for the church. Once dead, it was thought, the man watched jealously over the respect shown for his last wishes, going so far as to appear to survivors, first of all to his widow, to remind them of their duties. Let us also mention the symbolic status of the widow and her confused feeling that her remarriage (if she was young enough and had the financial means to remarry) would go against a sort of prohibition, in spite of the denials of the church. And in the opposite case, the widow felt it was her obligation to devote herself forever to devotions, to prayer for the dead, in the first row of which was her dead husband. It is thus from the wife's point of view that our texts stress the importance, in marriage, of the carnal and affective bond: the dead husband haunts the conjugal bedroom (in the case of the invisible spirit of Gui de Corvo of Alès) or, like an incubus, enters the bed and lies down on his wife (in Buckinghamshire, according to William of Newburgh).[68]

The apparition reminds the widow of the alternative presented by the death of her husband: remarriage or entering the orders. Guibert of Nogent's mother, a young widow of good lineage, had to resist the pressures of her own parents and of a nephew of her dead husband so there would be, writes her son, "no loosening of the ancient union of their bodies by substitution of other flesh."[69] A century later, according to Caesarius of Heisterbach, the widow of the usurer of Liège similarly proclaims that she is "part of her husband's body." Not only did she in fact obtain permission from the pope for the body of the usurer, deprived of a Christian grave, to be buried in the cemetery, but she also had a tomb built for him and locked herself up there as a recluse in order to pray continually for him. While appearing to her in her funereal place of reclusion, the dead man encouraged her to persist in her praying and then told her of his liberation from purgatory.[70] On the other hand, Gervase of Tilbury tells of the case of a widow who is tempted by remarriage in spite of her promise of perpetual faithfulness to her husband. The dead husband, invisible, smashes her head with the blow of a mortar.[71]

In a more or less dramatic way, all of these tales highlight the psychological and social wrenching caused by the death of a husband. Torn between the temptations of the world and reclusion in prayer, the widow was left to her remorse and her phantasms. Virtually placed back into the matrimonial market and subject to the pressures of her family, the widow—if she was young and had property—saw suitors pour in. Widowhood offered the opportunity for a renewal of social ties, but it was necessary first to appease the first husband, to complete the "work of mourning." The threat of the mortar was to fantastic tales what the charivari was to ritual procedures of social control.

In the society of the time, if marriage in principle assumed the consent of the couple, it above all represented the alliance of two lineages, that of the father of the bride and that of the bride's husband. As for the woman, she simply passed from one to the other, giving children to the lineage of her husband before returning, if she became widowed, to her father. Unlike a man, she was therefore caught between two lineages and had to be careful not to injure either one. In Florence of the Quattrocento, it was not uncommon for sons orphaned of their father to accuse their mother of abandoning them and, above all, of casting them aside when the woman returned, as a widow, to her father's home.[72] In Yorkshire around 1400, the apparition of the dead sister of Adam of Lond illustrates the same problem. She was condemned to wander all night long on the road because of the deeds she had given illegally to her brother, to the detriment of her husband and her own sons. The latter were therefore deprived by their brother-in-law and their uncle, Adam of Lond, of their house and their land. In vain William Trower, the beneficiary of the apparition, attempted to convince the guilty man, to whom his sister appeared directly the following night, but with no more success. The matter was not settled until the next generation.[73]

Kinship: Filiation

Although a dead child, like little Alberto Morelli, occasionally appeared to one of the parents, the opposite case was by far more frequent. Demography was not the only reason; social roles that were attributed to each generation also played a part. From father or mother to son or daughter, all types of apparitions were encountered in documents. The dead person, male or female, might appear to a close relative to bear testimony to the punishment caused by past misbehavior or, on the contrary, to warn the survivor against sinful ways. Often a dead mother was an affectionate adviser not only to her living daughter but also to her son, especially when he was a priest. According to the English chronicler Ranulf Higden, the future archbishop Edmund of Canterbury (d. 1240) was still a student when he dreamed that his recently deceased mother appeared to him to ask him the meaning of the geometric figures he was drawing. Unhappy, she traced, using her hand, three circles containing the faces of the Father, the Son, and the Holy Spirit, adding: "It is to these figures that you must henceforth devote yourself." The dead woman intended to convert the future prelate to the science of God by taking him from the sciences of the world.[74] It is perhaps possible to see in the privileged relationships, beyond death, between the mother and her cleric or monk son a testimony to the affective and educative role played by mothers in the training of future men of the church. For some, such as the monk Guibert of Nogent, the earthly mother and the spiritual mothers—which were, in various capacities, the Virgin and the church—were very nearly one and the same.

When the father appeared, he was generally authoritarian and vindictive toward his sons or daughters, whom he castigated for their behavior, even if he himself had died in sin. Thieving knights, drunkards, or usurers in the tales of Caesarius of Heisterbach assailed their daughters or sons. One brandished the stein that he had used to drink in excess,[75] and another hung fish caught in hell on the door to his house, fish that at dawn turned into toads and snakes.[76]

Two *miracula* from Peter the Venerable similarly portray the relationships between dead fathers and their sons, but these tales follow a more complex narrative structure. Lord Geoffroy of Semur appears in a dream to the recluse nun Alberée so that she will ask his son, also named Geoffroy, to cancel the exorbitant fee the father instituted while he was alive.[77] Likewise, Lord Guichard of Beaujeu, who is dead, does not appear directly to his son, Humbert. He has himself represented by another dead man, his vassal Geoffroy of Ion, who appears first to another knight, Milo of Anse. The two knights, the dead one and the living one, are of equal rank, and they belong to the same hunt. Milo is assigned the task of passing on Guichard's message to his son, Milo's master Humbert of

Beaujeu. But since Humbert turns a deaf ear, Milo ultimately appears to him directly to implore him to be concerned with the salvation of his dead father.[78] This complex tale is interesting in that it intersects relationships of natural kinship with vassalic ties, of which we will speak again later.

However, tales of apparitions of the dead deal with many other forms of natural kinship: between brothers, between sisters, between brother and sister, between uncle or aunt and niece or nephew,[79] and between cousins (between male and female cousins in the affair of Beaucaire, which Gervase of Tilbury recounts). All these apparitions indicate well the extent to which duties of natural kinship were important, and not only when an inheritance was at stake (most often that concerned only the relationship between husband and wife or between father and son). The burning memory of the dead person, the affection (or the hatred) that the survivor preserved for the dead person, the concern that the living person had with salvation and with the sense of spiritual duties toward the deceased, and the reminder of the sins of the dead person and the weight of the survivor's own sins were all integral elements of these tales. Sometimes an entire extended network of relatives was revealed on the occasion of an apparition: a young nun who died eight years earlier complains to a Cistercian abbot of having been abandoned by her entire natural family, which included her father, her mother, a maternal aunt (*matertera*) who was also a nun, and two married sisters of her mother, as well as one of their daughters.[80]

Kinship: Spiritual

Relationships of spiritual kinship in medieval society played a no less fundamental role than did those of natural kinship. They intersected, increased, and extended the networks of solidarities that gave force and cohesion to society, notably by including the memory of the dead in the thoughts and activities of the living. The models are numerous and complementary. From the start, all of Christendom considered itself a single large family whose members, by virtue of their baptism, were "brothers" and "sisters" in Christ and were thus connected to the *caritas*, to a reciprocal love of divine origin that, for example, justified charity toward the poor, the sick, and the afflicted as well as solidarity among the living and the dead.[81] The possibility of suffrages for the dead, then, at the end of the Middle Ages and the idea of the "communion of the saints," according to which the dead could also intercede next to God for the living, ideally found their justification in the notion of Christian fraternity.

In the first centuries of Christianity, monasticism developed a model of a spiritual "family" within the confines of Christendom. Among themselves, the monks and the nuns, the religious men and women, especially if they belonged to the same order, thought of themselves as—and called the others—"brothers" and "sisters," "fathers" and "mothers" (with regard to the abbots and abbesses). These networks of spiritual kinship were all the more dense in that the monasteries and convents organized among themselves, and with the descendants of their lay benefactors, "fraternities" of prayer intended to ensure for their dead members the suffrages of all the surviving "brothers" and "sisters." Inscribing the names of the dead in the necrology or the obituary, transporting the "rolls of the dead" made up of all the death "announcements" of the monks or nuns from one monastery to another,[82] guaranteed the liturgical exercise of that solidarity. In the middle of the twelfth century, the series of tales of miracles from the monastery of Marmoutier spoke explicitly of the *debitum fraternitatis* that the monks owed to their dead.[83] It showed how the apparitions of dead monks benefited the extended monastic "family," thanks to the associations of prayer connecting different establishments, even beyond the English Channel.[84]

Often, the spiritual kinship of the "brothers" or "sisters" in religion within a certain monastery was combined with earlier ties of natural kinship. This accumulation of kinship ties—brothers in Christ, through flesh and in religion—is mentioned in tales as a factor favorable to the apparition of a dead person. A dead monk who was a "brother" (*frater*) in the monastery and also a brother by blood (*germanus*) appeared to a monk of Marmoutier. We encounter identical cases in the monasteries of Cistercian nuns, who often recruited the younger members of the same aristocratic families, strong in an extended natural family.[85] In the monastery of Charlieu, a dependency of Cluny, a young monk was the beneficiary of the apparition of a dead superior who was also his paternal uncle (*patruus*).[86] If the antagonistic demands of the two types of kinship, natural and spiritual, were a commonplace in religious literature (for example, Saint Francis's relationship with his father), our tales show rather how the identity of blood and that of religion accumulated their effects to revive the memory of the dead by recalling the duties of solidarity for the benefit of the deceased.

Our tales also portray, although in a less ponderous way, forms of spiritual kinship that came out of baptism. Baptism in fact instituted a double relationship: on the one hand, between godfather (or godmother) and godson (or goddaughter) and, on the other hand, between *compères* and *commères*, that is, the natural parents and the spiritual parents of the same child. Well noted as of the sixth century, compaternity was, in the central Middle Ages, a strong social link that implied duties of protection and assistance.[87] Ethnologists have been able to show that godparenting and compaternity fulfilled, among other functions, that of intercession beyond death, as is illustrated up to the present time in tales of apparitions of the dead.[88] My own collection of texts sheds light only on relationships of compaternity. In the eleventh century a few ghost tales announced the strength of the ties between parents and godparents.[89] In Rome, according to Peter Damian, during the night of the Feast of the Assumption of Mary, a woman was visited by the "godmother" Marozia, who had died a year earlier and was freed that very day by the Virgin. We might think that one was the mother and the other the godmother of the same child and that it was this indirect connection that warranted their solidarity beyond death. Similarly, a priest sees in a dream the father of his godson and follows the man into a gathering of saints; most likely, this priest was the godfather of the son of the dead man.[90] In the middle of the twelfth century the miracles of Marmoutier illustrated another interesting case of relationships between fathers and godfathers: a priest who amassed a large fortune in the world bequeaths it to the monastery at the time of his death, specifying that the monks must pray for his salvation. He also asks his *compater et familiaris* (most likely the father of his godson) to reimburse the monks the sum of sixty pounds, which the man secretly owed him, when the time came. Their pact was sealed with "a holy kiss of faith and of peace," the creditor dispensing the debtor (weren't they father and godfather?) from a more constricting oath, which would have been a mark of disrespect. The status of father-godfather therefore indeed created a privileged relationship, beyond the usual social norms.[91] According to Peter Morone (the future Pope Celestin V), Peter's father had appeared to Peter's godmother to tell his son how happy he was that his widow had given instruction to Peter.[92] This tale shows the godmother integrated into the family, where she played, several years after the death of the father, the role of a "messenger of souls."

The *familia*, or the feudal-vassalic hunt, was also, in its own way, a sort of hierarchical and also egalitarian "family" kept together through exchanges of largesses and services, through communal activities of war

and hunting, and through the division of the profits from seignorial dom-
ination. Symbolic gestures of faith and homage consecrated these ties.[93]
As we have seen in Peter the Venerable's tales of apparitions, vassalic
kinship did not disappear after the death of the lord or of his man. It was
through the intermediary of their vassals—one dead, the other alive—
that the old and the new lords of Beaujeu, the dead father and the living
son, enter into a relationship. In a contemporary miracle concerning
Saint Foi of Sélestat, the dead count Conrad of Hohenstaufen appears to
his vassal the knight Walter. "By virtue of the vassalic faith that he swore
to [the count] and the largesses that he always received from his lord,"
the dead man asks Walter to beg the count's surviving brothers to give
generous gifts to the new church.[94]

In the *familia* that was sheltered and formed by every "house" worthy
of that name (as Christiane Klapisch-Zuber has shown, "house" must be
understood in both a material and a symbolic sense),[95] relationships of
dependency, including salaried ones, were not easily distinguishable from
the affective ties that united true "relatives." Peter the Venerable gathered
the tale of Peter Engelbert, the master of a house, to whom the servant
Sancho, who had been his "mercenary," that is, his employee, had appeared to ask him to use, for Sancho's salvation, the few wages he still
owed his employee.[96] Similarly, in Yorkshire two centuries later, the dead
"mercenary of a head of the family" requested, through an interposed
informant, that his master pardon him for his professional misconduct
and endeavor to free him from his punishment.[97]

Curiously, at least one form of spiritual kinship does not appear in
our tales even though it became increasingly important at the end of
the Middle Ages: the kinship formed by confraternities and lay charities,
especially in urban environments. It is true that the role of these collective institutions in assisting the dying, in burying the dead, and in praying for the souls of the dead showed rather strong regional disparities.[98]
This gap in our tales perhaps also comes from the relative autonomy
of the life of the confraternities as compared with the apostolate of the
preachers. Generally, confraternities rarely figure in the literature of the
exempla. All the same, the very frequent theme, in this literature as well,
of the two friends who promise each other that the first to die will visit
the survivor can be connected to the ideal of spiritual solidarity developed in the heart of the confraternities.

Assuming they were not hermits, people in the Middle Ages were never
alone. Even in their dreams, where the educated of the twelfth century

had the experience of a certain form of subjectivity, they encountered other *personae*, as texts sometimes say—dead people belonging to their natural or spiritual *familia*. The success of ghost tales, enhanced by the entire chain of oral and written tradition, derived from the fact that they always placed at least two people in a relationship—a dead person and a living person, united beyond death—and most often many other people as well.

NINE

DESCRIBING GHOSTS

Not all ghosts wanted to be seen. Some sources (up to Johannes Gobi) reported that they heard only noises or voices interpreted as being those of ghosts. In asserting that a dead person appeared clearly to someone who was awake, certain autobiographical accounts (from Thietmar of Merseburg to the emperor Charles IV) were more hesitant than were the tales handed down for a long time by word of mouth. The former were dreams and confused impressions of noises and voices, rather than apparitions in a clear vision. How a dead person was made visible was therefore indeed an effect of the social construction of the tale. Just as doubts and hesitations about the appearance of the dead person corresponded to the subjective and oneiric experience of the apparition, so did an objectivization of the ghost go hand in hand with the socialization of the tale.

Sometimes the dialectic of the invisible and the visible served as a motif for the tale: a dead person who at first was invisible later agreed, at the request of the living, to show himself or herself. According to an old hagiographical model that went back to Gregory the Great, the dead person might also visit only one person, refusing to appear to anyone else: the ghost was visible to that person alone (but in certain cases, others could hear the dead person) or might disappear if an intruder entered. This was the case in the tale of the ghost of Beaucaire, when the parents of the young girl appeared on the threshold of the bedroom.

The Body of Appearances

When visible, the dead person normally had a human form; ghosts were the same age they had been and appeared with the same features they had had at the time of death. This enabled the beneficiary of the apparition to recognize the ghost, which might also have exhibited a distinctive physical mark. For example, a knight who died in combat or during a tournament might have the still-bleeding wound that had caused him to pass from life to death. But a ghost did not always have a human appearance. In reported tales, unlike autobiographical tales, the dead person sometimes took on the shape of a material object (a haystack) or, more often, of an animal—a bird, a dog, a reptile, or a horse. In the metamorphoses that such tales attributed to them, the dead had a rich bestiary at their disposal, the symbolism of which was highly significant. Sometimes such transformations manifested the evolution of the spiritual state of the dead person. In Yorkshire, according to the account of the monk of Byland, the spirit of the former "mercenary" of Rievaulx appeared first in the form of a horse that reared up, then as a haystack, and only the third time "in the shape of a man." Another dead man, who had been excommunicated, appeared successively to the tailor Snowball in the form of a crow that fluttered miserably, a dog that was able to talk like a man, a goat, and finally, a very tall man. Even the spirit of old Heinrich Buschmann appeared the first time in the form of a mean dog and only afterward as the old man of eighty-eight that he had been when he had died. These tales probably bear the mark of very old representations of the soul in the form of animals, such as reptiles and birds.[1] But we must be careful not to see in these metamorphoses only the "remnants" of a pre-Christian folklore: Christian art also, especially until the twelfth century, often represented the soul or the spirit in the form of a bird.[2] In addition, clerics believed that the metamorphoses of the dead, like their changes in color (especially from black to white), provided a measurement of the progression of their souls in purgatory toward their liberation. Let us recall once again that the content of texts or illustrations cannot be studied independently from the logic of the textual, narrative, and iconographical genres to which they belonged or from the functions they fulfilled.

The Spiritual and the Corporeal

At death, the body and the soul separated, remaining apart until the resurrection of the dead and the Last Judgment. The soul was "spiritual" but "passible," capable of feeling: it was tortured in hell or in purgatory by a fire or a cold that the people of the Middle Ages—or some of them, following Gregory the Great—imagined so concretely that they called these conditions "corporeal." In fact, medieval Christianity was never able to resolve the contradiction between two of its profound exigencies: on the one hand, the desire to deny the body in order better to serve God, and thus the association of the "spiritual" with the immaterial; and on the other hand, the necessity to *imagine* the invisible and thus to situate it in space and time, to conceive of the places, the forms, the volumes, and the bodies in the very place where they should have been excluded. The monk Guibert of Nogent, a fervent "spiritualist" in the tradition of Saint Augustine, laughed at those who imagined that souls had a body because painters represented them in the form of a little naked child coming out of the mouths of the dying.[3] Indeed, some authors of tales of visions and voyages to the hereafter, such as the famous *Vision of Tnugdal*, concerned with establishing a continuity between earthly life and the Christian afterworld, encouraged, against the advice of the more "spiritualist" theologians, the granting of a certain degree of "corporeity" to souls in purgatory.[4]

All ambiguity in fact came from the word "spiritual." In the Middle Ages the notion of "spiritual" was intermediate and ambiguous. Just as "spiritual vision" slipped in between "intellectual vision" and "corporeal vision," the spirit (*spiritus*) had its place—according to the great theologian of the twelfth century, Hugh of Saint Victor—between the soul (*anima, mens*, pure reason) and the body (*corpus*). Neither the "spirit" of a living person, who thought and imagined, nor the "spirit" of a dead person was an immaterial "pure spirit." By definition, these spirits were not corporeal either. The spirit was something in between, and this is why, said Alcher of Clairvaux, not without some unease, the spirit was "something": "All that is not a body and which however is *something* is said rightly to be 'spirit.'"[5] The spirit was not a body, and yet it was in league with the body.

For "spiritual images," notably those produced by an apparition, the relationship to the body was presented in three ways:

• Far from concerning only the "spirit" of the dreamer or the visionary, the images could act on the dreamer's body.
• Far from being completely immaterial, they could have a certain "corporeity."
• Far from being completely detached from the body of the dead person, they could, in the case of the apparition of a dead person, maintain a relationship with the cadaver.

Spiritual images acted not only on the spirit but also on the body of the one who perceived them. We have seen, above, how the monk Otloh of Saint Emmeram reported in his *Liber visionum* four personal dreams connected to his conversion and to the conflicts that put him in opposition to other monks.[6] One night he dreams that a "man" (*vir*) is violently whipping him. After awakening, he feels a great pain and realizes that his back is covered with blood. Questioned, a young oblate states that he heard no disturbance during the night. Otloh is shocked, then collects himself. He had forgotten that "spiritual things occur with no corporeal sound"— but not without an effect on the body: the marks of the whipping on his back are the proof of the truth of the vision. In the next century Guibert of Nogent himself is caught in the same contradictions. On the one hand, he speaks of the "appearance of bodies" (*species corporum*) of the souls that manifest themselves to the living; on the other, he reports that a nun of his acquaintance saw in a dream two demons strike a dead sister with a mallet, the blows producing sparks, one of which penetrated the eye of the sleeping woman. The pain awakened her, and the wound in her eye remained as the proof of the truth of the dream.[7]

Like demons, ghosts could produce material effects on the objects or living bodies that they touched on earth.[8] In particular were burns when they brought the "corporeal fire" that was afflicting them in the afterworld with them and introduced it among the living, as proof of their lamentable fate. A famous *exemplum* of the thirteenth century tells of the apparition of a dead disciple to a university teacher, Master Serlo. To convince the teacher of the vanity of his knowledge, the ghost drips onto his hand a drop of incandescent sweat, which instantly goes right through his hand.[9] Another level is reached in Yorkshire at the end of the twelfth century in the tales reported by William of Newburgh. There the ghosts were not evanescent appearances of souls in purgatory requesting suffrages but were the evil-doing dead, like those described in sagas: "pestilential monsters" that attacked people, killed them, and drank their blood.[10] This was confirmed by the monk of Byland two centuries later when he told, for example, how the spirit of the dead curate of Kirkby returned at night to gouge out one of the eyes of his ex-mistress.

Our tales portray dead figures who, in varying degrees and in a troubling way, display a consistency, a density, a resistance to physical contact with the living. Questioned by his young cousin, the ghost of Beaucaire explains his nature as a ghost: he defines himself not only as an "image of a body" that is not a body but also as an "aerial body."[11] Both of these notions come from Saint Augustine, from his theory of "spiritual vision" and from his demonology. The latter theory in fact attributes to demons an "aerial body" with which they move through the air, just above the earth, much more rapidly than people move on earth; thus they are able to anticipate human actions and thoughts.[12] The ghost of Beaucaire also says that he does not suffer in his "body" but as a "spirit," so delicate that the lightest weight—that of the stole with which the priest wants to "tie him"—is unbearable to him. Although invisible, the spirit of the citizen of Alès, Gui de Corvo, also reveals that he is an aerial body: his widow and the prior of the Dominicans, Johannes Gobi, sense movement in the air at the moment he leaves them. Around the same time, in Montaillou, Arnaude Ribes saw wandering souls who exhibited true bodies; according to Guillaume Fort's account of the event before the inquisitor, the souls of the evil, Arnaude said, had "skin, bones, and all their limbs, such as a head, feet, hands, and all the other limbs."[13] Around 1400 in Yorkshire, ghosts were even more corporeal: they came out of their graves, scattered outside the cemetery, and physically attacked the villagers. A woman was seen carrying a "spirit" on her back: she dug "her fingers deeply into the flesh of the spirit, as if the flesh of that same spirit were a putrid phantasm, and not solid."[14] It was as if, says the monk of Byland, the ghost was only a cadaver in appearance, a sort of soft or hollow body that, when hit, sounded like a pillow or a bed being struck.[15] These spirits were so concrete that the living could grab them and grapple with them: young Robert Foxton managed to hold a spirit at the exit of a cemetery against the door of the church.

It is therefore not surprising that many tales establish a strict relationship between the apparition of the dead person and the cadaver that was in the grave but that, it seems, escaped from the grave at night. To relieve their worries, the young men of Yorkshire opened a grave and verified the condition of the body. This specification was not characteristic only of Yorkshire. According to Caesarius of Heisterbach as well, a knight who attempted in vain to pull a dead woman from the clutches of an infernal knight ended up with only a lock of her hair in his hand. The next day, after opening the grave of that woman, he discovered that the cadaver was missing the lock of hair.[16] This interdependence, indeed this identity of the cadaver with the ghost, finds an echo in certain funerary practices. Well before William of Newburgh and the monk of Byland told how the young men of Yorkshire dug up the cadavers and burned them to prevent the return of evil spirits, Burchard of Worms denounced the Christians who put a stake through the cadavers of women who had died in childbirth and of stillborn children in order to prevent their ill-fated return.[17]

Behind these practices and tales, one might glimpse the idea that the curse weighing on an evil-doing dead person first affected the cadaver. Not only did the dead person return to haunt the space of the living, but the cadaver—and everything was connected—was condemned not to decompose in the ground. That such conceptions were ancient and foreign to Christianity cannot be doubted. But they found their place in Christian representations of death by echoing and at the same time opposing the official representations of the bodies of saints. Diametrically opposed to the ragtag of the Christian dead were the evil-doing dead, such as the excommunicated, which shared a destiny with the saints: their bodies were imputrescible. The fact was well-known for saints: from their graves emanated the "odor of holiness," which revealed the miraculous preservation of the flesh. Whether for the better (the saints) or for the worse (our corporeal ghosts), the same distance, though inversed, from the norm is observed. Thus the unique fate of such cadavers is a reminder that most ordinary Christians—those who were neither saints nor excommunicated—were subject to the common law of a triple progressive disappearance: of their physical remains in the grave, of their soul beyond purgatory, and of their memory in the minds of the living.

The Language of the Dead

The fact that the dead person spoke and that the words were most often reported in a direct style continued to add to the impression of a physical presence. The apparition was a sonorous phenomenon as much as it was visual and tactile. The visit of a ghost could be reduced to noises, more or less audible words, or even a "voice without words," according to the expression of the monk Guibert of Nogent.[18] Sometimes one could distinctly hear a ghost speaking and even converse with it, but without seeing it: this is what happened to the prior of the Dominicans of Alès, Johannes Gobi. The dead man "appeared in voice" (*apparuit in voce*) to his widow. The expression echoes the one that Rabanus Maurus used when he spoke of an "image of voice."[19] Some tales also suggest a gradation in a ghost's revelation: the dead person at first speaks and then agrees to appear.[20] Next, the usual dialogue between the living and the dead could begin. Often the scribe reported only the dead person's words in the direct style, reserving the indirect style for the questions of the living person. Thus, paradoxically, the most lively voice is that of the deceased. A voice from beyond the grave and thus one of authority had to be reported as faithfully as possible, just as it was heard. With some exceptions, this voice was not characterized by any form of glossolalia;[21] nor, even when the dead person was an *illitteratus* who did not know Latin, was the vernacular substituted for the scholarly language (that of the scribe). It is rare, in our clerical tales, to encounter intrusions of the vernacular.[22] Sometimes the manner of speaking combined with the physical appearance to facilitate recognition of the dead person by the living one: Peter the Venerable, concerned with faithfully transcribing the words of the dead monk William of Roanne, whom he heard in a dream, went so far as to reproduce the stuttering that had characterized William while the monk was alive.[23]

How could a ghost talk? Several tales stress that the spirit possessed a linguistic faculty different from that of the living body. When the cleric Raoul watched over the cadaver of his friend Cecilia in his house, he heard himself called by the spirit of the young girl from outside the house.[24] The spirit of Gui de Corvo himself explains the origin of his voice. The prior Johannes Gobi asks him, "How can you speak, you who have no mouth or tongue, which are the instruments of language?" Gui de Corvo answers that in a living body, the tongue does not have the power to speak by itself; it is but the tool of the soul, in which all power resides, including that of speaking. Thus when the soul is separated from the body, it has no trouble speaking, nor do the incorporeal angels.[25] The ambiguity of the spiritual and the corporeal applied both to the appearance of the bodies and to the voices of the dead. Moreover, some spirits spoke even though they had no tongue. The monk of Byland confirmed this: the tailor Snowball studies "the insides [of the spirit] through its mouth [while the spirit] forms its words in its intestines and does not speak with its tongue."[26] Another ventriloquist spirit "spoke from within its guts and not with its tongue, like in an empty jug."[27]

The Clothing of the Dead

Clothing was never used simply to protect the body. In medieval culture it was also a sign of belonging to a social "estate"; it situated the individual and the group within the hierarchy of the *ordines*. It was also perceived as one of the modes of expression of the moral or religious value of a per-

son. Moreover, it became one with the person who wore it and participated in that person's being, like a second skin.[28] But clothing was a skin
that could be changed, that could be exchanged; its dynamism, consequently, added more to its power as a symbol. In the realities of social
action as in those of the imaginary, the fact of dressing oneself, of un-
dressing oneself, of changing clothes, of altering them, or of giving them
away illustrated a person's transformations, worth, and spiritual being.

Like all other stages in life (birth and baptism, initiation into knighthood, taking on the monastic habit, marriage, etc.), the clothing of a
dead person was distinctive. Clothing concerned the deceased (it was
fitting, for example, that a monk be buried in the robe of his order) as
well as the close survivors (who, at the end of the Middle Ages and in
certain places, at least, wore a color of mourning, which commonly became black).[29] Clothing was a part not only of funerary rituals but also
of the imaginary of death and the hereafter. When the soul is depicted
as a little child who comes out with the last breath from the mouth of
the deceased, it is often nude. It is also nude in the torments of hell or
purgatory, as are the bodies that emerge from their tombs at the time
of the resurrection of the dead and at the Last Judgment. The elect, on
the contrary, are frequently dressed by the angels in lavish clothing, symbols of their glorious bodies.[30] The dialectic of nudity and of clothing
organizes the imaginary's representation of the fate of souls in the hereafter.

For ghosts, the situation was more complex, for they were not yet
completely detached from the world of the living. What they wore depended, therefore, on several factors, such as their past adherence to a
given order of society, which was often characterized by a specific type
of clothing. They continued to wear—in the memories, dreams, and
tales of the living—the clothing for which they were known and which
helped the living to recognize them. Their spiritual state in the hereafter
was likewise expressed by the nature, the condition, and the color of
their clothing. The use that the dead made of their clothing before their
death and the use that the survivors made of the clothing after the death
were also significant, in particular if the survivors made a charitable gift
of the clothing to a poor person.

Before the end of the Middle Ages, ghosts were hardly ever described as being more or less naked cadavers or as wearing only their
shrouds. Dead knights appeared with the uniform and the weapons of
the knights they had once been, and dead monks wore their monk's habit.
According to Peter the Venerable, the dead knight Geoffroy d'Ion "ap-

peared in the clothing that was usual for him."[31] In a Cistercian tale, a knight who was "boastful, thieving, and lecherous" appeared to his wife or his mistress after his death: he entered into the garden, "seated on his superb war horse, wearing in the appropriate manner the weapons and the military insignia *with which he was familiar in his lifetime* and making gestures, by shaking his hair and with other movements of his body, *that he was used to doing* in tournaments."[32] Another very bad knight, Henry Nodus, from the province of Trêves, appeared to his daughter "wearing the sheepskin he was used to wearing."[33]

The very numerous monastic tales of apparitions confirm the funerary symbolism of the monk's clothing. From the day that he "took the habit" the monk never took it off, not while he was among the living, nor while in the grave, nor while in the imaginary future that the living attributed to his soul. His cape with a hood *(cuculla)* played a particular role in his passing from life to death and, vice versa, in the visit that the dead made to the living. As Caesarius of Heisterbach recounts, for example, the monk Lambert was sleeping in the choir of the church one Sunday night and saw in a dream the monastery cellarer, named Richwin, who had died a few years earlier, enter the church and gesture to him to follow Richwin in the direction of the Rhine. Knowing that Richwin was dead, Lambert did not move. The dead man then turned toward the monk Conrad, more than fifty years old, and made the same gesture to him. Without saying a word, Conrad lowered his hood over his head and followed the dead man. After lunch the monk Lambert told the dream to the aged Conrad and told him that he would soon die. Indeed, shortly afterward they buried him "in the same *cuculla.*"[34] It was in fact important that the monk die in his *cuculla,* for it would protect him in the hereafter from the traps of demons.[35] In monastic tales of apparitions, the *cuculla* is the distinctive sign of former monks, even when they died in the habit of a secular or lay cleric.[36] The funerary symbolism of the mantle and hoods of monks was probably the beneficiary of more ancient beliefs concerning the "hood" as a sign of recognizing the dead and as an instrument of their passing into the hereafter.[37] In Germanic folklore the *tarnkappe* (or *tarnhut* or *hüttlin,* the hood) gave a superhuman strength to whoever wore it, enabling the person immediately to go wherever he or she wanted or even to become invisible. It was also called *Hellekeppelin:* this was explicitly the headgear of Hellequin, the king of the dead.[38] Even more generally, headgear was the sign of a unique passage between earth and the hereafter: at birth, by portraying children "born with headgear," and inversely after death, for the dead who return to visit the living.[39]

The shoes of the dead were also supposed to help in their passage into the hereafter. In the thirteenth century the liturgist William Durand stated that if socks were placed on the legs of dead people and shoes on their feet, they would thus be prepared to confront their judgment.[40] In Avignon, during funerals, the bell ringer received the socks, shoes, and belt of the deceased as his fee; the dead person was not, however, deprived of them, for the person carried into the hereafter the spiritual benefit of those gifts.[41] As we are assured in the *Vision of Gottschalk* (in northern Germany in the twelfth century), whoever, while alive, gave shoes to the poor would find in the hereafter, hanging from a majestic lime tree, a plethora of good shoes.[42] On the contrary, according to an *exemplum* of Caesarius of Heisterbach, a priest's mistress who had herself buried with her beautiful shoes—objects of her greed and symbols of her lust—was carried off into hell by a diabolical knight and his cursed pack of dogs.[43]

The color of the dead person's clothing in particular took into account his or her fate, and possibly the improvement in this fate, in the hereafter. In the tale of Saint Foi of Sélestat, the contrast between red and white prevails. In general the contrast between black and white revealed, in the rhythm of apparitions, the improvement of the fate of the dead person, dressed first all in black, then half-black, next half-white, and finally all in white; thus the dead person came back one last time dressed all in white to show the living person, who had helped with prayers, that the dead person was finally saved.[44] The chromatics of ghosts was not very diverse, and it remained quite traditional: the characteristic binary contrasts came from the old Indo-European system of three basic colors (white, red, and black).[45]

Finally, clothing was a powerful operator of exchanges between the world of the living and that of the dead. The exchange could be positive. In a tale from Peter the Venerable, an old nobleman who died during a pilgrimage, Bernard le Gros, appears to a monk of Cluny wearing a fox skin; indeed, he made a gift of just such a skin to a poor person, and that skin is now serving him as a *refrigerium*; it is comforting him in his tribulations in the hereafter. The exchange could also be negative, as in all the tales of apparitions in which the dead person is naked or dressed oddly because he or she refused to clothe a poor person, stole a habit, or neglected to give back a borrowed article of clothing. This dead person returns to ask those close to him to "clothe him" by rectifying the wrong committed. Peter the Venerable tells of how the "mercenary" Sancho appeared—completely nude, with only a loincloth around him—before his former master because he had stolen ecclesiastical clothing in his life-time; he begged his master to give back to the church what he had stolen. Caesarius of Heisterbach reported the apparition of a knight who had died recently, Frederic of Kelle, who was wearing the sheepskins he had stolen from a poor widow.[46] In the long tale from Gervase of Tilbury, the young William first appeared completely nude to his cousin of Beaucaire. The second time he had recovered his clothing that his aunt, the mother of the young girl, had in the meantime given to the poor.[47] In the hereaf-ter, dead people, potentially naked and miserable, wear the clothing with which they themselves (or their heirs) parted, to the benefit of the poor. Clothing was both a transferable material object and the immaterial sym-bol of a charitable gift. Every offering of clothing was supposed to take place simultaneously on two indissociable planes, on earth and in the hereafter. The model for this correspondence beyond the limits of life and death is very ancient: Sulpicius Severus's *Life of Saint Martin* contains the famous episode of the sharing of the mantle to benefit a poor person. In Martin's dream, Christ appears wearing the mantle given to the poor man. This hagiographical tale could be connected to the one of the appa-rition of King Sancho in the *Chronicle of Iria*: forty days after appearing a first time to his widow, Godo, the king appeared to her another time wearing white clothing (the sign that he had been saved) and a fur that, to save his soul, he had given to a poor priest. Tearing a piece of the fur from the ghost, Godo took it to the monastery of San Esteban de Ribas de Sil, where the monks noted that a piece of equal size was missing from the fur given to the priest. The supernatural piece of fur that Queen Godo brought back was then added to the real fur in order to attest— along the lines of the divisionary deeds that the protagonists of a transac-tion divide among themselves—to the truth of the apparition and to the merits of suffrages for the dead.[48]

Illustrations of Ghosts

If the object of a "spiritual vision" was an "image," its figured representa-tions must be understood as "images of images," a concept that poses a great many questions. How are the material illustrations of ghosts differ-ent from depictions of other objects? What are the specific traits of the apparition among the modes of figuration in use in the medieval period? From what we learn from texts, can we deduce the parameters of the figuration of ghosts? There exists a priori an entire range of possibilities, from the representation of living flesh to a skeleton, going through the various states of the cadaver in decomposition. Will the ghost be depicted dressed in the clothing characteristic of the social status it enjoyed, in the shroud in which it was buried, or even in no clothes, naked like a miserable soul? Will we find in this age pictures of phantoms draped in a white shroud, as they have been depicted since the romantic period? What iconic markers will point out the supernatural nature of the apparition? In the medieval iconography of dreams, only the juxtaposition of the image of the sleeper and the object of the dream designated the oneiric nature of the vision.[49] But what about apparitions perceived in a wakeful state? Finally, what role should be given to history, to the chronological evolution of the modes of representation? Like the theoretical and narrative texts, the iconography of ghosts has undergone a long evolution in time. Compared with the narrative tradition or with other types of illustrations, this iconography was rather late (we do not encounter pictorial images before the end of the eleventh century) and was transformed progressively until the end of the Middle Ages. Finally, just as we have carefully distinguished the various narrative genres, let us be careful not to mix all the figured representations independently of the iconic groupings to which they belong.

Schematically, between the twelfth and the fifteenth centuries there were six distinct and partially successive modes of representing ghosts:

- The Lazarus: the ghost is depicted as being resuscitated
- The living dead: there is no perceivable difference between the ghost and the living person or persons to whom it appears
- The soul: the ghost takes the form of a small naked child, following the most frequent conventional mode of representing souls
- The phantom: the ghost appears enveloped in a diaphanous shroud
- The macabre: the ghost appears as a living cadaver in a more or less advanced state of decomposition
- The invisible: this is a borderline solution to the image, in strict dependency with regard to a text

The illustrations we have already encountered correspond to several of these types: the ghost of Alès is invisible in the miniature by Simon Marmion, just as he is in the tale of Johannes Gobi. However, the invisible spirit that disturbs the sleep of the emperor Charles IV in Prague is depicted once according to the type of the living dead (wearing a fashionable doublet) and once according to the type of the soul (as a little naked child). Between the twelfth and the fifteenth century the iconography of Samuel in the biblical episode of Endor explored almost all the available possibilities, beginning with the Lazarus type.

Representations of more ordinary ghosts were rare before the end of the Middle Ages. The oldest might go back to the eleventh century, the time when written accounts of ghost tales began to increase in number. Two miniatures dated precisely from 1071 and a storied capital of Fleury (today Saint Benoît-sur-Loire) illustrate the miracles of Saint Benedict according to Gregory the Great's tale in the second book of his *Dialogues*.[50] In Chapter 23 Gregory tells how two nuns who could not hold their tongues were punished with excommunication by the saint. They died and were buried in the church. But every time mass was celebrated there, "their nurse, who was used to bringing the offering of the Lord to them, saw them rise out of their graves and leave the church." The marvel continued until the saint agreed to lift their excommunication. Chapter 24 tells a comparable story: a young monk left the monastery without permission to go visit his parents. On the way there he died in an accident. His parents twice tried to bury him, but the body always refused to stay in the sarcophagus. As a last resort the parents threw themselves at the feet of Benedict, who ordered that a consecrated host be placed on the dead man's chest. Henceforth the cadaver stayed put. The two tales are very closely related. Besides the comparable role of their common hero, Benedict, they portray the same wonder of cadavers rejected by the tomb, and they suggest the same remedy to overcome those accursed bodies: the consecrated host, the body of Christ. Are the spirits still ghosts? Not in the sense of the apparitions that Gregory the Great himself talks about in Book IV of his *Dialogues*. However, they are still ghosts if we connect those two tales to later ones that, primarily in Yorkshire, associate "spirits" with cadavers that supposedly came out of their graves and that were physically forced to go back in.

In 1071 the abbot Desiderius of Monte Cassino—the abbey founded by Saint Benedict himself—brought together a group of abbots and prelates (including several champions of ecclesiastical reform, such as Peter Damian) to carry out with pomp the consecration of the new abbatial church. On that occasion he had a very precious *Lectionnaire* of the feast days of Saint Benedict, Saint Maurus, and Saint Scholastica composed, today preserved in the Vatican library.[51] Our two tales found a place in the rich iconography of this manuscript. The order in which they appear is partially reversed, each picture illustrating episodes in both of the two tales. In the first (fol. 57 r.), we see Saint Benedict giving an offering to a cleric so that he can force the two women of Chapter 23 to go back into their graves. But here we also see the cadaver of the young monk of Chapter 24 lying dead, his eyes closed and his hood lowered on his head, next to the open sarcophagus in which he will not stay. In the background we see the same sarcophagus, this time containing the body of the young monk, on whose chest a priest places the host (illus. 15). Turning the page, we see depictions of two other episodes of the story of the young monk: Saint Benedict receives in turn the father and then the mother of the dead man and gives the consecrated host to the mother (illus. 16). In this same picture we also see the rest of the story of the two nuns. They are sitting up in their tombs, like the resuscitated dead, enveloped in shrouds or voluminous veils, one red and the other blue, partially hiding their faces. They are not cadavers, as is the young monk in the preceding folio, but indeed are living dead women rising stiffly out of their tombs and perhaps represented by the painter following the model of a resuscitated Lazarus.

The same story inspired the sculpting of a capital of Saint Benoît-sur-Loire, also dated, but without great precision, from the eleventh century (illus. 17).[52] This capital, today removed, shows on one side Christ giving his blessing; behind him, smaller, is Saint Benedict, whose right hand is blended with the left hand of the Lord: in a gripping manner the image recalls that God is the true author of miracles performed by the saints. On the other side is the tomb that someone is trying to open. The two nuns are lying there, but their heads are emerging as if they were coming out. They are not upright, as in the illustration in the manuscript. They appear dead, lying horizontally, but their status remains ambiguous, as it does in the tale itself; it was their bodies that were expelled from the church, under the pressure of a supernatural force that associates them with some evil spirit.

Illustrations of ghosts began to multiply in the thirteenth century. An example is *Miracles of Our Lady*, composed in French between 1218 and 1233 by a monk of Saint Medard de Soissons, Gautier of Coincy. The success of this collection of fifty-five Marian miracles was enormous: we know of more than eighty manuscripts of them. In all of these miracles, the Virgin intervenes to protect or heal her devotees during their lifetimes or to save them at the hour of their deaths or from the individual judgment of their souls, even when they should be damned. Her mercy thus benefited a monastery prior who had committed great sins but who had never failed to honor the Virgin.[53] He died, and the brothers buried him normally. But exactly one year later, "at the head of the year," while the sacristan monk, Brother Hubert, is lighting the lamps of the church before matins, he hears his name being called by a strong and clear voice. "Hubert, beautiful brother," says the voice. Gripped with fear, he goes to bed and instantly falls back asleep. In a dream he sees the dead prior, who reproaches him for not responding to the prior's call. Then the prior tells Brother Hubert of the torments he has endured for a year, but he also reveals that the Virgin has freed him due to the devotion he had always shown her. The next morning the sacristan tells the vision to the abbot, who decides to pray to the Virgin with his monks. Shortly afterward, Brother Hubert in turn dies.

Of all the miracles of Gautier of Coincy, this is the only one that depicts a ghost. This ghost, more than the Virgin, is the main character of the tale. In the illuminated manuscripts of the *Miracles of Our Lady*, the miniature retains only the first intervention of the dead man, when he calls to the sacristan but the latter does not yet see him (illus. 18).[54] The illustration gives a body to this voice by depicting the ghost who enters into the space of the sanctuary and raises his finger, a gesture that means he is speaking. It also suggests the surprise of the sacristan, who, his face gripped with fear, turns around at the call of his name; it thus transforms into a visual image of an apparition the tale of the sonorous manifestation of the dead person. That dead man has the carnal consistency and the clothing of a living monk, but the way in which he tucks up his mantle over his naked leg and his foot (whereas the sacristan monk is shod, and his leg is hidden under his frock) distinguishes him as a supernatural being. The foot that is revealed and naked is here the sign of belonging to the hereafter as well as of the miserable condition that justifies the request for suffrages.

In another manuscript from the same work, the miniature is divided into four parts representing as many sequences of the miracle (illus. 19).[55] In it we see in succession the entrance of the ghost into the church behind the sacristan, who is busy at the altar; the oneiric apparition to the sacristan, who has taken refuge in sleep; the tale that the sacristan tells the abbot and the monks the next day; and finally, the funeral of the sacristan. In the first vignette the dead prior is half hidden by the edge of the picture, which suggests his incursion into the church and into the earthly space of the living. His head is covered by the hood, the *cuculla* on which so many monastic tales of ghosts insist and that here contrasts him with the living monk. He crosses the sleeves of his habit in front of him, a gesture that we have already encountered in the illuminated manuscripts of the autobiography of Charles IV and that might signify a lack of power and a humble request.[56] But there are no hands coming out of the sleeves (in contrast to the active hands of the sacristan), as if this habit was empty, in order perhaps to suggest that the "spiritual image" has no carnal consistency. Similarly, the feet are not visible. The second vignette presents a classic illustration of a dream: the curtains that are spread apart on both sides of the bed delimit the space of the oneiric vision. Without the help of the text and the knowledge of this conventional way of representing a dream, we could not distinguish the dead person from any living visitor at the foot of the bed.

The Birth of the Phantom

Another jewel of the medieval tradition of miracles of the Virgin is found in *Cantigas de Santa Maria*, written between 1267 and 1272 by King Alfonso X the Wise of Leon-Castilla. It is a massive work (it contains more than three hundred miracles) with a rich iconography (close to two thousand illustrations). Each tale of a miracle is accompanied by a single or double full page with six (or twelve) vignettes.[57] Two tales are stories of ghosts. One of them tells "how Saint Mary took a Minorite brother under her care against devils at the time he died."[58] The six corresponding miniatures (illus. 24) show successively the entrance of the brother into the monastery church; his death, in which the blackness of his face betrays that of his soul, which is being seized by demons; and the flight of the demons when the brothers put into the dead man's hand the candle that is the emblem (*signaculum*) of the Virgin, to whom, despite his sins, he always remained devoted. The dead man's face here becomes all white again. Next is the scene of the funeral. The fifth illustration shows the apparition of the dead man to two other brothers in the cloisters. Finally, once again in the church, the brothers give thanks to the Virgin. The illustration of the apparition in the cloisters does not indicate that a dead man is among the three brothers; only knowledge of the text of the miracle reveals his presence. He is distinguishable neither by his corporeal appearance nor by his habit. One might even hesitate to choose a figure for this role, but the absence of a book in the hands of the person on the left most likely designates him as the ghost. In this illustration, even more than in the earlier ones, the dead man gives the illusion of being alive. On this point the illustration is consistent with many tales of apparitions in which a living person is surprised to encounter a close friend or relative whose death has just been revealed but who seems alive to the visionary—unless the living person is unaware of the recent death and believes the friend or relative is still alive.

However, regarding another ghost tale, the same manuscript presents a quite different illustration (illus. 25).[59] The miracle tells how a demon killed a young barfly, a *tafur* who, after losing at a game, had blasphemed against the Virgin. The six miniatures show successively the players in the tavern; the moment of the blasphemy (expressed by a vigorous gesture aimed at the sky); and the demon as it immediately eviscerates the guilty man. In the next illustration "a dead man appears to the father of the *tafur* and tells him that his son is dead." The ghost is therefore not the young man who has just died: the ghost's role is that of a messenger from the afterworld and from the Virgin, who remains invisible. Informed—thanks to this ghost—the father, in the following illustration, goes to the cadaver and laments. Then he gives his son a worthy funeral. What is most strange in this series of illustrations is the phantom-like appearance of the dead man: unlike the living person who is standing in front of him, he is lacking all color and all material density; the description of his face and his clothing is reduced to a drawing that is uniformly diaphanous and scarcely visible.

Even though several hands contributed to the iconography of this large manuscript and even though we cannot therefore exclude differences in style, we must admit that there existed locally at least two ways of representing ghosts in the second half of the thirteenth century: in the manner of the living; and as partially incorporeal and translucent phantoms. The differences in these two illustrations comes perhaps from the status of the two dead men in question: whereas the Minorite brother, who is endowed with a strong corporeity, had just died, the dead man who appears to the father of the *tafur* had been dead for much longer. The appearance of this ghost perhaps indicates how much time has passed since the death, the distance placed between the living and the dead, and the likely completion of the process of decomposition of the flesh in the tomb. In addition, whereas the Minorite brother who had just died was known by his brothers and therefore his depiction could represent him as one of them, the ghost who tells the father of the tragic end of his son is for him a foreign and anonymous dead person, not a dead relative still present in his memory. Might not the phantom-like depiction in this illustration be a means of representing the anonymity of a dead person who had been dead for some time, who has no attachment to the living person to whom he is speaking, and who has no other purpose here than as a messenger from the world of the dead? Finally, the illustration strongly contrasts this phantom to the cadaver, lying just below on the bier: in contrast to the evanescence of the phantom-like representation is the strong density of a true cadaver, whose weight is measured by the effort expended by the men who are carrying it.[60] The phantom, while presenting the appearance of a body, is only an image—an image that is the very first, perhaps, in Western tradition and that announces from afar those that, since the nineteenth century, have been imposed on us to the exclusion of all others.

One might say that the Western phantom, that of cartoons and of fantastic films, was born at the end of the thirteenth century. For the miniature of *Cantigas* is not a unique case. Phantoms are also represented in certain illuminated manuscripts of *Pilgrimage of Human Life* by Guillaume of Deguileville. In this lengthy allegorical and religious poem, the author tells in the first person a dream that he supposedly had under the influence, he says in the prologue, of reading *Roman de la Rose*. Having fallen asleep (and it is in this state that the first miniatures of the very numerous manuscripts of the poem represent him), he dreams that his soul, taking on the appearance and the attributes of a pilgrim, leaves for Jerusalem. Jerusalem is described not only as a true city but also as the anticipation of the celestial Jerusalem. Moreover, the beautiful, young, crowned, and haloed woman who guides the soul on the pilgrimage is named Grace of God. In one of the many edifying vicissitudes during the journey, the pilgrim soul sees three dead people (ghosts) serve three living people at a table. The text of the poem inspired artists to highlight the contrast between the living and the ghosts. But from one manuscript to another, the solutions chosen differ and provide a very extensive range of possible representations. The pilgrim, recognizable by his large hat and his staff and accompanied by his guide, arrives at a refectory where the dead are serving the living:

> En refectoire apres je vis
> Ce dont moult fu plus esbahi
> Pluseurs mors tous ensevelis
> Donnoient a mangier aux vis
> Et les servoient doulcement
> A genouz et devotement

[Later, in the refectory, I saw something that astonished me even more. Many dead people, all in shrouds, were giving food to the living and serving them gently and devoutly on their knees.]

Accompanying this text, the illustration from an Oxford manuscript establishes the strongest contrast between the dead and the living (illus. 21).[61] The dead cannot stand up on their legs and seem to have difficulty pulling themselves up to the level of the table. Shrouds in the form of sacks of a nondescript beige color cover them entirely, including their faces. We find an almost analogous representation of them in a Parisian manuscript, but this time the dead, only two of them, are entirely white and seem to be covered with a film that sticks to their bodies (illus. 22).[62] The arms, legs, and head are well distinguished, but the features of the faces are no better drawn than in the Oxford manuscript. In another manuscript in the Bibliothèque Nationale, the three dead people of *Pilgrimage* have a more corporeal appearance (illus. 23).[63] Each is wearing a sort of white frock, out of which emerges a head, this time quite distinct from the habit. The head of each dead person has two black holes for eyes and a large mouth and big teeth. The representation is close to the macabre images of the time. It also evokes images found in the German wood carvings of incunabular editions.[64] However, the same scene also inspired very different representations of the three dead people—illustrations following the traditional mode of representing souls in the hereafter as naked and asexual (illus. 20).[65]

These variations are of interest, therefore, because they show, once again, that there was not just one but several ways to represent ghosts, including in contemporary manuscripts and in the illustrations of the same text. Among them, the macabre constitutes a new formula that tended increasingly to prevail at the end of the Middle Ages in illustrations of ghosts; the representation of the phantom, on the contrary, remained rare.[66]

Ghosts and the Macabre

If the evanescent representation of the phantom did not prevail more widely and more rapidly, the reason for this is perhaps that its diffusion was halted by the emergence of the macabre, which emphasized the corporeal, tactile, and horrible presence of the cadaver. The principal themes of the macabre are well-known, and it is beyond the scope of my work to speak of this other than in relation to ghosts. At the end of the thirteenth century appeared the theme of the encounter of the Three Living and the Three Dead: three young horsemen see three dead men, their doubles, standing in front of them; the doubles, who enjoin them

to prepare for their deaths, are undeniably ghosts.[67] A bit later the obsession with death and the macabre found a chosen field in the office of the
dead in the book of hours. The different emblematic themes of the macabre, beginning with "Death" itself in its allegorical representation, are
associated with the scene of an individual dying. Moving around under
its shroud and threatening the dying person with a javelin or a scythe,
Death is scarcely distinguishable from ghosts in the strict sense. The margins of a book of hours of Rouen (second half of the fifteenth century)
assemble emblems and figures of death: we see a living dead person, who
is naked or half draped in a white shroud, who has light skin and a still
rather full form, but whose eyes are reduced to two simple holes.[68] A
javelin and, in one case, a round shield enable us to identify the allegory
of Death. Glancing through the beginning of the manuscript, we see a
death's-head, a gravedigger at work, a coffin, and a cadaver sewn in a
white shroud. But one of these margins reveals a completely different
figure, all black and covered with a light-blue shroud (illus. 26). This is
undoubtedly a soul in purgatory or even a damned soul. Only the eyes,
the nose, and the mouth light up in this dark mass. As is normal in a
book of hours, the facing text gives no information about this marginal
illustration, the interpretation of which remains hypothetical. In many
books of hours the scene of funerals, very often represented for the office
of the dead, appears favorable to the fantastic manifestations of the world
of the dead. The story of Raymond Diocres was famous: seeing him
emerge out of his coffin right in the middle of his funeral service, Saint
Bruno was said to have decided to leave for the "desert," where he
founded the Grande Chartreuse.[69]

Manifestations of the dead could also be collective. Starting in 1425
the theme of the "danse macabre," or "Dance of the Dead," began to
spread; it portrayed a series of couples, each formed by a dead person
and a living person incarnating an "estate" of society. The danse macabre
was different from representations of the dance of the dead in the cemeteries: in the latter the graves open up, and the dead, like living cadavers,
rise up, move around, and dance. In a very beautiful fifteenth-century
Flemish manuscript of the *Golden Legend* by Jacobus da Voragine, the same
miniature shows two distinct passages from the chapter devoted to the
Day of the Dead on November 2 (illus. 29).[70] Jacobus da Voragine became the echo of the contemporary *exempla* regarding the usefulness of
prayers for the dead. A man used to pray for the dead whenever he went
across the cemetery. One day, when he is pursued by his enemies, he sees
the graves open and the dead come to his aid. The illustration renders

perfectly the dramatic nature of the scene, even observing a sort of gradation between the dead who are beginning to emerge from their graves
and those who are already rushing at the assailants. The other side of the
illustration, in a different mode, portrays the apparition of a ghost to a
friend, who is lying in his bed with his wife. The dead man complains of
the unbearable weight of the mantle he stole while he was alive. In the
cohort of the dead in this manuscript, as a bit later in the dance of
the skeletons engraved for *Liber chronicarum* by Hartmann Schedel under
the title *Imago mortis*,[71] it is indeed a matter of ghosts. These images of
living dead in the fifteenth century translated a greater attention to the
future of the cadaver and to the stages of its decomposition: sometimes
the flesh is still firm, sometimes the bones stick through the skin, which
bursts and reveals the skeleton, and sometimes time has left only a whit-
ened skeleton.[72] But the images are interesting for other reasons. Guided
by profane literature, the iconography of the time also discovered the
province of the fantastic.

The French illuminated manuscripts of the works of Boccaccio,
translated by Laurent de Premierfait for the king and the princes of the
line at the beginning of the fifteenth century, provide two remarkable
examples of this. The superb Arsenal manuscript of the translation of the
Decameron offered to Charles VI in 1414 presents an illustration of the
novella entitled "Dioneo" (Seventh Day, Tenth Story) of the *Decameron*
(illus. 27).[73] It is a dual representation: one side shows a meal in the
course of which two friends, Tingoccio and Meuccio, seated at a table,
mutually promise each other that the first to die will appear to the survivor to inform him of the dead one's fate in the hereafter; at the same table
the mother of Tingoccio's godchild, who is also his mistress, is seated.
Tingoccio soon dies from the excesses of that incestuous love, and as
promised, he appears to his friend. The apparition pulls Meuccio from
his sleep. He is sitting up in his bed, completely awake. At the foot of
the bed, the ghost is only partially visible, for the windowsill somewhat
hides him from the viewer. This cutting off, as in the miniature of *Miracles
of Our Lady* by Gautier of Coincy, perhaps has the function of recalling
that the ghost does not belong to this world, that he comes from elsewhere.[74] The illustration shows an emaciated body, mostly covered with
a white shroud; the body does not have the appearance of a skeleton but
rather of a living cadaver or a man who, compared with the friend of his
age to whom he is speaking, appears to have aged by several decades in
a few days. Another French manuscript of Boccaccio, also preserved in
the library of the Arsenal, presents an even more extraordinary miniature.

215

Although it might seem to illustrate the same tale, in fact it does not belong to the *Decameron* but to a work written a bit later in Latin and translated by Laurent de Premierfait in 1409, *De casibus virorum illustrium* (On the fates of famous men) (illus. 28).[75] Of more humanist inspiration, this work presents, in nine books, a gallery of illustrious destinies from antiquity, from the Scriptures, or from more recent history. Chapter 19 of the second part is devoted to the truth of dreams. Among other examples the author cites the tale of the poet Simonides, who in a dream received the announcement of the visit of a man arriving by ship. No one came, but soon afterward the body of a drowning victim was discovered on the shore; the poet had it buried correctly before returning to his rest. *Et tandis qu'il dormoit, une vision lui vint que le corps qu'il avoit fait ensevelir lui defendoit qu'il n'entrast point sur mer le prouchain jour ensuivant* ["And while he was sleeping, he saw in a vision the body of the man he had had buried, who ordered him not to go to sea the following day"]. Simonides obeyed the "message of the dream," but his companions did not believe it and died the next day in a tempest. The miniature shows the poet, asleep in his bed and covered with the most beautiful red cloth. From behind the canopy the dead man slides into the room, or rather into the dream; he is wrapped in a shroud that reveals the characteristic gesture of crossed arms. His face, uncovered, is not that of a cadaver but of a sort of sleeping person who, from his not completely closed eyes, seems to observe the sleeping poet. This is not a representation of a phantom but is not really the macabre either. The image is tied rather to the type of the resuscitated, though giving to the ghost a freedom of movement that makes this intruder a strangely familiar figure.

The macabre art that took hold of ghosts at the end of the Middle Ages underwent strong evolutions at the turn of the sixteenth century, as Jean Wirth has shown well for Rhenish Germany. The painter Hans Baldung Grien replaced the representation of the skeleton and even of the fleshless and animated cadaver with that of a young girl, scarcely dead and with voluptuously full flesh.[76] Sometimes the dead girl, at the moment when she seeks to flee from her tomb, is forcefully called back by Death or by a dead person whose flesh is half decomposed, the sign of a less recent death. In every case, this horrible figure is brandishing a half-empty hourglass to remind us of the ephemeral nature of a life that a *mors immatura*—premature death—has too soon interrupted; the decomposition of the flesh is used as a marker to measure the flow of time in the hereafter.

A new theme also made its appearance, that of the double macabre portraits. On the opposite side of a bust portrait of a very living person, lay or ecclesiastical, the same person was painted in the reduced state of a cadaver, but with the bust standing just as erect as the one of the living person, whose posture and anguished gesture it reproduced.[77] This type of representation participated in the tradition of vanities (in which the presence of a skull recalled the ephemeral nature of existence), but it gave the tradition an otherwise dramatic presence. The doubling of the living person with a dead one also entered into the logic of the danse macabre but replaced the tableau of the various "estates" of society carried away in death with the much more tragic one of an individual destiny. The double portrait thus translated a deepening reflection on the meaning of the vitalized portrait that was initially thought of as a memorial representation intended to keep alive, to immortalize, the image of the person who inevitably would one day be dead. We can therefore also speak here of an illustration of a ghost, especially since this double representation was not anonymous but concerned a specific and named person.

Thus, using entirely new means, the portrait sealed the dialectic that was at the heart of the issue of ghosts: that of the memory and the death of the individual. The means used in painting during the Renaissance were unprecedented. But as we know, the question raised had already found an original answer in the funerary art of earlier centuries.

Recumbent Figures: Are They Ghosts?

At least three traits justify a priori the connection between recumbent figures and representations of ghosts.[78] The recumbent figure is the image of a specific dead person, whose memory it contributes to keeping alive. After a very long hiatus from late antiquity (for example, the funerary masks of Fayyum or the mosaics from Roman Africa), funerary effigies—of stone, bronze, or wood in relief—reappeared in the West at the end of the eleventh century.[79] All the while evolving and presenting varied types (for example, the double effigy, the type of someone praying in contrast to the recumbent figure, etc.), effigies continued until the eighteenth century. Their historical duration was therefore somewhat similar to the evolution of the body of ghost tales. In addition, recumbent figures display formal traits that connect them to ghosts as described in texts and as depicted by certain miniatures or paintings. They have the appearance of living dead, even keeping their eyes open, at least in northern

217

Europe. All the same, their stone eyes do not watch the earthly world but rather symbolize the eyes of the soul open onto the eternal realities of the hereafter. Their hands are joined in the posture of prayer, a sign of awaiting resurrection.[80] But sometimes the recumbent figures cross their hands on their chests or on their stomachs, a gesture that also characterizes certain ghosts in iconography[81] and that in both cases might express the quest for and the expectation of suffrages from the living. Moreover, none of these signs are univocal: if the recumbent figures have their eyes open onto an eschatological world as yet invisible to the living, concretely, in the space of the church, they are looking at their living relatives who contemplate them—especially since the recumbent figure, although lying on a horizontal slab, is in fact often portrayed as if it were upright. The feet are resting on a table or, more frequently, on an animal—a lion or a dog—whose emblematic value and probable apotropaic function Michel Pastoureau stresses at the same time: is the animal there to protect the dead one or to protect the living one from a return of the dead?[82] Moreover, the recumbent figure is not always fixed forever in an attitude of prayer. In England, the recumbent figures of knights were depicted crossing their legs and drawing their swords: is this the ultimate gesture of defense of a living knight against the death that comes to take him? Or is it a symbolic gesture of the soul that seeks to protect itself from the assault of the devil? Or did the sculptor want to eternize the posture of the warrior at the instant when his life was taken from him?[83] The nature of the clothing confirms the profound ambiguity of the postures: the dead man is wearing the clothing he wore while he was alive, and he sports the insignia of his status (the cleric in his robe, the knight in armor, the bishop with his cross and his miter), just as the tales of ghosts make the clothing of the dead person a sign of recognition for the one to whom the ghost appears. Sometimes the recumbent figure does not assume the fixed position of a dead person in prayer. The figure gives a sad look to the living who pass close by in the church or the cloisters, the body slightly leaning, the free hand held to the side, in an expression of great lassitude and of waiting for aid or for a few comforting words, those that the living who look at the figure will alone be able to give (illus. 30).[84]

In spite of all these parallels, let us nevertheless reject a hasty interpretation that would turn the recumbent figure into a portrait of a ghost. Whatever the proximity of certain formal traits, these representations fulfilled different and even opposite functions. The ghost made a return into the memory and the dreams of the living, even while the living sought, through rituals and prayer, to be separated from the dead person, to make the ghost a *true* dead person well separate from the living and gradually sent on to oblivion. The dead person was manifest "warm" when a desirable, normal relationship could not be established between the living and the dead. The recumbent figure, in contrast, showed a dead person whose image was fixed in stone and whose name remained inscribed in the epitaph, to be deciphered without emotion by generations to come, the generations for whom, indeed, this dead person would be nothing but a name. The recumbent figure consecrated and perhaps favored a normalization of relationships between the living and the dead, once that dead person was buried and the mourning of the family was in the process of easing. The recumbent figure was not the exacerbated product of an enduring memory. In the familial necropolis where the descendants of the dead person trampled on the stone slabs, the recumbent figure recalled, on the contrary, that the dead person had taken a place in the long memory of his or her lineage. Tombstones, with their epitaphs and their effigies, ticked off the list of a "cold" memory, the names of the dead who no longer frightened. By contrast the single ghost, who came back shortly after death, attached itself, grew, threatened, and refused to go away. The recumbent figure, in stone or in bronze, sanctioned the success of a rite of passage; the ghost, on the other hand, manifested the failure of the same rite of passage.

"The dead grasps the living." This old adage of common law in the Middle Ages expressed the continuity of the succession from father to son in an ordinary lineage and then in the royal dynasty.[1] In tales of apparitions of the dead as well, the ghost, who was often the father, seemed "to grasp the living" (his son, his heir) when he recalled himself to his son's memory and enjoined his heir to have masses said for his salvation. The adage seems especially appropriate in that tales of ghosts were also known to concern the succession of goods and power. But must we not reverse the proposition and say, rather, that it was the living who seized the dead? It was in fact the living who granted the dead a sort of postmortem existence. If the living had the impression that the dead took the initiative in appearing to them, it was the living alone, in their tales and their images, their phantasms and their dreams, their feelings of guilt and their greed, who fashioned the return of the dead.

To account for the facility that the living had in imagining and telling about the return of the dead, we have had to cease claiming that, in traditional cultures such as that of the Middle Ages, there existed an immutable "belief in ghosts," an a priori given that was distinct from the subjects of the enunciation and that went without saying. It has been more useful to question the modalities of the statement of belief, the way in which the belief was never a given but was always in the process of being shaped and transformed. The documents themselves, their origin, and their generic form have therefore not been considered as illustrations of a belief completely formed outside of them but as part of the process of believing, of the complex modalities of the statement of belief in which doubt is blended with the affirmation and the concrete representation with the phantasm. We have therefore paid the greatest attention to the nature of the documents, first by pointing out the difference between the autobiographical tale, in which an educated person writes down his or her experience, and the reported tale, which relates the experiences of others and relies on a primarily oral transmission. This first distinction has enabled us to show that the subjective and autobiographical experience of the return of the dead was normally that of a dream, in which the ghost was characterized by an uncertain and ambivalent appearance, whereas the reported tale usually mentioned a conscious vision, one with a clear and objective form. From this we have derived our hypothesis that an objectivization of the vision and the image of the ghost goes hand in hand with the socialization of the tale, its transmission and its legitimation through the authorized writing of a cleric, and its use for all sorts of ideological ends. However, this initial hypothesis still cannot account for the diversity of the documents that tell of these "socialized" and "objectivized" visions—thus the necessity to distinguish, on the one hand, between the tales and the illustrations (essentially miniatures), without ever reducing the ones to the others and especially not the latter to the former, as is still all too often done, and on the other hand, between the different narrative and textual genres—*miracula, mirabilia, exempla,* and opuscules coming out of the *discretio spiritum.* Thus we have analyzed, as precisely as possible, diverse treatments of the question of ghosts throughout the period from the fifth century to the fifteenth.

This method supported a deliberate choice: that of dealing with the question of ghosts as a subject in social history. I have attempted to analyze and explain the modalities and functions of tales and illustrations in the *present* of each historical moment considered. Following a universally chronological unfolding, I have also tried to show the *transformations* of these modalities of believing and of their social uses in the long duration of the social and cultural system of Western Christendom, from late antiquity up to the dawn of modern time. In doing this, I have deliberately rejected two methods used by certain historians. The first is the search for a universal symbolism. This is reductive, since it sees specific historical phenomena only as unique illustrations of an unconscious characteristic of human nature, or of man's confused relationship with the forces of nature, or even of a transcultural cosmology of which each religion would be simply a specific mode of expression. In my opinion the historian, just like the ethnologist in the field, has almost nothing to gain from these speculations. The second path that I have deliberately rejected is the search for origins, whether or not that path deviates toward the theory of "remnants." Since this theory seems to fit better within a continuous span of historical time, it has seduced more than one historian. For this theory, the myths and the rituals of the Middle Ages would be the expression or even the "remnants" of old pre-Christian "beliefs" durably handed down by Celtic, Greco-Roman, Germanic, or more generally, Indo-European paganisms. Obviously, the influence of very ancient cultural substrata and the reality of syncretisms resulting from the temporal succession of great social and religious systems cannot be denied. The only question is whether the historian must reduce the meaning of historical phenomena to ancient and more or less well established layers, or whether the historian must show how these inheritances have continued to be reworked into the *present* functioning of societies and cultures at each moment of their history. I have given priority to this latter approach, by seeking to show how medieval society, in all its institutional and ideological functions and in the historical course of its transformations, specifically raised and resolved the issue of the remembering and the forgetting of the dead. Even though the phenomenon of ghosts is universal, I have not attempted to find the somewhat analogous traits that are provided by the history and ethnography of many other civilizations in the Middle Ages or in other times. Nor have I looked systematically behind our tales—even if they are the "wildest," such as those that deal with Hellequin's hunt—for the "remnants" of pre-Christian beliefs. Instead I have tried to see how that society never ceased to rework and rethink its past while it continued to create innovations to respond to its unique demands; thus the solidarity of lineal kinship beyond death and the articulation of spiritual and natural kinship largely explain "the invasion of ghosts" that characterized the turn of the millennium. Likewise, the conflictual relationships at the heart of feudal society between the church and the warring aristocracy and the issue of social violence, in my opinion, largely account for the appearance and the development of the theme of Hellequin's hunt, inseparable from the institution of the Peace of God. Likewise too, out of the church's religious, ethical, and ideological harnessing of laypeople after the turn of the twelfth century there flowed, into the hands and the mouths of the brothers of the Mendicant orders, the development and the efficacy of the *mass media* of the Middle Ages: the massive and stereotypical narrative collections of *exempla*. These tales, products of an oral tradition, in spreading by word of mouth through almost all the regions of Christendom, transformed and saved the ghost story. In this capacity, depending on their circulation and reception, and perhaps for the first time in Western history, they fulfilled a decisive role of acculturation.

We have repeated this many times: the dead had no other existence than that which the living gave them. The individual and the social imaginary (dreams, tales, shared beliefs), the socialized speech (at mourning, in preaching), made ghosts move and speak. Thanks to those images and words heard in dreams, derived from conversations, noticed in rumors, or received from atop the pulpits, the living fashioned a life after death for themselves and maintained, even if they sought not to do so, an imaginary relationship with those who had left them. This relationship simultaneously tied new bonds between the living, through the circulation of property between lay houses and the church, through alms given to the poor, and through the participation of natural or spiritual "relatives" in the rituals (funerals, anniversary masses) celebrated for the salvation of their common ancestors or their dead brothers. Through its material and symbolic effects, the imaginary of death and the dead supported the social ties bound among the living. Out of the same movement, the living constructed and considered their relationships with the imaginary beings of the hereafter and with others on earth. They took for themselves the space and the time that the tales portrayed. Thus people could situate themselves in the continuous chain of relatives, witnesses, informants, preachers, and authors who ensured the transmission of tales, and to these tales each person could add that of his or her own dreams. The living therefore made the voice of the dead their own, a voice that, strong with the authority conferred on it by its supernatural origin, reminded them of all the norms of Christian society.

I have deliberately made the end of the fifteenth century the chronological end of this study. I could have carried it farther, undoubtedly to the eighteenth or nineteenth century. Indeed, up to that time the material and ideological structures characteristic of that "long Middle Ages," as Jacques Le Goff calls it, were maintained.[2] But I would have to have considered major transformations: the impact of Protestant reform (with, at least officially, the rejection of souls in purgatory and the increased diabolization of ghosts);[3] the link established between the apparition of spirits and sorcery; the progressive rendering into folklore, accentuated by the Enlightenment, of an entire part of what would soon be called "popular beliefs"; the substitution of spiritualists for the traditional "messengers of souls";[4] and the evolution of attitudes regarding death—including, according to the terms of Philippe Ariès, the passage from the "tame death" of traditional societies to the "death of the other" characteristic of the nineteenth century, before the "invisible death" of today. Above all, I would have needed to pursue this study from a perspective of comparative history, which would have enabled us to confront the old modalities of believing and of making others believe with new modalities, to evoke documents unique to the modern period (for example, those of the theater),[5] and to analyze the transformation of functions assigned to ghosts or even the inflection of the debates concerning ghosts. For if we judge by the apologetic literature of the seventeenth and eighteenth centuries, ghosts lost nothing of their contemporary reality. *Traicté de l'apparition des esprits* by Nicolas Taillepied, published in 1600, and then *Discours des spectres ou visions et apparitions d'esprits* by Pierre Le Loyer, in 1608, count among the milestones of this reflection, which is inscribed in the more general framework of demonological literature.[6] Then we find *Dissertation sur les revenants* by Dom Augustin Calmet in 1751. The author intends "to show that in all times and among all policed nations," apparitions of the dead have authenticated the thesis of the immortality of the soul. "The feeling of the immortality of the soul [. . .] is one of those truths that the length of the centuries has not been able to erase from the mind of peoples," he writes, among other things.[7] But to demonstrate this in the midst of the Enlightenment, Calmet had to distinguish himself from the gullibility judged to be excessive among the medievals—the gullibility vis-à-vis the *exempla* of Mendicant preachers, who were too naive for his taste—as much as from the "rules of philosophy" that fed skepticism, about which the scholarly Benedictine abbot was all the better informed since he had welcomed Voltaire into his abbey of Senones. A few years later, with a completely different freedom, the *Encyclopedia* listed the "five different opinions on spectres," in contrast to the "three classes of philosophers" who had denied their existence.[8] From that time, a belief in ghosts, having lost the legitimacy that was conferred on it by the all-powerfulness of the Catholic Church and the cult of souls in purgatory, was pushed into the realm of "superstitions."[9] It was there, in the ambiguous realm of "popular beliefs," that nascent ethnology would attempt to find it.[10]

What is the status of ghosts today? Faced with the reassuring idea of a continuous progress of rationalism benefiting from the loss of members in traditional religions and, inversely, from the rise of modern science and technology, we must resolutely note the no less obvious vogue of research in parapsychology or metapsychology, of spiritism and clairvoyance services. Such phenomena are not as marginal as one might think or want. Moreover, relaying the fantastic literature of the last century, film, television, and their "special effects" have profited from this interest and have had great success with the irrational: they may indeed fill the void left by the ghost tales of old.

Explanations, in truth rather uninspired, do immediately come to mind. One might, without really believing in it, invoke "continuities" or "reappearances" or might more seriously question the reciprocal effects of a weakening of the structuring framework of traditional churches. Contemporary spiritism, a sort of new secularized religion, could satisfy a "need to believe" that no longer finds its expression in the rituals and formulas of the past.[11] But more positive factors must also be mentioned. The recent efforts of communication techniques have made us familiar with the abolishment of any distance between the here and elsewhere and the blending of limits between the visible and the invisible. And the media, which have become an essential part of our daily lives, even in their name come from the family of mediums.

Within this general framework, we must ask the more specific question regarding death and the dead today. For the relatives of a dead person, all the problems of separation, pain, memory, and forgetting remain intact, especially when the living no longer receive from their friends and family, or from the fragmented society in which they live, the comfort once provided by kinship, the community, rituals, and old tales. Granted, the traditional ritual of death knew some failures—sudden death, murder, suicide, children who died without being baptized, the impenitent dead person, etc.—on which the imaginary of ghosts was fed, but everything was foreseen socially to deal with those ghosts as well: relays of speech, from the witness to the preacher or the exorcist, gave a structure of acceptance and provided the conditions for a social recognition of dreams and pain. But today, hiding death has taken over not only the ritual of death but also the usual treatment for its dysfunctioning: those stories of ghosts who freed people from anguish while appearing simultaneously to maintain it.

There thus remains open, for each of us, the question of the death of the other, especially when it occurs suddenly or prematurely. It is here that each individual, at least as much as in parapsychology and its doubtful enterprises, discovers the topicality and the generality of the issue of ghosts. How can one carry out the "work of mourning" today when solidarities of family and friendship fail, as does also the psychological help (but do we really know to what degree?) provided by the slow rites of separation, the shared beliefs, and the event of the death prolonged in a tale? This question concerns each one of us and dictates that, for the historian as well, ghosts cannot constitute simply an object on which it is sufficient to cast the cold look of the scientist. While reading, even though five centuries later, the autobiographical tale of Giovanni Morelli, haunted by the memory of his dead child, how can the historian remain unmoved by the poignant expression of such pain and by the familiar emotions that it awakens?

But death and the dead, memory and the impossibility of forgetting, are also today collective issues that are relevant to our civilization in its entirety. Granted, the furious troop of Hellequin has been chased from our culture. But our society also harbors its collective phantoms, ready to surge forth each time history and, in particular, political reason attempt to push them from the memory of the people. As long as justice has not been rendered at least to their memory, as long as our collective memory has not made peace with itself, many tragedies of contemporary history—treachery, tortures, and massacres, Vichy, Val'd'Hiv, Algeria, Vietnam, Auschwitz, Katyn, and the endless list of charnel houses and of all those lines of the living dead with emaciated bodies—will continue to break open the doors of guilty indifference and forgetting. What Freud said about individuals can also be applied to nations: "A thing that has not been understood inevitably reappears; like an unlaid ghost, it cannot rest until the mystery has been solved and the spell broken."[12]

Abbreviations

C.S.E.L.   *Corpus scriptorum ecclesiasticorum latinorum,* Vienna, 1866.

M.G.H. (S.S., Script.   *Monumenta Germaniae Historica; Scriptores,* or *Scriptores rerum*
rer. merov., Poetae,   *merovingiarum* or *Poetae,* etc.
etc.)

PL   J.-P. Migne, *Patrologiae cursus completus, series latina,* 222
vol., in 4°, Paris, 1844–1855.

Introduction

1. For an overview of medieval visions, see the synthesis by P. Dinzel-bacher, *Vision und Visionsliteratur im Mittelalter* (Stuttgart, 1981), who primarily stresses the "great visions" and somewhat neglects the more numerous shorter accounts (for example, in the *exempla*) that are the chosen ground for apparitions of the dead. By the same author, see the useful *"Revelationes,"* Typologie des sources du moyen age occidental 57 (Turnhout, 1991). See also Carolly Erickson, *The Medieval Vision: Essays in History and Perception* (New York, 1976). We await the publication, in French, of the important work on this subject by Claude Carozzi.

2. The notably ethnological bibliography on ghosts is extensive. See, for example, H. R. E. Davidson and W. M. S. Russell, *The Folklore of Ghosts* (Cambridge, published for the Folklore Society by D. S. Brewer, 1981). An indispensable historiographical perspective is D. Fabre (comp.), "Le retour des morts," *Ethnologie rurale* (1987), pp. 105–106. A rather uninspired attempt at a "history of ghosts" through the centuries is R. C. Finucane, *Appearances of the Dead: A Cultural History of Ghosts* (London, 1982). From the point of view of historical anthropology, but above all dealing with Marian apparitions, is W. A. Christian, *Apparitions in Late Medieval and Renaissance Spain* (Princeton, 1981). For the Middle Ages, from a perspective different from my own, see below the works of Claude Lecouteux.

3. See, for example, Dante's encounter with Charles Martel of Anjou, king of Hungary, who died in 1295, in song VIII of *Paradise,* analyzed through its

symbolic and political dimensions by G. Arnaldi, "La maledizione del sangue e la virtù delle stelle. Angioini e Capetingi nella 'Commedia' di Dante," *La Cultura* XXX, 1 (1992): 47–216. For a very different period, I will later discuss visions concerning the Carolingian rulers, such as the *Vision of Wetti*. The principal medieval tales of voyages to the hereafter are very well grouped and translated by A. Micha, *Voyages dans l'au-delà d'après les textes médiévaux. IVe–XIIIe siècle* (Paris, 1992).

4. Peter Brown, *The Cult of the Saints: Its Rise and Function in Latin Christianity* (Chicago, 1981).

5. A good presentation is J. Delumeau, *La Peur en Occident (XIVe–XVIIIe siècle). Une cité assiégée* (Paris, 1978), p. 86, based on a study of five hundred contemporary tales of ghosts gathered in the Polish countryside by L. Stomma, *Campagnes insolites. Paysannerie polonaise et mythes européens* (French translation, Lagrasse, 1986). Here we see, notably, that stillborn babies, victims of abortions, and those who died without being baptized represent 37 percent of the ghosts, suicides account for 9 percent, and the rest are divided, for the most part, between women who died during childbirth and women who died at the time of their marriage.

6. Claude Lecouteux, *Fantômes et revenants au Moyen Age* (Paris, 1986). All of the proposed interpretations are taken up in a synthesis in *Fées, sorcières et loups-garous au Moyen Age* (Paris, 1992), especially pp. 171–175. On sagas, see R. Boyer, *Le Monde du double. La magie chez les anciens Scandinaves* (Paris, 1986) (this author also wrote the prefaces to Claude Lecouteux's two works cited above).

7. Philippe Ariès, *Essais sur la mort en Occident du Moyen Age à nos jours* (Paris, 1975) and *L'Homme devant la mort* (Paris, 1977). [The English edition of the latter book is *The Hour of Our Death*, trans. Helen Weaver (New York, 1981). Any citations from this work will be taken from the English edition.] These books offer a periodization of Western attitudes toward death: (1) "tame death," in the long continuity of pre-Christian and then Christian peasant societies; (2) the "death of the self" or "death untamed," starting at the end of the Middle Ages, with the horror of death and the fear of the judgment of the soul; (3) the "death of the other," in the nineteenth century, with the exaltation of mourning and the cemetery; and (4) the "invisible death" or "death denied," in the present time. For a different and sometimes critical point of view, see more recently M. Vovelle, *La Mort et l'Occident de 1300 à nos jours* (Paris, 1983).

8. Jacques Le Goff, *La Naissance du purgatoire* (Paris, 1981). [English edition: *The Birth of Purgatory* (Chicago, 1984). Any citations from this work will be taken from the English edition.]

9. Let us above all emphasize the importance of the work of German historians, gathered notably in the volume compiled by K. Schmid and J. Wollasch (eds.), *Memoria. Der geschichtliche Zeugniswert des liturgischen Gedenkens im Mittelalter*, Münstersche Mittelalter-Schriften 48 (Munich, 1984). See also H. Braet and W. Verbeke (eds.), *Death in the Middle Ages* (Louvain, 1983), notably the essential article by O.-G. Oexle, "Die Gegenwart der Toten," pp. 19–77. Several of the

same authors are again found in D. Iogna-Prat and J.-Ch. Picard (eds.), *Religion et culture autour de l'an mil. Royaume capétien et Lotharingie* (Paris, 1990), including J. Wollasch, "Les moines et la mémoire des morts," pp. 47–54. For the end of the Middle Ages, especially noteworthy is J. Chiffoleau, *La Comptabilité de l'au-delà. Les hommes, la mort et la religion dans la région d'Avignon à la fin du Moyen Age (vers 1320–vers 1480)* (Rome, 1980). We await the publication of a book commended for raising the issue of the dynamic transformation in attitudes regarding the dead between those two periods: M. Lauwers, *La Mémoire des ancêtres et le souci des morts. Fonction et usage du culte des morts dans l'Occident médiéval (diocèse de Liège, XIe–XIIIe siècle)* (Paris, E.H.E.S.S., doctoral thesis directed by J. Le Goff, 1992), 2 vols., typed. A general study of the ties between visions of the hereafter and of the dead and the liturgical remembrance of the dead between late antiquity and the thirteenth century is offered by Fr. Neiske, "Vision und Totengedenken," *Frühmittelalterliche Studien* 20 (1986): 137–185.

10. See the rich collection of anthropological essays collected by M. Izard and P. Smith (eds.), *La Fonction symbolique. Essais d'anthropologie* (Paris, 1979); M. De Certeau, "Croire: une pratique de la différence," *Documents de travail et prépublications,* Centro Internazionale di Semiotioca e di Linguistica, Università di Urbino, 106, Series A (1981): 1–21; and M. De Certeau, *L'Invention du quotidien,* vol. I, *Arts de faire* (Paris, 1980), pp. 299–316 ("Croire/Faire croire"). For a historical perspective of the notion, see J. Wirth, "La naissance du concept de croyance (XIIe–XVIIe siècle)," *Bibliothèque d'humanisme et de Renaissance* 45 (1983): 7–58.

11. On these issues, see *Faire croire. Modalités de la diffusion et de la réception des messages religieux du XIIe au XVe siècle,* presented by A. Vauchez (Rome, Ecole française de Rome, 1981).

12. For the psychoanalytical approach that inspires some of these thoughts, we will look at the classic works of Sigmund Freud. ["Mourning and Melancholia" (1917) in *Papers on Metapsychology,* and "The 'Uncanny'" (1919) in *Papers on Applied Psycho-Analysis,* both in *Sigmund Freud: Collected Papers,* Vol. 4, authorized translation under the supervision of Joan Riviere (New York, 1959), pp. 152–170, 368–407] See also M. Schur, *La Mort dans la vie de Freud* (Paris, 1975).

Chapter One. The Rejection of Ghosts

1. Homer, *The Illiad,* XXIII, lines 59–107.

2. Jean-Pierre Vernant, *L'Individu, la mort, l'amour. Soi-même et l'autre en Grèce ancienne* (Paris, 1989), p. 86.

3. Lucretius, *On the Nature of Things,* I, vv. 130–135, and IV, vv. 58–62.

4. J. Scheid, "Contraria facere," *Annali del Istituto Orientale di Napoli* 6 (1984): 117; and more generally, J. Scheid, *Religion et piété à Rome* (Paris, 1985), pp. 54–55.

5. *Draugr* is a word that comes from the same root as *dream* or *Traum,* in modern German. Cf. G. D. Kelchner, *Dreams in Old Norse Literature and Their Affinities in Folklore, with an Appendix Containing the Icelandic Texts and Translations* (Cambridge, Eng., 1935), pp. 66–72.

6. Saxo Grammaticus, *Gesta Danorum*, V, ed. A. Holder (Strasbourg, 1858), p. 162. [English edition: *The History of the Danes*, trans. Peter Fisher, ed. Hilda Ellis Davidson (New Jersey, 1979)]

7. *The Saga of Grettir the Strong: A Story of the Eleventh Century*, translated from the Icelandic by G. A. Hight (London, Toronto, New York, 1914; 2d ed., 1929), chaps. XVIII and XXXII–XXXV, pp. 42–45, 86–100. Cf. Cl. Lecouteux, *Fantômes et revenants au Moyen Age*, p. 103.

8. Jesus resuscitates the daughter of the head of the synagogue (Matt. 9:23; Mark 5:42; Luke 8:54), the son of the widow of Nain (Luke 7:15), and Lazarus, the brother of Mary Magdalene.

9. Matt. 17:3.

10. Peter Comestor, *Historia scholastica*, chap. XXV (Lyon, 1539), pp. 104–105.

11. Guyart des Moulins, *Bible historiale* (Paris, first quarter of the fifteenth century), New York, Pierpont Morgan Library, MS M394, fol. 127 v.

12. Jean-Claude Schmitt, "Le spectre de Samuel et la sorcière d'En Dor. Avatars historiques d'un récit biblique: I Rois, 28," *Etudes rurales* 105–106 (1987): 37–64, ills. 6–10.

13. *Gumbertsbibel* (Germany, before 1195), Erlangen, Universitätsbibliothek, MS 1, fol. 82 v.

14. Bamberg, Staatliche Bibliothek, MS 59, fol. 3 r.

15. Guyart des Moulins, *Bible historiale* (France, c. 1291–1294), London, British Library, MS Harley 4381, fol. 127; and the fifteenth-century copy cited in note #11, above.

16. *Bible moralisée* (early thirteenth century), Oxford, Bodleian 270 b, fol. 144, and *Tickhill Psalter* (England, early fourteenth century), New York Public Library, Spencer Collection, MS 26, fols. 43 and 42 v.

17. *Kayserchronik* (Bavaria, c. 1375–1380), New York, Pierpont Morgan Library, MS M769, fol. 172.

18. Tertullian was undoubtedly acquainted with *Passio S. Perpetuae et Felicitatis* [Passion of Perpetua and Felicitas] in which the future martyr—this will be discussed in the next chapter—is the beneficiary of the apparitions of her young brother Dinocratus. The first ghost tale noted in Christian literature, from the second half of the second century, is found in *Life of Saint Thecla*: a dead young woman appears to the saint, whom she asks to pray for her salvation and to take her place alongside her mother. Cf. Fr. Neiske, "Vision und Totengedenken," pp. 137–139.

19. Tertullian, *De anima*, 57, 3–10, ed. J.-H. Waszink, Corpus Christianorum, Series latina, II (Turnhout, 1954), pp. 779–869.

20. Lactantius, *Divinae Institutiones*, II, 2, 6, Corpus Christianorum, Series latina, 19, p. 104. The idea that the pagan gods were deified dead heroes refers to the tradition of euhemerism.

21. Augustine, *Epistolae*, 158, 3–10 (letter from Evodius to Augustine)

(C.S.E.L., 44, Vienna and Leipzig, 1904), pp. 488–497. Cf. M. Dulaye, *Le Rêve dans la vie et la pensée de saint Augustin* (Paris, 1973), pp. 210–225. Origen also expressed the belief that the souls of the evil "wander here below and are vagabonds; they wander around the graves where one sees the phantoms of the souls like shadows; they wander simply around the earth." Origen, *Contre Celse* [*Contra Celsum*], ed. M. Borret, t. IV (Paris, 1969), pp. 22–23.

22. Augustine, *De cura pro mortuis gerenda ad Paulinum liber unus*, in *Patrologia latina* (henceforth cited as *PL*), vol. 40, cols. 591–610; J. Zycha (ed.), C.S.E.L., 41 (Prague, Vienna. and Leipzig, 1900), pp. 621–660. See the commentaries by P. Courcelle, *Les Confessions de saint Augustin dans la tradition littéraire* (Paris, 1963), pp. 595–600; M. Dulaye, *Le Rêve*, pp. 113–127; P. Brown, *The Cult of the Saints*, p. 35.

23. Augustine also expresses his hostility toward the traditional funerary customs in *City of God* (VIII, XXVII), in which he contrasts the cult of the martyrs to the sacrifices that the pagans "offer up to the dead as if they were gods," and in *Confessions* (VI, II), in which he praises his mother, Monica, for submitting to the prohibition made by the bishop Ambrose against bringing food to the graves of the saints.

24. He gives the same answer concerning the gestures of prayer that raise the soul up to God: Jean-Claude Schmitt, *La Raison des gestes dans l'Occident médiéval* (Paris, 1990), p. 291.

25. Augustine, *La Genèse au sens littéral en douze livres* [*De Genesi ad litteram libri duodecim*], book XII, VIff., ed. P. Agësse and A. Solignac (Paris, 1972), p. 346.

26. A complete discussion of this is found in D. C. Lindberg, *Theories of Vision from Al Kindi to Kepler* (Chicago, 1976).

27. See, for example, the description that William of Saint Thierry gives of this process in *De la nature du corps et de l'âme* [*De natura corporis et animae*], edited and translated by M. Lemoine (Paris, 1988), pp. 112–113.

28. A. Vöbus, "Böser Blick," *Lexikon des Mittelalters*, II, 3, col. 470–472.

29. Augustine, *De cura*, II, 4, col. 594: "Proinde ista omnia, id est curatio funeris, conditio sepulturae, pompa exsequiarum, magis sunt vivorum solatia, quam subsidia mortuorum." (The concern with funerals, the condition of the sepulcher, the pomp of the funeral service aim more to console the living than to help the dead.)

30. Guibert of Nogent, *A Monk's Confession: The Memoirs of Guibert of Nogent*, translated and with an introduction by Paul J. Archambault (Pennsylvania, 1996), p. 117. [See also *Self and Society in Medieval France: The Memoirs of Abbot Guibert of Nogent (1064?–c. 1125)*, ed. John F. Benton (New York, 1970) and *The Autobiography of Guibert Abbot of Nogent-sous-Coucy*, trans. C. C. Swinton Bland, with an introduction by G. G. Coulton (New York, 1925).] According to William Durand, the thirteenth-century bishop of Mende, the ancients called the souls of the recent dead *umbrae*, those who still wandered around the graves; however, *animae* applied only to the soul inhabiting a living body; *manes* referred to the souls that were in hell and *spiritus* to those that rose up to heaven. In practice, which is

otherwise diverse, tales of apparitions of course take no such typology into account.

31. A few examples of doubt about the identity of such *personae*: Caesarius of Heisterbach, *Dialogus miraculorum*, ed. J. Strange (Cologne, Bonn, and Brussels, 1851), I, 32; IV, 4; XII, 29. [In subsequent notes, I will refer to the English edition of Caesarius's *Dialogus Miraculum: The Dialogue on Miracles*, trans. H. von E. Scott and C. C. Swinton Bland, with an introduction by G. G. Coulton (London, 1929).]

32. Augustine, *De cura*, XII, 14, col. 602.

33. "In somnis deludens, modo laeta, modo tristia, modo cognitas, modo incognitas *personas* ostendans": Reginon de Prüm, *De synodalibus causis et disciplinis ecclesiasticis*, II, 371, ed. F. G. Wasserschleben (Leipzig, 1840), p. 356.

34. Jean-Claude Schmitt, "Les masques, le diable, les morts dans l'Occident médiéval," *Razo. Cahiers du Centre d'études médiévales de Nice* 6 (1986): 87–119.

35. Augustine, *De cura*, XVII, 21, col. 608.

36. Augustine, *De Genesi ad litteram libri duodecim*, books XII, XIII, 27–28, pp. 371–375.

37. M. Dulaye, *Le Rêve*, pp. 113–127.

38. Julian of Toledo, *Prognosticorum Futuri saeculi libri tres*, II, chap. XXX, ed. J. N. Hillgarth, Corpus Christianorum, Series latina, t. 115 (Turnhout, 1976), pp. 67–68.

39. Gratian, *Decretum*, II, Causa XIII, Qu. II, chap. XXIX, ed. A Friedberg (Graz, 1959), pp. 730–731.

40. Honorius Augustodunensis, *Elucidarium*, III, 8, in *PL*, vol. 172, col. 1162D.

41. Honorius Augustodunensis, *Gemma animae*, 1, 121, in *PL*, vol. 172, col. 583; Jean Beleth, *Summa de ecclesiasticis officiis*, 161, ed. H. Douteil (Turnhout, 1976), vol. 2, pp. 315–316; William Durand, *Rationale divinorum officiorum*, 7, 35 (Lyon, 1592), pp. 864–865.

42. *Liber de spiritu et anima*, in *PL*, vol. 40, cols. 779–832. Cf. G. Raciti, "L'autore del 'De spiritu et anima,'" *Rivista di filosofia neo-scolastica* LIII (1961): 385–401; L. Norpoth, *Der Pseudo-augustinische Traktat "De Spiritu et anima"* (Ph.d. diss., Munich, 1924) (reprinted, Cologne and Bochum, 1971); M. Putscher, *Pneuma, Spiritus, Geist. Vorstellungen vom Lebensantrieb in ihren Geschichtlichen Wandlungen* (Wiesbaden, 1973).

43. On this hierarchical typology and its dissemination, see Jacques Le Goff, "Le christianisme et les rêves (IIe–VIIe siècles)," in T. Gregory (ed.), *I Sogni nel Medioevo* (Rome, 1985), pp. 183–184 (pp. 171–218), taken up again in J. Le Goff, *L'Imaginaire médiévale. Essais* (Paris, 1985), pp. 265–316. [English edition: *The Medieval Imagination*, trans. Arthur Goldhammer (Chicago, 1988), pp. 202ff. All subsequent citations will be taken from the translated edition.]

44. Constantius of Lyons, *Vie de Saint Germain d'Auxerre* [*Vita Germani*], ed. R. Borius (Paris, 1965), chap. 10, pp. 138–143. It is probable that these *insepulti*

dead were massacred during the revolt of the Bagaudae: cf. chap. 28, pp. 174–175.

45. Sulpicius Severus, *Vie de Saint Martin*, 11, 3–5, ed. J. Fontaine (Paris, 1967), p. 276.

46. *Tripartite Life of Patrick*, edited and English translation by Whitley Stokes, I (1887) (reprinted, New York, 1965), pp. 124–125. Saint Patrick was accustomed to stopping and praying in front of all the crosses with which he had marked the territory of the new faith. One day he neglected to pray in front of one of them because it had erroneously been placed on the grave of a pagan; it had been intended for a young Christian's grave, where the saint immediately returned it. This *Life*—in Irish, with passages in Latin—dates from around 900. I want to thank Michael Richter for telling me about the text.

47. Peter Brown, "Sorcery, Demons, and the Rise of Christianity from Late Antiquity into the Middle Ages" (1970), reprinted in *Religion and Society in the Age of Saint Augustine* (London, 1972), pp. 119–146 (p. 137, regarding John Chrysostom, who died in 407).

48. *Miracula Stephani*, 1, 6, in *PL*, vol. 41, col. 838.

49. *Benedictio salis et aquae* (tenth century?), in *PL*, vol. 138, col. 1048.

50. Gregory of Tours, *Liber in gloria confessorum*, 72, in *Miracula et opera minora*, ed. B. Krusch, M.G.H. Script. rer. merov., Hanover, 1885, I, 2, pp. 340–341. Cf. Peter Brown, *Society and the Holy in Late Antiquity* (Berkeley, 1982), p. 190; Brown even suggests that Gregory was "oppressed" by the very small number of graves of the blessed in this pagan necropolis.

51. Gregory of Tours, *Liber in gloria confessorum*, 62, ed. H. L. Bordier (Paris, 1862), vol. 3.

52. Compare this with sagas, with the story of Asvith and Asmund told around 1200 by Saxo Grammaticus, or even with the *Chronicle of Salerno* in the tenth century: the Lombard king Arechis delivers an assassin to the cadaver of his victim, who is the husband of his lover. Three days later the husband's body is found in the tomb, lying on that of his murderer; the mouth and the nose of the killer appear completely eaten away. Cf. H. Taviani, "L'image du souverain lombard de Paul Diacre à la Chronique de Salerne (VIIIe–Xe siècle)," *Atti del 6° Congresso internazionale di Studi sull'alto Medioevo* (Milan, October 21–25, 1978), Spolète, Centro italiano di studi sull'alto medioevo (1980), p. 685.

53. F. Graus, *Volk, Herrscher und Heiliger im Reich der Merowinger. Studien zur Hagiographie der Merowingerzeit* (Prague, 1965).

54. B. Krusch (ed.), *Vita Amati abbatis Habendensis*, 13–15, M.G.H. Script. rer. merov. 4 (Hanover and Leipzig, 1902), p. 220. Cf. A. Angenendt, "Theologie und Liturgie," in K. Schmid and J. Wollasch (eds.), *Memoria*, pp. 166–167.

55. R. Hertz, "Contribution à une étude sur la représentation collective de la mort" (1907), reprinted in *Sociologie religieuse et folklore* (Paris, 1970), pp. 1–83.

56. Saint Gregory the Great, *Dialogues*, translated by Odo John Zimmerman, O.S.B. (New York, 1959), IV, 57.

57. Ibid., IV, 42.

58. Jacques Le Goff, *The Birth of Purgatory*, pp. 88–96.

59. Saint Gregory the Great, *Dialogues*, IV, 57.

60. Jacques de Serugh, *Poème sur la messe des défunts*, cited by C. Vogel, "Le banquet funéraire paléochrétien," in B. Plongeron and R. Pannet (dir.), *Le Christianisme populaire. Les dossiers de l'histoire* (Paris, 1976), pp. 61–78 (I want to thank Anca Bratu for telling me of this text). On prayers for the dead, see also Dhuoda, *Manuel pour mon fils*, ed. P. Riché, B. de Vregille, and Cl. Mondésert (Paris, 1991), pp. 316–317.

61. Gregory of Tours, *Historia Francorum*, III, chap. XXXVI, ed. R. Latouche, Classiques de l'Historie de France au Moyen Age 27, vol. 1, pp. 176–177.

62. Bede the Venerable, *Historia ecclesiastica*, IV, 8 and 9 (a.664) and V, 9 (a.690), ed. C. Plummer (Oxford, 1896). [See also *Baedae Opera Historica*, with an English translation by J. E. King (New York, 1930).] A monk who will die within the year announces to a recluse nun that she will die at dawn; the abbess Ethelburga, who died three years earlier, warns her sister Tortgyth that she will join the abbess in death the next day; Boisil, the former prior of the monastery of Melrose, begs a brother to dissuade another monk, Egbert, from going to preach in Germany. Cf. P. F. Jones, *A Concordance to the Historia Ecclesiastica of Bede* (Cambridge, Mass., 1929) s.vv. "apparitio," "apparere," "spiritus." Cf. for a few other tales of apparitions of the dead, notably in the letters of Saint Boniface: Fr. Neiske, "Vision und Totengedenken," pp. 148–152.

63. J. Ntedika, *L'Evocation de l'au-delà dans la prière pour les morts. Etude de patristique et de liturgie latine (IVe–VIIIe siècles)* (Louvain and Paris, 1971). See notably Amalarius of Metz, *Liber officialis*, III, ed. J. M. Hanssens (Rome, 1948) vol. 2, p. 535.

64. *Vie de Raban Maur*, in *Acta Sanctorum*, February 1, 1668, p. 532.

65. *Annales Fuldenses*, III (auct. Meginhardo), M.G.H. S.S. in usum scholarum (Hanover, 1978), p. 82. Cf. Cl. Carozzi, "Les Carolingiens dans l'au-delà," in *Haut Moyen Age. Culture, education et société. Etudes offertes à Pierre Riché*, comp. M. Sot, Nanterre, Université de Paris-X (1990), p. 369. It has been shown that this tale coincided in Fulda with the beginning of the lists of the dead that the monks were to commemorate: O.-G. Oexle (dir.), *Die Uberlieferung der fuldischen Totenannalen (Die Klostergemeinschaft von Fulda im früheren Mittelalter . . .)* (Munich, Münstersche Mittelalter-Schriften 8/2.2, 1978), p. 461, and Fr. Neiske, "Vision und Totengedenken," p. 156 and n. 118.

Chapter Two. Dreaming of the Dead

1. Thietmar of Merseburg, *Chronicon*, ed. R. Holtzmann, M.G.H. S.S., Nova Series 9 (Berlin, 1955), vol. I, pp. 11–14.

2. H. Lippelt, *Thietmar von Merseburg, Reichsbischof und Chronist* (Cologne and Vienna, 1973), especially pp. 48ff., and p. 193 "Der Character des Chronistes und die Memorial-Struktur seines Werkes." On the historical context, see H. Mayr-Harting, "The Church of Magdeburg: Its Trade and Its Town in the

Tenth and Early Eleventh Centuries," in D. Abulafia, M. Franklin, and M. Rubin (eds.), *Church and Society, 1000–1500: Essays in Honour of Christopher Brooke* (Cambridge, Mass., 1992), pp. 129–150.

3. Thietmar of Merseburg, *Chronicon*, III, 13, pp. 112–113.

4. Ibid., III, 15, pp. 114–117.

5. Ibid., VI, 76, pp. 364–367.

6. Ibid., I, 13, pp. 18–20.

7. *Vita Karoli Quarti. Karl IV. Selbstbiographie* (Hanau, 1979), pp. 74–77. Cf. P. Dinzelbacher, "Der Traum Kaiser Karls IV.," in A. Paravicini Bagliani and G. Stabile (eds.), *Träume im Mittelalter. Ikonologische Studien* (Stuttgart and Zurich, 1989), pp. 161–172 (especially pp. 167–168 and ill. pp. 202–203).

8. Vienna, Österreichische Nationalbibliothek, MS Ser. N. 2618, fol. 18 v. (1472), and 581 (1470–1480). I want to thank Mr. Gerhard Jaritz (Institut für Realienkunde des Mittelalters und der frühen Neuzeit, Krems) for providing me with these two photographs.

9. Paul Amargier, *La Parole rêvée. Essai sur la vie et l'oeuvre de Robert d'Uzès O.P. (1263–1296)* (Aix-en-Provence, 1982), p. 96 (Vision 29). See also p. 86 (Vision 3), the apparition of a "spectre of a man" in which the Virgin is substituted for the Child. The Latin text is in Jeanne Bignami-Odier, "Les visions de Robert d'Uzès," *Archivum Fratrum Praedicatorum* XXV (1955): 258–310. See also P. Amargier, "Robert d'Uzès revisité. Annexe: les testaments de Robert d'Uzès (1293)," in *Cahiers de Fanjeaux* 27 (1992), "Fin du monde et signes des temps. Visionnaires et prophètes en France méridonale (fin XIIIe–débout XVe siècle)," pp. 33–47, and in the same volume, M. Tobin, "Les visions et révélations de Marie Robine d'Avignon dans le contexte prophétique des années 1400," pp. 309–329.

10. Gertrude of Helfta, *Le Héraut*, V, in *Oeuvres spirituelles*, V, edited and translated by J.-M. Clément, the recluse nuns of Wisques, and B. de Vregille (Paris, Cerf, 1986), pp. 19ff.

11. J. Ancelet-Hustache, "Les 'Vitae sororum' d'Unterlinden. Edition critique du Ms. 508 de la Bibliothèque municipale de Colmar," *Archives d'histoire doctrinale et littéraire du Moyen Age* 5 (1930): 317–513, notably chaps. XII, XXIII, XXVIII, XXXIV, XXXVI (apparition during the sister's prayer), XL, XLIII (apparition in the sisters' cemetery).

12. Ibid., chap. XXXVIII, p. 454.

13. Ibid., chap. XLVIII, p. 480.

14. This is confirmed in the tales concerning other female mystics of this period, such as Lutgarde, according to the *Vita Lutgardis* of Thomas of Cantimpré, *Acta Sanctorum*, June III, books II and III, pp. 244ff.

15. Jacques Le Goff, "Les rêves dans la culture et la psychologie collective de l'Occident médiéval" (1971), reprinted in *Pour un autre Moyen Age. Temps, travail et culture en Occident: 18 essais* (Paris, 1977), pp. 299–306 [English edition: "Dreams in the Culture and Collective Psychology of the Medieval West," in *Time, Work, and Culture in the Middle Ages*, trans. Arthur Goldhammer (Chicago, 1980), pp. 201–

204]; J. Le Goff, "Le christianisme et les rêves (IIe–VIIe siècle)" (1985), reprinted in *The Medieval Imagination*.

16. Eusebius, *Ecclesiastical History*, V, 1, 20 ("The Martyrs of Lyon"), cited by Peter Brown, *The Making of Late Antiquity* (Cambridge, Mass., 1978), p. 56.

17. *La Règle de saint Benoît*, edited and translated by H. Rochais (Paris, 1980), LVIII, 25, cited by Jean-Claude Schmitt, *La Raison des gestes dans l'Occident médiéval*, p. 78.

18. C. van Beek (ed.), *Passio sanctarum Perpetuae et Felicitatis* (Nimegue, 1936). Undoubtedly written by Tertullian, the *Passio*, the authenticity of which leaves no doubt, is in the form of an autobiography. Cf., for its contribution to the history of places in the hereafter, Jacques Le Goff, *The Birth of Purgatory*, pp. 48–51.

19. Ambrose, *De excessu fratris sui Satyri*, I, 72, in *PL*, vol. 16, col. 1370, cited by M. Dulaye, *Le Rêve*, p. 66.

20. Agius, *Dialogus de morte Hathumodae*, M.G.H. Poetae III, ed. L. Traube (Berlin, 1896), pp. 372–388. On this work's position in literary tradition, see P. von Moos, *Consolatio. Studien zur mittelalterlichen Trostliteratur über den Tod und zum Problem der christlichen Trauer*, 4 vols. (Munich, 1971–1972), vol. 1, pp. 169ff.

21. The most complete study is that of H. Schauwecker, *Otloh von St. Emmeran. Ein Beitrag zur Bildung- und Frömmigkeitsgeschichte des 11. Jahrhunderts*, Studien zur Mitteilungen des Benediktiner Ordens ud seiner Zweige 74, 1963, Heft I–IV (Munich, 1964), pp. 1–240.

22. K. Hallinger, *Gorze-Cluny. Studien zu den monastischen Lebensformen und Gegensätzen im Hochmittelalter*, 2 vols. (Graz, 1971), vol. 1, pp. 618–628; H. Jakobs, *Die Hirsauer. Ihre Ausbreitung und Rechtstellung im Zeitalter des Investiturstreites* (Cologne and Graz, 1961), pp. 8–12.

23. On the autobiographical and visionary aspect, see G. Misch, *Studien zur Geschichte der Autobiographie*, vol. I, *Otloh von Sankt-Emmeran. Bekehrungsgeschichte, Visionsgeschichte, Schriftstellers- Autobiographie*, Nachrichten der Akademie der Wissenschaften in Göttingen, I. Phil.-Hist. Kl. 5 (1954), pp. 123–169; G. Vinay, "Otlone di Sant'Emmeran ovvero l'autobiografia di un nevrotico," in *La storiografia altomedievale*, Settimane di Studio del Centro italiano di studi sull' alto medioevo, XVIII (Spolete, 1970), vol. I, pp. 13–37. Generally these studies take into account only the first four visions of the *Liber visionum*, as is also the case, for the most part, in H. Röckelein, *Otloh, Gottschalk, Tnugdal: Individuelle und kollektive Visionsmuster des Hochmittelalters* (Frankfurt, New York, 1987).

24. From the fifth to the eighteenth, as well as the twenty-third and last, which Otloh says he forgot to report earlier.

25. Only four tales come from written sources. No ghost is mentioned in them: they are visions of punishments in the hereafter, the first one cited from a letter from Saint Boniface to a nun and the three others from Bede's *Ecclesiastical History*. There is supplemental proof of the relative novelty of ghosts in the eleventh century: more ancient texts rarely providing any resources, authors around

the year 1000 had to have recourse either to their own dreams or to oral tales that they could glean around them.

26. *PL*, vol. 146, cols. 359–361.

27. The pope was formerly a bishop, Bruno of Toul, and was closely connected in that role to the monastic reform of Gorze, which inspired that of Saint Emmeran.

28. *PL*, vol. 146, cols. 361–363.

29. Ibid., cols. 366–368, 371–373.

30. Trusting in the word of his son, who had in fact lied to him, the father had sworn to his lord that his son had not killed one of the lord's lambs.

31. Guibert of Nogent, *A Monk's Confession*, pp. 51–53.

32. Ibid., p. 52.

33. Unless the swimmer ghost, although he is damned and requests no suffrages, is for Guibert a literary recollection of the *Dialogues* of Gregory the Great. The two hypotheses are not irreconcilable, since the memory of a lived experience might blend into the literary topos.

34. Ibid., pp. 64–69.

35. *"Nollite eam tangere"*: the evangelical reference, in spite of the reversal of the subject and the object, is clear and seems to designate Christ as the one who speaks and Guibert's mother as Mary Magdalene.

36. Regarding this tale, see Jacques Le Goff, *The Birth of Purgatory*, pp. 181–186.

37. Jean-Claude Schmitt, *Le Saint Lévrier. Saint Guinefort guérisseur d'enfants depuis le XIIIe siècle* (Paris, 1979). [English edition: *The Holy Greyhound: Guinefort, Healer of Children since the Thirteenth Century*, trans. Martin Thom (Cambridge, Eng., 1983)]

38. Thomas of Cantimpré, *Bonum universale de apibus*, II, 53, 32, ed. Douai (1627), pp. 513–514.

39. Peter Morone, *Autobiographia*, ed. A. Frugoni, "Coelestiana," in *Studi Storici*, 6–7 (Rome, 1954), p. 62. See also p. 57, the tale of the apparition of his father to his godmother.

40. M. Zink, *La Subjectivité littéraire. Autour du siècle de saint Louis* (Paris, 1985), p. 234 (and pp. 219–239). [The translated citation is from *The Life of St. Louis by John of Joinville*, trans. René Hague (New York and London, 1955), pp. 218–219.]

41. Jacques Le Goff, *Saint Louis* (Paris, 1996).

42. Giovanni di Pagolo Morelli, *Ricordi*, ed. Vittore Branca (Florence, 1956), pp. 455–516. See the very fine analysis by Richard C. Trexler, *Public Life in Renaissance Florence* (New York, 1980), pp. 161–186.

43. Christiane Klapisch-Zuber, *La Maison et le Nom. Stratégies et rituels dans l'Italie de la Renaissance* (Paris, 1990), especially pp. 249–262.

44. R. C. Trexler, *Public Life*, especially pp. 172–185.

45. Ibid., p. 174.

46. Ibid., pp. 174–75, speaks of "communication" with the soul of the son, but not of necromancy.

47. The child was, however, nine years old. It was accepted that the inno-
cence of the young baptized ended at the age of seven, the "age of reason." One
might compare his fate with that of Dinocratus, the young brother of Perpetua
(cf. n. 18, chapter I, above).

48. R. C. Trexler, *Public Life,* p. 177.

49. Ibid., p. 182. This notation should be added, of course, to the inquiry
initiated by Philippe Ariès into the "discovery of the feeling of childhood."

Chapter Three. The Invasion of Ghosts

1. Saint Gregory the Great, *Dialogues,* IV, 43.

2. Thietmar of Merseburg, *Chronicon,* p. 16.

3. Guibert of Nogent, *De pignoribus sanctorum,* IV, 1, in *PL,* vol. 156, col.
668A. They do not appear to him to be inferior to those of Gregory the Great
or of Bede.

4. Peter the Venerable, *De miraculis,* I, XXVII and XXVIII (pp. 87 and 94).
Another mention of noticing, in this period, "many examples and revelations of
souls" is Hugh of Saint Victor, *Summa de sacramentis,* in *PL,* vol. 176, col. 586CD.

5. William of Newburgh, *Historia rerum anglicarum usque ad annum 1198,* V,
chap. XXIV, ed. R. Howlett, *Chronicles of the Reign of Stephen, Henry II, and Richard I*
(London, 1884), vol. 1, p. 477. For a slightly different translation, see Claude
Lecouteux and Ph. Marcq, *Les Esprits et les Morts textes traduits du latin, présentés et com-
mentés* (Paris, 1990), p. 171.

6. See P. A. Sigal, *L'Homme et le miracle dans la France médiévale (XIe–XIIe siècle)*
(Paris, 1985).

7. Ekkehard of Saint Gall, *Vita S. Wiboradae,* chap. XXIII, ed. W. Berschin,
Mitteilungen zur vaterländischen Geschichte 51 (St. Gallen, 1983), pp. 63–67.
See M. E. Wittmer-Butsch, *Zur Bedeutung von Schlaf und Traum im Mittelalter* (Krems,
1990), p. 287.

8. R. Rigodon, "Vision de Robert, abbé de Mozat, au sujet de la basilique
de la Mère de Dieu," *Bulletin historique et scientifique de l'Auvergne* LXX (1950): 27–55,
especially pp. 48–50. On this document, see Jean-Claude Schmitt, "L'Occident,
Nicée II et les images du VIIIe au XIIIe siècle," in F. Boespflug and N. Lossky,
Nicée II 787–1987. Douze siècles d'images religieuses (Paris, 1987), pp. 271–301.

9. M. C. Diaz y Diaz, *Visiones del Mas Alla en Galicia durante la alta Edad Media*
(Santiago de Compostela, 1985), pp. 63–81, especially pp. 75–76.

10. E. de Certain (ed.), *Miraculi sancti Benedicti* (Paris, 1858) (reprinted, New
York and London, 1968). Apparitions of Saint Benedict: I, 20, 40; IV, 7; VII, 12,
13, 15; IX, 10.

11. H. Hoffmann (ed.), *Chronica monasterii Casinensis,* M.G.H. S.S. XXXIV
(Hanover, 1980). See IV, 99, p. 561 (to take the abbey's treasure from the greed
of King Roger of Sicily); other visions: II, 21; IV, 30, 102; apparitions of Saint
Benedict: II, 22; III, 20; IV, 101. While he was alive Saint Benedict had, ac-

cording to Gregory the Great, accomplished miracles regarding the dead. On the Cassinian interpretation of this tradition under the abbacy of Desiderius (eleventh century), see chapter IX, below.

12. Fridolin Dressler, *Petrus Damiani. Leben und Werk* (Rome, 1954); Jean Leclercq, *Saint Pierre Damien. Ermite et homme d'Eglise* (Rome, 1960).

13. Peter Damian, *Epistolae*, VIII, 20, in *PL*, vol. 144, cols. 403–404.

14. Peter Damian, *Opuscula*, XXXIII and XXXIV, in *PL*, vol. 145, cols. 559–572, 571–590. On these tracts, see Jacques Le Goff, *The Birth of Purgatory*, pp. 177–180.

15. Fr. Dressler, *Petrus Damiani*, p. 88 n. 372 (lists the tales that Hugh told him during the voyage to Cluny, Saint Martial de Limoges, and Chalon, where Peter Damian imposed a respect for the independance of Cluny on Bishop Drogo of Mâcon).

16. Peter Damian, *Opuscula*, XXXIII, chaps. V, VI, VII, and *Opuscula*, XXXIV, *Disputatio*, chap. V, in *PL*, vol. 145, cols. 567–570, 588–590.

17. Peter Damian, *Opuscula*, XXXIV, *Disputatio*, chaps. III, IV, V, in *PL*, vol. 145, cols. 585–590.

18. See D. Iogna-Prat, "Les morts dans la comptabilité céleste des Cluni-siens de l'an Mil," in D. Iognat-Prat and J.-Ch. Picard, *Religion et culture autour de l'an mil*, pp. 55–69.

19. Jotsuald, *Vie de saint Odilon*, in *PL*, vol. 142, cols. 926–928, written by Peter Damian, *Vie de saint Odilon*, in *PL*, vol. 144, cols. 933–938, and then by many authors (Sigebert of Gembloux, Vincent of Beauvais, Jacobus da Voragine, etc.).

20. Peter Damian, *Epistolae*, VI, 2, col. 372C. See Fr. Dressler, *Petrus Damiani*, pp. 53, 83.

21. *De rebus gestis in Majori Monasterio saeculo XI* [sic], ed. Dom J. Mabillon, *Acta Sanctorum Ord. S. Ben.*, VI, 2 (Venise, 1733–1745), p. 400, reprinted in *PL*, vol. 149, cols. 403–420. On this collection, see J. Van der Straeten, "Le recueil des miracles de saint Martin dans le ms. 117 de Charleville," *Analecta Bollandiana 94*, 1–2 (1976): 83–94 (especially pp. 89–92). On the history of the prestigious abbey, ruined in the Revolution, see Ch. Lelong, *L'Abbaye de Marmoutier* (Chambray, 1989) (briefly). See, above all, S. Farmer, "Personal Perceptions, Collective Behavior: Twelfth-Century Suffrages for the Dead," in R. C. Trexler (ed.), *Persons in Groups: Social Behaviour as Identity Formation in Medieval and Renaissance Europe*, Medieval and Renaissance Texts and Studies (Binghampton, 1985), pp. 231–239, and since then, by the same author, *Communities of Saint Martin: Legend and Ritual in Medieval Tours* (Ithaca and London, 1991), especially pp. 135–149, in which she rightfully insists on the exclusively monastic identity of the dead who appear.

22. *PL*, vol. 149, cols. 415D, 417A ("nostris temporibus").

23. Ibid., col. 416D.

24. Ibid., col. 411D: "sollicitos nos esse conveniat, ne defunctis fratribus debitum suum exsolvere negligamus."

25. Ibid., col. 412B.

26. In fact fifteen, if we exclude one tale that is absent from the manuscript of Charleville. See S. Farmer, *Communities of Saint Martin*, p. 135 n. 47.

27. Tales 3, 5, 6, 7, 11, 14, 16.

28. Tales 12, 13, 15. One day of Pentecost, Count Fulk has a vision of the abbey glowing in the fire of the Holy Spirit; another time, old Hildebrand forces the relics of Saint Corentin to participate in the procession against the drought; finally, Saint Martin saves a shipment of fish, intended for the provisions of the monks, from a shipwreck on the Loire.

29. Tale 4: a brother who recently died appears in a dream, at midnight, to his confessor Hildebrand to complain that his confession did not spare him all the punishments in the hereafter; the confessor takes responsibility for the man's sins, and he is freed. Tale 10: two dead brothers appear three times to Ulric, the steward of the priory of Tavant, to scold him, then to threaten him, and finally to beat him severely because he stole their "right." Tale 2: two dead brothers appear to the abbot Bartholomew so that he will privately reprimand the monks guilty of negligence in their prayers for the dead.

30. Tale 8.

31. Tale 9.

32. Tale 17.

33. S. Farmer is right to stress the exclusively monastic sphere of the figures in these tales. The same cannot be said of other collections (see, below, Peter the Venerable, Caesarius of Heisterbach, etc.).

34. S. D. White, *Custom, Kinship, and Gifts to Saints: The Laudatio Parentum in Western France, 1050–1150* (Chapel Hill and London, 1988), p. 22. These lay benefactors of Marmoutier are well identified: they are the provosts of the chateau of Vendôme, the lords of Lavardin, Count Fulk the Rich, whom we encountered in one of the tales, etc. It is they who enabled the formation, throughout all of western France, of the "ecclesiastical empire" of Marmoutier. See O. Gantier, "Recherches sur les possessions et les prieurés de l'abbaye de Marmoutier du Xe au XIIIe siècle," *Revue Mabillon* 53 (1963): 93–110, 161–164; 54 (1964): 15–24, 56–67, 125–135; 55 (1965): 32–44, 65–79. See the study that ignores our document, by D. Barthélemy, *La Société dans le comté de Vendôme de l'an mil au XIVe siècle* (Paris, 1993).

35. Peter the Venerable, *De miraculis libri duo*, ed. D. Bouthillier, Corp. Christ. Cont. Med. LXXIII (Turnhout, 1988). This edition replaces the one in *PL*, vol. 189, cols. 851–954. The complete French translation is *Pierre Le Vénérable, Les Merveilles de Dieu*, presented and translated by J.-P. Torrell and D. Bouthillier (Paris, 1992). By the same authors is *Pierre le Vénérable et sa vision du monde. Sa vie, son oeuvre, l'homme et le démon* (Louvain, 1986). On apparitions of the dead at Cluny, see J.-Cl. Schmitt, "Les revenants dans la société féodale," *Le Temps de la réflexion* III (1982): 285–306.

36. J.-P. Torrell and D. Bouthillier, *Pierre le Vénérable*, p. 138, and in more

detail, by the same authors, "'Miraculum'. Une catégorie fondamentale chez Pierre le Vénérable," *Revue thomiste* LXXX, 4 (1980): 549–566. A different point of view is found in J. P. Valéry Patin and J. Le Goff, "A propos de la typologie des miracles dans le *Liber de miraculis* de Pierre le Vénérable," in *Pierre Abélard, Pierre le Vénérable. Les courants philosophiques, littéraires et artistiques en Occident au milieu du XIIe siècle* (Paris, 1975), pp. 181–187.

37. All of the many vitae of Saint Hugh tell of the apparition, with swollen lips, of Durannus, the former bishop of Toulouse and abbot of Moissac, to whom the abbot of Cluny had predicted that he would be punished in the afterlife for having, through his chatting, incited his monks to laugh. Informed of the apparition, Hugh twice orders seven days of fasting, until Durannus comes back to say that he is saved. See H. E. J. Cowdrey, *Two Studies in Cluniac History* (*1049–1126*) (Rome, 1978), pp. 43–110, and Fr. Neiske, "Vision und Totengedenken," p. 167.

38. The research of the editors, adding to the chronological specifications given by Peter himself, enable us in almost all cases to appreciate the temporal distance between the date of the death, the supposed apparition of the dead person, and the writing down of these tales around 1135: I, 10, dead in 1105–1106, thirty years earlier; I, 11, dead in 1070, apparition in 1076 or 1080, fifty-five years; I, 24, dead in 1119, apparition after 1125, fifteen years; I, 26, dead in 1123, apparition after 1123, twelve years. This new edition enables me to specify and correct my initial analysis of these tales, an analysis I had proposed using the Migne edition, in "Les revenants dans la société féodale."

39. Two tales written in 1142: I, 27, death and apparition in 1141, one year; I, 28, death and apparition in 1114, twenty-eight years earlier, but gathering of information in 1142.

40. II, 25, death and apparition in 1145; II, 26, death in 1148–1149, apparition in 1149–1150; II, 27, death in 1145, apparition in 1145?

41. Peter the Venerable, *De miraculis*, I, 26, p. 81: this is the case of the recluse nun Adèle of Blois in whom the beneficiary of the apparition, Sister Albérée, confided. The daughter of William the Conqueror, the mother of the king of England, Stephen, Adèle was of the noblest blood.

42. Ibid., II, 26: the monk Enguizo, a former knight to whom his companion in arms, the knight Peter of la Roche, who died during the Crusades, appeared.

43. Ibid., I, 23: the priest Stephen, to whom the knight Guigo de Moras appeared three times.

44. Ibid., II, 25.

45. Out of ten dead people, four are knights who died in those times, and another is a former knight who became a monk. Out of the five others, four are monks, and one is the former bishop of Geneva.

46. See ibid., I, 23 and 27.

47. *Liber tramitis*, c. 33, ed. P. Dinter, in K. Hallinger (ed.), *Corpus Consuetudi-*

num Monasticarum, t. X (Siegburg, 1980), p. 277, cited by M. Lauwers, *La Mémoire des ancêtres, le souci des morts*, vol. 2, p. 469.

48. Peter the Venerable, *De miraculis*, I, 27, p. 86.

49. See J.-P. Torrell and D. Bouthillier, *Pierre le Vénérable*, p. 169.

50. Ibid.

51. Peter the Venerable, *De miraculis*, I, 27, pp. 84 and 86: Geoffroy of Ion has Humbert of Beaujeu told that Geoffroy died in his service for an unjust cause (*non satis iusta de causa cum eo veneram*) and that God disapproves of his war against Amadeus II of Savoy. On this theme, see Fr. H. Russell, *The Just War in the Middle Ages* (Cambridge, Eng., 1975) (reprinted, 1979).

52. J.-P. Torrell and D. Bouthillier, *Pierre le Vénérable*, pp. 66–67. See J. M. Lacarra, "Una aparicion de ultratumba en Estella," *Principe de Viana* 15 (1944): 173–184. On the political context and Peter the Venerable's voyage to Spain, see Ch. J. Bishko, "Peter the Venerable's Journey to Spain," in G. Constable and J. Kritzeck (eds.), *Petrus Venerabilis, 1156–1956: Studies and Texts Commemorating the Eighth Centenary of His Death* (Rome, 1956), pp. 163–175; B. F. Reilly, *The Kingdom of Leon-Castilla under King Alfonso VI (1065–1109)* (Princeton, 1988), pp. 211ff.; M. R. Astray, *Alfonso VII Emperador. El imperio hispanico en el siglo XII* (Leon, 1979), p. 161s.

Chapter Four. The Marvelous Dead

1. Gervase of Tilbury, *Otia imperialia*, III, prologue, ed. G. W. Leibniz, Scriptores rerum Brunswicensium I (Hanover, 1707), pp. 960–961. French translation: *Le Livre des merveilles*, ed. A. Duchesne, preface by Jacques Le Goff (Paris, 1992), p. 20. Another contemporary author, the Welshman Giraldus Cambrensis or de Barri, who was very close to Gervase of Tilbury, also reflects on the notion of the marvelous at the beginning of the second part of his description of Ireland, an island that is "far from the center of the earth" and that has many "marvels of nature," distinct from the "miracles of the saints." See, finally, J.-M. Boivin, *L'Irlande au Moyen Age. Giraud de Barri et la "Topographia Hibernica"* (1188) (Paris, 1993), pp. 84–88, and the text by Giraldus, p. 197. See Jacques Le Goff, "The Marvelous in the Medieval West," republished in *The Medieval Imagination*, pp. 27–44, and also by Le Goff, "Le merveilleux scientifique au Moyen Age," in J. F. Bergier (ed.), *Zwischen Wahn, Glaube und Wissenschaft* (Zurich, 1988), pp. 87–113.

2. One finds a curious example of this "experimental" spirit in thirteenth-century Italy, as reported in a manuscript from the following century. Since a peasant had been fasting for forty days, he was bled by a barber to be sure that he still had blood and was therefore "not a spirit, but a man." See R. Creytens, "Le Manuel de Conversation de Philippe de Ferrare o.p. (d. 1350)," *Archivum Fratrum Praedicatorum* XVI (1946): 116 n. 36.

3. William of Newburgh, *Historia rerum anglicarum*, II, chap. XXVIII, vol. 2, pp. 84–87.

4. J. Marx, *La Légende arthurienne et le Graal* (Paris, 1952), pp. 281–284; F. Du-

bost, *Aspects fantastiques de la littérature narrative médiévale (XIIe–XIIIe siècle). L'autre, l'ailleurs, l'autrefois* (Paris, 1991), vol. I, pp. 410–430. On a specific theme that we will see again in the *exempla*, see D. Bohler, "Béances de la terre et du temps: La dette et le pacte dans le motif du Mort reconnaissant au Moyen Age," *L'Homme* 111–112 (1989), XXIX, 3–4, pp. 161–178.

5. *Historia Regum Britanniae* and *Vita Merlini*, by Geoffroy of Monmouth, are the first literary forms of the "Matter of Britain," almost immediately put into French by Wace and Robert of Boron. [Regarding the author's reference to Brutus, I would like to cite the useful text by Norris J. Lacy and Geoffrey Ashe, *The Arthurian Handbook* (New York and London, 1988), p. 314: "*Brutus*—According to a confused Welsh legend in the *Historia Brittonum* Brutus (or Britto) was a great-grandson of the Trojan Aeneas, hero of Virgil's epic. In the twelfth century B.C. he led a party of migrant Trojans to Britain, then called Albion, and they took possession. Geoffrey of Monmouth vastly elaborates the story, telling how the island was renamed Britain after Brutus, and its new people were called Britons. He traces a long succession of kings, including Arthur. Since Britain's legendary monarchy starts with Brutus, various works based directly or indirectly on Geoffrey use his name as their title, the chief being Wac's *Roman de Brut*, Layamon's *Brut*, and a number of Welsh chronicles."]

6. R. D. Ray, "Medieval Historiography through the Twelfth Century: Problems and Progress of Research," *Viator* 5 (1974): 33–59.

7. R. Thomson, *William of Malmesbury* (Woodbridge, 1987), pp. 22–23.

8. William of Malmesbury, *De gestis regum Anglorum libri quinque*, ed. W. Stubbs (London, 1887), II, 204, pp. 253–256: "non superno miraculo, sed inferno praestigio."

9. Ibid., II, 124, pp. 134–135: "has sane naenias sicut caeteras. Angli pene innata credulitate tenent."

10. Ibid., III, 257. Another apparition of the deceased: ibid., III, 293.

11. William of Newburgh, *Historia rerum anglicarum*, V, chaps. XXII–XXIV, pp. 474–482: "His diebus in pago Bukingamensi prodigiosa res accidit[. . . .] In aquilonalibus quoque Angliae partibus aliud non dissimile et aeque prodigiosum eodem tempore novimus accidisse[. . . .] Item aliud non dissimile[. . . .] His itaque expositis, ad historiae ordinem redeamus."

12. In the preface to the *Otia imperialia*, Gervase of Tilbury says he wrote a *liber facetiarum* for Prince Henry the Young King; judged by its title, this must have been rather similar to the *De nugis curialium* of Walter Map: ed. G. W. Leibniz, Hanover, Scriptores rerum brunsvicensium, t. I (1707), p. 883. See the remarks by A. Duchesne, translation cited, p. 2. On the court clerics, see E. Türk, "Nugae curialium," *Le règne d'Henri II Plantagenêt (1154–1189) et l'éthique politique* (Geneva, 1977).

13. *Walter Map, De nugis curialium. Courtiers' Trifles*, edited and translated by M. R. James, revised by C. N. L. Brooke and R. A. B. Mynors (Oxford, 1983) (1st ed., 1914). See also the French translation by M. Perez, *Contes de courtisans*.

Traduction du "De nugis curialium" de Gautier Map, Lille, Centre d'études médiévales et dialectales de l'université de Lille III, s.d. (doctoral thesis, defended in 1982).

14. *Walter Map*, introduction, p. xxxiii: the editors place these "trifles for the courtiers' spare time, idle tales to amuse them," between "Mirrors for Princes" and a collection of *exempla*.

15. Ibid., Dist. II, chaps. XI–XVI, and Dist. VII, chaps. IX–X.

16. See F. Dubost, *Aspects fantastiques* (notably vol. I), pp. 31–45. See also S. Auroux, J.-Cl. Chevalier, N. Jacques-Chaquin, Ch. Marchello-Nizia (eds.), *La Linguistique fantastique* (Paris, 1985), and T. Todorov, *Introduction à la littérature fantastique* (Paris, 1970).

17. Robert Bartlett, *Gerald of Wales, 1146–1223* (Oxford, 1982). On Giraldus and Wales, see M. Richter, *Giraldus Cambrensis: The Growth of the Welsh Nation* (Aberystwyth, 1976).

18. Giraldus Cambrensis, *Expugnation Hibernica*, I, XLII, ed. J. F. Dimock, *Opera*, V (London, 1867), p. 295. Reprinted and English translation: *The Conquest of Ireland by Giraldus Cambrensis*, ed. A. B. Scott and F. X. Martin (Dublin, 1978), pp. 116–119.

19. Giraldus Cambrensis, *De invectionibus*, XV, 18, ed. J. S. Brewer, *Opera*, I (London, 1861), p. 170.

20. This lost work is mentioned in the prologue to Gervase of Tilbury, *Otia imperialia*.

21. Ibid., III, chap. XC, "De coemeterio Elisii campi et illuc advectis," pp. 990–991.

22. Ibid., III, chap. XVII, "De Johanne episcopo et animabus mortuorum," pp. 965–966.

23. Ibid., III, chap. XCIX, "De mortuo qui occidit uxorem quondam suam," pp. 993–994.

24. "Mortuus mortario erecto": note the play on words and the sexual symbolism of the instrument associated with the pilon (phallic?).

25. Gervase of Tilbury, *Otia imperialia*, III, chap. CIII, "De mortuo qui apparet virgini, mira dicit et annunciat," pp. 994–1000. The French translation of this tale and a close study: H. Bresc, "Culture folklorique et théologie. Le revenant de Beaucaire (1211)," *Razo. Cahiers du Centre d'études médiévales de Nice* 8 (1988): 65–74. Since then, see A. Duchesne, *Le Livre des merveilles*, pp. 112–128.

26. Ernst H. Kantorowicz, "Mysteries of State: An Absolutist Concept and Its Late Medieval Origins," in Ernst H. Kantorowicz, *Selected Studies* (New York, 1965), pp. 381–398.

27. H. Bresc, "Culture folklorique et théologie," p. 70. My interpretation appears reinforced by the last words of the ghost, not translated by Henri Bresc; these words concern the "linking power" of the priest in confession (Gervase of Tilbury, p. 999).

28. A. Duchesne stresses the anti-Albiginsian meaning of all of Gervase of Tilbury's *Otia imperialia*.

Chapter Five. Hellequin's Hunt

1. H. Wolter, *Ordericus Vitalis. Ein Beitrag zur Kluniazensischen Geschichtsschreibung* (Wiesbaden, 1955), insists on the Clunisian influence that Marjorie Chibnall, *The World of Orderic Vitalis* (Oxford, 1984), tends on the contrary to limit, placing more emphasis on the attention that Orderic paid to the Anglo-Norman aristocracy.

2. In any case, it was not as widely read. Similarly, unlike the *Gesta regum Anglorum* of the contemporary English chronicler William of Malmesbury, Orderic's *History* remained unrecognized until the sixteenth century.

3. Orderic Vitalis, *Historia ecclesiastica*, III, 8–9. See M. Chibnall (ed.), *The Ecclesiastical History of Orderic Vitalis*, 6 vols. (Oxford, 1969–1980), vol. IV, pp. 212–215.

4. M. Chibnall, *The World of Orderic Vitalis*, pp. 37–38: he tells of his shock when a storm killed only those animals of the female gender, both human and otherwise, and he recalls his participation in the general chapter of Cluny in 1132, in which no fewer than 1,212 monks were gathered.

5. Orderic Vitalis, *Historia ecclesiastica*, introduction to vol. IV (p. xix).

6. Ibid., VIII, 17 (IV, 1973), pp. 236–250.

7. This temporal specification is, of course, important, It signifies that the dead person will still experience the trials of Lent before finding the hope of salvation. It also connects the symbolism of the rise of the liberated soul to paradise, to the entrance to Jerusalem, and to the beginning of Holy Week.

8. See C. Ginzburg, "Charivari, associations juvéniles, Chasse sauvage," in Jacques Le Goff and Jean-Claude Schmitt (eds.), *Le Charivari* (Paris, New York, 1981), pp. 134–136, and Brian Stock, *The Implications of Literacy: Written Language and Models of Interpretation in the Eleventh and Twelfth Centuries* (Princeton, 1983), pp. 495–497.

9. Here I see a folkloric theme linked to death, rather than the inexplicable metaphor of the apostles envisioned by Brian Stock, *The Implications of Literacy*, p. 497: "the four medlars, possibly representing the apostles, are balanced by the four condemned riders of the miniature apocalypse."

10. Georges Duby, *Les Trois Ordres ou l'Imaginaire du féodalisme* (Paris, 1978). [English edition: *The Three Orders: Feudal Society Imagined*, trans. Arthur Goldhammer, with a foreword by Thomas N. Bisson (Chicago, 1980)]

11. On the themes of the Peace of God and the just war, in regard to the *Ecclesiastical History*, see M. Chibnall, *The World of Orderic Vitalis*, pp. 132–145. Lastly, see the study by J. Flori, "L'Eglise et la Guerre sainte: De la 'Paix de Dieu' à la 'croisade,'" *Annales. E.S.C.* 2 (1992): 453–466.

12. L. L. K. Little, "La morphologie des malédictions monastiques," *Annales. E.S.C.* 1 (1979): pp. 43–60, and P. Geary, "L'humiliation des saints," ibid., pp. 27–42.

13. Bernard of Clairvaux, *Eloge de la nouvelle chevalerie*, edited and translated by P.-Y. Emery (Paris, 1990), pp. 58ff. [See also the English-language edition:

The Works of Bernard of Clairvaux, Vol. VII, Treatises III: "On Grace and Free Choice," trans. Daniel O'Donovan, introduction by Bernard McGinn, and *"In Praise of the New Knighthood,"* trans. Conrad Greenia, introduction by R. J. Zwi Werblowsky (Kalamazoo, 1977).]

14. The work of the German Volkskunde in the 1930s—in which ideological prejudices coexist with the best scholarship—remain required references, notably O. Höfler, *Kultische Geheimbünde der Germanen* (Frankfort, 1934). Regarding Hellequin's hunt, the Volkskunde material is reflected in the more recent works of J. H. Grisward, *Archéologie de l'épopée médiévale* (Paris, 1981), pp. 183–228, and of C. Ginzburg, *Le Sabbat des sorcières* (1989), French translation by M. Aymard (Paris, 1992), pp. 313–314 nn. 46–48. Although I do not attribute great importance to the etymological research (it must not be substituted for a sociohistorical interpretation), I believe there is less reason to connect Hellequin's hunt to a pre-Christian Celtic substratum—see Ph. Walter, *La Mythologie chrétienne* (Paris, 1992)—than to Germanic traditions, which the name appears to indicate more directly.

15. I will not take up again the endless discussions on this etymology and refer the reader instead to H. Flasdieck, "Harlekin. Germanischer Mythos in romanischer Wandlung," *Anglia* 61, Heft 3/4 (1937): 225–340 (especially pp. 270, 312s.).

16. *Vie d'Isidore d'Alexandrie,* cited by K. Meisen, *Die Sagen vom Wütenden Heer und Wilden Jaeger* (Münster, 1935), pp. 22–23.

17. Augustine, *Concerning the City of God against the Pagans,* II, 25, a new translation by Henry Bettenson with an introduction by David Knowles (London, 1972), p. 81: "[these malignant spirits, *maligni spiritus*] were, indeed, seen joining battle among themselves in a wide plain in Campania, shortly before the citizen armies fought their shameful battle in that very place. For first a terrible din was heard there, and before long many people reported that they had seen two armies fighting for several days. And when the fighting stopped men found what looked like the tracks of men and horses, such as could have been left on the ground as a result of that encounter." Augustine's description is inspired by Julius Obsequens's *Book of Wonders.*

18. Paul the Deacon, *Historia Langobardorum,* II, 4 (anno 570), ed. G. Waitz, M. G. H. Script. rer. Germ. in usum schol., Hanover (1878), pp. 86–87. Cited by K. Meisen, *Die Sagen vom Wütenden Heer,* pp. 23–24.

19. For example, in Peter the Venerable, *De miraculis,* I, 23, pp. 69–70, the ghost says he heard "behind his back the din of a huge army," and at I, 28, the ghost Sancho says that the "large army" of the dead is waiting for him outside the house.

20. Raoul Glaber, *Les Cinq Livres de ses histoires (900–1044),* ed. Maurice Prou (Paris, 1887). Since then, see *Rodolfo Il Glabro, Cronache dell'anno Mille (Storie),* a cura di Guglielmo Cavallo e Giovanni Orlandi (Milan, 1989), and *Rodulfi Glabri,*

historiarum libri quinque: Rodulfus Glaber, the Five Books of the Histories, ed. John France (Oxford, 1989).

21. D. Milo, *Trahir le temps (histoire)* (Paris, 1991).

22. Brian Stock, in *The Implications of Literacy,* commenting on this vision, rightly stresses the terms that mark the community *(plebs, professio, vocatio, collegium)* but asserts—wrongly, in my opinion—that the *viri* that accompany the bishop are "laymen." In my opinion, they are, on the contrary, the *religiosi* who had to take up weapons against the Saracens to defend themselves and who became martyrs.

23. Fr. Cardini: *Alle radici della cavalleria medievale* (Florence, 1981) and *La Culture de la guerre. Xe–XVIIIe siècle* (1st Italian edition, 1982; French translation by A. Levi, Paris, 1992).

24. *Liber miraculorum sancte Fidis,* ed. A. Bouillet, Collection de textes pour servir à l'étude et à l'enseignement de l'histoire, 20 (Paris, 1897), pp. 269–275 (from the Sélestat manuscript, twelfth century, in which two pages telling our tale were added in the thirteenth century). The best edition, from the Saint Gall manuscript (twelfth century), is O. Holder-Egger (ed.), *De fundatione monasterii S. Fidis Sletstatensis,* M.G.H. S.S., XV-2 (Hanover, 1888), pp. 996–1000. The outside dates are those of the death of Abbot Bégon, mentioned in the tale, and of the advent of the Hohenstaufen to royalty (Conrad III in 1138) or even to the empire (Frederick Barbarossa, in 1155), following the predictions of the tale.

25. A parallel can be noted between the renewal of the pilgrimage of Conques at the beginning of the eleventh century, owing to the completely new statue-reliquary *(majestas)* of the saint and to a first miracle of healing, and the renewal of the monastery of Sélestat at the end of the century, following this apparition, which also was considered miraculous.

26. We know, moreover, that Conrad's body had not been buried at Sélestat; in the thirteenth century at least, its presence was noted in the family sepulchre of the abbey of Lorch, another foundation of Frederick of Büren: H. Pertz (ed.), *Historia Frederici,* M.G.H. S.S., XXIII (Hanover, 1874), pp. 384–385. A dead person could appear far from where the body was buried and therefore provoke an even greater surprise. This text includes a summary of our tale, with several transformations: it asserts in particular that Conrad appeared directly to his brother, the bishop Otto, and not to the knight Walter.

27. When Conrad and Otto had gone to Conques, they had put their arms in the *strevile,* or stirrup, of Charlemagne. Unlike the rather frail arm of the bishop Otto, the thick arm of the warrior Conrad had filled up the space. Wasn't that stirrup Charlemagne's "A," still present in the treasure of Conques? Furthermore, the two brothers had asked for hospitality in a house, and Otto had been recognized after revealing his episcopal ring.

28. G. Livet and F. Rapp, *Histoire de Strasbourg des origines à nos jours* (Strasbourg, 1981), II, p. 24.

29. "Cruciatus avernales" and not "Arvernales" (sic), as A. Bouillet writes on p. 274 of his edition.

30. "usque Nivellam in quodam monte tartareas flammas." There were many mountainous mouths of hell (we will recall later that this description was connected to Etna). It is necessary to know whether this tradition is confirmed elsewhere.

31. *Cartulaire de Conques*, #575, cited by A. Bouillet in his edition of *Liber miraculorum sancte Fidis*, p. 275.

32. Gervase of Tilbury, *Otia imperialia*, III, chap. XLI, p. 974.

33. *Vie de Bernard de Tiron*, II, 17, in *PL*, vol. 172, col. 1379AB; B. Stock, *The Implications of Literacy*, p. 463, rightly connects this passage of the apparition of the dead-elect to Vulferius, according to Raoul Glaber. But he underestimates in the latter the reference to warriors in the procession of the dead religious figures.

34. *De rebus gestis in Majori Monasterio saeculo XI*, #17, in *PL*, vol. 149, col. 417–420.

35. William of Malmesbury, *De gestis regum Anglorum*, I, pp. 256–258. On the tradition of this tale, see P. F. Baum, "The Young Man Bethrothed to a Statue," *Publications of the Modern Language Association of America* 34 (1919): 523–579; Jean-Claude Schmitt, "Ecriture et image: Les avatars médiévaux du modèle grégorien," *Littérales*, 4 (*Théories et pratiques de l'écriture au Moyen Age*), University of Paris X, Nanterre, Cahiers du Département de français (1988), pp. 119–154.

36. Giraldus Cambrensis, *Expugnation Hibernica*, I, IV, p. 235.

37. *The Anglo-Saxon Chronicle*, edited and translated by D. Whitelock, D. C. Douglas, and S. I. Tucker (London, 1961) (2d ed., 1965). Original text: *Two of the Saxon Chronicles: Parallel, with Supplementary Extracts from the Others*, ed. Ch. Plummer and J. Earle, reprinted by D. Whitelock (Oxford, 1965) (1st ed., 1892), p. 258. (I want to thank Michael Richter for indicating these texts to me.) See K. Meisen, *Die Sagen vom Wütenden Heer*, pp. 38–39. A first version must have been copied on the order of King Alfred around 890; it was then pursued by increasing large annual notices, until the death of King Stephen of Blois and the advent of the Angevin King Henry II Plantagenet in 1154. The manuscript of the Anglo-Saxon chronicle stops in 1154, which does not mean that the chronicle stopped after that date. In this case it is probable that the Anglo-Saxon language must not have continued to be used for very long. In any case, the advent of the Plantagenets indeed marked a break.

38. *Actus Pontificum Cenomannis in urbe degentium* (chap. XXXVII: *Gesta Hugonis ep.*, anno 1135), ed. J. Mabillon, *Vetera Analecta* (Paris, 1723), p. 326. Partial translation and commentary in Cl. Lecouteux and Ph. Marcq, *Les Esprits et les Morts*, pp. 113–116, who rightly see in Garnier a type of the poltergeist, the "striking spirit."

39. The same is true, for example, in the tale by Peter the Venerable (*De miraculis*, I, 28) regarding the *exercitus sociorum* who, outside the house, awaits the dead Sancho, who alone appeared.

40. Ekkehardi Uraugiensis, *Chronica*, ed. G. Waitz, M.G.H. S.S. VI, p. 256.

See Cl. Lecouteux and Ph. Marcq, *Les Esprits et les Morts*, p. 147, who confuse this chronicler with Ekkehard IV of Saint Gall (d. c. 1060), but note another interesting version of this tale that appears in the *Chronicle of Brunswick*, dated 1125: the incandescent phantom carries a milestone, undoubtedly one he displaced while he was alive.

41. E. Uraugiensis, *Chronica*, p. 261. See K. Meisen, *Die Sagen vom Wütenden Heer*, p. 38.

42. Walter Map, *De nugis curialium*, I, 11, and IV, 13, pp. 26–30 and pp. 370–373.

43. Jean-Claude Schmitt, "Temps, folklore et politique au XIIe sicle. A propos de deux récits de Walter Map, *De Nugis curialium*, I, 9 and IV, 13," in *Le Temps Chrétien de la fin de l'Antiquité au Moyen Age, IIIe–XIIIe siècle* (Paris, 1984), pp. 489–516.

44. Cl. Lecouteux: "Zwerge und Verwandt," *Euphorion* 75 (1981): 366–378, and *Les Nains et les Elfes au Moyen Age* (Paris, 1988).

45. G. Gatto, "La christianisation des traditions folkloriques: Le voyage au paradis," *Annales. E.S.C.* (1979), pp. 929–942.

46. Helinand of Froidmont, *De cognitione sua*, chaps. X–XIII, in *PL*, vol. 212, cols. 721–736. Helinand wrote, moreover, "A Mirror of the Prince" (*De bono regimine principis*), a moral treatise (*De reparatione lapsi*), a universal chronicle (in which he takes up the famous "Tnugdal's Vision"), and in Old French, the famous *Vers de la mort* (see the commentary and translation into modern French by M. Boyer and M. Santucci, H. Champion, 1983). Helinand's tales were taken up in the thirteenth century by Vincent of Beauvais in his *Tractatus consolatorius de morte amici* (letter addressed to Louis IX on January 15, 1260, to console him on the death of his eldest son), published in *Opera* (Basel, 1481), *in folio*, chap. VII (I am grateful to M.-A. Polo de Beaulieu for this reference).

47. To see Charles V, the king of France (1364–1380), in Hellequin, K. Meisen, *Die Sagen vom Wütenden Heer*, p. 49 n. 1, is forced to assume that the original text underwent an interpolation.

48. Herbert, *Libri de miraculis cisterciensium monachorum libri tres*, in *PL*, vol. 185, col. 1274. (Cf. K. Meisen, *Die Sagen vom Wütenden Heer*, p. 60.) Other apparitions (individual) of the dead are in ibid., cols. 1335–1337.

49. The aerial movement of Hellequin's hunt is also mentioned in the fourteenth-century French poem *Richard-sans-Peur*. The hunt travels on a sort of flying carpet, which enables the hero in a few moments to cover the entire distance between the monastery of Sainte-Catherine-du-mont-Sinai and Normandy. See Denis Joseph Conlon (ed.), *Richard Sans Peur: Edited from Le Romant de Richart and from Gilles Corrozet's Richart sans Paour* (Chapel Hill, 1977), pp. 73–77.

50. J.-Cl. Bonne, *L'Art roman de face et de profil. Le tympan de Conques* (Paris, 1984), pp. 271–274.

51. Caesarius of Heisterbach, *Dialogus miraculorum*, Dist. XII, chaps. XVI–XVI.

52. Ibid., III, 58.

53. Ibid., II, 12. Thus in this tale Etna plays the role that Arthurian legend usually bestowed on the Lost Isle of Avalon, where a wounded Arthur enjoys a sort of immortality. See G. Ashe, *The Quest for Arthur's Britain* (London, 1969), and A. Graf, "Artù nel Etna," in *Mitti, leggende e superstizioni del Medio Evo* (Milan, 1984), pp. 321–338.

54. The bibliography for this is huge. See, notably, R. S. and L. H. Loomis, *Arthurian Legends in Medieval Art*, Modern Language Association of America, Monograph Series IX (New York, 1938) (reprinted, 1966), especially p. 36.

55. W. Haug, *Das Mosaïk von Otranto. Darstellung, Deutung und Bilddokumentation* (Wiesbaden, 1977), pp. 87–91.

56. For a much more cautious look, after a meticulous discussion of the various interpretations proposed, the most complete study remains that of Ch. Settis Frugoni, "Per una lettura del mosaico pavimentale della cattedrale di Otranto," *Bolletino del'Istituto Storico Italiano per il Medio Evo e Archivio Muratoriano* 80 (1968): 213–256 (especially pp. 237–240) and 82 (1970): 243–270 (especially pp. 249–250).

57. Caesarius of Heisterbach, *Dialogus miraculorum*, Dist. XII, chaps. XII–XIII. In book XII, completed in 1223, Caesarius says that the event, reported by two abbots, involving Emperor Frederick, unfolded "three years ago," thus in 1220, which is indeed the date of Frederic II's ascent to the imperial throne.

58. "Inclitus rex Brittonum" (illustrious king of the Britons)—it is thus that William of Malmesbury designates Arthur with regard to the church of Glastonbury, which claimed possession of the tomb of the legendary king. See John Scott (ed. and trans.), *De Antiquitate Glastonie Ecclesie: The Early History of Glastonbury* (Woodbridge, 1981), pp. 82–83. This does not indicate a Celtic origin for the tradition of King Herla and the *familia Herlethingi*: the etymology, the reference by Walter Map to the Anglo-Saxon invasion, and the diffusion of the theme, on the contrary, underline its Germanic origin.

59. Stephen of Bourbon, *Tractatus de diversis materiis praedicalibus de septem donis Spiritus Sancti*, ed. A. Lecoy de la Marche (Paris, 1877), #365, p. 321.

60. The ethnological literature on the hood is quite vast. See G. Widengren, "Harlekintracht und Mönchszkutte. Clownhut und Derwischmütze," *Orientalia Suecana*, vol. II, fasc. 2/4 (Upsala, 1953), pp. 41–111.

61. William of Auvergne, *De universo*, III, chap. XII, in *Opera omnia* (Paris, 1674), I, pp. 593–1074 (excerpts in K. Meisen, *Die Sagen vom Wütenden Heer*, p. 53).

62. "nec tamen certum est eos malignos spiritus esse"

63. Regarding the apparition of Sancho to Peter Engelbert in Spain, Peter the Venerable (*De miraculis*, I, 28), a century earlier, had already noted the appellation *exercitus sociorum* for the troop of the dead waiting outside for this ghost. Locally, the name *huesta antigua* is noted in the fifteenth century in Alfonso de Spina, *Forsalitium fidei*, 1458 (ed. 1494, fol. 281 v.), cited by Th. Wright, *A Contemporary Narrative of the Proceedings against Dame Alice Kyteler Prosecuted for Sorcery in 1324, by Richard de Ledrede, Bishop of Ossory* (London, 1843), p. xl. It is interesting to

discover William of Auvergne's passage in the manuscript of this Irish witchcraft trial dated 1324. On the relationships between Hellequin's hunt and witchcraft, see C. Ginzburg, *Le Sabbat des sorcières*, pp. 113ff.

Chapter Six. The Imaginary Tamed?

1. Jacques Le Goff and Jean-Claude Schmitt, "Au XIIIe siècle, une parole nouvelle," in J. Delumeau (comp.), *Histoire vécue du people chrétien* (Toulouse, 1979), vol. I, pp. 257–279.

2. Cl. Bremond, J. Le Goff, J.-Cl. Schmitt, *L'"exemplum,"* (Brepols, Typologie des sources du Moyen Age occidental, fasc. 40, 1982), especially pp. 37–38 and the following definition of the medieval *exemplum:* "a brief tale presented as true and intended to be inserted into a speech (in general, a sermon) to convince an audience through a salutary lesson." Two indispensable research tools are F. C. Tubach, *Index exemplorum: A Handbook of Medieval Religious Tales* (Helsinki, 1969) (FFC 204), and its complement, J. Berlioz and M. A. Polo de Beaulieu (eds.), *Les Exempla médiévaux. Introduction à la recherche, suivie des tables critiques de l'Index exemplorum de Frederic C. Tubach* (Carcassonne, 1992).

3. Jacques Le Goff, *The Birth of Purgatory,* notably pp. 293ff.

4. Bernard of Clairvaux, *Vie de saint Malachie,* V, 11, ed. P.-Y. Emery (Paris, 1990), pp. 210–213: the saint having failed to pray for his sister, she appears to him in a dream at the end of thirty days to demand her suffrages; afterward, three other successive apparitions testify to the progressive improvement of her fate, until her definitive salvation.

5. If the apparitions of Saint Bernard himself increased on the day of his death, the apparitions of other dead are absent from the *vita prima* of the saint (written successively by William of Saint Thierry, Arnold of Bonneval, and Geoffroy of Auxerre) but appear in the *vita secunda* by Alan of Auxerre. See *PL,* vol. 185, cols. 490–491 (the apparition to Saint Bernard, at night, of the dead monk Gaudry of Clairvaux), and ibid., cols. 699–704 *(Defunctorum apparitiones).*

6. Conrad of Eberbach, *Exordium magnum cisterciense,* ed. Br. Griesser (Rome, 1961). The author wrote the first two books of this work at Clairvaux, where he was a monk, between 1186 and 1193, and then wrote the following two at Eberbach between 1206 and his death in 1221. Two other books were added later and come from the collection of Herbert of Clairvaux. In all I count nine ghost tales: Dist. I, chap. XXII; Dist. II, chap. I, II, and XXXIII; Dist. VI, chap. V, VI, VII, VIII, IX.

7. Herbert of Clairvaux, *De miraculis libri tres,* in *PL,* vol. 185, cols. 1271–1384. Herbert was a monk at Clairvaux, the abbot of Mores in the Jura, and then bishop of Torres (Sassari) in Sardinia. His collection of 118 chapters in three books had to include up to 150 chapters; it strongly influenced later Cistercian collections and was partially published by the Dominican Vincent of Beauvais. It provided an important account of Hellequin's hunt (col. 1274) and other tales of apparitions of the dead (cols. 1335–1337). A fundamental study of this col-

lection is Br. Griesser, "Herbert von Clairvaux und sein *Liber miraculorum,*" *Cistercienser Chronik* 54, NF 2 (1974): 21–39, 118–148.

8. Paris, Bibliothèque Nationale (hereafter cited as B.N.), MS Lat. 15912, around 1200. Especially chapter 79, *De memoria mortis,* fols. 127b–128b, the transcription of which I owe to Marie-Anne Polo de Beaulieu: the dead monk Benedict, from the abbey of Fontaine, appears to the doctor monk Herbert, who was watching over his body. The entire tale bears on the simultaneity of the presence of the cadaver and of the apparition of the spirit of the dead man.

9. The study by Br. Griesser, "Ein Himmeroder *Liber miraculorum* und seine Beziehungen zu Caesarius von Heisterbach," *Archiv für mittelrheinische Kirchengeschichte* 4 (1952): 257–274, includes an introduction to and the publication of the twenty-four chapters of the collection, written between 1213 and 1220, along with the mention of Caesarius of Heisterbach's tales, several of which concern apparitions of the dead.

10. Caesarius of Heisterbach, *Dialogus miraculorum,* 2 vols. Caesarius himself estimated that he wrote thirty-six works. On the sources, see B. P. McGuire, "Written Sources and Cistercian Inspiration in Caesarius of Heisterbach," *Analecta cisterciensa* 35 (1979): 227–282. On the author, see H. Herles, *Von Geheimnissen und Wundern des Caesarius von Heisterbach* (Bonn, 1990), bibliography on pp. 300–301. Preceded by a good introduction, a French translation is in progress: Caesarius of Heisterbach, *Le Dialogue des miracles,* livre I, *De la conversion,* French translation by A. Barbeau, abbey cistercienne de Notre-Dame-du-Lac (Canada), coll. Voix monastiques 6 (1992). The issue of ghosts in the tales of Caesarius of Heisterbach has been addressed in the study (in Polish, with a summary in English) by Edward Potkowski, *Dziedzictwo wierzén pogánskich w średniowiecznych Niemczeh. Defuncti vivi* (The Heritage of Pagan Beliefs in Medieval Germany: Defuncti vivi) (Warsaw, 1973).

11. *Die Wundergeschichten des Caesarius von Heisterbach,* ed. A. Hilka, vol. 1, *Einleitung, Exempla und Auszüge aus den Predigten des C.v.H.* (Bonn, 1933), pp. 110ff., for numbers 121, 131, 218, 307, 310, and vol. 3, *Die beiden ersten Bücher der Libri VIII Miraculorum* (Bonn, 1937), pp. 61ff., for numbers I:34, 44, 45 and II:2, 4, 5, 49. This second volume also includes the vita of Engelbert, the archbishop of Cologne (d. 1225), whose process of canonization Caesarius wanted to bring up, and a vita of Saint Elizabeth of Thuringen.

12. Caesarius of Heisterbach, *Dialogus miraculorum,* Dist. XII, chap. XXIV.

13. Ibid., chap. XXXII. The monk was a son of his time: wasn't the thirteenth century the great century of the cult of the Eucharist?

14. Ibid., Dist. I, chap. XXXIII: he cites the *Liber Visionum Claraevallis.* See B. P. McGuire, "A Lost Exemplum Collection Found: *The Liber Visionum et Miraculorum* Compiled under Prior John of Clairvaux (1171–1179)," *Analecta cisterciensia* 39 (1983): 27–62.

15. Caesarius of Heisterbach, *Dialogus miraculorum,* Dist. XII, chap. XXIX: Caesarius obtained this tale of the apparition of a dead monk of the monastery

of Preuilly (diocese of Sens) from "our abbots when returning the preceding year from a general chapter."

16. Ibid., Dist. III, chaps. XXIV and XXV. Only seven apparitions out of fifty are dreams.

17. Ibid., Dist. XII, chaps. XXV, XLIII, XLIV.

18. Ibid., chap. XXXIII.

19. Ibid., chap. XXVI.

20. Ibid., chap. V.

21. Ibid., chap. XIV.

22. Ibid., chap. XVIII.

23. See, concerning this tale and the "impulse of repetition," J.-Cl. Schmitt, "Les revenants dans la société féodale," especially p. 301.

24. *Die Wundergeschichten*, vol. 3, pp. 61–63.

25. Caesarius of Heisterbach, *Dialogus miraculorum*, Dist. XII, chap. XVII (and for a tournament of demons, reported by the same monk, see chap. XVI).

26. Ibid., Dist. XII, chap. XXIV. On this tale, see Jacques Le Goff, *La Bourse et la Vie* (Paris, 1986), pp. 90ff. [English edition: *Your Money or Your Life: Economy and Religion in the Middle Ages*, trans. Patricia Ranum (New York, 1988), p. 85]

27. Caesarius of Heisterbach, *Dialogus miraculorum*, Dist. XII, chap. L. On the three prayers necessary and sufficient for the simple faithful—Our Father, Credo, Ave Maria—see J.-Cl. Schmitt, "Du bon usage du Credo," in *Faire croire* (presented by A. Vauchez), pp. 337–361.

28. See, for example, in the middle of the thirteenth century, the numerous tales of ghosts in the section "Du don de crainte," especially those tales regarding the fear of death, of hell, of purgatory, and of judgment, in the collection of *exempla* by the Dominican Stephen of Bourbon, *Anecdotes historiques, légendes et apologues . . .*, ed. A. Lecoy de la Marche (Paris, 1977), pp. 22ff. More generally, see Barthelemy Hauréau, "Mémoires sur les récits d'apparitions dans les sermons du Moyen Age," *Mémoires de l'Institut. Académie des inscriptions et belles lettres* XXVIII, 2 (1876): 239–263.

29. A. G. Little (ed.), *Liber exemplorum ad usum praedicantium [. . .]* (Aberdeen, 1908), I, 43 and 44, pp. 25–28.

30. Ibid., II, 62, pp. 38–39, and II, 167, pp. 99–100. Other tales of ghosts are II, 121, p. 171 (against those who steal the church's property), II, 157, pp. 95–96 (*De gula*: the dead drunkard who appears to his friend, the miser), and II, 166.

31. Thomas of Cantimpré, *Bonum universale de apibus*.

32. Ibid., II, 53, chaps. XIff., pp. 498–515.

33. *Liber exemplorum*, II, 166, pp. 98–99 (*De indulgenciis*).

34. Thomas of Cantimpré, *Bonum universale de apibus*, II, chap. LIII, 27, p. 508.

35. See F. C. Tubach, *Index exemplorum*, nos. 3976, 2207. Among others are *Liber exemplorum*, II, 157, and Johannes Gobi, *Scala Coeli*, ed. M.-A. Polo de Beaulieu (Paris, 1991), 320 (p. 300), 490 and 491 (pp. 368–369): the spirit of the

friend of a priest appears in the form of a "shadow" that flutters around the tabernacle during mass to bear witness to the benefits that the host brings to souls in purgatory.

36. Caesarius of Heisterbach, *Dialogus miraculorum*, Dist. I, chap. XXXIII, Dist. XII, chaps. XXXI, XLI, XLIV.

37. Anonymous collection of *exempla* in alphabetical order (Auxerre, Bibliothèque municipale, MS 35), s.vv. "Elemosina" and "Penitentia."

38. See the marvelous story of two lovers, Cecilia and Radulf, the latter of whom supposedly wrote the tale: Paul Gerhard Schmidt, "Die Erscheinung der toten Geliebten," *Zeitschrift für deutsches Altertum und deutsche Literatur* 105, 2 (1976): 99–111.

39. Erich Kleinschmidt, "Die Colmarer Dominikaner-Geschichtsschreibung im 13. und 14. Jahrhundert. Neue Handschriftenfunde und Forschungen zur Überlieferungsgeschichte," *Deutsches Archiv* 28 (1972): 447–449. The dead man assigns him a mission to go to the count of Schwarzenburg: he is to tell the count to leave for the Crusades. The count laughs at the messenger and is killed shortly afterward. The story is cited among other political prophecies that predicted to Rudolf of Habsburg that he would become king of the Romans.

40. Conrad of Eberbach, *Exordium magnum*, VI, 7, pp. 358–359; Paris, B.N., MS Lat. 14896, fol. 174, and MS lat 15971, fol. 121. See also J. Klapper, *Exempla aus Handschriften des Mittelalters* (Heidelberg, 1911), 38, p. 33.

41. For example, see Conrad of Eberbach, *Exordium magnum*, VI, 6, pp. 356–358, cited from Herbert of Clairvaux; Caesarius of Heisterbach, *Die Wundergeschichten*, II, 49, vol. 3, p. 140. The same tale is in Stephen of Bourbon, *Speculum Laicorum*, in *Alphabetum Narrationum*, s.v. "Suffragium," which cites as an origin Peter the Chanter (end of the twelfth century), and is in Johannes Gobi, *Scala Coeli*, in a fifteenth-century manuscript edited by J. Klapper, *Exempla*, 43, pp. 35–36.

42. This is already in Peter the Venerable, *De miraculis*, I, 1, in *PL*, vol. 189, col. 851. In the thirteenth century, it appears in works by Caesarius of Heisterbach (*Dialogus miraculorum*, VII, 4), Stephen of Bourbon, Humbert of Romans, Thomas of Cantimpré, Vincent of Beauvais (*Speculum historiale*, VII, 173), and Jacobus da Voragine—*The Golden Legend: Readings on the Saints*, translated by William Granger Ryan (Princeton, 1993)—and then in *Alphabetum narrationum*, s.v. "Sacerdos." See also J. A. Herbert, *Catalogue of Romances in the Department of Manuscripts in the British Museum*, vol. III (London, 1910), 383, p. 158, and J. Klapper, *Exempla*, 36, p. 32.

43. J. Klapper, *Exempla*, 46, "De ebrio qui defunctum invitavit," pp. 36–38. On this narrative motif, see F. C. Tubach, *Index exemplorum*, nos. 767, 797, 1013.

44. Rudolf von Schlettstadt, *Historiae memorabiles. Zur Dominikanerliteratur und Kulturgeschichte des 13. Jahrhunderts*, ed. E. Kleinschmidt (Vienna and Cologne, 1974), nos. 20, 21, 32, 34, 45, 47.

45. Ibid., 20: "Wer ich da zw kurtzhaim, als ich bin zw langhaim, so wölt ich vor meinem ende gütz vil beywenden und für mich sendenn" (If I had known

briefly on earth what I am enduring for a long time beyond the grave, I would have behaved myself better before my death, to my advantage).

46.	*Nos qui sumus in aperto,*
	Vox clamantis in deserto,
	Nos desertum, nos deserti,
	Nos de penis sumus certi.

47. K. A. Barack (ed.), *Zimmerische Chronik,* reprinted by P. Hermann (Meersburg and Leipzig, 1932), vol. 4, pp. 86, 119–120, 127. The author is Wilhelm Werner von Zimmern (1485–1575), the uncle of Froben Christoph von Zimmern (d. 1566), who copied the MS Donaueschingen 704 from the preacher Rudolf von Schlettstadt.

48. J. Duvernoy (ed.), *Le Registre d'inquisition de Jacques Fournier, évêque de Pamiers (1318–1325)* (Paris, La Haye, and New York, 1978), especially vol. I, pp. 158–171, and vol. II, pp. 439–449. See E. Le Roy Ladurie, *Montaillou, village occitan de 1294 à 1324* (Paris, 1975), pp. 585ff. [English edition: *Montaillou: The Promised Land of Error,* trans. Barbara Bray (New York, 1978), pp. 342ff.] Another approach is Matthias Benad, *Domus und Religion in Montaillou* (Tübingen, 1990). The issue of ghosts from the testimony of Jacques Fournier is studied in detail in the unpublished state doctoral thesis by Michelle Fournié, *Le ciel peut-il attendre? Le culte du purgatoire dans le Midi de la France (vers 1320–vers 1520),* under the direction of Professor B. Guillemain, University of Bordeaux-III (1993), vol. II, pp. 375ff.

49. C. Ginzburg, *Le Sabbat des sorcières.*

50. Montague Rhodes James, "Twelve Medieval Ghost Stories," *English Historical Review* 147 (July 1922): 413–419, from London, MS British Museum, Royal 15 A XX (manuscript of 164 folios from the end of the twelfth century or the beginning of the thirteenth century, with two additions dated around 1400, sometimes illegible, fols. 140b–143a and 163b–164). I had access to the microfilm available at the I.R.H.T., Paris. A description of the manuscript is in Sir G. F. Warner and J. P. Gilson, *Catalogue of Western Mss. in the Old Royal and Kings Collections* (Oxford, 1921), vol. II, p. 147.

51. Let us recall that Montague Rhodes James, a scholar and publisher of these tales, was himself the author of fantastic tales: *Ghost Stories of an Antiquary,* with four illustrations by James Mc Bryrde and a new introduction by E. F. Bleiler (New York, 1971). The Middle Ages is generally represented in this work by the figure of a medievalist scholar subject to apparitions of spirits.

52. He does so only once, in the tale ending with the separation of a couple; he comments that this "divorce" must have displeased God: tale XI, p. 421 (the numbering is that of M. R. James).

53. Tale X is a story of divination, which I exclude from my analysis.

54. Tale V.

55. Notably tales II and XII.

56. Tales VII and II.

57. Tale XI, p. 421 n. 2: M. R. James notes the frequency of the apparitions

of the army of the dead as well as the exceptional nature of these *mortuaria*, which he explains by the persistence of pagan funerary practices.

58. Tale I
59. Tale II.
60. Tale III.
61. Tale IV.
62. Tale VIII.
63. Tale XII.
64. Tale IX.

65. P. Paravy, "Angoisse collective et miracles au seuil de la mort: Résurrections et baptêmes d'enfants mort-nés en Dauphiné au XVe siècle," in *La Mort au Moyen Age*, colloque de l'Association des historiens médiévistes français (Strasbourg, 1975), Publications de la Société savante d'Alsace et des régions de l'Est. Recherches et documents, XXV (Strasbourg, 1977), pp. 87–102; J. Gelis, *L'Arbre et le Fruit. La naissance dans l'Occident moderne (XVIe–XIXe siècle)* (Paris, 1984), especially pp. 490ff.

66. Tale V: "unus retulit quod vidit manus mulieris demergentes in carne spiritus profunde, quasi caro eiusdem spiritus esset putrida et non solida sed fantastica."

67. Tale III.

68. Ibid., p. 418: "loquebatur in interioribus visceribus et non cum lingua, sed quasi in vacuo dolio."

69. Tale II, p. 416: "et conspexit per os eius sua interiora et formavit verba sua in intestinis et non loquebatur lingua."

70. H. Martin, "A la recherche de la culture populaire bretonne à travers les manuscrits du bas Moyen Age," *Annales de Bretagne et des pays de l'Ouest (Anjou, Maine, Touraine)* 86, 4 (1979): 631–633. On the role of preachers in the penetration of the Christian doctrine in Brittany, see H. Martin, *Les Ordres mendiants en Bretagne (vers 1230–vers 1530)* (Paris, 1975). In the modern era, behavior mostly conformed with the expectations of the clergy: A. Croix, *La Bretagne aux XVIe–XVIIe siècles. La vie, la mort, la foi* (Paris, 1981), vol. II, pp. 1058–1060.

Chapter Seven. The Dead and Power

1. Editing, French translation, and commentary by M.-A. Polo de Beaulieu, from the manuscripts and incunabular editions. I thank the author for sharing her entire file, which will soon be published. On J. Gobi, see Johannes Gobi, *Scala Coeli*, pp. 13–77.

2. J. Chiffoleau, *La Comptabilité de l'au-delà*, p. 405, rightly speaks on this subject, on "the regenerative exorcism of Johannes Gobi [which] consists of engaging the ghost in dialogue, of changing it into a talkative and reasoning spirit," and he compares the Dominican's role as interpreter and mediator to that of the "messenger of souls," Arnaud Gélis in Montaillou.

3. Jacques Le Goff, *The Birth of Purgatory*, pp. 267ff. See Thomas Aquinas,

Summa theologica, vol. V, *Supplementum Tertiae Partis* (Ottawa, 1945), pp. 295a–329b: the *Quaestiones* 69, 70, and above all 71 *De suffragiis mortuorum,* of which articles 12, 13, and 14 (pp. 327a–329a) raise questions that are found word for word in the dialogue of Johannes Gobi. Do the suffrages intended for a specific dead person benefit the other dead? Inversely, do common suffrages benefit each dead person individually, including those for whom special suffrages were not intended?

4. Malibu, J. Paul Getty Museum, MS 31, fol. 7. Manuscript of 1437 written in French by David Aubert, miniature attributed to Simon Marmion, reproduced in Th. Kren and R. S. Wieck, *The Visions of Tondal from the Library of Margaret of York* (Malibu, 1990), p. 32.

5. W. Seelmann, "Arndt Buschmanns Mirakel," *Jahrbuch des Vereins für niederdeutsche Sprachforschung. Niederdeutsches Jahrbuch* VI (1880): 32–67. I want to thank Peter Dinzelbacher for pointing this text out to me, and Matthias Grässlin for helping me translate it.

6. Ibid., p. 41, chap. II, in which the text switches abruptly, in the same sentence, from "Arndt" to "ich."

7. Ibid., p. 64, chap. XXXVIII.

8. See, respectively, chaps. IX, XII, XXIX, pp. 45, 48, 59.

9. Th. Hohmann, *Heinrichs von Langenstein "Untersuchung der Geister." Lateinisch und Deutsch,* Texte und Untersuchungen zur Übersetzungsliteratur aus der Wiener Schule (Zurich and Munich, 1977). See, more generally, R. Kieckhefer, *Magic in the Middle Ages* (Cambridge, Eng., 1989), pp. 151–175, chapter VII: "Necromancy in the Clerical Underworld."

10. P. Boland, *The Concept of "Discretio spiritum" in John Gerson's "De probatione spiritum" and "De Distinctione verarum visionum a falsis"* (Washington, D.C., 1959).

11. On the symbolics of fasting and its relationship with the visionary mystic of the end of the Middle Ages, see C. W. Bynum, *Holy Feast and Holy Fast: The Religious Significance of Food to Medieval Women* (Berkeley, Los Angeles, and London, 1987).

12. See the incunabular edition of Cologne, 1496, in 4° (B.N. Res. D 8204), where the *Vision of Tnugdal* is also printed.

13. I readily espouse this oral suggestion, made by Father P. M. Gy, o.p., a critic on this point, regarding the great book by A. Franz, *Die kirchlichen Benediktionen im Mittelalter* (Fribourg-en-Brisgau, 1909).

14. An example was Emperor Charles IV in Prague (see above).

15. Fr. Neiske, "Vision und Totengedenken," pp. 152ff.

16. P. Dinzelbacher, *"Revelationes,"* pp. 79–80.

17. Norman Cohn, *The Pursuit of the Millennium: Revolutionary Millenarians and Mystical Anarchists of the Middle Ages,* revised and expanded edition (New York, 1970), p. 111. On the political aspects of prophetism at the end of the Middle Ages, see A. Vauchez, *Les Laïcs au Moyen Age. Pratiques et expériences religieuses* (Paris, 1987), pp. 237ff. An excellent look at the Portuguese "Sebastianism" in the mod-

ern era is Lucette Valensi, *Fables de la mémoire. La glorieuse bataille des trois rois* (Paris, 1992).

18. C. Beaune, *Naissance de la nation France* (Paris, 1985), pp. 100–101, and John W. Baldwin, *The Government of Philip Augustus: Foundations of French Royal Power in the Middle Ages* (Berkeley, 1986), pp. 391–392.

19. Stephen of Bourbon, *Anecdotes historiques, légendes et apologues*, 323, pp. 271–272.

20. Gervase of Tilbury, *Otia imperialia*, III, 103, p. 123.

21. This continuation of the tale, which is indeed part of the same chapter, was not translated by H. Bresc. "Culture folklorique et théologie," pp. 65–74.

22. The *Epître* of Philippe de Mézières was published by Kervin of Letten-hove, *Oeuvres de Froissart, Chroniques*, vol. XVI, *1397–1400* (Brussels, 1872), pp. 444–523. I thank Colette Beaune for pointing this text out to me. On the author and this letter, see N. Iorga, *Philippe de Mézières (1327–1405) et la croisade au XIVe siècle* (Paris, 1896) (reprinted, Geneva, 1976), pp. 503–504.

23. Gervais du Bus, *Le Roman de Fauvel*, ed. Arthur Långfors (Paris, 1914–1919). The interpolation of manuscript E that is of interest to us is reproduced on pp. 164–167, without the other pieces or drawings. See also the facsimile edition of Pierre Aubry (Paris, 1907), and for the "[lai] of the hellequines," see E. Dahnk, *L'Hérésie de Fauvel* (Leipzib, 1935), fols. 35ff. [For the translation, see the English-language text: Samuel N. Rosenberg and Hans Tischler (eds.), *The Monophonic Songs in the Roman de Fauvel* (Lincoln, Nebr., 1991).]

24. On this interpretation, see notably H. Rey-Flaud, *Le Charivari. Les rituels fondamentaux de la sexualité* (Paris, 1985). The little bald characters in the drawings are also interpreted as children who died without being baptized.

25. There have been many studies since P. Fortier-Beaulieu, "Le Charivari dans le Roman de Fauvel," *Revue de folklore français et colonial* XI (1940): 1–16.

26. Nancy F. Regalado, "Masques réels dans le monde de l'imaginaire. Le rite et l'écrit dans le Charivari du *Roman de Fauvel*, Ms. B.N. Fr. 146," in M.-L. Olier (ed.), *Masques et déguisements dans la littérature médiévale* (Montreal, 1988), pp. 111–126.

27. C. Ginzburg, "Charivari, associations juvéniles, chasse sauvage," pp. 131–140.

28. Adam de la Halle, or Adam le Bossu, thirteenth-century Artesian minstrel, *Jeu de la feuillée*, ed. E. Langlois (Paris, 1923), vv. 590ff.

29. See, for example, in the collected volume *Le Charivari*, the contribution of Cl. Karnoouh, "Le charivari ou l'hypothèse de la monogamie" (pp. 33–44).

30. Jean-Claude Schmitt, "Les masques, le diable, les morts dans l'Occident médiéval," pp. 87–119.

31. I am grateful to Elizabeth A. R. Brown for these suggestions, presented during a seminar at the E.H.E.S.S.

32. The son of Louis X, John I (called "the Posthumous" because he was born after the death of his father on June 5, 1316), formally reigned for only a

few months, under the regency of his uncle Philip, until his death on November 20, 1317.

33. See Andrew W. Lewis, *Royal Succession in Capitian France: Studies on Familial Order and the State* (Cambridge, Mass., 1981).

Chapter Eight. Time, Space, and Society

1. Jean-Claude Schmitt, "Temps, folklore et politique au XIIe siècle. A propos de deux récits de Walter Map, *De nugis curialium*, I, 9, and IV, 13," in *Le Temps chrétien de la fin de l'Antiquité au Moyen Age. IIIe–XIIIe siècle* (Paris, 1984), pp. 489–516.

2. Jacques Le Goff, "Le temps du purgatoire (IIIe–XIIIe siècle)," in ibid., pp. 517–530.

3. All Saints' Day has been celebrated by the church on November 1 since the eighth century. The liturgists of the twelfth and thirteenth centuries stressed the connection between the two feast days: Jean Beleth, *Summa de ecclesiasticis officiis*, pp. 243, pp. 306–319; William Durand, *Rationale divinorum officiorum* (Lyon, 1672), pp. 451ff.

4. Iogna-Prat, "Les morts dans la comptabilité céleste," p. 56.

5. Ibid., p. 64.

6. J.-L. Lemaitre, *L'Eglise et la mémoire des morts dans la France médiévale*, Communications de la table ronde du C.N.R.S. of June 14, 1982 (Paris, 1986), pp. 14–17.

7. A. Van Gennep, *Manuel de folklore français contemporain* (Paris, 1958), I, VII, p. 2860.

8. Ibid., pp. 3013ff. See M. Meslin, *La Fête des calendes de janvier dans l'Empire romain. Etude d'un rituel de Nouvel An* (Brussels, 1970).

9. Otloh of Saint Emmeran, *Liber visionum*, 12, ed. P. G. Schmidt, M.G.H. Quellen zur Geitesgeschichte des Mittelalters 13 (Weimar, 1989), p. 80.

10. Cl. Gaignebet and M. Cl. Florentin, *Le Carnaval* (Paris, 1974), p. 138. The hypothesis is taken up again by Ph. Walter, *La Mythologie chrétienne*.

11. Raoul Glaber, *Les Cinq Livres de ses histoires*, II, 19 and 20, pp. 46–47. Five months later—*in December,* specifies Raoul Glaber—the monk, as if called by the dead he had seen, left this world.

12. Isidore of Seville, *Regula monachorum*, XXIV, 2, in *PL*, vol. 83, col. 894.

13. E. Martène, *De antiquis ecclesiae ritibus*, IV (Anvers, 1764), pp. 164–166.

14. See M. Bloch, *La Société féodale* (1939) (reprinted, Paris, 1968), p. 436 [English edition: *Feudal Society*, trans. L. A. Manyon (Chicago and London, 1961), p. 313], for a comparison with initiation in "primitive societies."

15. I. Levi, "Le repos sabbatique des âmes damnées," *Revue des études juives* 25 (1892): 1–13, and "La commémoration des âmes dans le judaïsme," ibid. 29 (1894): 43–60.

16. Benedeit, *Le Voyage de saint Brendan*, vv. 1309–1322, ed. E. Ruhe (Munich, 1977), pp. 110–111.

17. Gervase of Tilbury, *Otia imperialia*, II, 12, p. 921; and Stephen of Bourbon, *Anecdotes historiques, légendes et apologues*, p. 33. See Arturo Graf, "Il riposo dei

dannati," reprinted in *Miti, Leggende e Superstizioni del Medio Evo* (Milan, 1984), pp. 151–166.

18. Raoul Glaber, *Les Cinq Livres de ses histoires*, V, 1, p. 118, mentions an apparition of a dead man one Sunday.

19. M.-A. Polo de Beaulieu, "Lundi jour des morts, de l'origine d'un rituel," in *Le Récit des origines*, Actes des rencontres de Carcassonne (December 1988), Carcassonne, Garae-Hesiode (forthcoming) and "Recueil d'*exempla* méridonaux et culte des âmes du purgatoire," in *La Papauté d'Avignon et le Languedoc, 1316–1342, Cahiers de Fanjeaux* 26 (1991): 257–278.

20. Thomas of Chobham, *Summa confessorum*, ed. F. Broomfield (Louvain and Paris, 1968), p. 128. See F. C. Tubach, *Index exemplorum*, no. 2424B, and, for example, Johannes Gobi, *Scala Coeli*, no. 741, p. 483.

21. Thietmar of Merseburg, *Chronicon*, I, 12, p. 16: "Ut dies vivis, sic nox est concessa defunctis."

22. Caesarius of Heisterbach, *Dialogus miraculorum*, XII, 17 and 20: "sacerdos quidam [. . .] dum in crepusculo noctis transiret de villa in villam, vidit," "nocte sequenti longe ante lucem, luna splendente, miles quidam."

23. Walter Map, *De nugis curialium*, II, 30, p. 207: "A knight of Northumberland was seated alone in his house after dinner in summer *about the tenth hour* after lunch." Rudolf von Schlettstadt, *Historiae memorabiles*, 20, p. 92: "Bene dormivit et, cum dulcem somnum perfecisset usque ad horam undecimam, vigilavit."

24. *Die Chronik des Klosters Petershausen*, III, 18, ed. Otto Feger (Lindau and Constance, 1956), p. 134: "Visio Bernardi. Post medium noctis, cum pulso torpore somnia sunt verissima, interim scilicet dum pulsabantur matutine, videbar."

25. M. R. James, "Twelve Medieval Ghost Stories": "et solebat egredi in noctibus usque Kereby et quadam nocte." See also II, p. 415.

26. Thietmar of Merseburg, *Chronicon*, I, 13, pp. 18–20.

27. Helinand of Froidmont, *De cognitione sua*, chap. XII, in *PL*, vol. 212, cols. 731–736: "Cum autem circa meridiem apud quoddam nemus appropinquassemus."

28. Rudolf von Schlettstadt, *Historiae memorabiles*, 20, p. 72.

29. J. Delumeau, *La Peur en Occident*, and *Le Péché et la peur. La culpabilisation en Occident (XIIIe–XVIIIe siècle)* (Paris, 1983). On the "night police," see the wonderful study by E. Crouzet-Pavan, "Recherches sur la nuit vénitienne à la fin du Moyen Age," *Journal of Medieval History* VII (1981): 338–356, taken up again in his thesis: *"Sopra le acque salse." Espaces, pouvoir et société à Venise à la fin du Moyen Age* (Rome, 1992), II, pp. 802ff. On all the reglementary and symbolic aspects, see the studies gathered by M. Sbriccoli (comp.), *La Notte. Ordine, sicurezza e disciplinamento in èta moderna* (Florence, 1991).

30. M. R. James, XI, p. 421. See also J. Delumeau, *La Peur en Occident*, pp. 75ff.

31. W. Seelmann, "Arndt Buchmanns Mirakel," 15, p. 50.

32. *De rebus gestis in Majori Monasterio saeculo XI*, 8, in *PL*, vol. 149, col. 410C.

33. Jacques Le Goff, *The Birth of Purgatory*, p. 47.

34. See, for example, several *exempla* of Caesarius of Heisterbach, *Dialogus miraculorum*: I, 33 (eternal damnation of a necromancer), II, 6 (a murdering robber), II, 15 (an impenitent canon), and XII, 5 (the Count of Juiliers), 14 to 20 (accursed knights, concubine of a priest, etc.). As we have seen, Caesarius attempts to say that the dead were induced by the harshness of their torment to confuse purgatory and hell.

35. Peter the Venerable, *De miraculis*, I, 28, p. 89. Theologians themselves had doubts: Hugh of Saint Victor (*De sacramentis*, II, XVI, 4, cited by J. Le Goff, *The Birth of Purgatory*, p. 144) admits: "The place where this pain is suffered is not definitely fixed, although many instances in which afflicted souls have appeared suggest that the pain is endured in this world, and probably in the places where the sin was committed, as an abundance of evidence proves. It is hard to know whether these pains are inflicted in other places."

36. *Die Chronik des Klosters Petershausen*, III, 20, p. 142: "nam eius judicio mihi pro pena concessum est, angulos huius claustri circuire et observare."

37. This idea might go back to the very ancient representation according to which the elect were called to replace the fallen angels next to God. I thank Jérôme Baschet for suggesting this to me.

38. W. Seelmann, "Arndt Buchmanns Mirakel," chap. XXXIII, p. 62.

39. On the limbo of the patriarchs, a place emptied of its occupants by Christ and distinct from the limbo of unbaptized children, see J. Le Goff, "Les limbes," *Nouvelle revue de psychanalyse* XXXIV (1986): 151–173.

40. J. Le Goff stresses this in *The Birth of Purgatory*, p. 331.

41. At the beginning of the sixteenth century, Geiler von Kaysersberg, the preacher from Strasbourg, gave a sermon maintaining the impossibility that a house could be haunted: souls make no noise; those that are in hell do not leave it; those that are in heaven "are not concerned with such foolishness"; and those in purgatory "have other things to do." Geiler von Kaysersberg, *Die Emeis* (Strasbourg, 1516), fol. 44, cited by J. Wirth, *La Jeune Fille et la Mort. Recherches sur les thèmes macabres dans l'art germanique de la Renaissance* (Geneva, 1979), p. 73.

42. Peter the Venerable, *De miraculis*, I, 28, p. 89.

43. Caesarius of Heisterbach, *Dialogus miraculorum*, XII, chap. XVIII.

44. Peter the Venerable, *De miraculis*, I, 27, p. 86: as soon as another person crosses the *limen domus*, the apparition fades away, a sign that it is reserved for one person alone. Gervase of Tilbury, *Otia imperialia*, III, 103: when the young girl's parents, alerted by the sound of voices, appear on the threshold of the door to her bedroom, they neither hear nor see their dead nephew.

45. Raoul Glaber, *Les Cinq Livres de ses histoires*, V, 1, 6, pp. 117–118.

46. Rudolf von Schlettstadt, *Historiae memorabiles*, 20, p. 72.

47. Ibid., p. 90: "in inferiori fenestre margine residentem."

48. Jacques Fournier, *Le Registre d'Inquisition*, vol. I, pp. 158–160.

49. Philippe Ariès, *The Hour of Our Death*.

50. R. Fossier, *Enfance de l'Europe. Aspects économiques et sociaux,* vol. I, *L'Homme et son espace* (Paris, 1982), p. 193, and J. Chapelot and R. Fossier, *Le Village et la maison au Moyen Age* (Paris, 1980), pp. 46–47.

51. P. Duparc, "Le cimetière, séjour des vivants (XIe–XIIe siècle)," *Bulletin Philologique et historique,* 1964 (Paris, C.T.H.S., 1967), pp. 482–504.

52. L. Gougaud, "La danse dans les églises," *Revue d'histoire ecclésiastique* 15 (1914): 5–22, 229–245. A remarkable case is E. Schröder, "Die Tänzer von Kölbigk. Ein Mirakel des II.Jahrhunderts," *Zeitschrift für Kirchengeschichte* 17 (1897): 94–164. For a more anthropological interpretation, see J.-Cl. Schmitt, "'Jeunes et danse des chevaux de bois,'" *La Religion populaire en Languedoc du XIIIe siècle à la moitié du XIVe siècle, Cahiers de Fanjeaux* 11 (1976): 127–158, and more broadly, *La Raison des gestes dans l'Occident médiéval,* pp. 90–92.

53. A. M. Cadot, "Le motif de l'aître périlleux," *Mélanges C. Foulon* (Rennes, 1980), II, pp. 27–35. See notably around 1190–1220, *Amadas et Idoine* (ed. J. R. Reinhard, 1925, vv. 4662ff.): a troop of fantastic knights led by the "Maufe" [the devil] seeks to violate the enclosure of the cemetery to take out the body of Idoine, an action that Amadas prevents. For a systematic treatment, see A. Guerreau-Jalabert, *Index des motifs narratifs dans les romans arthuriens français en vers (XIIe–XIIIe siècle). / Motif-Index of French Arthurian Verse Romances (XIIth–XIIIth Cent.)* (Geneva, 1992), p. 77: F778.1 (G) "Extraordinary Graveyard," with references to the *Première Continuation de Perceval,* to the *Continuation de Perceval* by Manessier, to the *Chevalier de la Charrette* of Chrétien de Troyes, and to the *Merveilles de Rigomer.*

54. Peter the Venerable, *De miraculis,* II, 27, in *PL,* vol. 189, col. 942D. This would be the oldest known mention of a lantern of the dead: see J. de Mahuet, "Lanterne des morts," *Catholicisme. Hier, aujourd'hui, demain,* vol. VI (Paris, 1967), col. 1811–1812, and F. Hula, *Mittelalterliche Kultmale. Die Totenleuchten Europas. Karner, Schalenstein und Friedhofsoculus* (Vienna, 1970), p. 20. Light was believed to have a protective function over the souls of the dead. But the general chapter of the Cistercian order in 1218 prohibited the monks' custom (undoubtedly judged to be "superstitious") of letting lamps burn on the tombs of their brothers. See J.-M. Canivez, *Statuta capitulorum generalium Ordinis Cisterciensis,* 2 vols. (Louvain, 1933) (38, anno 1218).

55. M. R. James, "Twelve Medieval Ghost Stories," VI, p. 419: the place of the apparition is undoubtedly explained by the profession of the beneficiary, who is *magister aratorum.* This head of the farmers was, quite naturally, crossing a field when a dead canon from Newburgh appeared to him. See also, in Brittany, the story of the dead baker who avoids paths and collects all the mud of the fields.

56. Caesarius of Heisterbach, *Dialogus miraculorum,* XII, 17.

57. Le Roy Ladurie, *Montaillou,* pp. 345ff.

58. Walter Map, *De nugis curialium,* I, 11, p. 31.

59. J.-Cl. Schmitt, "Le suicide au Moyen Age," *Annales E.S.C.* (1976), pp. 3–28.

60. M. R. James, "Twelve Medieval Ghost Stories," I, p. 414: he refuses to carry the sack of beans—legumes that symbolize funerals—of the living man he is accompanying any farther.

61. Ibid., II, p. 417.

62. Orderic Vitalis, *Historia ecclesiastica,* VIII, 17, vol. IV (1973), pp. 237–238.

63. Cl. Lecouteux, *Fantômes et revenants au Moyen Age,* pp. 24–25.

64. Roger of Wendover, *Flores historiarum,* ed. H. O. Coxe (London, 1841–1845), IV, p. 206 (anno 1229).

65. William of Auvergne, *De universo,* II, chap. III, p. 1069, col. 1a.

66. Gervase of Tilbury, *Otia imperialia,* III, 17, p. 35.

67. Robert of Uzès, Vision 29, French translation in P. Amargier, *La Parole rêvée,* p. 96.

68. William of Newburgh, *Historia rerum anglicarum,* V, chap. XXII, pp. 474–475. Compare with the incubus demon that assailed Guibert de Nogent's mother at the beginning of her widowhood: "As she choked in agony of spirit and lost all use of her limbs, being unable to make a single sound," she mentally implored the Virgin, who immediately came to her aid. It was then that she vowed not to remarry (Guibert of Nogent, *Autobiography,* pp. 47–48). See also Caesarius of Heisterbach, *Dialogus miraculorum,* XII, 19, for the story, which was "very famous in Bavaria," of the dead knight who, pushed by the devil, entered his wife's bedroom. But his wife, in no way afraid, made him sit on her bed and gave him her blanket to warm him up.

69. Guibert of Nogent, *A Monk's Confession,* p. 42.

70. Caesarius of Heisterbach, *Dialogus miraculorum,* XII, 24. On this tale, see J. Le Goff, *Your Money or Your Life,* pp. 78ff. In contrast to the final salvation of the ursurer are two apparitions: of the sinning knight who reveals his wanderings to his wife (or his mistress) and tells her that after the Last Judgment, he will go to hell; and of another knight who is damned for his past lechery and who appears to a nun but, paradoxically, asks her not to pray for him, for it would be of no use to him. *Die Wundersgeschichten des Caesarius von Heisterbach,* vol. III, ed. A. Hilka (Bonn, 1937), pp. 73–75, 44 and 45.

71. Gervase of Tilbury, *Otia imperialia,* III, 99, pp. 109–110.

72. Ch. Klapische-Zuber, "La 'mère cruelle.' Maternité, veuvage et dot," in *La Maison et le nom,* pp. 249–262.

73. M. R. James, "Twelve Medieval Ghost Stories," XII, p. 422.

74. *Polychronicon Ranulphi Higden monachi Cestrensis (d.c. 1364),* ed. J. Rawson Lumby (Script. Rer. Brit.), vol. 8 (London, 1882), pp. 220–222. On ghosts of mothers, see also Caesarius of Heisterbach, *Dialogus miraculorum,* XI, 34, and Giraldus Cambrensis, *Expugnatio Hibernica,* 42, pp. 116–119.

75. Caesarius of Heisterbach, *Dialogus miraculorum,* XII, 15 and 41.

76. Ibid., XII, 18.

77. Peter the Venerable, *De miraculis,* I, 26, pp. 80–82.

78. Ibid., I, 27, pp. 82–87.

79. Caesarius of Heisterbach, *Dialogus miraculorum*, XII, 50.

80. Ibid., XII, 26.

81. A. Guerreau-Jalabert has revealed this notion of *caritas* at the heart of the specific spiritual kinship of medieval Christian culture. See notably: "La parenté dans l'Europe médiévale et moderne: à propos d'une synthèse récente," *L'Homme* 110 (1989): 69–93; "Inceste et sainteté. La vie de saint Grégoire en français," *Annales. E.X.C.* 6 (1988): 1291–1319; and "Aliments symboliques et symbolique de la table dans les romans arthuriens (XIIe–XIIIe siècle)," ibid. 3 (1992): 560–594.

82. J.-Cl. Kahn, *Les Moines messagers. La religion, le pouvoir et la science saisis par les rouleaux des morts, XIe–XIIe siècle* (Paris, 1987).

83. *De rebus gestis in Majori Monasterio saeculo XI*, 9, col. 410B.

84. Ibid., col. 411.

85. Caesarius of Heisterbach, *Dialogus miraculorum*, XII, 35.

86. Peter the Venerable, *De miraculis*, II, 27 in *PL*, vol. 189, cols. 941–945.

87. J. H. Lynch, *Godparents and Kinship in Early Medieval Europe* (Princeton, 1986); Ch. Klapisch-Zuber, "Parrains et filleuls. Etude comparative" and "Compérage et clientélisme," in *La Maison et le nom*, pp. 109ff.; B. Jussen, *Patenschaft und Adoption im frühen Mittelalter* (Göttingen, 1991) (Veröffentlichungen des Max-Planck-Instituts für Geschichte 98). The church forbade sexual relationships between parents and godparents. Novella VII, 10 of Boccaccio's *Decameron*, relativizes the importance of this prohibition, since the ghost Tingoccio says to his friend Meuccio that he endures no additional punishment in the afterworld for having slept with his godchild's mother.

88. F. Zonabend, "La parenté baptismale à Minot (Côte d'Or)," *Annales. E.S.C.* (1978): 656–676, and A. Fine, "Le parrain, son filleul et l'au-delà," *Etudes rurales* 105–106 (1987): 123–146.

89. Just as tales of ghosts were rare before the eleventh century, this implication of compaternity beyond death must have been new in the time of Peter Damian. See B. Jussen, *Patenschaft*, p. 300.

90. Peter Damian, *Disputatio*, 3 and 4, in *PL*, vol. 145, col. 584.

91. *De rebus gestis in Majori Monasterio saeculo XI*, 8, col. 410. The expressions used to describe their pact are: "osculo sancto pacis et fidei" and "jusjurandi sacramentum."

92. Peter Morone, *Autobiografia*, p. 57.

93. J. Le Goff, "The Symbolic Ritual of Vassalage," reprinted in *Time, Work, and Culture in the Middle Ages*, pp. 237–287, especially pp. 257–58.

94. *Liber miraculorum sancte Fidis*, p. 272: "per fidei sacramentum, quo te mihi conjunxisti, per beneficia plurima que tibi contuli."

95. Ch. Klapisch-Zuber, *La Maison et le Nom*.

96. Peter the Venerable, *De miraculis*, I, XVIII, p. 91: Sancho is called "unum ex mercennariis mercede mihi servientibus."

97. M. R. James, "Twelve Medieval Ghost Stories," VII, p. 419: "mercennarius cuiusdam patris familias."

98. C. Vincent, *Des charités bien ordonnées. Les confréries normandes de la fin du XIIIe siècle au début du XVIe siècle* (Paris, 1988), pp. 143ff.

Chapter Nine. Describing Ghosts

1. Cl. Lecouteux, *Fées, sorcières et loups-garous.*

2. J. Baschet, s.v. "Anima," *Enciclopedia dell'arte medievale,* vol. I (Rome, 1991), pp. 804–815.

3. Guibert of Nogent, *De pignoribus sanctorum,* IV, 4, in *PL,* vol. 156, cols. 675–678.

4. Cl. Carozzi, "Structure et fonction de la Vision de Tnugdal," in *Faire croire* (presented by A. Vauchez), pp. 223–234. The author establishes a distinction between two theological currents, "spiritualist" and "corporealist." The first, the issue of the teaching of the Greek Fathers, including Origen, and also of the Augustinian tradition, ended in the ninth century with John the Scot Erigena and in the twelfth century with Honorius Augustodunensis *(Scala Coeli),* Guibert of Nogent, and Abelard or Richard of Saint Victor, in the affirmation that the punishments in the hereafter are only "spiritual," that there is nothing material about them. The other current, the "corporealist," derived its arguments from Gregory the Great, who asserted that souls, in the hereafter, endured a "corporeal fire." This view was represented in the twelfth century in the *Vision of Tnugdal* by the monk Marc, in the *Elucidarium* of Honorius (who afterward adopted, from one work to another, noticeably different points of view), and in the work of other important theologians, such as Hugh of Saint Victor *(De sacramentis)* and William of Saint Thierry *(De la nature du corps et de l'âme).* According to these authors, after death the soul preserves a certain "passibility" in the torments that it endures (temporarily or permanently) due to the sins committed. Jacques Le Goff *(The Birth of Purgatory,* p. 136 n. 2) criticizes the too rigid nature of the contrast between these two currents and makes a case for a more nuanced concept of the notion of "spiritual"; as he rightly points out, "spiritual" does not mean "disincarnate."

5. Alcher of Clairvaux, *Liber de spiritu et anima,* in *PL,* vol. 40, col. 797: *"Spiritu autem corporum similitudines intuentur. Quidquid enim corpus non est et tamen aliquid est, recte jam* spiritus *dicitur"* (my emphasis).

6. Otloh of Saint Emmeram, *Liber visionum* (Visio 4a), in *PL,* vol. 146, col. 348, edition replaced by that of P. G. Schmidt, M.G.H. Quellen zur Geitesgeschichte des Mittelalters 13, pp. 54ff.

7. Guibert of Nogent, *A Monk's Confession,* p. 86.

8. The "Museum of Purgatory" at the church of the Prati in Rome displays a series of cloths, missals, and night tables that date from the seventeenth to the beginning of the twentieth centuries and that bear the marks, in the form of burns, of the dead person who visited a relative to implore suffrages. See *La*

Chiesa del S. Cuore del Suffragio e il "Museo del Purgatorio," Arciconfraternita del S. Cuore del Suffragio (Rome, n.d.).

9. This story is found in most of the collections of *exempla* and in *The Golden Legend* of Jacobus da Voragine.

10. William of Newburgh, *Historia rerum anglicarum*, V, chaps. XXII–XXIV, vol. 2, pp. 474–482.

11. Gervase of Tilbury, *Otia imperialia*, chap. CIII, *De mortuo qui apparuit virgini*, p. 997: "Interrogatus, respondit corporis effigiem, quam praetendit, corpus non est nisi aereum, ipsum asserens non posse pati, sed tantum spiritum, neque posse onus quamvis levissimum sustinere."

12. Augustine, *De divinatione daemonum* c. (ed. C.S.E.L., 41, p. 603). In *Exordium magnum cisterciense*, I, 22 (p. 81), the Cistercian Conrad of Eberbach, regarding a dead brother who appeared to the abbot Stephen, says: "he seemed more to be transported through the air than to rest on the ground" (ita tamen magis in aere ferri quam in terra consistere videretur).

13. Jacques Fournier, *Le Registre d'Inquisition*, vol. II, p. 444.

14. M. R. James, "Twelve Medieval Ghost Stories," V: "unus retulit quod vidit manus mulieris demergentes in carne spiritus profunde, quasi caro eiusdem spiritus esset putrida et non solida sed fantastica."

15. Caesarius of Heisterbach, *Dialogus miraculorum* XII, 15: "talem ex se sonum emittens, ac si mollis lectus percuteretur."

16. Ibid., XII, 20.

17. Burchard of Worms, *Decret*, X, 13 and 14, in *PL*, vol. 140, col. 1066; Cl. Lecouteux and Ph. Marcq, *Les Esprits et les Morts*, p. 17.

18. Guibert of Nogent, *A Monk's Confession*, p. 51.

19. *Vie de Raban Maur*, p. 532: phantoms pummel the monk with blows, "horribili vocis imagine consonantes."

20. Caesarius of Heisterbach, *Dialogus miraculorum*, XII, 26.

21. On glossolalia and the fantastic, see various contributions to S. Auroux, J.-Cl. Chevalier, N. Jacques-Chaquin, Ch. Marchello-Nizia, *Linguistique fantastique.*

22. Let us recall a few exceptions: *Liber exemplorum ad usum praedicantium*, II, 62, pp. 38–39, in which a dead woman speaks in English to her sister; and Rudolf von Schlettstadt, *Historiae memorabiles*, 19, 20, 21, pp. 70–73, in which the dead in the cemetery sing in German.

23. Peter the Venerable, *De miraculis*, II, 25, p. 145.

24. P. G. Schmidt, "Die Erscheinung der toten Geliebten," pp. 99–111.

25. Johannes Gobi, *Disputatio*, Qu. 21. The same reasoning is held by the spirit of old Heinrich Buschmann: W. Seelmann, "Arndt Buschmanns Mirakel," chap. XII, p. 48. This is one of the passages that appear to attest to an influence of the text of Johannes Gobi on the German text.

26. M. R. James, "Twelve Medieval Ghost Stories," II, p. 416, see pp. 172 and 282, nn. 68–69.

27. Ibid., III, p. 418, see pp. 172 and 282, nn. 68–69.

28. In his thesis at the E.H.E.S.S. (1994) devoted to the symbolics of clothing, Pierre Bureau insists on the parallel between skin and clothing.

29. After the death of Charles VIII, the queen of Brittany went into mourning in black, as was the custom in Brittany, and not in white, as was the custom in the kingdom of France; this was interpreted as a political gesture. See the contribution of Ph. Braunstein to Ph. Ariès and G. Duby (eds.), *Histoire de la vie privée* (Paris, 1985), vol. II, pp. 570–571. See the importance of black in the illustrations of the Office of the Dead from the fifteenth-century book of hours. See R. S. Wieck, *Time Sanctified: The Book of Hours in Medieval Art and Life* (New York, 1988), pp. 124ff.

30. William Durand, *Rationale divinorum officiorum*, VII, *De officio mortuorum*, 43: "Quaeritur etiam utrum homines erunt nudi post diem iudicii an vestiti, et videtur quod vestiti." For the iconography, see the remarks—too systematic, however—of J. Wirth, "L'apparition du surnaturel dans l'art du Moyen Age," in F. Dunand, J.-M. Spieser, and J. Wirth, *L'Image et la production du sacré* (Paris, 1991), pp. 139–164.

31. Peter the Venerable, I, 27, p. 85: "*ei mane iam clara die in lecto iacenti ac vigilanti, sese visibilem demonstravit. Nam lecto eius assidens et formam quam habuerat vestitum quo usus fuerat, letale vulnus quod die mortis susceperat velut abuc recens pectore ac dorso pretendens*" (my emphasis).

32. Caesarius of Heisterbach, *Die Wundergeschichten*, III, 43, p. 73.

33. Caesarius of Heisterbach, *Dialogus miraculorum*, XII, 15.

34. Ibid., XI, 33.

35. Ibid., XI, 36, and XII, 39, and also XII, 25.

36. Ibid., II, 2 and 3, and XII, 21.

37. In Montaillou the *armarié* Arnaud Gélis sees the dead wearing white linen, their heads uncovered, with the exception of religious figures who wear the habit of their order and have their heads covered (Jacques Fournier, *Le Registre d'Inquisition*, vol. I, p. 163).

38. H. Wolf, "Das Predigtexempel im frühen Protestantismus," *Hessische Blätter für Volkskunde* 51–52 (1960): 353 (regarding what Martin Luther said about the headgear).

39. N. Belmont, *Les Signes de la naissance. Etude des représentations symboliques associées aux naissances singulières* (Paris, 1971).

40. William Durand, *Rationale divinorum officiorum*, cited by K. Stüber, *Commendatio animae. Sterben im Mittelalter*, Geist und Werk der Zeiten, 48 (Berne and Frankfort, 1976), p. 140: "Nec debent indui vestibus communibus prout in Italia. Etiam, ut quidam dicunt, debent habere caligas circa tibias et sotulares in pedibus, ut per hoc ipsos esse paratos ad judicium repraesentetur."

41. J. Chiffoleau, *La Comptabilité de l'au-delà*, pp. 120–121.

42. E. Assmann, *Godeschalcus und Visio Godeschalci*, Quellen und Forschungen zur Geschichte Schlesswig-Holsteins 74 (Neumünster), and W. Lammers,

"Gottschalks Wanderung im Jenseits. Zur Volksfrömmigkeit im 12.Jahrhundert nördlich der Elbe," *Sitzungsberichte der Wissenschaftlichen Gesellschaft an der Johann Wolfgang Goethe Universität Frankfurt am Main* 2 (1982): 139–162, n. 2. On the motif of the shoes of the dead person in Germanic traditions, notably in the saga of Gisli Sursson, see Cl. Lecouteux, *Fantômes et revenants au Moyen Age*, p. 39.

43. Caesarius of Heisterbach, *Dialogus miraculorum*, XII, 20.

44. Ibid., II, 2: the former monk who became a robber knight is taken from purgatory through the suffrages of a bishop. At the time of his first apparition, one year after his death, his clothing is dark. At the end of twelve years, he reappears with the white hood of the monk he had once been.

45. M. Pastoureau, "Du rouge au bleu: étoffes et colorants," in *Couleurs, images, symboles. Etudes d'histoire et d'anthropologie* (Paris, 1989), pp. 20–30.

46. Caesarius of Heisterbach, *Dialogus miraculorum*, XII, 14. The knight is also wearing a clot of dirt on his shoulders because he had usurped a field.

47. Gervase of Tilbury, *Otia imperialia*, III, 103, pp. 112ff.

48. M. C. Diaz y Diaz, *Visiones del Mas Alla en Galicia*, pp. 63–81.

49. On the medieval iconography of the dream, see A. Paravicini Bagliani and G. Stabile, *Träume im Mittelalter*.

50. Gregory the Great, *Dialogues*, II, 23 and 24.

51. Vatican Library, MS Vat. Lat. 1202, fols. 57 r. and v.; facsimile edition: *Lektionar zu den Festen der heiligen Benedikt, Maurus und Scholastika, Vat. Lat. 1202*, Belser Verlag, Codices e Vaticanis selecti L, 2 vols. (Zurich, 1981). See B. Brenk, "Il significato storico del Lezionario di Desiderio Vat. Lat. 1202," in *L'Età dell'Abate Desiderio, II. La decorazione libraria*, Atti della Tavola rotonda, Montecassino, 17–18 maggio 1987, Miscellanea Cassinese 60 (Montecassino, 1989), pp. 25–39.

52. Reproduction in *Val de Loire roman*, La Pierre-Qui-Vire (2d ed., 1965), fig. 8.

53. "D'un moigne qui ne seoit mie as heures Nostre Dame," *Les Miracles de Nostre Dame par Gautier de Coinci*, ed. V. F. Koenig (Geneva and Paris, 1970), pp. 255–260.

54. Paris, B.N., MS Nouv. acq. fr. 24541 [fol. 60 v.]. See H. Focillon, *Le Peintre des Miracles Notre Dame* (Paris, 1950), Pl. XV (painted by Jean Pucelle, 1330–1334).

55. Paris, B.N., MS Fr. 22920, fol. 105.

56. See F. Garnier, *Le Langage de l'image au Moyen Age. Signification et symbolique* (Paris, 1982), p. 216.

57. Escorial, MS TI1. This manuscript of 212 folios contains 1,262 miniatures but represents only two-thirds of the original manuscript. The last third is preserved in Florence, Biblioteca Nazionale, MS BR 20, which comprises 131 folios and 91 full illuminated pages. After nine miracles there is always a nonnarrative *cantiga de Lor* or praise of the Virgin. Between two *cantigas de Lor*, the fifth miracle always portrays its miniatures on two full pages, doubling their number (twelve instead of the usual six).

58. Ibid., fol. 174, *Cantiga* CXXIII.

59. Ibid., fol. 106 v., *Cantiga* LXXII.

60. I am grateful to Jérôme Baschet, who, in the course of our discussions, enabled me to broaden my interpretation of this illustration.

61. Oxford, Bodleian Library, MS Douce 300, fol. 115. [The English translation of the text is from Guillaume de Deguileville, *The Pilgrimage of Human Life (Le Pèlerinage de la vie humaine)*, trans. Eugene Clasby (New York and London, 1992), p. 175.]

62. Paris, B.N., MS Fr. 823, fol. 89. I owe the discovery of this miniature and of the following one to Anca Bratu, who studied them from another perspective in her thesis *Images d'un nouveau lieu de l'au-delà: le purgatoire. Emergence et développement (vers 1350–vers 1500)* (Paris, 1992), vol. I, pp. 228ff., and vol. III, ills. 63 and 65.

63. Paris, B.N., MS Fr. 376, fol. 83.

64. In particular, see the illustrated editions of the *Romance of Melusina*, to which Danièle Alexandre-Bidon kindly drew my attention.

65. Paris, Bibliothèque de l'Arsenal, MS 5071, fol. 80 v.

66. See, for example, a miniature in the *Chemin de Paradis* by Jean Malliard (England, first half of the sixteenth century), Oxford, Bodleian Library, MS Bodl. 883, fol. 10 v., in which the poet, fallen prey to melancholia, falls asleep on a path and dreams that his soul, incapable of reaching paradise, wanders among the tombs of the cemetery. The dream anticipates the death and the wandering of the phantom covered with a white shroud. An indirect account is also found in an illustration in the manuscript, from around 1330, of *Sachsenspiegel* by Eike von Repgow, reproduced in W. Koschorreck, *Der Sachsenspiegel in Bildern* (Frankfort, 1976), p. 97, from the MS Heidelberg Cod. Pal. Germ. 164. This common law goes back to the first third of the thirteenth century. The compensations (*Wergeld*) were all the lower when the social status of the victim was lower, victims such as illegitimate children, children of priests, and jongleurs of servile condition, to whom one gave as compensation only "the shadow of man" by whom they had been offended. They could metaphorically attack the shadow but not really the guilty person. The corresponding illustration shows, opposite the jongleur who is carrying his instrument, not, as one might expect, a shadow projected horizontally on the ground but a shadow standing up like a phantom. The words *umbra* or *umbraticus* very commonly indicated ghosts. Similarly, here the shadow that is portrayed standing signifies the incorporeal image substituted for the absent guilty party, even if that person was alive. On the shadow in Germanic traditions, see J. von Negelein, "Bild, Spiegel und Schatten im Volklsglauben," *Archiv für Religionswissenschaft* 5/1 (1902): 1–37.

67. In a vast bibliography, see notably A. Tenenti, *La Vie et la Mort à travers l'art du XVe siècle* (Paris, 1952). For a long-term placing in perspective, see Ph. Ariès, *Images de l'homme devant la mort* (Paris, 1983) [English edition: *Images of Man and Death*, trans. Janet Lloyd (Cambridge, Mass., 1985)]. A very nice example is

Heures de Louis de Laval (around 1480), Paris, B.N., MS Lat. 920, fol. 190: the encounter takes place in front of a gravestone, where a recumbent figure with joined hands is represented. See V. Leroquais, *Les Livres d'heures manuscrits de la Bibliothèque nationale* (Paris, 1927), Pl. LXXIX, and also *Livres d'heures. Manuscrits enluminés français du XVe siècle* (Leningrad, 1991), 6, Musée historique, MS 3688, fol. 17 (Tours, 1460).

68. *Heures à l'usage de Rouen* (fifteenth century), Paris, B.N., MS Lat. 1178, fols. 107 v. and 124. Other "macabre" margins are in fols. 106 and 119 (heads of the dead), 108 (gravedigger), 109 and 109 v. (coffins), and 112 v. (cadaver). An analysis of the manuscript is V. Leroquais, *Les Livres d'heures manuscrits*, vol. I (Paris, 1927), 43, pp. 117–118.

69. New York, Metropolitan Museum. The Cloisters, *Belles Heures de Jean de France, duc de Berry,* fol. 94 v. (Frères Limbourg, c. 1410); see the facsimile edition: J. Porcher (Paris, 1953). A comparable image of the funeral of Diocres is in *Très Riches Heures* (fol. 86 v.), created for the same prince and by the same artists; see Millard Meiss, *French Painting in the Time of Jean de Berry: The Bouricaut Master* (London, 1968), nos. 146 and 578.

70. Mâcon, Bibliothèque municipale, MS 3, fol. 25 v. On the complex codicology problems raised by this manuscript (the major part of which is today found in the Pierpont Morgan Library of New York), see J. M. Caswell, "A Double Signing System in the Morgan-Mâcon *Golden Legend,*" *Quaerendo: A Quarterly Journal from the Low Countries Devoted to Manuscripts and Printed Books* X, 2 (1980): 97–112. The manuscript bears the arms of Jean d'Auxi, knight of the Toison d'or and chamberlain of the count of Charolais, the future Charles the Bold. For the text, see Jacobus da Voragine, *The Golden Legend.*

71. Hartmann Schedel, *Liber chronicarum* (Nurenberg, 1493), in fol. 264, Paris, B.N., Rés. G. 500.

72. These hesitations are clear in the many vignettes in the manuscript of Bernard Gui, *Les Fleurs des chroniques,* Besançon, Bibliothèque municipale, MS 677 (anonymous translation, end of the fourteenth century–beginning of the fifteenth century), notably fol. 48 v. (of a dead *clavelière* nun [the keeper of the keys] who leaves her tomb to return the keys she was responsible for to the abbess: a type of living dead), and several macabre illustrations: fol. 57 (of a king of Germania who appeared to his son), fol. 53 v. (of a dead man's head that appeared outside his tomb), and fol. 65 v. (of a priest who appeared to his companion).

73. Paris, Bibliothèque de l'Arsenal, MS 5070, fol. 273 (Parchement, 395 sheets of 402 x 285mm, 100 miniatures). Reproduction in Boccaccio, *Le Decameron. Manuscrit enluminé du XVe siècle,* texts by E. Pognon (Paris, 1978), p. 89. The modern French translation was presented and annotated by V. Branca (Paris, 1962), pp. 636–643, with an engraving, also double but rather different from the miniature: on one side, Tingoccio entwines his godchild's mother onto a bench; on the other, he appears, dead but this time *in the form of a skeleton,* to

Meuccio, seated on his bed. I thank Danièle Alexandre-Bidon for leading me to this text.

74. See the same device, but much later (eighteenth century), in an illustration of the episode of Endor. See J.-Cl. Schmitt, "Le spectre de Samuel et la sorcière d'EnDor," ill. 10.

75. *Cas des nobles hommes et femmes*, Paris, Bibliothèque de l'Arsenal, MS 5193, fol. 76 v. This voluminous manuscript (405 parchment sheets, 402 x 298mm) contains 150 miniatures. It was intended for the duke Jean of Berry or the duke John the Fearless of Burgundy. Compare it with MS 5192, Bibliothèque de l'Arsenal, which is of the same origin and size but which, for chapter II, 19, presents a completely different scene: the author (?) welcomes two other figures in his office (fol. 62 v.).

76. J. Wirth, *La Jeune Fille et la Mort*, pp. 61ff., figs. 55, 64–69.

77. Ibid., figs. 33–34.

78. The most insightful historical analysis remains that of Ph. Ariès, *The Hour of Our Death*, pp. 240ff. The work of art historians is more useful for its archaeological descriptions: E. Panofsky, *Tomb Sculpture: Four Lectures on Its Changing Aspects from Ancient Egypt to Bernini* (New York, 1964); A. Erlande-Brandenburg, *Le roi est mort. Etude sur les funérailles, les sépultures et les tombeaux des rois de France jusqu'à la fin du XIIIe siècle* (Paris, 1975). The best work is incontestably that of K. Bauch, *Das mittelalterliche Grabbild. Figürliche Grabmäler des 11. bis 15. Jahrhunderts in Europa* (Berlin and New York, 1976). An interesting approach is *La Figuration des morts dans la chrétienté médiévale jusqu'à la fin du premier quart du XIVe siècle*, Abbaye royale de Fontevraud, Centre culturel de l'Ouest (Cahiers de Fontevraud, I, 1988).

79. The earliest cases are, foremost, one of the oldest sarcophagus covers, that of the abbot Isarnus of Saint Victor-de-Marseille, who died in 1048 (see its reproduction in Ph. Ariès, *The Hour of Our Death* p. 204j and p. 241), and also, in the church of Merseburg, the funerary plaque in bronze of King Rudolf of Swabia, killed by the Imperials in the battle of Elster in 1080 (see K. Bauch, *Das mittelalterliche Grabbild*, pp. 12–13, ill. 4). The king's violent death connects his situation in the hereafter to that which characterized many ghosts. The ostentatious sepulchre in the cathedral is explained, according to the terms of the epitaph, by the fact that he died "for the Church" in his battle against the emperor Henry IV.

80. An engraving from the *Romance of Melusina* by Jean d'Arras perhaps enables us to go even further in connecting the ghost and the recumbent figure. Even if obscurities remain, I am indebted to Danièle Alexandre-Bidon and Véronique Frandon for pointing me in this direction. The fairy Melusina's son, "large-toothed Geoffroy," conquers the giant Grimolt and penetrates into a mountain, where he discovers his grandfather Elinas of Albania's tomb, covered with the gold-cast recumbent figure of the king, his arms crossed on his stomach. Geoffroy also finds the alabaster statue of the queen, who is carrying a tablet telling of the entire adventure. Quite different from the 1474 edition, the 1478 edition

represents next to the recumbent figure the statue of the queen, her arms crossed over her chest, and, with an identical posture and the same type of hollow eyes, an old man whom the text does not mention but who might be the double of the dead king. In this case the image would explicitly connect the recumbent figure to the phantom. Text in L. Stouff (ed.), *Mélusine. Roman du XVe siècle, par Jean d'Arras* (Paris and Dijon, 1932), p. 265. A wood carving of the incunabulum is in W. L. Strauss (ed.), *The Illustrated Bartsch: German Book Illustration before 1500, Part II, Anonymous Artists (1475–1480)*, vol. 82 (New York, 1981), p. 106 (19.353), to contrast with ibid., vol. 80, p. 220 (3.197). Another, slightly different version is (Geneva, 1478) in fol. 1 (p. 164), Paris, B.N., Rés. Y2, 400.

81. In the Fr. MS 22920 of *Des Miracles Notre Dame* by Gautier of Coincy, cited in note 54, above. See also note 53.

82. M. Pastoureau, "Le Bestiaire des morts: Présence animale sur les monuments funéraires (Xe–XIXe siècle)," in *La Figuration des morts*, pp. 124–137 (p. 132).

83. See the case of the tomb of a knight buried in the church of Dorchester (Oxfordshire). Reproduction in E. Panofsky, *Tomb Sculpture*, p. 56, ill. 219. On the crossed legs of the English recumbent figures, see also M. Clayton, *Catalogue of Rubbings of Brasses and Incised Slabs* (London, 1968).

84. Wurtzbourg, Marienkapelle. Tombstone of the knight Konrad von Schaumberg, 1499.

Conclusion

1. J. Krynen, "'Le mort saisit le vif.' Genèse médiévale du principe d'instantanéité de la succession royale française," *Journal des savants* (July–December 1984), pp. 187–221. The author shows how this expression of common law was taken up again beginning in the fourteenth century to establish the idea of a royal succession at the death of the sovereign, without waiting for the coronation of the heir ("Le roi est mort, vive le roi" [The king is dead, long live the king]).

2. Among the many accounts concerning ghosts in the modern era, see *Chronique de Lucerne* in German by R. Cysat, *Collectanea Chronica und Denkwürdige Sachen pro Chronica Lucernensi et Helvetiae*, ed. Josef Schmid, Quellen und Forschungen zur Kulturgeschichte von Luzern und der Innerschweiz, 4, 2 (Luzern, 1969), pp. 591–609 (I thank M. Norbert Schindler, of the University of Constance, for pointing out this precious reference to me). Although very allusive, see R. C. Finucane, *Appearances of the Dead*.

3. N. Z. Davis, "Ghosts, Kin, and Progeny: Some Features of Family Life in Early Modern France," *Daedalus* 106, 2 (1977): 87–114. Luther preferred to equate ghosts to demoniacal manifestations.

4. D. Fabre, "Le retour des morts," p. 11. The very "Londonian" Society for Psychical Research, founded in 1882, assigned itself the task of putting together a corpus of all the phenomena of this type and of carrying out experiments to which nascent photography would bring the guarantee of modern technology;

the slides of the so-called phantom of Kathie, taken by William Crookes starting in 1874, have remained famous. See W. Crookes, *Recherches sur les phénomènes du spiritualisme. Nouvelles expériences sur la force psychique* (Paris, 1923) (1st English ed., 1878). See G. Pareti, *La Tentazione dell'occulto. Scienza ed esoterismo nell'età vittoriana* (Turin, 1990), pp. 183ff., and ill. outside the text.

5. Let us remember the specters in the theatre of Shakespeare, *Hamlet*, I, 5, v. 91 (the final words of the specter) and vv. 110–112 (when they are written by Hamlet for his own use): "So, uncle, there you are. Now to my word; It is 'Adieu, adieu! remember me.' I have sworn't."

6. J. Delumeau, *La Peur en Occident*, pp. 76ff.

7. Dom Augustin Calmet, *Dissertation sur les revenants en corps, les excommuniés, les oupires ou vampires, brucolaquies* (1751), reprinted with a preface by R. Villeneuve (Paris, 1986), pp. 341–342.

8. Diderot and d'Alembert, *L'Encyclopédie* (Paris, 1752), s.v. "spectre," with references to the articles "shadows," "ghosts," and "apparitions." The five opinions on specters are presented in a way that strangely recalls the scholastic discussion on the apparition of Samuel: "Some have believed that it was the souls of the deceased that return and show themselves on earth; others that it was a third party of which man is formed; others have attributed apparitions to elementary spirits; some have seen spectres as the effect of exhalations of bodies that are rotting; finally, the fifth opinion gives as the cause of spectres diabolical workings."

9. On this evolution of society as much as mentalities, see the synthesis by M. Vovelle, *La Mort et l'Occident.*

10. Arnold Van Gennep intended to propose a "general theory of ghosts and hauntings," a theory that he did not complete. See A. Van Gennep, *Manuel de folklore français contemporain*, I, vol. 2, p. 791. See D. Fabre, "Le retour des morts," p. 13. For a general anthropological approach, we can always refer to E. Morin, *L'Homme et la Mort* (Paris, 1970).

11. On the assessment of the new forms of the religious by a sociology of religions forced to reformulate its approaches, see D. Hervieu-Leger, *La Religion pour mémoire* (Paris, 1993).

12. S. Freud, "Analysis of a Phobia in a Five-Year-Old Boy: Little Hans," in *The Standard Edition of the Complete Works of Sigmund Freud*, translated from the German by James Strachey (London, 1955), vol. X, p. 122.